Uprooting and Integration in Simone Weil

American University Studies

Series VII
Theology and Religion

Vol. 20

PETER LANG
New York · Bern · Frankfurt am Main · Paris

Betty McLane-Iles

Uprooting and Integration in the Writings of Simone Weil

PETER LANG
New York · Bern · Frankfurt am Main · Paris

Library of Congress Cataloging-in-Publication Data

McLane-Iles, Betty.
  Uprooting and integration in the writings of Simone Weil.

  (American university studies. Series VII, Theology
and religion ; vol. 20)
  Bibliography: p.
  Includes index.
  1. Weil, Simone, 1909–1943. I. Title. II. Series:
American university studies. Series VII. Theology and
religion ; v. 20.
  B2430.W474M34   1987   194   86-20822
  ISBN 0-8204-0348-2
  ISSN 0740-0446

CIP-Kurztitelaufnahme der Deutschen Bibliothek

McLane-Iles, Betty:
Uprooting and integration in the writings of
Simone Weil / Betty McLane-Iles.—New York ;
Bern ; Frankfurt am Main : Lang, 1987.
  (American university studies : Ser. 7, Theology
  and religion ; Vol. 20)

ISBN 0-8204-0348-2
NE: American university studies / 07

© Peter Lang Publishing, Inc., New York 1987

All rights reserved.
Reprint or reproduction, even partially, in all forms such as microfilm, xerography, microfiche, microcard, offset strictly prohibited.

Printed by Weihert-Druck GmbH, Darmstadt (West Germany)

To Genevieve, Clifford, Carol, and Diana,
my family,
and
my husband, Lawrence

As I present this book to the public, I do so with the hope that the entirety of Simone Weil's writings be understood, that her status as a philosopher and scholar be more fully grasped, and that each of her contributions to the fields of philosophy, science, politics, history, religion, folklore, and literature be recognized, each constituting a work of great merit and scholarship.

—B. McLane-Iles

Contents

Preface

Introduction 1

1. "Science et Perception dans Descartes," Simone Weil's Early Views on Perception, The Self, and The Transcendency of The Ego 11

    The Self and the World: The Ambiguity of Limits • Consciousness • Existence Through Power • The World and Freedom • The Act of Understanding: Connaître • Thought–Infinite and Continuous Movement • Continuous Movement Reoriented • Le Travail • The Self and Others as Instruments of Knowledge and Action • Le Travail Effectif • Collective Forces of Perception • Weil's Views on Freedom, Perception, and Necessity in Relation to Traditional West European Philosophy

2. A Study of *Leçons de Philosophie*: Méthodologie de l'Action ...43

    Search for Order: Materialist vs. Idealist Philosophies • The Materialist Approach to Knowledge: The Influence of Exteriority • The Influence of the Body on Action • Influence of the Body on Emotion • Influence of the Body on Thought • *Imagination and Memory* • *Imagination* • *Memory* • *Influence of the Body on Reasoning* • The Power of Self-Interiority •*Thought as Will and Consciousness* • *Identity* • *Judgment* • Methodical Action • *Recreation Through Reasoning and Language* •*Language* • *Objectification* • Recurring Themes of the Roanne Lectures in Simone's Weil's Philosophy

3. The Deconstruction of Power 73

    Biographical Note • Freedom and Oppression • *Freedom* • *Theory of Oppression: Conditions of Existence* • *Divison of Labor* • *The Other* • *Centrality of Power and Knowledge* • *Power: 'La Course au Povoir'* • Myth and Deconstruction of Power • Myth and Heroism • The Myth of the Great Beast • The Myth of the State • La France Eternelle • L'Eternelle Allemagne • La Patrie et la Nation • The Colonial Empire • The Myth of Revolution and The Social • Revolution and History: The Failure of Liberation • *Spontaneous Mass Action* • *Revisionism* • *The October Revolution* • Marxist Critique • Militarism • Bureaucratic Rule • *German Reformism* • *National Socialism* • *German Communist Party* • *The Soviet Union* • Technocracy and Machinism • *Factory Life: The Effects of Machinism and Rationalism* • Conclusion • Traditional Religion and The Social

4. Science and Uprootal 161
   Introduction • Early Writings—Reintegration of Theory with Action • A Comparative View of the Periods of Scientific Development • Greek Science • *Algebra—Symbol and Meaning* • Classical Science • *Work* • *Necessity and Entropy* • Modern Science • The Crisis of Determinism and Acausality • *Philosophical Climate* • *Determinism* • *Quantum Theory and Quantum Mechanics* • Discontinuity and Continuity • Irreversibility • Probability and Chance • Space and Time • *Space* • *Time* • Conclusion

5. Deconstruction of Self 221
   Le Processus Décréateur—The Deconstruction of Self • Creation • Autonomy • Anguish and Total Detachment • Attention—The Mediating Power of Intelligence

6. The Reintegration of Meaning, Through Language, History, Mythology, and Poetry 235
   The Reconstitution of Symbol • The Reconstitution of Historical Meaning • *Violence and Language* • *Mediation and Violence* • *Violence and Myth* • *Violence and Poetry*

Conclusion 259

Bibliography 267

Index 273

Preface

Nearly eight years have passed since my year of final research on Weil in France. Many memories of that period remain vivid yet fleeting, as the precious crystallizing moments of one's life can be. In the context of these memories I would like to acknowledge and express deep gratitude to those individuals whose time and guidance enriched my journey into Weil's thought, life and writings.

The culmination of my study was the year 1979-1980. It was during that period that I served as a "lectrice de langue anglaise" at Lycée Henri IV, the school where Weil had done her preparatory work for examinations that would later allow her entrance into l'Ecole Normale Supérieure. It was to the classrooms of Lycée Henri IV that Weil had often returned, following completion of her secondary studies, to attend the lectures of her mentor, Alain. On many occasions I prepared lesson plans under the gaze of Alain, whose lifelike portrait hung prominently in the Salle des Professeurs. Alain's influence on the school and on Modern French Rationalism remains strong. As one would expect, walking the halls, working and visiting with the students, reading in the peaceful courtyard, in nearby cafés, in the Luxembourg Gardens close by, my days were evocative of past times and a glimpse at the cultural "ambiance" of Weil's schooldays. I am deeply appreciative of my appointment for that year and wish to thank the administrative staff and the instructors of English of Lycée Henri IV for their guidance and support. I thank in particular the manual workers, the classroom monitors, the cooks and painters boarding at the school who gave so generously of their time, friendship, and hospitality to make me feel at home, to advise me on politics and interview techniques for those of Weil's family and friends I was preparing to meet. I will not forget their warmth and kindness.

I am indebted as well to the librarians of Lycée Henri IV, who encouraged me in my studies and arranged my meeting with Camille Marcoux, a former classmate of Weil's and a retired professor of Henri IV. Monsieur Marcoux gave me considerable insight into Weil's early rationalist period as well as her final days. "Je fais mon paquet," he said calmly at the end of our talk, having brought back to life for a few moments the emotions and friendships of earlier days. I am deeply grateful to Monsieur Marcoux and realize the pain of old memories.

I thank as well Madame Simone Pétrement, the major biographer of Weil and a very close friend of Weil and her family since the early period of Weil's life. I am appreciative of the courteous time she graciously gave me in her home one peaceful afternoon in Enghien-les-Bains. I still retain in my possession the flowers Pétrement cheerfully gave me at the moment of my departure.

I thank Gustave Thibon for his time and for the course of a day during which discussions of Weil's *La Pesanteur et la Grâce* alternated with family gatherings. Thibon, writer and philosopher, had sheltered Weil and given her agricultural work during the period of Vichy's racist laws.

I thank also Father Joseph-Marie Perrin for the precious time he gave me both in Aix-en-Provence where his religious ministry was based, and in Paris. Father Perrin is a Dominican priest who had known Weil well during the last period of the war and had shared her unofficial conversion to Catholicism. He also had been entrusted with the manuscripts later published under the title, *Attente de Dieu*. Having kindly summoned me to Paris during his visit there he gave me one of the first editions of *Attente de Dieu*. He urged me to visit Malu Blum, the former supervisor of Weil in the Resistance.

I will not forget Malou Blum who had supervised Weil's work for *Le Témoignage Chrétien*, an underground publication founded by Perrin; and I remember vividly the hours Malou Blum and her husband spent with me, evoking the complexities of an assimilated Jewry in war-time France, laughing about Weil's own audacious humor. I am grateful for their time and for the determination I share with them to retain an understanding of Weil's philosophy, untarnished by hagiography.

Of all the people who had known Weil, I am particularly grateful to Dr. André Weil, who generously welcomed me into the Weil family home on Rue Auguste Comte. He, more than anyone, has contributed most to an understanding of Weil's writings and has sought to retain the integrity of his sister's beliefs, protecting her work from exploitation of any kind. I respectfully thank Dr. Weil.

I must also express my appreciation to my advisor, Dr. Stanley Gray, for his invaluable direction and support in the course of my writing. I am grateful as well to Dr. Bernice Carroll with whom I studied Weil's political philosophy, to Dr. Evelyne Accad and to Professor André Devaux of the Sorbonne, and to l'Association de l'Etude de la Pensée de Simone Weil. My deep thanks are expressed to the staff of Northeast Missouri State University for its assistance, particularly Mrs. Teresa Wheeler and Mrs. Paula Presley for their help in preparation of the final manuscript and typography. I would like to thank the publishers Editions Gallimard and Librairie Plon for permission to quote from most of Weil's published writings. I am deeply appreciative as well to the Bibliothèque Sainte Geneviève where, at the time, most of Weil's published writings were available to the public. I acknowledge as well the assistance given me at the Bibliothèque Nationale where I was able to study the original manuscripts. I appreciate also the resources made available to me at the Bibliothèque de la Sorbonne and at the British Museum Library. I thank my francophone friends from Africa, the Middle East, and Asia as well as Europe, for their warmth and perception which among other things helped me to deal with the complexities of the question of "déracinement."

Lastly and finally, I thank my family for their support and particularly my husband for the unfailing assistance and strength he has given me.

Betty McLane-Iles

Kirksville, Missouri
June, 1986

Introduction

In the years following the death of Simone Weil in August 1943, Gustave Thibon and Father Joseph-Marie Perrin gathered together the manuscripts Weil had left in their care, edited and had them published under the titles *La Pesanteur et la Grâce* (1947),[1] and *L'Attente de Dieu* (1950).[2] The rest of her religious thoughts and writings were published shortly afterwards. Apart from the legend that had resulted from Weil's political activity, the public's image of Weil was determined by the deluge of spiritual and religious writings published posthumously. Despite the publication, in Albert Camus's "Collection Espoir" of the essays on politics and science collected in *L'Enracinement* (1949),[3] in *Oppression and liberté* (1955)[4] and, after Camus's death, in *Sur la Science* (1966),[5] attention to this work was overshadowed by that given to her religious meditations. In the last thirty years most critical studies of Weil have been devoted to the understanding of her religious writings. Some of these commentaries have been valuable and analytical. Others have been emotional, subjective, and in some cases detrimentally hagiographic.

Most of the biographies of Weil have contributed interesting historical detail on both Weil's life and times. Thibon and Perrin wrote together and published in 1952 a biography of Weil based on the latter period of her life, the period of their acquaintance with her, *Simone Weil telle que nous l'avons connue*.[6] Jacques Cabaud wrote the first major biography of Weil in 1957, *L'Expérience vécue de Simone Weil*.[7] Sir Richard Rees, one of the major translators of Weil's writings on politics and science, wrote a shorter critical biography, *Simone Weil, Sketch for a Portrait*.[8] Simone Pétrement, a close friend and classmate of Weil, wrote and published in two volumes (1973) the most complete biography of Weil, *La Vie de Simone Weil*.[9] It is unfortunate that much substantive material in this work was not included in its translation into English.[10] In this book, the two extensively detailed studies by Pétrement and Cabaud are the main source of biographical information.[11]

The major critical works which I found helpful to an understanding of Weil's religious philosophy are Miklos Vëto's important analytical study of "décréation," *La Métaphysique religieuse de Simone Weil* (1971),[12] and Michel Narcy's book *Malheur et beauté du monde* (1967).[13] Marie Magdeleine Davy's early critical study, while tending to the hagiographic, has the merit of situating Weil within the European literary and philosophical tradition, and illuminating particularly relations between her work and that of Plato and Kierkegaard.[14] Gaston Kempfner also explored Weil's religious mysticism. His allusions to Oriental and European literature serve to illustrate stages of

Weil's concept of "décréation" in his book, *La Philosophie mystique de Simone Weil*.[15] Perrin and Thibon have both contributed to the great number of commentaries on Weil. In 1964, Perrin published a collection of essays addressing Weil's religious doubts, *Résponses aux questions de Simone Weil*.[16] In the spring of 1980, Gustave Thibon gave a series of interviews to Radio France in Paris, discussing her life and religious writing. He occasionally published excerpts of his correspondence with Weil.[17] Paul Giniewski has also published a very controversial work on Weil, taking an unusually critical, but much too biased, stance against Weil's views of Judaic theolgy, called *La Haine de Soi*.[18] In recent years, most commentary has appeared in the quarterly publication of *Cahiers Simone Weil*.[19] Some of the articles in this publication have been biographical studies, but a great deal of valuable critical analysis has appeared there also, although most of it concerns religious philosophy. There is a new generation of critics whose commentary has appeared in *Cahiers* or who have presented papers at colloquia in France or in the United States. Among these are Peter Winch and Eric Springsted who have worked in depth with Weil's concept of Necessity.[20] David Raper has written a major study on the influence of Oriental religious concepts on Weil.[21] I have also found Janet Patricia Little's studies on myth, work, and the Social to be the most penetrating commentary of Weil yet written.[22] Wladimir Rabi, with the encouragement of Emmanuel Levinas, has produced a significant study examining parallels between Weil's concept of "décréation" and Cabbala, the Jewish tradition of mysticism.[23]

In contrast, there are only a few significant studies of Weil's political and social thought. I cite in particular Marcel Corte's article "La Pensée Sociale de Simone Weil," (1947), an early essay on Weil's critique of symbol and language, valuable but strangely ignored.[24] Luce Blech-Lidolf's book, *La pensée philosophique et sociale de Simone Weil* (1976) has been helpful to my understanding of Weil's concept of methodical action.[25] In 1956, Ivo Malan wrote an interpretative essay on *L'Enracinement*, Weil's final political work. His book was entitled, *L'Enracinement de Simone Weil, an Interpretative Essay*.[26] Malan constructed a conservative image of Weil in this work, identifying her as a monarchist. Ten years later Roy Pierce wrote a piece entitled "Simone Weil: Sociology, Utopia, and Faith" in his book *Contemporary French Political Thought*.[27] He too saw in Weil a political conservative, basing much of his commentary on *L'Enracinement* and on her religious works. Despite the political distortion I see in this judgment, I find his essay useful for its remarks on Weil's analysis of power. His consideration of Weil alongside Aron, Sartre, Jouvenel, Maurras, and Alain, is an implicit recognition of her stature as a political philosopher. The kind of assessment which places Weil on the right, politically, is probably most pronounced in the work of an extreme leftist, Philippe Dujardin, whose *Simone Weil, idéologie et politique* (1975).[28] detects in her a series of fragmentary, contradictory personalities evolving towards a reactionary political position, bordering on fascism.

On the other hand, the most recent treatment of Weil's political thought is a collection of essays edited by George Abbot White, entitled *Simone Weil; Interpretations of a Life*,[29] It includes two essays (by the editor and by Staughton Lynd), which relate Weil's labor experiences and her critique of Marxism to some of the concerns of the American New Left.[30] George Abbot White should be generally recognized for his insightful exploration of significant parallels between the writings and experiences relating to the concept of work of Simone Weil in northern industrialized France, of Dorothy Day of the Catholic Worker Movement in New York, and of George Orwell (Eric Blair) in his documented descriptions of the slums of London and Paris.[31] Notable also in this collection is Michael Ferber's interpretation of *L'Iliade, ou le Poème de la Force*. His reading, which explores the theme of necessity, sees in this work an anticipation of later religious concepts.[32]

Most neglected have been Weil's writings on Descartes and on science, writings which are especially important for an understanding of the theme I examine in this book.[33] Little analysis of the early essay on Descartes has appeared, and on the *Leçons de philosophie*, there is only Peter Winch's preface to the translation by Hugh Price.[34] As for science, no extended commentary is in print, only a report on the 1975 MIT seminar on Weil.[35]

The political and historical essays included in *Ecrits historiques et politiques* have received little if any recognition. Dujardin does make occasional references to a few essays alongside biographical commentary. George Panichas included in his anthology, *The Simone Weil Reader*, a translation of Weil's essay "Ne Recommençons Pas la Guerre de Troie," preceded by a general introductory essay.[36] Although I am in debt to Panichas for drawing my attention to this essay, there are still implications and aspects of it which are yet unexplored.

In short, there has been fine commentary published on Weil, but there is room for more. The purpose of my study is two-fold: to discover a coherent pattern of analysis of Weil's philosophy, and, in doing so, help widen the range of study previously done on Weil.

I have chosen as the topic of my book an examination of the problem "déracinement/enracinement" in the writings of Simone Weil.

"Déracinement" and "Enracinement" are evident derivatives of the base word "une racine," meaning root. The former means, of course, to uproot, and the latter, to implant. The obvious and traditional polarization of the terms—"déracinement" meaning uprootedness, alienation and exile; "enracinement" meaning grounding, integration and belonging—has probably found its most familiar and compelling formulation in twentieth-century France in the works of Barrès and Gide. Barrès's belief that "déracinement" was a purely negative force opposed Gide's view favoring separation and change as a positive experience. Weil's usage of the terms in *L'Enracinement* and related essays, shows that she had been consciously referring during this latter period of her life to the problem of cultural alienation. In *L'Enracinement*, Weil uses the terms to describe the labor problem and the needed respiritualization of the worker, the rupture with our past caused by the overriding power of the nation concept and an increasingly technologically oriented society. She also used the terms to describe what she believed was a spiritual vacuum particularly acute among French peasants and agricultural workers, farmers, a social and economic class to whom she wanted to restore a sense of faith and identity. In these contexts where Weil specifically uses the terms "déracinement" or "enracinement" they express the movements of uprootedness and grounding. "Déracinement" describes the completely negative experience of uprootedness and exile.

> Le déracinement est de loin la plus dangereuse maladie des sociétés humaines, car il se multiple lui-même. Des êtres vraiment déracinés . . . tombent dans une inertie de l'âme presque équivalente à la mort, . . . ou ils se jettent dans une activité tendant toujours à déraciner. . . .[37]

"Enracinement" is, for Weil, the positive state of social reintegration. It is one in a series of primary human needs and values enumerated by Weil, what she calls "les besoins de l'âme."[38]

> L'Enracinement est peut-être le besoin le plus important et le plus méconnu de l'âme humaine. . . . Un être humain a une racine par sa participation réelle, active et naturelle à l'existence d'une collectivité qui conserve vivants certains trésors du passé et certains pressentiments d'avenir. . . .[39]

I believe that the value of the terms, "déracinement/enracinement" in Weil's philosophy extends beyond her own conscious usage of the terms. A reading of Weil's spiritual works had first led me to believe that there was a direct opposition between her usage of the term "déracinement" in a political and historical sense, and her concept of "décréation," an important principle of her religious philosophy. I realized later, however, that a reduction of these terms to a simple opposing pair would be a devaluation of the metaphoric power of "déracinement/enracinement." After further study I concluded that the movements of "déracinement/enracinement" occurred in various complex ways throughout Weil's writings on philosophy, power, myth, history, politics, science, religion, and language. In examining the entirety of her thought the terms acquire a complex, metaphorical meaning. Certainly the problem of alienation in its various forms is the major theme of Weil's work, which is discussed in this work. But each of the terms of the binary pair, "déracinement/enracinement" describe movements relating not only to the problem of cultural alienation but also to its solution. The two terms are both opposed and complementary to each other, and retain both detachment and cohesion in their relationship. This is particularly evident in Weil's writings on science and language. In some instances, one term functions as its opposite, as for example in Weil's rejection of the transcendental ego, in her deconstruction of myths of power, in the spiritual "décréation" of self. Each term has both negative and positive value. Each seems subversive in so far as one functions at times as the other. The substitution of one term for another, the value attributed to displacement and flexibility contribute to the ambiguity and complexity of "déracinement/enracinement." Thus, in Weil's writing and philosophy, the pair "déracinement/enracinement" poses a considerable problem. They are terms whose movement and relationship are not easily defined nor understood, and cannot be known in advance.

This book is based on an exploration of the various manifestations of "déracinement/enracinement" in order to better understand this problem. In this way I hope to express for myself the essential value of Simone Weil's philosophy. In doing so I have used a pattern of deconstruction present in her own analysis. This pattern in great part determines the structure of my thesis and the choice of chapters. The order of the chapters is not entirely chronological. The first two chapters discuss works representative of two consecutive periods of development in Weil's philosophy, "Science et Perception dans Descartes" (1929-1930) and *Leçons de Philosophie* (1934-1935). I have chosen to discuss these works not only because they have been undervalued both for their independent worth and for the transitional points they demonstrate in Weil's philosophy, but also because they lay the groundwork for Weil's later writings, and are consequently useful in helping me to explore all the dimensions of the problem "déracinement/enracinement." Weil wrote on politics and history from early adulthood to the time of her death. The chapter entitled, "Deconstruction of Power" deals with Weil's political and historical works of this period (1934-1943). As I have said, there has been limited treatment of most of Weil's political and historical essays, particularly those in the collection *Ecrits historiques et politiques and Oppression et Liberté*. There has not yet been a study that traces a coherent pattern throughout Weil's writings on history and politics. The following chapter on "Science and Uprootal" is, as the title indicates, a discussion of the essays contained in *Sur la Science*. Most of these date from the final years of her life (1941-1943), although the collection contains also the yet untranslated early essay "Science et Perception dans Descartes" and excerpts of letters dating from earlier years. When they have received attention at all, these essays, most of them written in the final period of her life, such as those on religion, have been studied only in a religious context, as an expression of her religious belief. I have chosen to separate my analyses of science and religion in order to do justice to each, and have placed the chapter on science before that on religion in order to avoid reading the former in terms of the latter. My chapter on religion, ("The Deconstruction of the Self"), which treats a much explored topic, attempts to relate the central idea of "décréation" to the opposition of "déracinement" and "enracinement" which I have examined in other contexts. The last chapter deals with the reintegration of symbol with original meaning. Here I have related the problem "déracinement/enracinement" to Weil's critique of language usage in a political and historical context and to her final preoccupations with mythology and poetry. This last area of Weil's thought has also received limited attention.

I believe that my study provides a different view of Weil and of the theme of "déracinement/enracinement." At the same time, I believe to have contributed to the range and depth of commentary on Weil. I hope the reader will obtain from a reading of this study a more coherent and meaningful understanding of Weil's philosophy.

Notes to Introduction

[1] Simone Weil, *La Pesanteur et la Grâce*, preface by Gustave Thibon (Paris: Plon, 1947).

[2] Simone Weil, *Attente de Dieu*, 1st ed., preface, comments and conclusion by J. M. Perrin (Paris: La Colombe, 1950).

[3] Simone Weil, *L'Enracinement: Prélude à une déclaration des devoirs envers l'être humain* (Paris: Gallimard, Coll. Espoir, 1949).

[4] Simone Weil, *Oppression et liberté* (Paris: Gallimard, Coll. Espoior, 1955).

[5] Simone Weil, *Sur la Science* (Paris: Gallimard, Coll. Espoir, 1966).

[6] Jean-Marie Perrin and Gustave Thibon, *Simone Weil Telle que Nous l'avons Connue* (Paris: La Colombe, 1952).

[7] Jacques Cabaud, *L'Expérience Vécue de Simone Weil* (Paris: Plon, 1957), translated *Simone Weil: A Fellowship in Love* (London: Harvill, 1964). Cabaud also wrote *Simone Weil à New York et à Londres: Les quinze derniers mois (1942-43)* (Paris: Plon, 1967).

[8] Richard Rees, *Simone Weil, A Sketch for a Portrait* (Carbondale: Southern Illinois University Press, 1966).

[9] Simone Pétrement, *La Vie de Simone Weil* (Paris: Fayard, 1973).

[10] Simone Pétrement, *Simone Weil, A Life*, tr. Raymond Rosenthal (New York: Pantheon Books, 1976).

[11] In addition, Maurice Schumann wrote an interesting biographical essay on Weil in his book, *La Mort née de leur propre vie—trois essais sur Péguy, Simone Weil, Gandhi*. Schumann had known Weil during the time she worked for Free France and had helped her in obtaining her post by his connections with DeGaulle. Of interest also is Bertolt Brecht's play, *The Visions of Simone Machard*; here the heroine, Simone Machard, is caught between the two opposing political positions represented by the characters Maurice and Le Père Gustave. Other details of the play indicate that Brecht is portraying Weil at the latter period of her life, although he has taken liberties with one biographical detail, interpreting her stay in a sanitorium during the final moments of her life as punishment for having worked against the French Collaborationist government. Although Weil's leg injury in Spain and her eccentricity as a political activist and religious mystic had already become legend among West European intelligentsia, it is curious that Brecht would have known about Weil's friendships with Gustave Thibon and Maurice Schumann. Thibon did not begin publishing Weil's writings until 1947, Schumann much later. Brecht's play was written in 1942-43 before any biography had been written on Weil. *La Mort née de leur propre Vie* (Paris: Fayard, 1974), "Les Visions de Simone Machard," *Théâtre complet VI* (Paris: l'Arche, 1957), 85-152.

[12] Miklos Vetö, *La Métaphysique religieuse de Simone Weil* (Paris: Librairie philosophique J. Vrin, 1971).

[13] Michel Narcy, *Simone Weil, malheur et beauté du monde* (Paris: Editions du Centurion, 1967).

[14] Marie-Magdeleine Davy, *Introduction au message de Simone Weil* (Paris: Plon, 1954), and *Simone-Weil, sa vie, son oeuvre avec un exposé de sa philosophie* (Paris: P.U.F., 1966).

[15] Gaston Kempfner, *La philosophie mystique de Simone Weil* (Paris: La Colombe, 1960).

[16] Perrin, Daniélou, Durand, Kaelin, Lochet, Hussar, Emmanuelle, *Réponses aux questions de Simone Weil* (Paris: Aubier, 1964).

[17] Gustave Thibon, "Correspondance: G. Thibon et Simone Weil," *Le Monde* le juin 1964. Also, "Souvenirs sur Simone Weil," *Bulletin des Lettres*, IX 90 (July 15, 1947), and "Simone Weil, Gustave Thibon, Correspondance," *Cahiers Simone Weil* (décembre 1981): 193-200.

8 Introduction

[18] Paul Giniewski, *Simone Weil ou la Haine de Soi* (Paris: Berg International Editeurs, 1978).

[19] *Cahiers Simone Weil*, published by the Association pour l'Etude de la pensée de Simone Weil, which organizes yearly seminars on Weil. Papers presented at one such meeting were published in *Simone Weil, philosophe, historienne, et mystique* (Paris: Aubier, 1978). (The seminar had taken place at Aix-en-Provence November 28-30, 1975.).

[20] Peter Winch, "Le Nécessaire et le Bien," *Simone Weil, philosophe, historienne, et mystique* (Paris, Aubier, 1978), 313-29. Eric Springsted, "Théorie weilienne et théorie platonicienne de la nécessité," *Cahiers Simone Weil* (septembre 1981): 149-67.

[21] David Raper, "Hindouisme et bouddhisme," in *Simone Weil, philosophe, historienne, et mystique*, 93-104.

[22] J[anet]. P[atricia]. Little, "La mythologie et les contes," *Simone Weil, philosophe, historienne, et mystique*, 105-22. Also, "Le refus de l'idolâtrie dans l'oeuvre de Simone Weil," *Cahiers Simone Weil* (décembre 1979); and "Action et travail chez Simone Weil," *Cahiers Simone Weil* (March 1979).

[23] Wladimir Rabi, "La conception weilienne de la création Rencontre avec la Kabbale juive," *Simone Weil, philosophe, historienne et mystique*, 141-60.

[24] Marcel de Corte, "La Pensée philosophique et sociale de Simone Weil," *Synthèses* 2: 9 (Brussels, 1947), 309-20.

[25] Luce Blech-Lidolf, *La pensée philosophique et sociale de Simone Weil* (Berne: Herbert Lang & Cie; Francfort: Peter Lang, 1976).

[26] Ivo Malan, *L'Enracinement de Simone Weil, essai d'interprétation* (Paris: Didier, 1956).

[27] Roy Pierce, "Simone Weil: Sociology, Utopia and Faith," *Contemporary French Political Thought* (London: Oxford University Press, 1966).

[28] Philippe Dujardin, *Simone Weil, idéologie et politique* (Grenoble: Presses Universitaires de Grenoble-François Maspero, 1975).

[29] George Abbott White, ed., *Simone Weil, Interpretations of a Life* (Amherst: University of Massachusetts Press, 1981).

[30] Staughton Lynd, "Marxism-Leninism and the Language of *Politics* Magazine: the First New Left . . . and the Third," *Simone Weil, Interpretations of a Life*, 111-35; and George Abbot White, "Simone Weil's Work Experience, From Wigan Pier to Chrystie Street," ibid., 137-79.

[31] Ibid., 137-79.

[32] Michael K. Ferber, "Simone Weil's Iliad," *Simone Weil, Interpretations of a Life*.

[33] "Science et Perception dans Descartes," in *Sur la Science* (Paris, Gallimard, 1966), 11-91.

[34] Simone Weil, *Lectures on Philosophy*, trans. Hugh Price, with introduction by Peter Winch (Cambridge: Cambridge University Press, 1973).

[35] "MIT Switches on to Weil," *Times Higher Education Supplement* (October 31, 1975): 14.

[36] "The Power of Words" (translated from "Ne Recommençons Pas la Guerre de Troie"), *The Simone Weil Reader*, ed. George A. Panichas (New York: David McKay Co., 1977), 268-85.

[37] Simone Weil, *L'Enracinement*, 66.

[38] Ibid., 61. The particular instances where Weil uses either of the terms "déracinement," "enracinement" occur principally in *L'Enracinement*, as explained. However, the term "déracinement" does occur in Weil's description of Israel in *La Pesanteur et la Grâce*, composed also during the final period of her life. In this instance, "déracinement" is used in an extremely negative sense. (Cf. Chap. 3, "Deconstruction of Power," Section on the Social.) Weil also uses the term "enracinement" in another passage of *La Pesanteur et la Grâce* in the section entitled "Le gros animal" where she criticizes the concept of nationalism. (Cf. Chap. 3, "Deconstruction of

Power.") Weil also uses the term "enracinement" to refer to the value placed on harmony and circularity in Greek philosophy (*Cahiers*, 1: 11, written 1940-41). (Cf. Chap. 4, "Science and Uprootal.) The term "déracinement" also appears in Weil's essay on colonialism, "A propos de la question coloniale dans ses rapports avec le destin du peuple français," and in her essay on a comparison between Roman culture and modern Germany, "Réflexions sur les origines de l'hitlérisme," *Ecrits historiques et politiques*. Both are critiques of French nationalism.

[39] Ibid., 61.

Chapter 1
"Science et Perception dans Descartes"
Simone Weil's Early Views on Perception, The Self and Transcendency of the Ego

'Déracinement' is a motif of the writings of Simone Weil. The first major expression of this theme appears in her diplôme d'études supérieures, "Science et Perception dans Descartes," written during the academic year 1929-1930, published in *Sur la Science* in 1966. It is one of the least known of Weil's writings and still remains to be translated. This study is of major importance for an understanding of her philosophical transition; it is also indicative of her participation in the early development of Existentialist philosophy.

'Déracinement' manifests itself initially through the simultaneity of uprootal and integration; six years before Sartre, Weil rejected total subjectivism and recognized social involvement as the sole means of self-determination. This initial manifestation of 'déracinement' determines the subsequent direction of Weil's philosophy. The rejection of the transcendental ego is the primary movement of uprootal; Weil's refusal of an essential moment in traditional philosophy. But this wrenching rejection of subjectivism brings with it the inevitability of involvement with the world, the inextricability of one's relation to exteriority which becomes the ethos of social commitment. This tension describes the general progression of 'déracinement' throughout Weil's writings, containing the opposing movements of exile and integration.

Simone Weil's discussion on Descartes's contribution to science and rationalism is the point of departure for her own study. Weil's affirmation that Descartes was the founder of modern sciences is easily justified and understood. The Cartesian method provided the basis for an analytical approach to knowledge by which all human science examined and comprehended its whole in terms of its simplest, most absolute units. Descartes was the first to understand that the most important objective of science was the measurable relationships between figures and movements; he subsequently applied algebraic science to express those infinitely applied relationships through arithmetic signs. Descartes propounded the idea of a universal mathematical science as a theory of knowledge based on absolute certainty and precision, in reaction to the predominance of Aristotelian logic. Mathematical concepts assured clarity and certitude in thinking; Descartes's perception on the validity of the emerging science of analytical geometry and physics, based on mathematical expression, provided a source of truth and security in an age of uncertainty and

12   *"Science et Perception dans Descartes"*

transition.

But this certitude, of which mathematics is the highest representation according to Plato, Descartes, and Weil, is based on the specificity of the relation between mind and matter; the mind provides the anchor, the source of method and innate understanding by which it determines the perception of exterior reality. Truth could be found neither through authority nor through the senses. The result was a sole reliance upon reason and mind.

Descartes's system was the triumph in Weil's view of 'la méthode a priori', of 'l'innéisme'. For Descartes the human spirit possesses truth in the form of innate ideas through which the ability to think or reason manifests itself.[1] Although Cartesian Idealism and Realism have given birth to opposing tendencies, the Idealism attributed to Descartes (i.e., "idées innées,") which Locke and other Empiricists later rejected is not in opposition, as Weil sees it, to his Realism, that is, his tendency to explore the applications of scientific study.

Descartes's rejected of knowledge gained purely through sense perception and placed his faith in human reason, in innate ideas. This was a major source of uprootal from traditional thought. Weil, in this early period of her life, was greatly influenced by these ideas, as were many others among the early twentieth century rationalists. His method and perceptions form the point of departure for her own exploration of and attempt to order exterior reality.

I am concerned mainly with her ideas on perception as expressed in the second part of her thesis. In the first part, Descartes is the mainspring from which she discussed the evolution of modern science. In the second part of her thesis where she expresses her ideas on perception, she speaks in the persona of a fictitious Descartes, "un Descartes ressuscité."

> ... tout commentateur doit se faire au moins pour un moment cartésien. ... c'est croire à rien qu'en sa propre pensée, dans la mesure où elle est claire et distincte, et sans accorder le plus petit crédit à l'autorité de qui que ce soit, et non pas même de Descartes.
>
> Ne nous faisons donc aucun scrupule d'imiter, en commentant Descartes, la ruse cartésienne. Comme Descartes, pour former des idées justes au sujet du monde où nous vivons, a imaginé un autre monde, qui commencerait par une sorte de chaos, et où tout se réglerait par figure et mouvement, de même imaginons un autre Descartes, un Descartes ressuscité. Ce nouveau Descartes n'aurait du premier ni le génie, ni les connaissances mathématiques et physiques, ni la force du style; il n'aurait en commun avec lui que d'être un être humain, et d'avoir résolu de ne croire qu'en soi.

Selon la doctrine cartesienne, cela suffit; Écoutons donc ce penseur fictif. . . .[2]

Weil was using this persona to discuss and extend certain ideas of Descartes. Although this is clearly not an attempt to rewrite the *Discours*, the tone is very much like that of Descartes's *Méditations*—lyrical, searching, introspective. Two viewpoints are expressed: 1) the actual Descartes of whom she speaks occasionally, and 2) the fictitious Descartes whose "je" expresses the Cartesian principles of autonomy of reason, and, at the same time, Weil's own uncertainty. The "je" is a device used to show the ambiguity of self and the involvement of self with the world, in recreating, as Descartes tried to, an ordered universe whose logic and order was determined by the self.

The application by Weil of "the ruse cartésienne" constitutes the point of departure for her study on perception. As Descartes envisioned a chaotic world from which emerged truth, order, and precision, the resuscitation of Descartes invites one to shed the polemical divergencies of his interpretors in an effort to purify, to implant oneself once again within the limits of the original Cartesian search and purpose. It is a return to the authentic capacities of human reason and common sense. In this manner, the creation of this 'autre, nouveau Descartes" is, in fact, a purification, an uprootal.

It is significant that Weil's usage of the term "creation" is ambiguous. In her thesis on Descartes as in her other works, the act of creation by both the divine and human spirits is an abdication and a search for purity, authenticity. Self-affirmation is paradoxically achieved through doubt, the only manifestation of thought and of being. Creation is ambiguously envisioned as both uprootal and implantation, "déracinement," and "enracinement."

Yet from the beginning, Weil views the solipsism and unresolved mind/body dualism of Cartesian philosophy as major obstacles in her attempt to perceive order and being. The "cogito ergo sum" affirms the "I" as the only reality. Yet, unlike Descartes, Weil saw the "I" as inextricably involved with and determined in great part by what lies outside of it; she rejected the separation of mind and body, believing rather in the natural dependence of perception and thought. The complexity of freedom and necessity, or power and its limits, are also involved in this question of the separation of mind and body. Descartes presents "l'être pensant" as the definition of being or existence; if one assumes that human thought and ideas are infinite, one has difficulty with Descartes' definition of the human being as imperfect and finite. The uncertainty lies there, in the ambiguity between freedom and its limits. As Pétrement states in a brief commentary on Weil's early philosophical beliefs, the self is power. It is the world that opposes our freedom. Yet the world that oppresses is not oppressive insofar as it is exterior, but interior. Because of the primacy of imagination over perception, thought relinqishes individual sovereignty, yet this sovereignty is regained in part by order conceived subjectively. Order is the alteration of which the mind disposes, the mind's only support.[3] In the Cartesian manner, immediate experience is expressed without commitment to any conception of a spatio-temporally ordered world of physical objects. As Peter Winch remarked in his preface to an English translation of Weil's subsequent work *Lettres de Philosophie*, Weil was trying to take such a phenomenological stage as a starting point, to trace how the conception of such a world can develop from it. The distinction between "I" and "the world" which confronts me but to which I also in some sense belong, arises through an ordering of the phenomenological world.[4] As this essay on Descartes is discussed, one will see whether, in her attempt at ordering phenomenologically the exterior world, she consistently upholds the command of the subjective "I."

Through Weil's exploration proceeding from a fictional "doublement" of Descartes, the rational being is continually haunted by the ambiguity of perception and existence. Recreating "un autre Descartes" without genius or knowledge, Weil applies her "ruse cartésienne." Through the mind and perception of this fictitious Cartesian thinker Weil underlines the aspects of existence that render ambiguous and uncertain the perception and understanding of a simple rational being in an attempt to re-order experience. To be underlined as this discussion progresses are the following ideas: 1) self as power, 2) exteriority opposed to freedom of the self, 3) this exteriority, as interiority, opposing freedom in the form of self-estrangement, 4) the mind/body dualism as originally defined by Descartes persisting in Weil's concept of the co-existence of the passive/active forces of the individual, 5) the application of Descartes' original delineation of all simple movement as straight and continuous to the process of thought, 6) her usage of Descartes' concept of all object and movement in terms of its most simple, absolute units, to re-order the complexity of the self and its exteriority, 7) his concept of "la droite," or "straight line movement," 8) the striking parallel between thought and labor, 9) the expansion of physical, mental capacities through a) a decentering of "la droite," and through b) the physical self as well as "the other," both human and inanimate, conceived as tools, 10) analysis of collective forces of perception in terms of combinced units of simple movement. These are the points by which can be followed Weil's application and extension of Cartesian principles in a re-ordering of the universe surrounding the self.

THE SELF AND THE WORLD: THE AMBIGUITY OF LIMITS

> ... la présence du monde est avant tout pour moi ce sentiment ambigu...[5]

In a controlled, lyrical passage Weil underlines the indivisibility of pain and pleasure, a manifestation of the mutual dependence of the living creature and its world. Objects are sources of pleasure if they extend the living creature's power and dominance. Pain manifests itself by the presence of objects that impose limits. Such limitations alienate one from the world. Yet estrangement is incomplete because no dependence on the world exterior to oneself is without reciprocity; there is no complete polarization. One's relationship with the world is a mixture of dependence and estrangement. The individual relationship to the exterior world is confused and ambiguous, inextricably determined by both liberty and necessity. Pleasure is the reaction to objects or elements of the outside world that extend individual freedom whereas pain expressed the limits imposed on this freedom by necessity; by the limiting presence of elements and individuals beyond oneself. Yet, no experience, no action, nor any emotion is only pleasurable or only painful, no situation completely determined either by liberty or necessity. Every pleasure is marred by the desire of greater joy, and by an awareness of the insatiability of one's own desires. Pain is in part a voluptuous expression of life, of self-awareness. Her discussion of this inextricable relation of pain to pleasure, underlines early in Weil's lifetime an uncertainty that she would always seek to explore and resolve, that is, a world and its creatures fluctuating between domination and dependence.

> Selon que je sens cette chose étrangère me soumettre ou m'être soumise, je sens plaisir ou peine....[6]

CONSCIOUSNESS

Our existence manifests itself only through appearances. Things are present to us only in so far as they are inextricably involved with our own being. The perception of the subject determines the presence of the exterior world, yet this perception is in turn dependent upon the physical state or the manifestation of the world to us. Our perception of the world is the only means of grasping it, but the accuracy of our perception in capturing reality is unverifiable.

> rien de ce qui se passe dans ma conscience n'a d'autre réalité que la

> conscience que j'en ai. . . .⁷

Weil viewed ideas and representation as no less uncertain as the world of feeling and sense perception. She saw the human creature as passive and powerless in relation to ideas, to the intelligible world. It is not the individual who grasps and develops ideas. It is the idea which, in a chaotic world determined by chance, is imposed in a particular form, or denied.

> Les idées m'imposent leurs manières d'être, me tiennent, m'échappent. . . .⁸

One's reasoning power reveals to oneself, not the individual self but the consciousness one has of the individual self. In the same way reasoning does not reveal the outside world, but only the consciousness or awareness one has of it. This leads to Weil's first positive affirmation: "I do have consciousness. I do think." It is not, however, the experience of thinking and reasoning in itself which leads to an affirmation of the existence of the self, unlike Descartes. It is rather a question of power. One doesn't think what one wants. Instead one is assailed by exterior things in a chaotic world. The exterior world imposes and eludes. One retains only a distant grasp of oneself, having obtained through reason only consciousness of the consciousness of self.

EXISTENCE THROUGH POWER

Weil views the rapport of self to exteriority as a displacement of power. The exterior, material world dominates. The as yet-undeveloped consciousness of the self is seemingly challenged and stimulated by the consciousness of exteriority, of being in the world. The belief in the dominating presence of physical, exterior reality is the basis of resistance by which the self struggles and affirms its own power. The transcendency of the ego becomes a struggle for freedom and autonomy of the self. Consciousness of the self remains unposited until it transcends the "illusion" of exterior domination and returns to itself through doubt and challenge resulting in affirmation of its power and identity.⁹

> . . .elles (les choses) me font illusion de leur puissance propre. Elles m'empruntent ma croyance. La puissance que j'exerce sur ma propre croyance n'est pas une illusion; c'est par cette puissance que je sais que je pense. Par cette puissance de douter, je sais que je suis . . . *Je puis, donc, je suis.* . . .¹⁰

The self exists through its freedom and power. Self affirmation is paradoxically achieved through the power to doubt as the only valid manifestation of thought and of being. The active power of the individual manifests itself through doubt. Belief is passivity, nonexistence of the self. To doubt, to challenge is an act. To believe is to flow and acquiese. All real power is infinite. If the individual self were alone in the world, this being would exercise absolute freedom, depending only upon the self. One's existence is determined by one's power, by one's act.

> ... Je connais ce que je fais ... du moment que je fais, je fais que j'existe ... je n'existe qu'autant que je me créé, je suis Dieu. ...[11]

Never again does Weil express such a degree of self affirmation power and autonomy. The images and ideas in this passage echo Nietzsche's *Zarathoustra*, a position from which Weil retreats, and condemns later in life as arrogant and egotistical. Usurpation of divine prerogative becomes for her a subject of deep moral contention. It leads to the formulation of her metaphysical philosophy, rather her spiritual search, be it a quest for uprootal or implantation.

THE WORLD AND FREEDOM

On the phenomenological level, Weil's Cartesian spokesperson recognizes as the principle of exteriority as the source of limits imposed on individual freedom and will. Existence manifests itself through the power to think and subsequently doubt. Ironically this freedom or power cannot assert itself except through a subject of thought whose presence imposes limitations on the freedom of the thinker.

The only power which belongs absolutely to the individual is freedom. Therefore, there is something beyond this subject, something other. The exterior world dominates the subject whenever the individual's thought is determined by something other than that person's own will. One is free only in so far as one is able to release or extricate one's will from domination by the exterior world. Freedom, the capacity for self-determination and autonomy distinguishes the self from the 'other' or from exteriority. Yet one overcomes with difficulty the control by exteriority. This is due to its semingly inextrical be involvement with personal will. Again one remarks the ambiguous delineation between the two forces of freedom and the world.

Descartes had argued the existence of God through a belief in perfection, the absolute represented by a divine presence, in contrast to the imperfection of the human spirit. Weil argues that the complete freedom, power of the human being is a reflection of the true, absolute power of the divine creator.

Human freedom limited and elusive shares and reflects the infallibility of God.

In this early stage of her writing, Weil vacillates but does not distinguish clearly between two types of necessity: 1) the limitations on power, limits imposed by physical necessity, that is, by the presence of 'l'autre,' and 2) the necessity of inevitable limits imposed by the very nature of human freedom itself. Only later does one become aware that in Weil's writings, exteriority and the obstacles its presence imposes on the self is encompassed by divine, universal necessity. For this reason, human freedom is seen as limited not only by the presence of exterior things and beings, but by its very nature.

> Si j'arrive à me heurter à la limite de mon pouvoir, je ne connaîtrai à la rigueur pas autre chose sinon de quelle manière Dieu m'empêche d'être Dieu....[12]

THE ACT OF UNDERSTANDING: CONNAÎTRE

Weil considers thoughts to be signifiers. Thoughts are signifiers of both the "self" and the "Other" because of the inextricable relationship of the two forces.

> Connaître c'est lire en une pensée quelconque cette double signification, c'est faire apparaître en une pensée l'obstacle en reconnaissant dans cette pensée sa propre puissance....[13]

Connaître is to *se connaître*, that is, to understand one's role in the determination of the self.

But one is impenetrable to oneself because one is not entirely responsible for the creation of the self. One does not totally control one's thought nor one's perception. The act of doubting encompasses the fusion of acceptance and challenge, passivity and action. The entire world challenges the individual's capacity for resistance and self-determination. But Weil's concern is that this act of tension and doubt, this verb, *connaître*, expressing human freedom and comprehension of its limits does not give us the means to understanding the exteriority over which we have no power.

IMAGINATION

Weil perceives a third faculty ambiguous in nature, made up of an entanglement of the world's powers and those of the self. Weil reminds us that such a being was recognized in Ancient Greece. People of that time habitually sought assistance with great problems and decisions at Delphes. There the enigmatic responses came from a female being constituting this fusion of the self and the world. In contrast to "le moi" which thinks, "l'entendement," and "le moi" which receives or feels "la sensibilité," Weil recognizes this encounter and fusion of subjectivity and exteriority as the zone of imagination. Imagination is all the more complex as it encompasses that zone of our existence where the delineation between what belongs to the self and what is exterior to the self is obscure and ambiguous. Imagination is by its very nature, twofold, contituting both the passions the individual imposes and those by which one is controlled, both one's freedom and its limits. Significantly, only for the person who acts are there obstacles since only through the act of doubt does one distinguish one's existence from that of others.

Most significantly imagination is a tool. The mind uses it to take hold, to impose itself on the world. It fulfills that function of mediation, of fusion. Weil paradoxically maintains that imagination, the provider of error and uncertainty, is our most valuable source of instruction. If there were no fusion through imagination, each of the individual's powers for thought and feeling would remain isolated and one-dimensional. If there where no imagination, beyond the certainty of one's own being, there would be no belief or prejudice, no passion and no error because the human being is more closely determined by its imaginative powers.

THOUGHT-INFINITE AND CONTINUOUS MOVEMENT

The primary task of the mind is to suppress or minimize "le hasard" the contingency of the world. Inevitably the world limits the sovereign power of the self. The mind, through ideas developed by imagination and attention can only partially shift the hegemony of power held by the outside world. Yet the capacity for infinite thought, that is, the perpetual addition of one finite thought to another enables human thought to transcend the limits of physical reality through vision and conceptualization. It is clear that the value of the individual, in Weil's view, finds its origin in thought and that the reasoning capabilities of oneself transcend the obstacles imposed by the outside world.[14] In the voice of her Cartesian spokesperson, Weil reminds the reader of the power of doubt by which one delivers oneself from a chaos of passion, domination and defeat. It is the way by which one grasps an understanding of one's presence. Once one has reaffirmed one's own power and autonomy, imagination provides a means for comprehending the limits imposed on the freedom and power of the self. The world is not beyond one's thought and grasp. Exteriority is within me, that seed of estrangement and passion planted by imagination, establishing and limiting my freedom.

Thus, as stated earlier, the mind through its infinite value escapes domination by exteriority. Simple, clear ideas by themselves are insufficient. The act of understanding and thought occurs only when one idea is added to another, complementing it and orienting its direction. At that time one understands that the value of the mind manifests itself through this infinite addition and reorientation of ideas. It is a model, a plan for potential action that is infinite.

CONTINUOUS MOVEMENT REORIENTED

The world is the source of my thoughts produced by the complementary forces of perception and imagination. I act indirectly upon the world; as the indirect source of thought and that towards which human action is directed, the world receives the action of "le mouvement droit." The struggle of the world as it encounters and receives the opposing human action is also a series of complementary "mouvements droits." Thus the encounter of the self with its world is a tense wrestling between two straight line movements. The self pulls an object in one direction and "the other" pulls the same object in the opposite direction. The result is that the object moves in an oblique direction in relation to each of the movements it has sustained. Weil initiates without completing the example of one's house as a manifestation of one's power and limitations. One's habitation is indeed, as Weil suggests, more than a secret threatening mass of exteriority. The identification of oneself with one's habitation is based on the feeling that one's home is primarily the object of one's own action. One's home is also, as Weil points out, the resistance to one's own act. Such resistance can only be conceived in the same terms, as parallel to my own, neither as thought, will, passion, but as movement. One could further pursue Weil's use of this analogy by recognizing that appropriation or identification with an exterior object is not only an affirmation of one's power over the world and oneself; it also represents a loss of identity, the relinquishing of complete self-determination because that exterior object represents the world's resistance and power over the individual self.

Weil applies to this study of human power and perception the Cartesian method of reduction to simple units for the purpose of analysis. All movement, affirms Weil, is uniform, its initial impulsion reproducing itself. The only possible way of understanding these infinite movements of resistance to the self is to conceive an innumerable series of movements, each conceived separately. Thus the world, exteriority, which deforms my movements, redirects and controls its course, is reduced to an indefinite quantity of simple movements.

The individual's conceptualization of exteriority as infinite movement is reduced to a series of simple units of motion. This reduction of the power of the other to units of movement is a crucial moment in the development of modern Existentialist thought. It thus gives one a certain hold, control within the world. The perpetual movement of the universe corresponds to the infinite series of thought by which I define and measure it.

It is valuable to note parallels between the German phenomenologist developing notions of intentionality and Weil's definition of action directed towards either the world or oneself as 'le mouvement droit'. But more significantly, Weil has applied the Cartesian idea of thought as straight line movement to action and perception. Using Descartes' method of reduction and analysis, she has reduced human action and perception to a level that increases our sense of self-determination and our understanding of power and its limits.

LE TRAVAIL

Weil underlines the duality of the being. Each individual is both a passive and active being. By geometry, in Weil's view, that these opposing tendencies can be brought together. Although they cannot be joined directly, they can be brought together indirectly, by the principle of work (labor) "le travail." Through labor that reason touches, reaches the world, and thus participates in part in determining the movements and changes imposed upon itself.

It is a body, "une chose étendue" which receives this movement and provides the point of encounter, of coming together of these two movements. In this body beyond the self and within the world the two types of imagination come together. In Weil's analysis there are two functions of the imagination: 1) that which allows for conceptualization, for geometrical reasoning, through its mediating power between feeling and thought, and 2) that which provokes emotion and passion. One's perception of exterior things, including one's own body involves the fusion of these two types of imagination.[15]

One cannot receive or sustain directly one's own action. Thus work or labour must constitute indirect action. Sensations received, cannot be interpreted as direct signifiers of unexplainable elements one can only receive as signifiers of an obstacle. One receives sensations as indications of the exteriority which obstructs. They provide intermediary experiences through which the individual passes before acting, before grasping the object of one's labor. In describing the process of perception, Weil reviews Descartes' famous discussion of "Le bâton de l'aveugle." The blind person does not feel directly the pressures of the stick, but uses the stick to contact things indirectly.

The blind man feels indirectly, through his stick and contacts the obstructions through intermediary sensations received through his contact with the stick. As the sharpened sense of perception through touch compensates for the absence of visual perception, the blind man's stick becomes an essential appendage, a part of his own body. In the same way, for each of us, the blind man's stick is one's own body, a means by which the human mind indirectly comprehends the limits of its powers, through perception.

> Le corps humain est pour l'esprit comme une pince à saisir et palper le monde...[16]

Weil seems to distinguish the conceptual I from the physical I. One does not easily rule the movement of one's own body. The movements of one's body correspond to each of one's thoughts. But, all that one has the power to do is to impose a unit of movement whose direction is reoriented by the body.

The physical presence of the self is portrayed by Weil as estranged from the rest of the individual being. One's body constitutes the obstacle. The mind must assume the task of indirectly controlling this physical potential for movement and direction.

Weil traces movement in the guise of her Cartesian spokesman as a series of simple movements increasing in complexity as they are combined. The conceptual self does not conceive the complexity of movement other than as a combination of units of simple movement. One does not know what is involved in making a circular gesture, but "l'étendue du corps" by the attachment of the arm to the shoulder reorients, by necessity, the straight movement of the arm. Thus by the physical impediments or presence of the body one combines units of movement. As the right angle helps one to understand the mathematical complexity and creation of a circle, so can the action of running be understood by reduction to principles of unified movements, each individually reoriented and combined by the body's mechanism.

One perceives through the senses. In the same way, maintains Weil, one perceives indirectly only through acting and touching. Weil applies and develops Descartes' comparison of a being's eyes to two sticks which touch the world directly. Having become conscious of one's own body as a part of this outside physical world, one now has seized exteriority, one has a hold on the world through conscious usage of one's body. The body itself has become an instrument of domination of the exteriority of which it is a part. Therein lies again the ambiguity of the self, inextricably part of both the objective (exterior) and subjective (self) worlds. Thought, as discussed earlier, is not a mere expression of one's freedom and power. It also is the way in which the world manifests its presence to the individual being. As my being is fused with that of the "other" or to the exterior world, so is the world fused with mine. As Sartre would later maintain in a more revolutionary statement on existence, Weil is already on the track of the individual inevitably 'en situation."

> Dès que mon corps est ainsi à moi, je ne conçois plus seulement,

comme la géométrie me le permettait, qu'on puisse louvoyer en cette mer du monde; j'y louvoie, non seulement, j'ai prise sur le monde, mais ma pensée est comme un élément du monde, tout comme le monde, d'une autre manière, fait partie de ma pensée, de ce moment, j'ai part à l'univers, je suis au monde. . . .[17]

THE SELF AND OTHERS AS INSTRUMENTS OF KNOWLEDGE AND ACTION

Despite the body's role in fusing the self with exteriority described in the last section, the body is also an obstacle. The body is ill-suited for work, for satisfaction of personal need and desire, and thus for affirmation of one's presence in the world. The physical self is inevitably alienated by the movements necessary for work because the desires and needs of the individual are indirectly satisfied by a series of movements constituting labor, actions seemingly unrelated to the individual. Although one's body is an ambiguous means of individual identification with the world, nevertheless, the body is also a tool. It is an instrument of knowledge and action, as are other people and other bodies. One's own physical self, and those of others, human and inanimate, may become instruments, to be possessed and to execute the series of indirectly-related simple movements comprising labor. Such tools expand one's reach, relating to the individual self in the same way as one's own body. Despite the limitations constituted by tools, as a part of exteriority, they enable one to transform one's drives into more composite movements. Because of its attachment to the shoulders, an arm can trace a circle. The circular movement of the arm must always have the shoulder, the body as its center but a wheel and a crank allow for a displacement, a transferral of power. The vertical movement of a lever provides the power displaced for the impetus of a greater vertical movement. Each of these tools independently provides for no greater complexity of movement than that of the body. In the same way that the individual movement becomes effective through an increase in complexity, power expands through the combination of movements and capacities of simple tools. Industry, as the application of the principle of de-centering of power and movement, complements labor.

The increasing complexity of human potential through the combined usage of tools approaches, without ever attaining, the infinite complexity of the universe. In labor the ambiguity of theoretical geometry disappears. Through work, the manifestation of geometrical action, one is able to distinguish between the direction of movement and the impediment to the directed action. The element or part of order, pertaining, belonging only to the exterior world, becomes the object of consciousness—what Weil terms as "ordre immédiat."[18]

LE TRAVAIL EFFECTIF

Perception and understanding of one's sensations is, as Weil proves, a process of "travail effectif." "Par le travail, je le (le monde) saisis."[19] That is, a process of precisely definable, predictable and self-determined steps achieved physically or analytically as a human task. The writer receives sensations caused by the pen. Signifiers of the action of writing itself and the conditions of this action, these sensations relate only indirectly to the writer's consciousness of herself or himself. In the same way, the combination of visual perception received by the double contact of one's eyes relates only indirectly to the viewer's consciousness of self. It relates directly only to the object of perception whose size, distance and mass is determined by the varied movements of the viewer. Weil refers to such explorations as a form of work. Such an exploration receives these sensations as signifiers of the conditions of tasks to be completed. Through the exploration it provides of the perceived object or objects, this "travail effectif" strengthens the act of knowing and understanding. The parallel is drawn by Weil between the role of "travail effectif" in cognitive understanding and its importance in an applied work situation.

> Ainsi autant le monde est soumis à mon action, exercée au moyen du corps et des plus simples outils, autant je saisis l'étendue elle-même en mes sensations. . . .[20]

One's perception of a rock or small mass at the end of a lever is only indirect, through contact with the lever itself. In the same way, one's visual perception of the Pantheon is accomplished indirectly through the combination of visual sensations received by both eyes; the scope of one's gaze of visual perception is comparable to the lever and end of which is the perceived object.

COLLECTIVE FORCES OF PERCEPTION

"L'étendue" (or expanse) is intuitively understood because the imagination, the intuitive powers of the individual are the only means by which the reality of the exterior world can be possessed and dominated. But the powers of the imagination and intuition are deceptive. In perceiving the Pantheon, one views the edifice as the apex of the triangle traced by the distance between the eyes and the common direction of both tools of visual perception. One individual's power of visual perception is not always sufficiently powerful. Weil recognizes the flaw in the Cartesian analogy of vision compared to a pair of pincers. The physical instrument, pincers or pliers, have two ends both parts of which can be separated in order to grasp distant objects. But one's eyes cannot be displaced at will, as one may do with pincers. Therefore one individual's visual powers are not great enough to seize the reality of a distant object such as the sun. One can have, independently, no conception of the depth, of the distance between oneself and the sun. Yet, maintains Weil, if two or more individuals work together, they can arrive at a physical perception of the sun. It would be possible for them to determine their distance from the sun in the same way Weil perceived the Pantheon, determining the distance between them and the respective directions of their visual attention. The two observers of the expanse, the distance separating us from the sun are two eyes, "les deu bâtons" of humanity. Through the collective powers of perception, we may comprehend space. This collective level of "travail effectif" may be applied to industry, the expression of the collective level of labor performed by humanity.

> On peut dire que les deux observateurs qui mesurent la distance du soleil sont comme deux yeux de l'humanité, que l'humanité seule perçoit l'espace qui sépare la terre du soleil; tout comme on peut dire que, par l'industrie, c'est l'humanité qui travaille. . . .[21]

Deception originating through the inevitable link of imaginative powers and sense organs is minimized by observing the actual extent to which one is able to physically control one's environment. This control exists by our consciousness of its limits, that is, by the presence of elements we fail to grasp perceptively among those already defined. Weil explains the perception of unexplained phenomena in terms of use objects. As each tool or piece of machinery constitutes part of the whole mechanism, each perception of unknown, unexplained phenomena contributes to the entire construct, mechanism of science. Human vision is a tool that enables us to perceive space, "la géometrie la plus simple . . . enfermée en mon corps. . . ."[22] The enhancement of this sense through the astronomical invention of the telescope enables the individual to overcome the limits of his sense perception. The human creature is unable to perceive space; science enables one to comprehend expanse. Thus science fulfills the liaison established by the principle of work. Observed phenomena, each a simple tool, through combination, increase in complexity. Weil interprets knowledge through the mechanical vision of Descartes in terms of an analogy with labor, as the construct of a vast mechanism whose complexity increases with each addition of a simple tool; that is, with each new observed phenomenon. Yet the physical complexity of tools and machinery created as a result and in view of greater power and knowledge fall short of reproducing the complexity of the world. We have, at least, the advantage in our building tools and accumulation of knowledge, of organizing in a geometrical series from the simple to the more complex phenomena that we do not grasp directly through perception with those that we do directly comprehend. All the mechanical models of a particular phenomenon are equal and the unity of all such constructs can be defined by an algebraic formula expressing their common level of complexity. As Weil points out, each level of knowledge can be applied infinitely:

> Quand on a obtenu un modèle mécanique d'un phénomène, on en peut trouver une infinité.[23]

All wisdom consists in rendering oneself conscious of a world subject to change by labor, by human action. Wisdom is contained in a mere act of perception, in the simplest action or act of labor. The order governing the universal challenge and doubt of the existence of the self, God, of time and space, is the same analytical process contained in labor and science. For this reason, for the sake of the unity of our being and our labors, that is, our conceptual self and our physical self, Weil reinterprets the need for an understanding of perception and science as an expansion of knowledge in view of the original Cartesian quest.[24]

WEIL'S VIEWS ON FREEDOM, PERCEPTION, AND NECESSITY IN RELATION TO TRADITIONAL WEST EUROPEAN PHILOSOPHY

Weil's thoughts on perception as revealed in her thesis are essential not only for understanding of the opposing aspects of her philosophy, but as an expression of tensions on the history of French Rationalism in the years prior to the Second World War. In her essay can be noted the seeds of discontent, planted by Descartes, Spinoza, Kant, Hume and their resolution through Alain's voluntarist philosophy, bordering significantly on Existentialism.

It is of considerable importance to note conversations with Weil in this early period of her life related by Simone Pétrement to understand the orientation of these young rationalists toward the problems of perception, freedom and necessity.

Their discussions reflect the challenge and support of Cartesian philosophy provided by Spinoza's writings. Alain is said to have declared commentaries written by Weil on Spinoza of far-reaching significance.[25] Yet, as Pétrement notes, Weil's orientation was in the Rationalist tradition, mainly determined by Cartesian thought. It is striking that two survivors among

Weil's acquaintances retain in their possession a volume of Spinoza's works given to them by Weil in friendship; it is significant because each of these individuals represents in his relations with Weil, one of two opposing tendencies of her philosophical development, rationalist and spiritual.[26] In each of these periods, Spinoza's influence in the question of freedom and necessity was considerable. It is also important to note the intensive study of Kant and Hume demanded by both Alain and Brunschvicg. Cabaud relates that Weil was so heavily influenced by Kant that her classmates called her 'l'impératif catégorique en jupons."[27] Her information was during these years mainly determined by the Voluntarist philosophy of Emile Chartier (Alain) whose influence is evident in the discussion on perception, as well as in most of her works up until the war. Of particular importance is the parallel development of Existentialist and Voluntarist philosophies. Only a few months before Weil began writing her thesis on Descartes for the Diplôme d'Etudes Supérieures, Husserl had given at the Sorbonne a series of lectures explaining his philosophy, later published under the title *Méditations Cartésiennes*.[28] Parallels can be found in Weil's ideas on perception during this period with those of this existentialist philosopher, and, indeed, Weil's thesis foreshadows Sartre's rejection of the transcendental ego in 1936. This was, perhaps, the critical period determining the direction of her philosophical development. In her attempt to reorder the phenomenological world, she could not avoid the obscure delineation of a subject of consciousness as apart from exteriority. The limits of the self as separate from the world were determined not by a preconceived order, but only by the order imposed by Weil's system of thought. Although she would later believe that *essence* precedes *existence*, Weil believes at this time existence to be created through freedom, action, and awareness of one's inextricable involvement with the world—"Je n'existe qu'autant que je me crée." As my preceding discussion indicated, she reaches the point of declaring consciousness to be consciousness of being in the world—'Je suis dans le monde."[29]

Struggling with the conception of an ambiguously defined cogito and its inseparable involvement with the world, Weil is at the point in her development where a choice must be made. She seems to be on the brink of the momentous step taken a few years later by Sartre. One wonders what would have happened had she dared to take that step. The public would have certainly been deprived of the beauty of her spiritual writings. But perhaps there might have been less tension, less struggle, less polarization in her life and in her lifetime had she not subsequently sought the reconciliation of human reality with the divine. Had she continued in the line of thinking which led to a rejection of the transcendency of the self, the problem of 'déracinement" could have been resolved by a return to values enriching human reality. She could have thus avoided the complexity of her convictions; yet, admittedly, many enriching aspects of her philosophy stem from the polarizations, the complexity of her beliefs.

Weil owes her ideas on freedom and necessity to Spinoza for his extension of dualism recognized by Descartes. The incomplete freedom, the power of the human being in Weil's view is a reflection of the true absolute power of the divine being. The finality of the human being is reflected by the limits on human freedom. Human freedom limited and elusive shares and reflects the infallibility of God.

Freedom in Weil's view is opposed to limits of necessity manifested by the presence of exteriority, through nature and/or autonomy seeking to extend itself. As did Spinoza, Weil establishes, with the chaotic exteriority surrounding the self, an order based on the perception of structures and beings whose rules of existence and movement are identical to one's own.

> . . . la tristesse est . . . le fait par lequel la puissance . . . d'agir de l'homme est diminuée ou entravée. . . .[30]

Here again one recognizes the expansion and reduction of power recognized by Weil in terms of perception and sensation. Pleasure is that which bends to the power and domination of the self. Pain is that which reduces our power or autonomy.

In Spinoza's view, the only way to attain freedom was to be enlightened by "l'entendement." Understanding actively that which I experience passively is to find in "la connaissance" autonomy and self-fulfillment through awareness. To the extent that we understand the reasons for our unhappiness, we cease to be unhappy.[31]

This recalls passages from Weil's essay on perception where the transcendency by thought of the limits of exteriority is conceived as an act of human will; and more importantly, the infinite capacity of human thought is analyzed in terms of units of movements combined and reoriented by successive movements, the geometrical pattern defining the moment of encounter, and reorientation. It also helps to explain the meaning Weil will give to terms like *exister*, and *connaître*. A close rapport exists between Weil's understanding of activity as *connaître*, the final stage of comprehension and awareness, and Spinoza's "l'immanentisme" by which connaître is to "comprendre activement ce que j'éprouvais passivement," that is, in extending one's comprehension beyond the limits of physical reality, transcending the limits of one's autonomous existence.

The uncertainty of the role attributed by Weil to imagination in perception shows in large part the influence of Hume and Kant. Weil's view of the imagination, not only as a source of illusion and deception, but also as the means of fusion between feeling and thought, between exteriority and interiority, owes something to Hume who saw imagination as the means to identifying the self. The self being no more in his philosophy than a series of states and conditions, it is imagination which hides the discontinuity of all things slipping from one psychological state to another, constructing the myth of personality.[32] Kant, in his *Critique of Pure Reason*, a work closely studied by Weil, emphasized the importance of imagination for the process of thought, in fulfilling the function of synthesis, of fusion. He speaks also of what he calls "la synthèse transcendantale de l'imagination."

This tension in Weil's philosophy has been strongly influenced by Kant. The entirety of Kant's philosophy appears to be essentially tragic since it affirms simultaneously the necessity of nature (*Critique of Pure Reason*) and the demands of absolute freedom (*Critique of Practical Reason*). Nature is the domain of determinism and finality which appears notably in the harmonious organization of living beings but, as demonstrated in the *Critique of Pure Reason*, the existence of nature, of the world, depends upon subjective ordering. The order of things depends upon our perception.[33]

Voluntarism began as the philosophical doctrine according to which judgment is determined by will as well as thought. For Descartes our understanding is finite and limited in contrast to our will which is of infinite measure and capacity. As a philosophical doctrine, Voluntarism was most effectively strengthened and developed by the philosopher, Maine de Biran and his disciples in the eighteenth century. Maine de Biran had enormous impact on French and European thought of the late nineteenth and early twentieth centuries. Among the philosophers whose thinking was determined in great part by "Le Biranisme" were Ravaisson, Lachelier, Boutroux, Bergson, and Alain by whom Weil was greatly influenced.

Maine de Biran's examination of the interiorized encounter of exteriority (that is, outside resistance) aimed at showing by what process the self consolidated its force and being. The consciousness of existence is consciousness of the power of personal will. So, for Biran the "cogito ergo sum" becomes a "volo ergo sum." Freedom or the concept of freedom was seen as the awareness of our power to act, thereby creating and consolidating "le moi—C'est ainsi que le moi se saisit."[34]

One can easily see how Biranism offered a common denominator for Nietzsche's philosophy of the will, for Lagneau and Alain's philosophy of action, for Weil's affirmation of freedom and power as the measure of existence ("Je puis, donc je suis"), for Heidegger's concept of existence as human freedom, project and anticipation of the human being who will fling itself towards its own finality or death.

Through "le Biranisme" or what became known as "la philosophie volontariste," Weil's views on freedom and power are identifiable with this view of the Existentialist Heidegger, of the expansion of the self, of the infinite power of self through thought and action restrained by limits of the physical, finite self. One can also see "le Biranisme" and "le Volontarisme" as a common influence, not only upon Weil's development but on the eventual formation of the Existentialist ethic—that is, the human being condemned to freedom, whose existence depends on one's own creation of oneself through action, through inevitable choice "en situation."

"Le moi" of Biran consolidates itself through action, conflict, through resistance. However this resistance is not provided by the outside world. There is no direct confrontation between the subject as interiority and the outside world as exteriority; instead, it is a polarization, a struggle between the active and passive elements of the individual. Both aspects are an expression of interiority in Biran's view. Thus freedom of the self, as will, manifests itself through a struggle against the passive part of oneself. In Weil's essay on perception, the passive/active duality is expressed through the opposition of *ressentir* to *connaitre*, that is, the passivity of received sensation or being acted upon, surpassed by activity, acting upon others through thought or physical action. The reader is reminded of Weil's formula: exister, penser, connaitre as stages towards the manifestation of the self by *pouvoir*. Weil, as was Alain, is on the track of a philosophy of will and action; yet the evolving of her philosophy, as was Alain's, is held back. Weil and Alain's exploration of the potential and responsibility of human freedom comes to a standstill. It is blocked from the path eventually completed by Existential phenomenology by three main limitations: first, the duality of the self through which the identity of the physical self is ambiguous, simultaniously merging with exteriority and with the conceptual or spiritual self. (The inability to distinguish totally between self and exteriority was critical in the philosophical transition of the times, as revealed by Sartre's objection to Pétrement's insistence that self-estrangement was separate and distinct from estrangement from exteriority.[35] Given the closeness in viewpoint and intellectual formation of Pétrement and Weil, established in Pétrement's biography of Weil,[36] one could possibly assume that Weil would have agreed with Pétrement. But, given the ambiguous and unsure identity of the passive, physical self in Weil's ideas on perception, I believe that she had already begun to question the absolute distance and transcendency of the *Cogito*, and thereby its relation to the world.) Second, the impersonal force of necessity seen as the source of final and inevitable limits on freedom—"Ils meurent et ils ne sont pas heureux. . . ."[37] Third, the refusal to attribute to human freedom and responsibility the divine prerogative; in other words, the refusal to refuse God. As Pétrement indicates, Weil knew that Descartes could not equate the human mind with God.

> Peut-etre voudrait-elle franchir ce pas, comme fera Sartre, mais son respect pour Descartes le lui interdit . . . .[38]

Alain maintains, as had Descartes and Weil, that the world of feeling and sensation is deceptive, elusive and imaginary. The real world is that which is built by thought and understanding: the mind is the "pouvoir constructeur" which builds order and reality. Weil's view of work and labor comes from or is at least strikingly close to Alain's. Weil's concept of "le travail effectif" is brought to mind by Alain's view of perception as work, inspired in great part by Descartes' theory of relative movement. Sensory explorations are a form of work by their receiving of sensations as signifiers of the conditions of tasks to be completed. We have seen how Weil views labor as the potential fusion of the passive/active forces of the individual. It is through the principle of work that the individual touches and determines in part the world, thus participating in the indirect determination of the movements and changes imposed upon itself. Thus fusion is brought about on both the levels of cognitive understanding and physical activity, both means of grasping and acting upon the world.

Alain and Weil's view of perception as a form of "travail" resembled the phenomenologist's view of movement of the mind towards the objects of perception, the movement of anticipation and project similar to the existential phenomenologist's concept of project or "praxis."

Imagination, for Alain, is the main source of uncertainty; Alain viewed it as a force estranged from physical reality or exteriority. Alain thus committed the "erreur idéaliste" that he frequently criticized, that is, the separation of subjective realaity from the physical world. Alain believed in "la maîtrise de soi" overcoming all error, all deception which originates, in his view, from misperceiving from imagination. For Weil, the presence of freedom is still ambiguous, as "la maîtrise du soi" does not erase the uncertainty of the identity of the self from exteriority. Polarizing the two negative forces of imagination and exteriority precludes the triumph of the will; nevertheless Weil clings to her position, surprisingly close to a break in rejection of traditional philosophy.

Alain continues in his praise of Kant and his criticism of both Idealists and

Realists, refusing in the last analysis to face the impossibility of one's mastery over a physical universe upon which one depends. That is, that existence of the world precedes its essence, the creation by our minds of an ordered universe.[39] Yet, he maintains, the order we conceive, distant and willful, is the ultimate reality.

To be underlined, however, is the contribution of Voluntarism to the transition toward a resolution of the contradiction of Idealism and Realism, to the dual relationship of the self with the world. As Alain said:

> La pensee ne se prouve qu'en s'éprouvant. *Il faut aller au monde pour y trouver l'esprit.*[40]

The principle of strength and will obtained from *contact*, from *presence within the world*, provided the key. One must *go to the world*, because, as for Husserl, essence and existence are mutually and reciprocally determined because one's presence and freedom are in the world. The mistake, the confusion stemmed from the subsequent attempt at retreat, at withdrawal and distance of the self from the world in an effort toward integration of the self through a return to the traditional mind/body dualism; thus Alain's Voluntarist philosophy, like Husserl's affirmation of the transcendental ego, provided both advances and retreats in the effort to resolve the mind/body dualism.

One's existence according to Heidegger, consists in "ex-sister," in projecting oneself towards the world, in being "hors de soi." Elaborating on Husserlian intentionality, Heidegger defines the human being as project, as the projection of the self towards the world and towards the future. The human being is project, or worker. One's main project is expressed by the idea of "work"; all work has the double goal of production and completion.

The philosophies of both Alain and Husserl led to a denial of Idealism and Realism. Husserl says that one can speak of the soul or spirit only in function of the body:

> le moi n'est pas une intériorité subsistante: il est . . . porté par et vers l'extérieur . . . il est intentionnalité. . . .[41]

The same conclusion was reached by Weil:

> non seulement j'ai prise sur le monde, mais ma pensée est comme un élément du monde, tout comme le monde, d'une autre manière, fait partie de ma pensée; de ce moment, j'ai part à l'univers, je suis

> au monde. . . .[42]

Not just the spirit or the body, the entire unified self is Husserl's point of departure from which one observes that this integral self is not isolated, existing only for itself, but thrust into a world of people and things with which the self interacts.

As shown in Diderot's discussion of the blind mathematician, Saunderson and Weil's apropros of the tactile sensations received by Descartes' blind man ("Le Baton de l'Aveugle"), only through the association of tactile and visual sensations does one arrive at a consciousness of oneself within the world, a consciousness determined by one's *resistance* through movement and perception; both expressions of one's work or project.[43] Thus for both Weil and Husserl, the integration of the self comes about through action, that is, Biran's principle of *resistence*. (Resistence expresses what becomes Weil's principle of *work* and Sartre's idea of *project*, "praxis.")

Husserl's analyses enriched the study of phenomenology by showing the need to shift attention to the description of intentional objects, existent and non-existent. Understanding of the foundation of knowledge could not be limited to a study of the activities of consciousness alone. The principle of intentionality provided the key to understanding the involvement of the activities of consciousness with the intended objects of consciousness. Weil's notion of perception as "travail" may be understood as an expression of intentionality.

Sartre disagreed with Husserl's claim that consciousness was discovered following a "reduction" brought about by a transcendental ego. To affirm the presence of a transcendental ego retarded the advances of phenomenology toward the description of objects themselves. It was a return to the primary of the ego.

> le "Je" est un producteur d'intériorité . . . .[44]

In Sartre's opinion, it wasn't necessary for phenomenology to depend upon a unifying individualizing "Je." Consciousness is intentionality.[45] Consciousness transcends and unifies *through* intentionality. The ego exists neither "in" nor "behind" consciousness, only "for" consciousness; that is, the ego is the presence of "I" in the world, an object among objects. Consciousness does not involve the ego; it has no contents, constitutes nothing more than spontaneity, than projection toward the objects of consciousness. Consciousness becomes consciousness of being in the world, and the ambiguity of the self's identity as separate, yet inextricable, from exteriority is resolved. Husserl had tried to resolve this ambiguity by his conceptualization of the transcendental ego.

> si je vise exclusivement cette vie je me retrouve en tant qu'ego pur avec le courant de mes cognitations.... [46]

Sartre rejects this solution some years later as an illusion of immanence. The reality of the universe guarantees the cogito. His rejection of Husserl's transcendental ego leads Sartre to an existential ethic deriving from the notion of being in the world. As Weil's principle of work bridged an important gap between phenomenology and sociology, so Sartre's exploration of the principles governing perception lead to what becomes the basis for his social and political commitment.

> les idées simples... expriment... le passage que le monde laisse à l'esprit... plus de contradition entre liberté et nécessité....[47]

It is significant that Weil perceives in her essay that there is no direct consciousness of "I," but only awareness of a consciousness of activities of a subject referred to as "I."

Weil's synthesis of the two structures of consciousness (réfléchie et réfléchissante, in Sartre's terminology) through the principle of work, or "travail effectif" is very similar to Sartre's. Sartre's description of *la conscience nonpositionnelle*, of the *tramway devant être rejoint* brings out the same points as Weil's description of actions such as writing. Both underline the complete absence of "le moi," "sur le plan irréfléchi." One is aware only of being an object among objects in pursuing a projected point through immediate action; one's activities are seen as part of the exteriority needed to transcend toward one's goals.

Thus there are important parallels between Weil's early ideas of perception and Sartre's: 1) the strong influence of Voluntarist philosophy and the importance of will in the transition toward a philosophy of action; 2) the principle of work ("praxis") as intentionality; 3) the awareness of consciousness as consciousness of "being in the world." This last point is the crux of the problem of "déracinement" for Weil. It is the source of difficulty in resolving the conflict of freeom and oppression.

Weil's exploration of the self's involvement and merging with exteriority led her to the brink of Sartre's conclusion of total commitment to one's "being in the world."

ma pensée est comme un élemént du monde . . . j'ai part à l'univers, *je suis au monde*.⁴⁸

To find parallels between Weil's early views and existentialism is not to devalue the final direction of her philosophy. I have done so in order to understand the problem of "déracinement." In *Existentialisme est un Humanisme*,⁴⁹ as well as in *La Transcendance de l'Ego*, Sartre refers to the transcendent power of concerted action. Weil had demonstrated earlier in a similar fashion the transcendent power of human freedom and thought through the principle of work as an indirect "prise de possession" of the self upon one's environment. In addition, she brings out the potentialities of the collective perception of humanity; collective work effort is underlined as a means of transcendency.

> cette action qui saisit le soleil est collective . . . l'humanité perçoit l'espace qui sépare la terre du soleil, tout come on peut dire que, par l'industrie, c'est l'humanité qui travaille . . . le pouvoir de l'humanité réunit. . . .⁵⁰

This is the final step of her essay on perception which was, in reality, a beginning statement on freedom and its limits just as Sartre's initial analysis of perception led to the formation of an Existentialist ethic. Weil has arrived at a new concept of freedom and consciousness through her expansion of Cartesian principles involving the duality of self, the reduction of perception to simple units of movement, the principle of work, and the decentering of movement; freedom is consciousness of being in the world, consciousness of the limits and potentiality for transcendency through collective perception and labor.⁵¹

In this essay there are different levels at which the pair "déracinement/enracinement" functions. Descartes' philosophical contribution constitutes an uprootal from tradition and authority, through reliance upon one's own reason, but this uprooting failed to resolve the mind/body duality. Descartes' philosophical rebellion did not culminate in a stronger regrounding of the Cogito, of self with exteriority, nor of mind with body. Instead it became the theoretical basis for the opposing philosophical movements of Idealism and Materialism. Therefore at the level of Descartes' initial contribution, "déracinement" is a positive movement, weakened by the absence of *valid* regrounding. One can interpret this failure to achieve a philosophical resolution of the mind/body duality as the absence of "enracinement" (rooting, grounding) the necessary aaccompanying factor of "déracinement."

Weil's relation to Descartes is another level at which the pair "déracinement/enracinement" functions. Cartesian theory is both the base and point of departure for Weil. Her ideas are both an extension and an uprootal from the traditionally opposing legacies of Descartes (the opposition of Idealist/Materialist philosophies). As did Descartes she uproots herself from tradition. At the same time her study advances through an extension of Descartes' ideas on geometry and perception, providing a basis for Weil's concepts of power, displacement, and collective labor. The movements of uprooting and rooting are simultaneous. Weil's resuscitation of Descartes implies that the movements of "déracinement/enracinement" function also as a purification. Cartesian theory became the basis for a tradition, encumbered and implanted beneath centuries of polemical interpretation.

The creation of a fictitious Descartes allows Weil a base from which to advance from a purified notion of Cartesian principle to explore and possibly resolve basic uncertainties. The "je" which she uses to express her own certainty and the principles of automony and reason represented by her fictitious Descartes, is a necessary device which captures the essential ambiguity of self. It allows Weil the flexibility and displacement to explore the power of self and its extricable involvement with the world; it allows her to explore both the presence and absence of self within a world which resists and diminishes our freedom. It enables her to simultaneously retain and question, basic traditional principles. Thus the opposing movements of "déracinement/enracinement" funtion simultaneously at the level of Weil's relation to Descartes. Weil's analysis is both an extension and a departure from Cartesian theory. The terms "deracinement/enracinement" are opposing yet complementary to each other. In one sense they convey Weil's analysis as the attempt to purify and rediscover the essential Descartes; in this case "enracinement" describes a negative state of encumberment, immobility, and "deracinement" describes the movement of change, the reduction of Cartesian theory to a purified state. In the other sense, "deracinement/enracinement" convey the movements of uprootal/grounding. 'Deracinement' here implies Weil's positive movement of uprootal from tradition but the uprootal is not total because it is dependent upon the retention of certain Cartesian principles. At this point the reader perceives that each term, each movement is contained within the other.

At the level of Weil's own analysis, her rejection of the transcendental ego is the primary movement of uprootal, the primary movement of 'déracinement.' It is a total rejection of solipsism. The movement of "enracinement" is the process by which Weil affirms the involvement of self with the world. This is a more valid form of grounding than in Descartes' thinking because mind and body, self and the world are shown as inextricable and are thus rejoined. But the process of rejoining involves both "déracinement/enracinement" as opposing yet complementary movements; the rejoining of interiority and exteriority is based on encounter and resistence between the forces of mind and body, between those of self and the world. Here the two terms (déracinement/enracinement) express the opposing movements of detachment/attachment, or dispersion/cohesion. These movements describe the rapport between interiority and exteriority. "Déracinement/enracinement" are terms which I use at this level of discussion to express the tension between interiority and exteriority, essential for true cohesion and unit, true "enracinement.' The value of 'deracinement/enracinement' lies in the flexibility provided by this tension.

Thus, Simone Weil's essay on Descartes is of major philosophical value. Although Weil does not use the terms 'déracinement/enracinement' until later years, I have used them to convey the complexity of ideas within her essay and to define Weil's philosophical position at this early point in her life. Weil's rejection of the Cartesian solipsistic viewpoint lays the groundwork for a lifetime of social and political commitment. It also reveals the complexity of that commitment. In addition, Weil's rejection of the transcendental ego is an early expression of deconstruction and decreation, principles which determine the pattern of Weil's entire philosophy and her search for true 'enracinement.'

Notes to Chapter 1

[1] Sylvain Aurous and Yvonne Weil, *Dictionnaire des Auteurs et des Thèmes de la Philosophie* (Paris: Librairie Hachette, 1975), 129.

[2] Simone Weil, "Science et Perception Dans Descartes," in *Sur la science* (Paris: Editions Gallimard, 1966), 47.

[3] Simone Pétrement, *La Vie de Simone Weil*, Vol. 1, *1909-1934* (Paris: Librairie Arthème Fayard, 1973), 56.

[4] Simone Weil, *Lectures on Philosophy*, trans. Hugh Price, introduction by Peter Winch (Cambridge: Cambridge University Press, 1973), 4.

[5] Weil, *Sur la Science*, 50.

[6] Ibid., 49.

[7] Ibid., 53.

[8] Ibid., 52.

[9] Yet the neo-Kantian influence of the early twentieth century is apparent in this essay as Weil seems to succeed only in recognizing the impossibility of polarizing freedom and necessity, that is, the inextricability of the self and one's environment. Weil's initial search for a total displacement of power between the self and its world fails or, even more, leads us to an impasse particular to the development of continental philosophy of her time, as will be discussed further. Beyond the purposes of discussion of this essay, it is also indicative of the equilibrium between freedom and necessity, power and obedience, oppression and liberty, which she was to seek in her political and social involvement.

[10] Ibid., 54-55.

[11] Ibid., 55.

[12] Ibid., 62.

[13] Ibid., 61.

[14] The reader of literature is well acquainted with the treatment of this paradox. Camus's portrayal of the rebel (*L'Homme Révolté*) and his essay on Sisyphe are perhaps the most famous. It is interesting to consider the contrasting resolutions of Weil and Camus. The transcendence of the other, of exterior limits by the infinite value of the self's conceptual capacities is for both an affirmation of the self. For Camus it is not only an affirmation, but a challenge, as seen through the lucid bitterness he attributes to characters facing this paradox (i.e., Dr. Rieux, Sisyphe, Jean-Baptiste Clamence) and by the violence of his vocabulary used to describe consciousness or awareness—"Je me révolte, donc nous sommes." (Albert Camus, *L'Homme Révolté* [Paris: Editions Gallimard, 1951]) In this early period the influences of rationalism and politics on philosophical development are at their height. Yet one recognizes in this essay the tension between action and passivity, between obedience and domination. This tension between the infinite value of the human mind and the forces of necessity contribute to the importance of "l'enracinement" and "le déracinement." Confronting the two infinities once discussed by Pascal, the human creature wavers between affirmation and denial, between power and abdication. It is significant that this essay brings to light her closeness to the existentialist resolution during these early years;yet as shown in later works, Weil in her last few years seeks spiritual solace through obedience to necessity, identifying necessity with universal clarity and order, order seen as an expression of divine love. Despite the change of her philosophical direction Weil retained a deep consciousness and sense of responsibility of "being in the world" by affirming the power and freedom of the self within the limits of the physical contingencies of the exterior world. More so than Camus, she sought the ideal conditions by which the self can manifest its greatest freedom within the limita-

"Science et Perception dans Descartes" 39

tions of physical and social reality..

[15] The body is perceived by Weil, in part at least, as an expression of exteriority, of an exterior will and movement.

[16] Ibid., 85.

[17] Ibid., 86.

[18] Ibid., 88.

[19] Ibid.

[20] Ibid., 89.

[21] Ibid., 89-90.

[22] Ibid., 92.

[23] Ibid., 93.

[24] Although Weil's views on science are closely related to the subject of perception, they are discussed in a separate study. I prefer to follow without digression the continuity and development of Weil's thoughts on perception.

[25] These commentaries have, unfortunately, not been located among the papers of Weil.

[26] I am referring to M. Camille Marcoux, former classmate of Weil and Lecturer of Literature at Lycée Henri IV, and to M. Gustave Thibon, a close friend of Weil during the latter part of her life, following the capitulation of France.

[27] Jacques Cabaud, *L'Expérience Vécue de Simone Weil* (Paris, Librairie Plon,1957), 33.

[28] Edmond Husserl, *Méditations Cartésiennes-Introduction àla Phénoménologie* (Paris: Librairie Philosophique J. Vrin, 1953).

[29] Weil, "Science et Perception dans Descartes," 73.

[30] Benoît Spinoza, *L'Ethique* (Paris: Editions du Rocher, 1974), 197, 277.

[31] Vergez and Huisman, "Les Cartésiens," *Histoire des Philosophes*, 17.

[32] Brunschvicg had demanded of his students, among whom were Pétrement and Weil, an intensive study of *An Inquiry Into Human Understanding*.

[33] Kant's epistemology reveals the overlapping of feeling and thought, a system of preconceived structures by which "la sensibilité" belongs or is included in transcendental philosophy. It is in his work *Critique de la Raison Pure* that Kant defines and distinguishes between "l'esthétique transcendantale" as "la science de tous les principes a priori de la sensibilité."

[34] Vergez and Huisman, "Le Spiritualisme français au XIX^c et au XX^c siècles," *Histoire des Philosophes*, 334-37.

[35] Sartre, "La Liberté Cartésienne," 335.

[36] The reader is reminded that, although of Jewish origin, Weil had been raised as an agnostic and had not yet concerned herself with religious questions, still in what is called her "Rationalist Period." Pétrement states that Weil was, at this time, vacillating between two opposing philosophies. In her long biography of Weil, she recalls a conversation during which Weil fervently defended Alain's voluntarist philosophy in opposition to religious assertions. I also recall an incident discussed with me by Camille Marcoux during which Weil revealed her admiration and identification with a mutual friend entering a religious order.

[37] Albert Camus, *Le Malentendu, suivi de Caligula* (Paris: Editions Gallimard, 1958), 112.

[38] Pétrement, 160.

[39] As the Existentialist would later rearticulate, "Existence précède essence," resolving the question of will and freedom by acceptance of one's place in the world. Weil was progressing

beyond Alain's point of view towards recognition of one's freedom and consciousness as a question of "being and consciousness in the world." At no other point was she closer to the Existentialist viewpoint. Later, she was to progress in a different direction, where, "l'éssence précède existence."

⁴⁰Emile Chartier, *Les Idées et les Ages* (Paris, NRE, 1927), 107.

⁴¹Husserl, *Médiations*, 18.

⁴²Weil, "Science et Perception," 73.

⁴³Denis Diderot, "Lettre sur les Aveugles," *Oeuvres Philosophiques, Chronologie et Introduction par Antoine Adam* (Paris: Garnier-Flammarion, 1972).

⁴⁴Jean-Paul Sartre, "La Transcendance de l'Ego—Esquisse d'une description Phénoménologique," *Recherches Philosophiques* VI (Paris: Librairie A. Hatier, 1936-37), 88.

⁴⁵Ibid., 88-89.

⁴⁶Husserl, *Méditations Cartésiennes*, 18.

⁴⁷Sartre, "La Transcendance de l'Ego," 89.

⁴⁸Weil, "Science et Perception," 73.

⁴⁹Jean-Paul Sartre, *L'Existentialisme est un Humanisme* (Paris; Editions Nagel, 1965).

⁵⁰Weil, "Science et Perception," 91.

⁵¹Pétrement, in her biography of Weil, mentions the low mark Weil received on this essay and Alain's anger at Brunschvicg. Alain had rationalized this negative appraisal by saying "C'est parce qu'elle est juive." This as not probable, however, as Pétrement says, because Brunschvicg was of Jewish origin himself and had given a particularly high grade to another student also of Jewish background. Although Brunschvicg's objections to Weil's essay, "Science et Perception," were never explained other than his dislike of Weil's development of the theme of "travail" in association with a treatment of Cartesian thought, one can understand his antipathy to such a development of Alain's voluntarist philosophy of action. Brunschvicg and Alain were known rivals. His disapproval was of symbolic value because it indicates to us the resistance against the strong turn toward Materialism that was the result of Alain's Voluntarist influence and studies of phenomenology of the time. Brunschvicg himself was known for his Idealist philosophy, his own belief in the synthesizing force of the mind, unifying the phenomena of exteriority and interiority. The views of each, however, on work and the actual dynamics of this source of unity, synthesis of exteriority and interiority, differed significantly.

Chapter 2
A Study of *Leçons de Philosophie*: Méthodologie de l'Action

> ... diaspora. C'est ce mot qui nous servira pour désigner le mode d'être du Pour-soi: il est diasporique. ...
>
> Jean-Paul Sartre
> *L'Etre et le Néant*[1]

Weil recognized in her diplôme monograph the inevitability of freedom and involvement of the self in the surrounding world. In "Science et Perception Dans Descartes," Weil's exploration related to a world where there was no pre-established order; one floated in ambiguity, unsurely, across and between undefined limits. The essay maintains that it is only by the affirmation of will and power that one exists. Value and existence are one; will and action build the unity of self. Yet one's existence constitutes inevitable inextricability with exteriority. This is the point of departure for *Leçons de Philosophie*.

The collection, *Leçons de Philosophie*, is not a formal work by Weil. It is a student's careful compilation of lecture notes taken during Weil's third year as a philosophy instructor. Anne Reynaud-Guérithault offered as an insight to Weil's teaching and philosophy a transcription of her notes taken during her year of instruction under Weil at the Lycée de Jeunes Filles de Roanne, during the school year, 1933-1934.

In the course of these lectures, Weil credits and challenges both the Materialist and Idealist approaches to the analysis of perception and knowledge acquisition. The primary value of this collection rests on this opposition and its resolution through methodical action. Consequently, this chapter will focus on her presentation of this opposition and the measure of its influence on Weil's philosophy at this transitional point. One cannot be absolutely sure of Weil's own position at this stage, but the treatment of certain themes (methodical action, reciprocity and balance of the mind/body duality, the distinction between effort and will, etc.) takes a direction which can be seen clearly in her later work.

Of particular significance is the positive treatment of Materialist philosophy in these lectures. Weil does more that present the Materialist, Radical Empiricism of William James. She concurs with and even extends further most of his conclusions. Although she unfortunately does not always distinguish between the Behavioral Reductionism of Watson and Pavlov, and the radical empiricism of the major American and British pragmatists James, Mill and Dewey, the emphasis she places on these different aspects of modern materialist approaches to the acquisition of knowledge has particular relevance to her own philosophy. For this reason, *Leçons de Philosophie* should be recognized as the main work revealing the influence of empiricism on Weil's concepts of work and methodical action, as well as a reinforcement of her rejection of the transcendental ego discussed in the previous chapter. *Leçons de Philosophie* shows also the point at which Weil's background in rationalism and phenomenology was merging with the materialist, empirical aspects of the School of American Pragmatism represented by William James.

Weil's positive treatment of Materialism, and radical empiricism, constituted a symbolic effort to emerge from the isolation of the French Rationalist tradition. This effort to unite continental and non-continental philosophies, was perhaps not deliberate on Weil's part, but her attempt to resolve the contradictions of Materialist and Idealist philosophies certainly was intentional. This suggests the influence of Pragmatist, empirical philosophy on the development of phenomenology following the rejection of Husserl's concept of the transcendental ego. Weil's lectures indicate the influence of pragmatist, empirical philosophy on Modern Existentialist Phenomenology. The reciprocity of the mind/body dualism in the determination of perception and conscious acts is also prominent in the writings of Merleau-Ponty, who wrote some years after Weil. However the main interest of this chapter is to show the development of Weil's philosophy constituted a fusion of Pragmatic, Voluntarist, and Idealist philosophical traditions. The fusion of these philosophies resulted in the formation of Weil's concept of methodical action.

As Weil has in all the realms of her philosophy, she opposes in order to resolve, she valorizes opposition in order to synthesize or balance. Weil notes both the opposition and complementarity of Materialist and Idealist approaches to the acquisition of knowledge. Therefore in the intermediate stage of Weil's rationalist development, the powerful antithetical yet complementary forces of 'déracinement/enracinement' are strongly present. Throughout this work, Weil refuses entrenchment within one dogmatic philosophic resolution, rejecting complete acceptance of either of the final imperatives of Idealism or Materialism.

'Déracinement/Enracinement' manifests itself further by Weil's departure from the isolation of continental philosophy to integrate with European beliefs the enriching influence of Pragmatism, Behaviorism and Materialist philosophies. Both the forces of uprootal and integration are present working in opposition and as complementary powers.

In this stage of Weil's development as in all others the complementary opposition of the forces of 'déracinement/enracinement'" are powerfully present. the feeling and knowing individual self is in perpetual diaspora, integrated yet uprooted from both the world and the objective self. In this period as in others, Weil searches for resolution in the flexibility of balance, reciprocity and unity without plunging into the abyss of inflexible dogma.

Leçons de Philosophie reveals three main features of Weil's thought at this time which are major features of her later writing. *A Search for Order*, unlike her first main work which is discussed in the previous chapter, *Leçons de Philosophie*, reveals a progression of thought based on the idea of order as logically prior to action; order exists and needs to be affirmed and understood. We rebuild and transform this order through the study of body, mind, morality, and the measure of their interdependence.

Dualities necessitating unification, synthesis. The dualities of interiority and exteriority still persist in her thought but have taken a greater variety of forms: 1) Pantheistic belief in divine immanence vs. Cartesian belief in divine transcendency, that is, God's will is either determined and manifested by us or is pre-existent to all forms of life and being; 2) Materialist vs. Idealist philosophical approaches; 3) finite vs infinite; the opposition of limit and limitless; 4) consciousness vs. unconsciousness, their opposition and complementarity; presence or absence of consciousness determines the struggle between good and evil; 5) necessity vs. free will; and finally, 6) the unity of self vs. the division of self; in the distinction between "le je" and "le moi," the self as subject is separate and distinct from the self as object. Defined as the source of Kant's synthetic unity, "le je" links thought with exteriority. However, the predominance of the conceptual self necessary to build this relation increases the polarization between the active and passive selves, "le je" and "le moi." Paradoxically, unity and order in our perception are built through a state of objectification. The self is both unity and division. Weil does not escape that ambiguity even in her final conclusions.

A Methodology of Action is introduced to provide the synthesizing force resolving the dualities of the order Weil establishes. Not all of these oppositions are resolved but they are minimized by Weil's emphasis on our capacity for transfromation or reconstruction through methodical action. The establishment of unity, objectivity, and relation is a form of methodical action. Weil's theory of methodical action is, in fact, a transformation in itself of traditional philosophical problems of duality, synthesis, and order. At this point, it is not clear whether Weil truly seeks complete synthesis through action, complete unity of the interiority/exteriority duality, or rather an identification of principles and contingencies demanding different types of individual or concerted responses. However, the analysis of and need for effective, methodical action is the final and basic principle encompassed by this body of notes. Compared to her dissertation on Descartes, this is a more ordered and developed form of the existentialist ethic. Methodical action justifies time and brings eternity into ourselves.

SEARCH FOR ORDER:
MATERIALIST VS. IDEALIST PHILOSOPHIES

In contrast to "Science et Perception Dans Descartes," the basic premise of Weil's lectures at Roanne was that exteriority already exists in an ordered form and is the primary reality. It is through the world that one learns of oneself and exteriority. This is a departure from the Cartesian solipsistic view point that the existence of self is the only certainty. It is an obvious attempt to eliminate the obscurity prevalent in her dissertation of Descartes where perception was based on the primary reality of self, and self became distinguishable from exteriority only in so far as will and action provided an affirmation of being. Weil draws general conclusions on the effectiveness of the opposed schools of psychological study.

Weil rejects the simplistic solution sought either by a completely exterior, materialist approach, or through an entirely interior, intellectual and spiritual solution. The philosophies referred to are, respectively, Behaviorism, associated most closely at the time with the psychologist, Watson, and the psychology of intuition, the spiritual positivism of Bergson. Both are ineffective in Weil's opinion, because they suppress a necessary element of reality; the behaviorists ignore the element of spirituality and concentrate on physical states of the body; those of Bergson's following exclude the importance of physical reality and intelligence.

In observation of exteriority, Weil observes that knowledge of others is obtained through three different levels of action: Nature provides us with the *physical reflex* as a manifestation of the other's presence, both mental and physical. In society, custom and habit also perform this function. In addition to these forces of physical and social determinism, there is the level of *voluntary, conscious acts* whereby the individual manifests free will. Distinguishing between these three forms of motivation is impossible in Weil's opinion.

Concerning knowledge of oneself, that is, introspection, Weil is pessimistic. Introspection is incompatible with most forms of human activity, such as speculative thought, emotion, or physical activity, in which one's awareness is directed away from oneself. On those rare occasions when one directs one's thought solely upon oneself, it is impossible to grasp the reality of the self because one is constantly changing.

Introspection demands a deliberate effort of concentrated passivity by which we attempt to remove ourselves from the forces of exteriority which divert our attention from ourselves. In doing so, however, we are nullifying that which consolidates and justifies our being, that is, the action and resistance with which we sustain or dominate exterior forces. This state of self-observation is an indirect source of knowledge. In observing oneself, one can directly see only the self which observes, not the observed self. The observed self is therefore found indirectly. One can never know what one is at the present moment. The observing self can only reveal the observed self as it was at a moment prior to the present. Consequently, introspection can only provide information on past emotional states. Past emotional states are valuable only in so far as they are transformed into action. Weil concludes that both forms of psychology, that of the study of others through physical manifestations of their thought process, and that of introspection or the study of the self, provide us with no definite knowledge. In examining the acts of others we cannot distinguish their motivation, be it physically or socially determined or an expression of personal will. In examining ourselves, we can perceive nothing more than our own thought and we are blocked by the structure of consciousness.

Thus the solution in Weil's eyes is to seek, not a scientific theory on thought, but analysis. Thought is present only in so far as it is active, but as such, cannot be grasped for it is lost in the process of being observed. As the basis for her analysis, Weil hypothetically separates the exterior world from the self. Her object is to study carefully the influences each has upon the other, despite the knowledge that neither realm is an absolute determinant of reality. To do this, she discusses the acquisition of knowledge first from the materialist point of view and then from the Idealist. The value and limits of both are discussed in her lectures.

THE MATERIALIST APPROACH TO KNOWLEDGE: THE INFLUENCE OF EXTERIORITY

In her discussion of the materialist approach to knowledge, Weil limits exteriority to one's own physicality, and uses the influence of the body upon action, feeling, and thought as a measure of determiniation by exteriority. Her main sources of information and analysis are provided by two physical manifestations of individual existence—reflexes and instincts. Congenital and acquired reflexes provide a means by which to classify, to generalize our reactions in the world of objects. In addition, the generalization provided by our reflexes reveals that we react physically not to the details of our environment, but to impressions of forms and relationships between structures. Thus Weil concludes from the discoveries of Pavlov and German psychologists that reflexes are an indication of an ordered world. She further affirms the credibility of their conclusion, that it is our body, not our mind, that grasps structural relationships and order.

THE INFLUENCE OF THE BODY ON ACTION

Reynaud-Guérithault's notes reflect Weil's uncertainty as to the distinguishable differences between the body and mind as determinants of action. She recognizes, however, the extent to which action can be interpreted as conditioned reflexes. The body influences action particularly through reflexes. Custom, family tradition, morality, and language are forms of a conditioned reflex. Work is an extension of a conditioned reaction to the noticed presence or absence of the object of labor. Conformity can be interpreted as physically motivated, as is the imitative instinct. One could conclude that material and technological progress is assured and inevitable as mechanical reactions perpetually manifest themselves in adaptation to increasingly complex and superior ways of life. Weil considers actions as they manifest themselves physically, from an empiricist's view of exteriority; she concludes that there is truth in the behaviorist's argument that action is the result of a conditioned response to one's environment.

INFLUENCE OF THE BODY ON EMOTION

In her examination of the body's influence on feeling and emotion, Weil recognizes the coherence and logic of the ideas of Freud and James and their development of Rationalist and Determinist explanations of perception. James's Pragmatism was based on the idea that corporal movement is the principal manifestation of emotion. In turn, as perceived by Descartes, Spinoza, and Freud, the corporal movements composing these emotions result from instinct, natural and conditioned reflexes, or a combination thereof. This confirms the purely corporal basis for feeling and emotion; the body is both the origin and manifestation of emotional response.

Upon having established the Pragmatist's emphasis on the body and their argument that corporal movement is both the essence and product of emotion, Weil also develops a discussion centering around the idea that emotions are the medium of expression of physiological changes experienced in the course of a lifetime. She evidently bases her discussion primarily on examples drawn from Descartes' "Traité des Passions de l'Ame" (1649), additional support being found in the psychological studies taken from the writings of Stendhal, Byron, and Racine. Emotion is the expression or consequence of action. One's sense of resistance can be unconsciously projected into the object of one's combat and thereby lost. The transfer of one's power of resistance to the object of one's confrontation is the reason for the sense of fatality and mystery associated with that object in the mind of the subject. This suggests that Weil's later efforts to demystify structures of power had been motivated in part by the revelations of Materialist theory. The idea she developed later on the impossibility of stabilizing, possessing, or localizing power and violence suggests the influence of William James's analysis of the close reciprocity of emotion and movement. Weil's emphasis on the volatile nature of power may well be an extension of James's theory on the transferability of resistance and physical experience. There is, at least, a striking relation between the two concepts.

Weil is obviously in agreement with the Pragmatist's explanation. Weil illustrated further James's famous theory of the reciprocity of movement and emotion by examples in practical life where action reinforces the emotion it expresses and where one projects and transfers through imagination one's physiological experience into the body of the object of the action or project in question.[2] She thereby affirms that the pragmatist or radical empiricist explanation of emotion was fully credible, logical and consistent in the various aspects of the unified theory.

INFLUENCE OF THE BODY ON THOUGHT
Sensation. In Weil's view, Ghérithault does not reveal to us Weil's scepticism regarding the effectiveness of the body's influence on thought. Basic information is relayed by the body to the mind through physical sensation, but the senses are inefficacious because they provide us with a perpetually changing impression of reality. Sight alone gives no orientation as to distance, forms, distinction of color, or spatial reality. In looking at a chair, our sight does not enable us to distinguish the chair from its background, the seat, the legs as separate parts of a whole.

> Dès que deux couleurs apparaissent comme distinctes, elles le sont absolument. On n'établit pas de séries entre les deux cas car on ne peut ranger des couleurs en séries qu'en les rattachant à des quantités. . . .[3] (*Leçons*, 36-37)

Weil argues that sight by itself is incapable of providing us with the knowledge of quantitative differences. From the senses of touch, hearing, smell and taste, no more of an understanding is acquired. They provide no understanding of distance or space, nothing more than a heterogeneous group of impressions indistinguishable in quantity or degree. Consequently by the inability to distinguish quantitative differences, a sense provides no order, no relation between the sensations it communicates. They provide no structure to orient action. They only underline our passivity in relation to exteriority ("sentir, c'est toujours subir. . . ." [*Leçons*, 41]). They give us no information on temporal and spatial reality. Yet Weil recognizes the power of physical movement or thought.

Movement gives us the feeling of change, of transformation through touch, and pain. Still Weil warns it is limited to an awareness only of qualitative change.

Weil uses the concept of "series" to establish how one passes from a sense of movement, a state of qualitative change, to spatial understanding which constitutes an awareness of quantitative change. We arrive at an understanding of quantitative difference through experience with matter; during this contact an imaginary process of reconstruction takes place. This process is the mind's construction of a series. Thus the body cannot independently provide us with an ordered comprehension of reality. This is another proof of the inextricable mind/body, interiority/exteriority duality.

Whereas we have the need to distinguish qualitative from quantitative differences, we have an even greater tendency to confuse actions with their consequences. In her discussion of innervation Weil refers to the indirect awareness of one's own effort or action.

> Est-ce qu'on sent l'effort en tant qu'on le produit ou en tant qu'on en est victime? Sentons-nous seulement les conséquences de notre activité, ou notre activité elle-même?....(*Leçons*, 40)

Unavoidably we have become so conditioned that we confuse the cause of a sensation with the sensation itself; in the same way we define effort and action. We are unable to discern the difference between our action and its consequences. Weil concludes that effort is experienced; it is an experience passively undergone because it is inversely proportional to the presence of will. Dominance of the will occurs when effort gives way to ease and serenity. In the ultimate realization of the will, effort is absent, which leads Weil to conclude that effort, as a reaction to all physical experience and sensation, is a reflection foremostly of our passive self.

> la sensation est toujours subie, passive, même lorsqu'on sent la volonté s'exercer puissamment. . . . (*Leçons*, 41)

It is already possible to trace the spectrum of action in Weil's philosophy:

one awakens in a world without order, without limits defining what is the self and what is exteriority. Gradually, one arrives at a definition of oneself; one's being is inevitably defined as "being in the world" because one affirms one's existence only by will and action; one's sense of power and will is at its height. One is in the world. One lives in action with others although that involvement inevitably limits one's own sense of autonomy. In "Science et Perception Dans Descartes" Weil would propose an order by which to capture the exact measure of our capability for independent, effective action. In this order, the will manifests itself differently; the will acts "passively" through the height of awareness it has arrived at. The will remains active and in equilibrium with outside forces by the awareness it sustains of its own capabilities or incapabilities for advancement towards the state of greatest possible public happiness and for the fulfillment of private conscience as Weil states in *Leçons de Philosophie*. Camus also would later emphasize this form of will or "passivity." In view of the limits to which one's actions and finite state are bound, strength lies in awareness, lucidity, and the ability to define the situation and the force of one's own presence. For Weil, action would slowly become less and less a manifestation of freedom and will, until the will would, in the tension of personal spiritual experience, impose its own negation. In Weil's lifetime, and in her writings, one can see the expanse traveled between two kinds of passivity. As shown in her essay, "Science et Perception dans Descartes," involuntary passivity precedes the awakening of the will which struggles against the domination and resistance of exteriority. As Weil's ideas change, will is redefined, and in the later part of her lifetime, it manifests itself most fully in that form of 'concentrated passivity' that particularly characterizes her final spiritual writings. Evidently, in her lectures at Roanne, Weil had already begun to perceive abstention and passivity as an expression of will.

Imagination and Memory: In this study of the body's influence on the mind, there are two major sources Weil considers: imagination and memory. Weil equates memory with habit in relation to thought.

Imagination: Weil believed that imagination alone enables one to comprehend space, depth, and form. Space is conceived through the imagination which builds a relation between physical sensation and the physical self, a relation which incites action and contact.

> rapport qui consiste essentiellement dans un rapport entre les objets et moi, rapport qui consiste dans une certaine disposition à agir. . . . (*Leçons*, 46)

One's measure of depth results from the merging of two different images from each of our eyes, neither of which corresponds to the final assumed reality. One's body is so disposed as to unify two different visual images into one. Rapport and unity are created as images merge together. The imagination arouses this movement of the self's advancement through time and space.

Imagination enables us to comprehend form, also. At the sight of a point we project the line of movement unifying that point with ourselves. The presence of diversely arranged objects implies an order; it invites us to build upon them a unifying structure; in this way two points imply a straight line, and three a triangle. Their presence invites us to move, impose limits, shapes and form.

> Toutes les lignes qui limitent les objets, qui constituent des formes, nous sont données par nos réflexes, par notre propre mouvement. ... (*Leçons*, 49)

Weil thus identifies a basic geometrical sense present in our perception: The relation between exteriority and our perception. The relation between exteriority and ourselves is based on a sense of projected movement. In this manner the self's imaginative power bridges the gap between received impressions, thought and action. Once the imagination creates the illusion of movement, the body reacts to this projection.

Memory: In her discussion of the role of memory in perception, Weil establishes memory as the body's creation rather than that of the mind.

In Bergson's analysis "le souvenir" is the memory of a specific happening accompanied by all the details associated with its particular circumstances and place in time. "La mémoire," however, is the return of an isolated element of the past. Bergson associates "la mémoire" with the body as a physical reflex action responding to present circumstances. He considers "les images-souvenirs," although aroused by mood or feeling, as a part of thought. Time cannot touch much less destroy "le souvenir" because it has already reached a state of completion and specificity. An isolated part of the past, such as a song or verse recalled through memory, is perfected or improved in time through practice and repetition. "Le souvenir" remains the property of the mind whereas "la mémoire" is completed by the body and physical response. This is significant for Weil's claim that meaning is one of the two main sources of the body's influence on the mind. Bergson's definition of "Le souvenir" as the sole property of the mind and irreductible to any bodily influence is a theory with which Weil cannot agree.

Yet Bergson maintained that the body does influence the manifestation of the "souvenirs." In Bergson's view, the unconscious is a storehouse of memories, or "souvenirs." They are there, unconscious, inactive. Their simultaneous manifestation would be incompatible with the body's capabilities for physical and emotional response; so, in Bergson's opinion, our physical state is a discriminating force which determines in great part the manifestation of memories or "souvenirs." The body, the involvement of our physical being, draws "les souvenirs" out of the shadow of the unconscious.

Weil is skeptical as to the true existence of the unexpressed, unconscious "souvenir." This is consistent with her discussion of consciousness and reasoning in a later section of *Leçons de Philosophie*, where she maintains that full consciousness is the only point at which existence can be acknowledged and defined.

Weil reinforces the point of view that memory is a creation of our body rather than of our mind by an analysis of "le sosuvenir" as found in Proust's *A La Recherche du Temps Perdu*. She indicates that it was through a suppression of effort, a self-imposed flexibility and openness, that Proust gave room to the expansion of unconscious feeling that had begun with the taste of the tea and the madeleine. This is a form of self-imposed passivity by which the will leaves itself flexible and open.

> Dans la mesure où Proust cherche, il rejette le souvenir au lieu de l'évoquer. L'activité de l'esprit n'a donc rien à voir dans l'évocation du souvenir. . . . (*Leçons*, 55)

Departing somewhat from Bergson's viewpoint of "le souvenir," she defines it differently. In the context of Proust's writing it is a conditioned reaction to awareness of absence in the present, that is, to consciousness of something no longer existing. The memory of the past arrived to fill up the absence of the present. The object evoking this reaction brings with it a special form of perception, which is in itself, a physical response. This response or perception is disproportional to its cause. Objects take on their own power by the emotions they unleash. Elements of the physical world provide the basis for remembrance, the evocation of the past. Memories exist only at the point of consciousness, a stage reached through their involvement with the body. One entrusts objects with the guardianship of isolated moments, feelings and events. One hopes to perpetuate one's own presence through them and the memories their presence evokes in our absence. The physical world of which our body is a part, determines memory. Weil thus extends the role of the body because a memory, both the origin and the product of physical response, participates in perception.

Influence of the Body on Reasoning: Weil credits the body as well as the mind with power of clarification. This is evident in her discussion of 'comparison', where she continues to describe imagination and the relation it establishes as a function of the body. At this point, Weil is recognizing an order in which the body is distinct both from the world and from the self; in this order, the body is an instrument of generalization, and helps determine the supposedly purely mental processes.

Spinoza's influence should be noted in this discussion, his emphasis on the finite nature of our being; the body is so limited that it is capable of determining in itself only a predictable amount of images.

> Les 'images' sont les traces des choses sur le corps, traces qui sont en réalité celles des réactions du corps à l'égard des choses. . . .
> (*Leçons*, 58)

As Spinoza implies, these images which reinforce a dualistic view of ourselves vs. exteriority, are, in fact, ambiguous reflections of our limited, finite, physical beings. In addition, these images constitute the body's response to the need to generalize, to distinguish between the obscurity of impressions received by the mind. Beyond the dual distinctions of self and exteriority, the body builds general categories through its responses. These general distinctions clarified by the body descend thereby to the realm of the particular, through the mind.

In considering generalization, Weil is critical of the Nominalist school; she rejects absolute particularity as a definition of reality. True to the Cartesian tradition she identifies more closely with the Realist School which defines realities through generalization. Our physical responses to exterior elements constitute the relationship between exteriority and ourselves. The mind cannot build the relation that exists between generalized elements.

Weil claims that the process discussed and attributed to generalization applies also to abstraction. However, her discussion reveals a slightly different consideration. She makes an appropriate analogy between the particularization of elements within a general category, and the concretizing of abstractions.

But she states that it is, above all, emotion which leads to the expression of individuality, of the particular, through art and religion, as concrete manifestations of the abstract. This emotion that inspires the final concretization, the final particularization of individual elements, is considered part of the body; it is a consequence of the body's contact with exteriority and the subsequent relation built. This relation, however, is based on the tension created between feeling and reality as one takes hold of one's emotion and justifies order.

The body as an instrument of elucidation produces associated images and ideas. Thought as an association of images, manifests itself unconsciously in dreams and introspection, or consciously in rational judgment and mathematical analysis. Algebra is a manifestation of such association of thought and imagery, in its tendency towards the categorization and a grouping of similar terms. In geometry, reasoning takes place through association by the accumulative nature of knowledge itself—that it, the discovery of a theorem results from logical conclusions drawn directly from other theorems.

Psychological Atomism defines human thought as the gradual disassociation of imagery. In the views of philosophers such as Hume and Mill, the mind constructs no unity. Our impressions are distinct from each other. The associationists believe that impressions are disparate, distinct experiences whose autonomous occurrence is not determined by anything more than chance. Weil recognized the body's role in determining the association of images which in turn determines our perception and behavior; but she rejected the Associationist theory as the basis of perception. By her rejection of the Associationist theory, Weil has already implied her position as to the total rejection of causality and the crisis of determinism with which she would involve herself more fully in later years, particularly in her writings on science and the Quantum Theory. Her main argument, at this point, however, is that the process of perception establishes unity, structure, a rapport between elements of one's exteriority. The reception of sensations and imaginative powers synthesize this structural relationship.

THE POWER OF SELF-INTERIORITY

The encounter of thought with exteriority leads to the structuring of reality. Contingent thought is transformed into thought bearing the mark of necessity. This process is what Weil calls *the discovery of mind*. This encounter is the point of departure for her description of the mind and associated processes, that is, a description of interiority. A materialist approach was appropriate to describe the reception of information from exteriority prior to the encounter of exteriority and interiority. Following this encounter, interiority predominates.

Thought as Will and Consciousness: For most philosophers dealing with phenomenological questions, there is a force consolidating the unconscious with the conscious. In Weil's case, thought is a manifestation of consciousness. It was Leibnitz, she points out who first introduced a theory of perception based on the unconscious; particles of units of unconscious perception had to be consolidated before reaching the point of conscious perception and thought. In her own philosophy, Weil applies this concept of unconsolidated thought. "Les pensées contingentes," (*Leçons*, 119) are not recognized as true thought because they represent an unconscious which by its very nature remains unstructured, unconsolidated; the unconscious represents a stage prior to the essential encounter with exteriority; thought is consolidated by this encounter and until that point thought does not exist. That is why Weil refuses to describe the unconscious as a realm of thought. This is the basic reason for her challenge of Freud's theory of the subconscious and Bergson's theory of "le souvenir inconscient" and its creative 'élan.' The unconscious is reduced to define a second self, instead of consolidation through the will and the mind of this unconscious with consciousness. The unconsciousness unveiled by Freud's theory of psychoanalysis is the source of repressed identity condemned by society; in Bergson's theory it is the source of true creativity and fulfillment. Each of these theories polarizes the unconscious and the conscious, whereas Weil reintegrates the two. Although her contribution to Existentialism is the main point of this discussion, it cannot be denied that Weil's approach led her to a stoical but somewhat simplistic and erroneous devaluation of Freudian theory. Although it seems to discount the complexity of studies surrounding Freud's theory of the subconscious, Weil's rejection of the term "subconscient" in favor of "refoulement" is a deliberate effort to retain the role of will in determining consciousness.

Self-determination by the will pervades Weil's views on consciousness. She believed in the absolute moral responsibility one fulfills by an affirmation of will or by the voluntary choice not to exercise will. The choice between refusal or recognition of will reflects the power of will itself and is an unavoidable moral responsibility.

Identity:
> Aucun des faits qu'on peut alléguer sur les troubles de la personnalité, aucune lutte intérieure, aucune alteration de souvenir ne brise l'unité en nous. . . . (*Leçons*, 120)

In Weil's philosophy the interiority/exteriority duality is an essential trait of the self, without which the self could not authenticate and affirm itself. Only by one's affirmation of the dual nature of the self, does one affirm the unity of self through the presence of will and consciousness. This is an essential aspect of the problem of "déracinement" in Weil's writings. The self depends upon estrangement, duality, for a sense of unity and existence.

> ... dès lors qu'on dit qu'on est deux, c'est qu'on est un, puisqu'il y a *une seule conscience*. ... (*Leçons*, 117)

At this stage of Weil's philosophy, one notes that there are three kinds of consciousness of the self; consciousness of the self as a subject, consciousness of self as an object, and consciousness of the self as a synthesis of both subject and object. This last form is the normal state in Weil's view, consciousness of being both. The other two forms of consciousness are unhealthy states of mind, reflecting either a refusal to accept one's limits or a loss of identity. Still, in the consciousness of "je" as both the subject and object of thought, "je" as subject is the more dominant force in the unity of self and the search for order. Identity of the self in time is a merging of multiple personalities. In Weil's opinion, the self as subject predominates; it is as a subject rather than as an object that one remembers oneself, even though remembrance is an objectifying process.

> Tout ce que nous subissons échappe à notre souvenir; et nous nous le rappelons seulement dans la mesure où le subi est un obstacle à notre action. ... (*Leçons*, 120)

Judgment: Judgment is equivalent to will according to Weil's lectures, as surely as value is to existence. Through her discussion of Kant's categories of analytical and synthetic judgments, she emphasizes the predominance of the mind, of "je" as subject, the force which orders and structures reality.

It is significant that at this point in her philosophy Weil rejects the denial of free will and judgment by the determinist doctrines of materialism, associationism, fideism, and of Spinoza.

Judgment cannot be defined as an association of ideas because a judgment is absolute, that is, either as affirmation or negation of value. This corresponds to Weil's refusal of the concept of degrees of consciousness. Judgment, consciousness, and existence, one and the same are absolute in their presence or absence. That is, one exists, or one doesn't. Her rejection of the materialist denial of free will and judgment is based on the belief that judgment is that essential distancing of oneself that allows one to question the illusions of sense perception; therefore, one is not entirely determined by the sensations one receives. Her rejection of Fideism is based on the idea that belief is an act of will, not an inevitable emotional response. By one's capacity for doubt, one retains distance and free will in the final determination of one's own beliefs and ideas. This rejection of Fideism anticipates her later essays on social tyranny through emotional manipulation. Her attitude here helps to explain why in later years, although drawn towards mysticism and Christianity, Weil never converted officially. For this reason also, she never identified completely neither with political groups nor entities, avoiding the extreme degree of "enracinement."

Perhaps Weil's rejection of Spinoza's determinist argument is the most significant of this particular period. As established in the first chapter, Spinoza's example influenced Weil throughout her lifetime. While a young student, she preferred Spinoza's pantheistic beliefs to theistic forms of religious belief. In her later years as she came to believe in the greater strength of necessity as an impersonal divine presence and force, the evidence of her belief in Spinoza's Determinist theories was very great. However, at this mature point of her Rationalist period, she opposes Spinoza's denial of free will. Spinoza had challenged Descartes' concept of doubt. As Weil explains to her students, in Descartes' Fourth *Meditation*, he distinguishes between the capability for conceiving relationships, that is understanding, and capability for affirming relationships, or judgment. In Spinoza's view, Descartes' concept of judgment and its capacity for abstention through doubt, was not sufficient proof of the existence of the self and the independent will. There is always a cause of the suspension of judgment; it is never a consequence of an arbitrary decision or chance event; thus, free will cannot exist. Given the fact that the divine encompasses everything, one can think only because of that element of divine presence in each of us. I have shown in the first chapter how Weil's interpretation of Descartes led her to a critical point where she stopped short of denying God. Although the preceding discussion shows Weil at a time of belief in the predominance of the mind and the will, it would be simplistic to reduce Weil's own position at this time to a choice between two absolutes, that of free will or determinism. The philosophy of Descartes and Spinoza were not absolutely opposed in this fashion. Descartes, after all, qualified his equivalency of the human and divine persons; and in his Ontological Proof, he affirmed God as infinity and perfection, as points which we, finite and imperfect, can attain but only conceptually through our infinite capacity for progression of thought.

However, it is clear that at this time in her life, Weil, like Descartes, believed in the greater role of free will, mind and self-determination. Her discussion of Rousseau supports her belief in the equivalency of judgment, will, and value, whereby she affirms that the power to judge is the power of the will which is the determining power within oneself.

METHODICAL ACTION
Weil has brought her students from the tentative assumption that the world is ordered, only to arrive at the idea that the world is ordered *because of us*; we are in it and act upon it and by our action determine a definite order and structure.

> ... l'ordre n'est pas déterminé: un grain de sel ne sert absolument à rien, c'est une poignée de sel qui nous sert. ... (*Leçons*, 73)

Recreation Through Reasoning and Language:
> ... notre action n'est jamais créatice; elle est transformatrice. ... (*Leçons*, 133)

Weil views our action as transformative, not creative. Our power is not creation, but recreation or transformation. We do not have the power to create, only the capacity to transform. This, in Weil's view, is the basic difference between the divine and the human, an extension of Descartes' belief in the perfection of God and the imperfection of the human being endowed with the compensating power of reason.

This power to recreate is affected by exteriority, as Weil has shown. But, as she has also indicated, it is determined also by the mind; the subject, "je," structures and transforms exteriority into a form we can comprehend, into "reality" as Weil terms ordered exteriority. By reasoning and language, we act; we transform and recreate the creation by the movement and fabrication of our conceptual and physical powers.

Weil's discussion of reasoning provides a useful review and fusion of traditional philosophy, from Leibnitz's principle of non-contradiction and sufficient reason to Kant's categories of quantity, quality, relation, modality, and their respective *a priori* principles of synthetic judgments. The third and fourth categories, those of relation and modality, are particularly related to methodical action. Rapport, equilibrium, and action are key terms in describing the category of relation. Rapport between cause and effect rules every action and every change, and gives to events a temporal order.

Kant's systematized analysis of physical sensation, perception, thought and action are based on the same principle of unity and reciprocity of *a priori* and *a posteriori* phenomena, of interiority and exteriority, reviewed by Weil. In following Weil's discussion of Kant's fourth category, that of modality, one can see how Weil followed the same pattern of analysis. The category of modality explains the distinction between possibility, existence, and necessity; this relates appropriately to Weil's own views. Conceptual reconstruction synthesizes interiority with exteriority, the possible with the real. Formalism or theory expresses possibility through language, whose objectification of exteriority proposes a structure by which one may act effectively. If one does so, one's effective, methodical action determines reality by its contact with and elucidation of particular material conditions. Necessity, causality, is the objectified structure determined by the mind's conversion of exteriority.

> ... c'est l'ordre qui ne dépend que de nous qui apparaît objectif, comme une nécessité. ... (*Leçons*, 74)

In retracing the conceptual capacity for recreation and transformation, Weil shows how principles of traditional philosophy are products of this function for the rebuilding, ordering of exteriority. Necessity, Causality, is a notion pre-existent to ourselves, grasped only through a process of conceptual reconstruction; this is the reason for Weil's new definition of necessity, as the consequence of the objectification of exteriority. Only by rebuilding movement do we conceive of necessity, by re-enacting and becoming the instrument of limitation.

The continuum rebuilt by our powers of reasoning is an imitation of the universe. The establishment of continuum requires the dominant principle of relation. Consequently, reasoning is defined in terms of the conceptual processes which establish unit and relation, such as synthetic reasoning, deduction, analogy. *A priori* and *a posteriori* are terms describing different forms of knowledge acquired through the unified structure we impose and build. Time and space are sources of this structured continuum, two basic coordinates by which obstacles emerge from obscure, undefined exteriority

> Rapporter ainsi les choses au temps et à l'espace, c'est faire comme si nous avions fabriqué le monde par une action méthodique; nous n'avons pas d'autre moyen d'expliquer la nature.... (*Leçons*, 133)

Space is *a priori*, but our comprehension of it is a condition of experience. The same description applies to time, also *a priori*. Time is both a discovery and a preerequisite of change.

Language: Weil considers language also a form of action by which we structure reality. One rises from the animal level of physical response of sensations and impressions, to the level of objective, structured representations. Among all forms of animal life, spontaneous language expresses individual emotion, mostly a type of physiological response. But particular to human society is a reduction of thought and reality to a conventional code of symbols whose detachment from the things and phenomena they represent allows meaning to transcend its concrete base in reality.

Objectification: Language as a subject and an object expresses the duality, that is, the essential nature of our existence. We are both active and passive creatures by the fact that we think. Language is not only the vehicle of thought. Thought and language are identical. Language imposes and receives, as both a subject and an object. It is, on the one hand, an expression of will. Through language the will expresses itself and creates for itself conditioned reflexes and responses; this is accomplished through an awareness of the emotional power of a word, the imagery and memories it evokes, by a crystallization of feelings and association of images.

In the realm of one's private, personal life, words provide a fixity. They are a source of stability. Words are a human-made reality by which one can form for oneself the strength of reflexes associated with a name or a word. By the strength of one's own determination through language no subsequent, natural, unconditioned response will be able to subdue or destroy its meaning.

Language is thus a manifestation and an instrument of our will. By words, one determines one's own action. By words we determine and structure our behavior; in many cases, by our words responsibly, cunningly, or recklessly preferred, we inspire or limit the actions of others. By our selection of words we possess the power to discriminate as to the meaning, the aspects of reality to be grasped. In our emotional lives language is a source of stability and strength; by its transcendency and breadth of meaning it holds the past safe for us. But language can limit us rationally, intellectually; its fixity of meaning also imposes inflexible limits of understanding.

> ... le langage est précieux parce qu'il permet de se dédoubler; mais il est funeste quand on se laisse entraîner par lui complètement parce qu'alors il empêche de se dédoubler. (*Leçons*, 81)

In 1933-1934, Weil viewed the objectifying power of "dédoublement" as a tool for effective action. It was not until later in her essay, "Ne Recommencons Pas la Guerre de Troie," written in 1937, that Weil considered the negative as well as positive aspects of "dédoublement" through language. At this later point, she indicated that the symbol's power of "dédoublement" was a potential and historically proven form of alienation. Even in the earlier stage of the Roanne lectures, she is cognizant of the inflexibility that occurs when objectifying symbols and signifiers replace the signified; they become indistinguishable from their meaning. It is interesting to note the contrasting explanations Weil provides for the devaluation of meaning. In 1937, loss of meaning and rapport was one dangerous consequence of the symbol's power of "dédoublement." In her lectures at Roanne, Weil had atributed devaluation of meaning to the loss of this power of "dédoublement," the loss of the symbol's power of flexibility and transcendency; language becomes mechanical and loses its power of "dédoublement" and order. Symbols subsequently lose their force of detachment and meaning. For this reason, Weil advocates more conscious use of language to retrieve this balance and flexibility which is, in her view, the key to the happiness and fulfillment of the individual and society. This value placed on a conscious, methodical use of language was the basis of both her praise and criticism of the consequences of the symbol's "dédoublement."

The permanence, stability and artificiality of language show that it is also a recipient of action; it is an object. Language is an instrument and an expression of objectified reality.

> Le langage est un objet. . . . Dès qu'on a donne un nom à ses sentiments on peut les regarder comme un objet. . . . (*Leçons*, 69)

Because of language, we have a fixed artificial presence outside of ourselves. It provides us distance in defining ourselves consciously and objectively. But by that very distance, we are split in our identity; we are polarized from ourselves by the presence of two forms of reality, objective, and nonobjective. Words written down thus add another dimension of objectivity and, inevitably, alienation. Through language, one identifies oneself with a particular social structure and culture. We are objectified and categorized by language functioning as a social determinant.

> . . . grâce au langage, nous sommes baignés dans un milieu intellectuel . . . grâce au langage, nous avons avec la pensée d'autrui le même rapport que si elle était nôtre. . . . (*Leçons*, 80)

Through this objectification, each of our thoughts is communicated to others and thus becomes a part of the intellectual environment of society. Objectification through language provides the cathartic exteriorization of disturbing thoughts and feelings. Language is the source and basis for methodical action which transforms this new objectified order into concrete reality. Exteriority structured by language and by the action language governs is termed "réalité."

> Quand l'action vient après le langage et se règle sur lui, l'action apporte quelque chose de nouveau. . . . (*Leçons*, 75)

Objects constituting exteriority are unmanageable and hostile to us in so far as they are obstacles. Yet the object in question ceases to threaten us when our action is no longer blindly conceived. The obstacle which threatened or impeded gives way to effectively conceived action. Weil uses the example of a group of men who finally succeed in lifting heavy stone blocks through the use of a lever.

This brings us finally to Weil's redefinition of *existence*. In her essay "Science et Perception dans Descartes," existence is established through will and action. In *Leçons de Philosophie*, a more mature Weil defines existence and identity of the self as methodical action. This is a major point in the development of Weil's philosophy.

> La grandeur de l'homme existe seulement dans les moments où on a réellement conscience de la réalité. . . ce rapport entre le langage et l'action qui donne la réalité. . . . (*Leçons*, 75)

Weil claims virtue and sin to be the result of the presence or absence of this rapport. The traditional Cartesian equivalency between value and existence reappears in this argument: value and existence are one and the same consequence of this final, true state of consciousness established by the rapport between methodical language and the action it inspires.

RECURRING THEMES OF THE ROANNE LECTURES IN SIMONE WEIL'S PHILOSOPHY

These lectures indicate central questions which are important in Weil's later writings. In her lectures at Roanne, she criticized simplistic solutions sought in either a completely Materialist or Idealist approach and emphasized *the reciprocity of the Mind/Body forces*. This emphasis reappears in her criticism of the modern application of Marx's theory of Dialectical Materialism. In Weil's opinion the Marxist reversal of the dialectic had led to an intensification of machinism, and the failure to separate the problems of private property and bureaucracy had intensified the problem of alienation, the removal of thought from action. In a review written by Weil on Lenin's book, *Materialism and Empiriocriticism*, Weil is very critical of Lenin's devaluation of the Idealist approach to knowledge; her criticism of Lenin's scientific socialism and theory of materialistic determinism is based on what she believed was Lenin's disregard for the balance of forces between mind and body, interiority and exteriority.[4] Her fear of this disregard for the mind-body relation appears also in her writings on science where she discusses insufficiently understood formulae and symbol which have become the basis of technological advancement. She fears from this process the absence of individual understanding, the loss of a sense of the relation between mind and matter. Weil's notion of work is a resolution of this reciprocity of mind/body forces. Work, as encounter of the mind with exteriority, fuses together the active and passive selves.

> ... car, par cet intermédiaire, si je n'unis pas les deux parties de moi, celle qui subit, celle qui agit, je peux faire du moins que je subisse les changements produits par moi, que ce que je subis, ce soit ma propre action. . . .[5]

The suppression of this reciprocity, the equal participation of mind and body in action, is the basis of her critique of the technological age of machinism and specialization (cf. *La Condition Ouvrière*, and *Enracinement*). Towards the end of her life, Weil envisaged a decentralized system of labor, similar to the cultural order idealized by Tolstoy, Rousseau and Proudhon. That was one of her suggestions for the respiritualization of postwar society (cf. note *Myth of the Social*). "Enracinement" throughout Weil's writings is mediation (with detachment) between body and mind, action and thought.

In her lectures, Weil presents two conflicting descriptions of *Necessity*. *Necessity* is first described obviously as part of her review of traditional philosophy, as pre-existent to ourselves. Yet, as shown in the discussion on methodical action, she maintains that necessity is both the order that is pre-existent to ourselves and also the order we reconstruct through reasoning, action, and language.

Through work or action we reconstruct or transform necessity. Luce Blech-Lidolf describes Weil's concept of necessity as both recreation, and encounter or contact with pre-existent orders of space and time.[6] Radical empiricists and Pragmatists propounded a view of a meaningful world where order and value becomes evident only through conscious action. This relates to Weil's description of necessity as a pre-existent order which we reconstruct through methodical action.

> The individual lives in . . . an experienced world in which non-cognitive, pre-reflective acts take place and within which reflection arises. . . .[7]

Methodical action, expressed through work, reasoning, and language is a concept that was developing in Weil's own thought at the time of the Roanne lectures. It appears also in her later writings. In her later discussion of pacifism, power and language in "Ne Recommençons Pas la Guerre de Troie," she describes the need for precise language use as the basis for methodical action. Weil's concept of methodical action was part of her critique of the popular concept of revolution (cf. section on the Myth of Revolution). Spontaneous unprepared political action had proven ineffective in Weil's opinion. Her view on that point was summarized in a letter addressed to "Le Cercle communiste démocratique," discussing the difference between Bataille's and her own conception of 'revolution.'

> Or la révolution est pour lui le triomphe de l'irrationnel, pour moi, une action méthodique où il faut s'efforcer de limiter les dégâts. . .[8]

The concepts that Weil formulates in the course of these lectures on work, necessity and reconstruction through conscious action were determined by the combined influences of Empirical (Radical Empiricism of James, known also as Pragmatism), Idealist, and Voluntarist philosophies. From Idealist philosophy, Weil retains the traditional concepts of causality, necessity, continuum, and relation. Maine de Biran's and Alain's development of Voluntarist philosophy determined Weil's insistence on encounter, resistance, and conscious action as an expression of will. Weil's simultaneous retention, however, of two apparently contradictory conceptions of "Necessity," as well as the value she placed on work as a form of reconstruction or transformation, was due to the influence of Radical Empiricism. The Roanne lectures attest to the influence of William James's *Principles of Psychology* on Weil's developing theories of action and mediation. Weil's concepts of work and reconstruction have not yet been linked to the movement of American Pragmatism which was developing simultaneously with that of Voluntarist philosophy. The influence of Radical Empiricism and Pragmatism on Phenomenology in the twentieth century has been recognized, however. So it is logical to note a comparable influence on Weil's philosophy of work and action.[9]

THE ROANNE LECTURES AND EXISTENTIALIST PHENOMENOLOGY

Leçons de Philosophie further illustrates Weil's participation in the Existentialist Movement. By her theory of objectification and action, she attempted to overcome the legacy of the subject/object duality in traditional philosophy.

Whether she succeeded or not is questionable; but this methodology of action became the base for later philosophical development in phenomenology and Existentialism. This contribution deserves recognition.

The philosophies of Marcel, Weil, Sartre, de Beauvoir and Merleau-Ponty, progress through four major points to a methodology of action: 1) the inextricability of self with the world; 2) the duality of being as both interior and exterior, active and passive, infinite and finite; 3) Encounter and resistance as the basis for existence, followed by; 4) the objectification and detachment of self.

In the first chapter it was shown that Weil anticipated Sartre's rejection of the transcendency of the ego. Both subsequently concluded that one is *in* the world; one can define oneself only by one's involvement with the world.

Weil's discussion of the body's role shows the dual presence of interiority/exteriority that haunts our search for order. In doing so, she identifies the two structures of consciousness that Sartre later called "la conscience irréfléchie" and "la conscience réflexive."[10] In observing oneself, one can directly see only the self which observes, not the observed self. In "Science et Perception," Weil had already sensed the double structure of our consciousness, but in *Leçons de Philosophie*, her description is explicit.

> ... si on essaie de s'observer au moment présent, on ne trouve en soi que l'état qui consiste à s'observer. . . .[11]

The observing self and the observed self express the duality of our nature. We are both active and passive beings, both subjects and objects of action. For Merleau-Ponty, also, one is both an object and a subject; one is both a physical or material being, and a being with consciousness and the will to act.[12] Sonia Kruks states in her study, *The Political Philosophy of Merleau-Ponty*, that this double-sidedness of human existence makes meaning, structure and intention possible in Merleau Ponty's Existentialist philosophy; his use of the term 'body-subject' sums up this duality.[13]

Both Marcel and Sartre describe the notion of series as a conceptual attempt to resolve the dualism of our infinite and finite selves by this unity that the mind reconstructs. Weil describes series as part of the conceptual process of reconstruction and ordering; through the concept of a series one is finally able to distinguish between qualitative and quantitative change. The notion of series reveals in these philosophers the rejection of Idealism: they reject the dual presence of appearance and essence. Essence emerges through the unit of appearances. This reduction of the existent to its physical manifestation does not assuredly eliminate all duality.

> L'essence d'un existant . . . est la loi manifeste qui préside à la succession de ses apparitions . . . la série[14]

All of the Existentialist philosophers—Marcel, Weil, Sartre, Merleau-Ponty, and Camus—describe a moment of encounter and resistance of the self to exteriority as the basis for existence. At first, Weil defines existence as will and action in "Science et Perception." In the course of her lectures at Roanne she often referred to Kant's metaphor about the dove whose flight for freedom is made possible only through the air's resistance to the movements of its own wings. The air's resistance supports the flight of the dove;[15] Simone de Beauvoir later used the same reference in her collection of essays *Pyrrhus et Cinéas*;[16] both philosophers sought to express not only the consciousness aroused by the involvement of the self with exteriority, but also the interdependence of one's freedom with the freedom of others. Weil's years as a teacher of philosophy coincided with a period of heightened labor and political activism. It is logical that the development of her Existentialist ideas on action should coincide with her increasing involvement with the freedom of others.

De Beauvoir seems to have had less struggle than Sartre in the transition from individual salvation to collective struggle. For Weil and de Beauvoir, there is more of a natural reciprocity between individual and collective freedom; Sartre later drew similar conclusions in *Existentialisme est un Humanisme*, but only following a struggle with concepts of nothingness and duality.[17] Despite the Hedonism of *Noces*, Camus also came to base his philosophy on collective freedom and fraternity—"Je me révolte, donc nous sommes."[18] The value and purity of action and enterprise portrayed in the novels of Malraux and Saint-Exupéry contributed to the theme of "l'engagement" as a philosophical, artistic and political value. In Brecht's portrayal of Weil in his play *The Visions of Simone Machard*, the main character's purity of commitment contrasts with the ambiguous stance of the Collaborationists.[19] In de Beauvoir's portrayal of Weil in *Le Sang des Autres*, she devalues slightly the sense of ultimate sacrifice and altruism that was linked at the time to Weil's legend; but the conclusions of her main character, Bloomart, reflect the same ethos of commitment.[20]

> C'est la source du sentiment du néant de l'existence. . . .[21]

One attempts to render oneself eternal through a manipulation of exteriority. The continuation of time beyond oneself is at the root of one's own feeling of nothingness and futility. However, if time is eternal, there must be some element or part of eternity in life itself. One acts to allow that value and eternity to manifest itself in life. This is what Weil considers the meaning of action; the struggle against time is both a struggle against one's exclusion from eternity and a struggle for the particle of eternity one's action represents.

> Si on conçoit la mort comme un passage dans l'éternité, il faut necessairement concevoir qu'il y a eu quelque chose d'eternel dans la vie.[22]

But action is not enough. Action, though, is effective only in so far as it has become structured and methodical with a definite objective and understanding of the relative conditions necessary for the accomplishment of that objective. A stage of detachment and regression is necessary to convert thought into effective action; reasoning and language are manifestations of this process. By such a process, all action predetermined and assessed in terms of its effectiveness and value to oneself as an individual and as part of exteriority would inevitably be moral. The separation of the objective self from the subjective self is the means by which one appraises one's own actions and values. It prevents one from losing oneself in absolute, unreflected action.

> Il faut considérer ses actions non plus par rapport à soi, mais objectivement. . . . Dans toutes les circonstances, être un homme, c'est savoir séparer 'le je' et 'le moi'. . . .[23]

To be, 'être,' is to will and to act through an objectification of oneself, thereby elucidating and creating effective action. *Leçons de Philosophie* thus shows that Weil's theory of action culminated in a final stage of objectification and regression of the self. Sartre recommends a similar stage of detachment and objectification,[24]

> . . . la motivation de la réflexion consiste en une double tentative d'objectivation et d'intériorisation.[25]

"Enracinement" is central to the problem of duality in Existentialism. For Weil, "enracinement" is the self's integration into surrounding life. But true "enracinement" constitutes at the same time a certain measure of flexibility, detachment, interiorized "déracinement." As did those of other Existentialists, her attempt to resolve the ambiguity and duality of our nature failed. Synthesis through action was only momentary; in order for action to be effective, the self had to be objectified. Still, momentary synthesis through action provided a fuller comprehension of one's relation to the world. Complete integration into either exteriority or interiority is neither possible nor desirable. In Weil's philosophy of will and consciousness, physicality reveals creatures both dependent and autonomous; our intellect and sense of morality must remain flexible yet stable through a balanced dichotomy of interior/exterior elements. That is the problematic nature of "enracinement," and "déracinement"; they are inextricably related. As many who seek both stability and independence of thought, Weil lived detached from absolutes. For Weil and for the other Existentialists, our presence and involvement in the world is our diaspora, our exile.

Notes to Chapter 2

[1] Jean-Paul Sartre, *L'Etre et le Néant* (Paris: Librairie Gallimard, 1943), 182.

[2] This is a close version of the "James-Lange Theory of the emotions." ". . . the theory, . . . that an emotion is . . . the feeling of the bodily changes that follow the perception . . . which excites it." (A. J. Ayer, *The Origins of Pragmatism, Studies in the Philosophy of Charles Sanders Peirce and William James* [San Francisco: Freeman, Cooper & Co., 1968], 206.) James's theories had constituted a revolutionary departure from the school of scientific empiricism that had also repelled Husserl, Brunschvicq, and Weil. His theories had also constituted an attack on the English neo-Hegelians (i.e., Bradley, T. H. Green, McTaggart, Royce). "It was for their lofty indifference to matters of mere empirical fact that he chiefly censured his Hegelian opponents." *The Origins of Pragmatism*, 175. He indicated a reciprocity between mind/body forces which appears to have influenced Weil's theory of methodical action. This accounts in part for the difference of her approach from that of Husserl, Brunschvicg, and even Alain, her mentor. "He (James) insisted that the mind is essentially active and organic" (William James, *Psychology* (abridged version of *Principles of Psychology*) [Cleveland: World], viii).

[3] Simone Weil, *Leçons de Philosophie*, transcrites et présentées par Anne Reynaud-Guérithault (Paris: Librairie Plon, 1959), 36-37.

[4] Simone Weil, "Sur le Livre de Lénine, 'Matérialisme-Empiriocriticisme'," *Oppression et Liberté* (Paris: Gallimard, 1955), 45-53. (Originally appeared in *Critique Sociale*, novembre 1933).

[5] "Science et perception dans Descartes," *Sur la Science*, 83-84. This quotation was also noted by Luce Blech-Lidolf, *La pensée philosophique et sociale de Simone Weil* Serie XX, vol. 1, Bd. 23 (Berne [Suisse] and Francfort [RFA]: Publications Universitaires Européenes, Herbert Lang & Cie SA, and Peter Lang S.A.R.L., 1976), 146.

[6] Lidolf, *La Pensée philosophique et sociale de Simone Weil*, 146.

[7] Sandra B. Rosenthal and Patrick L. Bourgeois, "Book I - American Pragmatism–C. Method," *Pragmatism and Phenomenology: A Philosophic Encounter* (Amsterdam: B. R. Gruner Pub. Co., 1980), 27, 37. "Meanings, not only logical and mathematical meanings, but all meanings, are irreducible to physical causal conditions or to psychological acts. . . ." (*Pragmatism and Phenomenology*, 20-21)

[8] Simone Pétrement, *La Vie de Simone Weil-I (1909-1934)* (Paris: Fayard, 1973), 422.

[9] Recent works that bring to light this close relationship between Pragmatism and Existentialism are: *Pragmatism and Phenomenology: A Philosophic Encounter* by Rosenthal and Bourgeois (cf. note 7). "The Empirical and Transcendental Ego," *Literature, Philosophy, and the Social Sciences: Essays in Existentialism and Phenomenology* (The Hague: Nijhoff, 1962), 44-54); James Edie, "The Philosophical Anthropology of William James," *An Invitation to Phenomenology: Studies in the Philosophy of Experience* (Chicago: Quadrangle Books, 1965). It is also significant to note the similarity between Weil and Dewey, a famous American pragmatist who influenced applied theories of education in this country. Each developed a philosophy of action based on reconstruction and method, to fuse theory and application, mind/body forces. *Reconstruction in Philosophy*, John Dewey (Boston: Beacon Press, 1920).

[10] Jean-Paul Sartre, "La Transcendance de l'Ego–Esquisse d'une description phénoménologique," *Recherches Philosophiques* VI (Paris: Librairie A. Hatier, 1936-1937).

[11] Weil, *Leçons de Philosophie*, 19.

[12] Of all the Existentialist philosophers, Merleau-Ponty's philosophy of perception has been the most influenced by an empirical view of the self. Both Weil and Merleau-Ponty rejected the extremes of scientific empiricism and positivism like Husserl, but unlike Husserl, they tried to merge both the philosophies of Realism and Idealism. Rosenthal and Bourgeois note that in

Merleau-Ponty's *The Structure of Behavior*, there is a two-fold consideration of consciousness, similar to that which characterizes Pragmatist philosophy. Consciousness can neither be reduced to a physical causal condition nor to psychological acts and processes. (*Pragmatism and Phenomenology: A Philosophic Encounter*, 96-97) These viewpoints are discussed in Merleau-Ponty's introduction to *La Phénoménologie de la Perception*, "La méthode eidétique est celle d'un positivisme phénoménologique qui fonde le possible sur le réel. . . ." (Merleau-Ponty, *La Phénomenologique de la Perception* [Paris: Gallimard, 1945], xi-xii). Although Weil and Merleau-Ponty applied their respective philosophies of action at different historical moments and in different political contexts (see H. S. Hughes, *The Obstructed Path* for review of Merleau-Ponty's importance in postwar politics and for Existentialist Movement), each of their encounters with Empiricism and Pragmatist philosophy helped to determine their mutual emphasis on 'lived experience.' A comparison of the two would be the subject of an interesting study.

[13] Sonia Kruks, *The Political Philosophy of Merleau-Ponty* (Sussex: Harvester Press, 1981), 10.

[14] Sartre, *L'Etre et le Néant*, 12-13.

[15] Weil, *Leçons de Philosophie*, 98, 136.

[16] Simone de Beauvoir, *Pyrrhus et Cinéas* (Paris: Librairie Gallimard, 1944).

[17] Jean-Paul Sartre, *L'Existentialisme est un Humanisme* (Paris: Editions Nagel,1965). Anne Whitmarsh, *Simone de Beauvoir and the Limits of Commitment* (Cambridge: Cambridge University Press, 1981), 41-42. "Sartre was at first unable to take the step from individual salvation . . . to colléctive . . . . 'I could not submit to the discipline of solidarity with all men. . . . And I could not be free alone.'" (*Force and Circumstance*, 242-43).

[18] Albert Camus, *L'Homme Révolté* (Paris: Librairie Gallimard, 1951).

[19] Bertolt Brecht, "Les Visions de Simone Machard," in *Théâtre Complet*, VI (Paris, l'Arche Editeur, 1957).

[20] Simone de Beauvoir, *le Sang des Autres* (Paris: Librairie Gallimard, 1945).

[21] Weil, *Leçons de Philosophie*, 255.

[22] Ibid., 257.

[23] Ibid., 250.

[24] Luce Blech-Lidolf, *La Pensée Philosophique et Sociale de Simone Weil* (Berne: Herbert Lang & Cie SA, 1976), 65. "La Méthode de Simone Weil nous paraît présenter quelque analogie avec celle préconisée par Jean-Paul Sartre, . . . descriptif-Observation, . . .) analytico-regressif. . . . c) historico-génétique . . . .

[25] Sartre, *L'Etre et le Néant*, 200.

Chapter 3
The Deconstruction of Power

BIOGRAPHICAL NOTE

In 1934, Simone Weil began her first major political essay, "Reflexions sur les Causes de la liberté et de l'oppression sociale," extracts of which were originally published in issues of *Essais et Combats* from December 1937 to April 1938. In the years since her teaching at Roanne in 1933-1934, Weil had accumulated a variety of political experiences which had affected her views on freedom, oppression, and power. In the year following her teaching at Roanne, she had requested an official leave of absence from her academic post and had worked close to a year in the factories of Alsthom, Renault, and Carnaud & Forges de Basse-Indre. Following the rise of the Popular Front coalition government, Weil participated in the Republican struggle of the Spanish Civil War. She had criticized Blum's government for what she had judged to be its failure in establishing order and preventing further division; she had also become disillusioned with Blum's neutralist position towards Spain, interpreting it as an abandonment of the principles of worker solidarity which had been the political platform of the Popular Front. In the course of her participation in Spain with Durrutti's anarchist guerillas, she had encountered an even deeper disillusionment with the violence that had perverted the Republican cause. As the scale of violence increased, the struggle of the hungry peasants and workers had degenerated into an international war. Following a leg injury she returned to France only a few months before the Fall of the Popular Front.

Weil was among the pacifist writers supporting a compromise at Munich in 1938, but she did not support the Collaborationist government at Vichy. From 1936 until Hitler's invasion of Czechoslavakia in 1939, Weil had encouraged a national policy of non-violence and had made important anti-war statements, most of which have been published in the collections *Les Ecrits Historiques et Politiques* and *La Source Grecque*.

Weil escaped to Vichy with her mother and father a few days before the Germans marched into Paris. From September 1940 to May 1942, they lived in Marseilles where Weil entered into religious discussions with Father Joseph-Marie Perrin. Weil's association with Perrin led her to work for the Resistance in the distribution of *Le Temoignage Chrétien,* which Perrin had founded. Gustave Thibon, an acquaintance of Perrin, found agricultural work for Weil, whom the racist laws of Vichy had prevented from holding a teaching post. She worked in the farming regions of the Rhône Valley. In 1942, the

Weil family emigrated to the United States; a few months later, Weil made her way back to Europe. During the last year before her death, Weil worked for De Gaulle's Free French organization in London. Her major writings of this final period were later published under the collections *Enracinement, La Pesanteur et la Grâce, Attente de Dieu, Intuitions Pré-Chrétiennes*, and *Sur la Science*. In August 1943, Weil died of malnourishment and pulmonary tuberculosis.

The following section on freedom, oppression, and the deconstruction of power through myth reflects her philosophical and political development through the years 1934 to 1943 and the importance of the theme 'déracinement/enracinement' in the context of political history.

FREEDOM AND OPPRESSION

Freedom: In her analysis of oppression, Weil refines her methodology of action by a new definition of freedom. A new conception of liberty emerges from the contradictory nature of our existence. We are born and remain slaves to natural and human necessity but we feel predestined for an autonomous state of self-fulfillment. We were meant to be free, but we are not; in this antithetical state we either clash against the limits of our condition or, stoically and passively, bow to the demands of a predetermined order. Freedom is conceived either as an idyllic feature of the past or as a dream of the future. We have created for ourselves an antithetical structure of belief whose opposite poles are inflexible moral postures safe from demystification. This has paralyzed effective action and demanded a choice of either/or in determining individual and collective intitiative. The priest and the doctor of Camus's *La Peste* confront each other as did Job and God, and spirituality becomes incompatible with social reform and physical healing. Our freedom is realized only through the death of God. This leads to a self-defeating reliance upon our mastery of matter and of the forces that emerge from its various transformations. The vision of total freedom, conceived by materialists and idealists alike, is an opium dream. Weil uses this term in her own description of this phenomenon.

> Ce rêve est toujours demeuré vain, comme tous les rêves, ou s'il a pu consoler, ce n'est que comme un opium; il est temps de renoncer à rêver la liberté, et de se décider à la concevoir. . . .[1]

Freedom had to be conceived clearly and realistically. Perfect liberty had to be understood as an ideal by which to guide possible changes in our own situation, not as a realistic goal, but as a measure of assessment and improvement of actual conditions.

> C'est la liberté parfaite qu'il faut s'efforcer de se représenter clairement, non pas dans l'espoir d'y atteindre, mais dans l'espoir d'atteindre une liberté moins imparfaite que n'est notre condition actuelle; car le meilleur n'est concevable que par le parfait. . . .[2]

But then what exactly is perfect freedom? It is not the toppling of barriers to individual aggrandizement. It is not the increased satisfaction of desires which perpetually renew and augment in proportion to the technological development of society's resources. Weil defines perfect freedom as a state of conscious control through one's own participation in action and through comprehension of the steps to be taken to reach the projected goal. Enslavement is accordingly a self-alienating state whereby an individual's action and physical accomplishments are inspired and comprehended by minds other than her or his own. Weil considers perfect liberty the physical realization of the process and conceptual exercises involved in a mathematical problem.

This methodical action eliminates the factor of chance and uncertainty in ourselves; it only reduces its presence in the world. But the presence of the insurmountable is necessary resistance to our will, the source of our freedom. The absence of the unexpected would be undesirable as would that of necessity, an additional form of nature that obstructs our autonomy and expansion. However, even upon the determination of work and the scheme of tasks leading to its completion created by methodical thought and action, there is another obstruction to freedom. This obstacle stems from the difference between theory and action, between the theoretical resolution of a problem and even the most methodical completion of work. In the resolution of a theoretical problem one is conscious of the logical progression of one's advancement in elucidating and resolving the problem by advancing consciously in an increasingly complex chain of logic. But in completion of work, one's movements do not increase in complexity. Instead in the mind of the worker each unit of movement determines the one which follows. By its very nature thought unifies movement whereas work or execution of a task disperse it. For this reason, the individual cannot simultaneously execute a complex work task and conceive its unit and project. That would be perfect freedom. What is realistically sought by Weil and others is an equilibrium between the dual demands of our mind and our bodies so as to end the estrangement of a society whose economic and cultural welfare has been based on division of labor, machinism and an inflationary use of uncomprehended symbols.

The necessary separation in distinct stages of thought and action has led to an exaggerated division of labor whereby those who execute a methodically conceived task do not comprehend the entire process of its production. Method displaces itself and moves from the workers' minds to the movements themselves, eventually into the material produced. In the age of automation, this method has been entirely displaced into machines which have become not only the product but the instruments of creation. As science and technology progress in their accumulation of signs and their various combinations and formulas, ordinary individuals become increasingly powerless to understand the concepts that are used and manipulated. Thus, not only work itself but the conceptualization of its methodology is taken over by symbol and machines, without the direction of human thought or consciousness. The estrangement of mind from body, our dual nature, has reached dehumanizing proportions. That is why Weil proposes a new definition of freedom but insists that it is not a goal, but an ideal.

Thus ideal liberty would make all our actions the work and creation of our own thought. The utility of such an ideal hinges, however, upon our perception of what distances us from it and what possible changes in our respective situations could bring us closer to it, or further estrange us from its attainment. The main obstacle is of course nature; the world's expanse and complexity falls beyond the reach of our mind much less that of our physical capabilities. We are not presented in life with problems drawn to scale because of the infinite forms and expanse of energy and matter. In all situations, even in those demanding the most simple action, there is an unpredictable factor of chance whose forms are innumerable and elusive. Despite this factor of chance and unpredictability thought is not a futile exercise in the association of symbols. But this uncontrolled chance factor is minimized particularly in ourselves by the close direction of conscious thought and judgement. The conceptualization of a chain of possible unified intermediary actions leading to one's goal provides an abstract scheme of action; the mind does not thus eliminate but at least contains the factor of unpredictability by filtering it into well-defined series that correspond to the various sequences of planned action.

> Tous les outils sont ainsi, d'une manière plus ou moins parfaite, comme des instruments à définir les hasards. . . .[3]

Methodical Action as conceived by Weil was similar to John Dewey's philosophical school of Instrumentalism. According to this form of American Pragmatism, absolute knowledge would be replaced by methods of control;[4] a higher consciousness of oneself and the world would be accomplished neither by theoretical abstract knowledge nor by brainless doing but by a practical sense of learning—"... the heart of our best knowing is in doing, ... a doing which is more thoughtful, more intelligent."[5] It is very possible that Weil's ideas on freedom and methodical action were indirectly or directly determined by the Instrumentalist school of American Pragmatism represented by Dewey (1859-1952). There was at least a parallel development on both sides of the Atlantic; Voluntarist and Pragmatist philosophies both sought a higher level of consciousness in acting through theories of methodical action.

Weil's new conception of freedom, her functional theory of oppression and her studies on the natural instability and displacement of power form the basis for a methodical deconstruction of social, cultural myths. Immersed in the mood of social and political catastrophe and demoralization, this concept of freedom as a higher form of consciousness through methodical action led to her vision of reconstruction and respiritualization. This was accompanied by a perhaps idealistic, utopian hope for the reintegration of self with society and mind with body, retaining the antithetical tension of integration with detachment as the realization of true 'enracinement.'

Theory of Oppression: Conditions of Existence: Weil's sociological scheme of oppression is an application of biological principle, reflecting the strength of Darwin's influence on Weil's view of sociology. Weil sought to apply his discovery of the biological principle of 'conditions of existence' to sociological studies directed towards the improvement of society; she believed that it was necessary to identify the conditions of existence whereby the greatest state of equilibrium and stability can be maintained. Freedom manifests itself in the presence of stability and equilibrium of power.

Weil's interpretation of sociological development was based on this conception that material factors combine to determine the development both of the organism and of society. A certain point of correlation between components produces the greatest amount of equilibrium of a living metabolism and the least amount of oppression in society. Her view was strongly influenced by the proponents of Positivist and Materialist studies of society, Auguste Comte and Karl Marx.

Weil searches for the material conditions causing oppression in early societies. From this study, she discovers three main conditions that render a society oppressive: complexity of knowledge, division of labor, and the race for power.

The first known form of oppression was serfdom in Egypt. An irrigation system centered around the Nile determined the Egyptians' way of life. It transformed the nomads and hunters into farmers and laborers. Their claim to such valuable land was the source of economic rivalry and military confrontation with foreign armies. Armies were essential. Consequently, their warrior formed a privileged caste dominating their system of social hierarchy. Their geographic location determined their society economically and socially. As the Egyptians became dependent on irrigation as the sole means of effective cultivation, and as the social hierarchy would secure itself only through a system of stable production, forced labor came into being; only an involuntary system of labor could have obliged members of a formerly nomadic society to build the long canals and the pyramids.

> . . . à partir de l'Egypte, avec son Nil et ses guerres, on peut retrouver l'Etat égyptien, de la même manière qu'à partir de la mer, et de telle autre condition concrète, on peut retrouver les poissons. . . .(*Leçons de Philosophie*, 165)

There was slavery in Greece. There might have been slavery instead of serfdom in Egypt if Egypt had also been a country surrounded by the sea; slavery existed more easily in a maritime civilization; Greece's geographical location facilitated the seizure and abduction of foreign peoples and the establishment of a slave labor force. Yet the geographic factor that Greece was a maritime civilization also determined its political and social life in a positive way; the transient life of merchants and sailors prevented centrality of power and tradition which was fragmented among different states. It was a system that remained internally stable until Athens deteriorated into an imperialist power. Weil believed that Ancient Greece had achieved the greatest possible point of equilibrium; although the geographic factor was the cause of oppression, in the form of slavery, it compensated for the oppression because it also determined stability and freedom by the fragmentation of power.

In Rome, centrality of Egyptian power was imitated and magnified by the military. Military domination was the condition and purpose of Roman society. The Roman peasants who cultivated the land, the laborers who built the famous system of bridges and roads, existed to meet the needs of the military centralization of power. The Empire was the 'raison d'être' of political and social life. The absence of other material factors in Weil's explanation of the political and social life in Roman times is significant; it was to show that aggression was at the extreme point. This was a period of estrangement from natural, material rapport with nature. The intensification of centralized power was the furthest point away from a natural equilibrium of power.

> . . . il fallait des esclaves pour faire des routes et des routes pour

avoir des esclaves. . . . (*Leçons de Philosophie*, 166)

The intense centrality of Roman power disintegrated; feudalism came into being. Weil used the principle of natural selection to explain the transition towards feudalism. The king who reigned over the other feudal lords was the strongest, in the struggle for the survival of the fittest. Although the feudal land system was oppressive, Weil believes that this period of urban prosperity and craftsmanship provided a strong sense of equilibrium and freedom. Urban workers were craftsmen organized in corporations and were accorded the dignity of their profession. The value and pride of workmanship and skill motivated a sense of worth and a love for work and production. Weil believed that freedom was at a high level in this society because of the comprehension and consciousness which dignified work. The decentralized power divided among feudal lords allowed for a greater individualism and independence of thought. Although the feudal system was tyrannical and arbitrary it reinforces in Weil's mind the certainty that individualism, consciousness and independence of thought decrease in proportion to an increase in centrality of power and division of labor. In Weil's analysis the complexity of knowledge through centralization of power in the hands of an elite, privileged class, and the division of labor are two main conditions of existence for an oppressive society.

Division of Labor: It is necessary to understand the distinction Weil makes between force and oppression in order to comprehend her social theory. Force originates in nature. Oppression is the human abuse of force once force has been removed from nature, transferred to our realm of power and intensified by certain objective conditions. The first of these objective conditions is specialization or division of labor. This is the qualitative transformation of production methods whereby society becomes dependent on the exploitation of its own members. In a society dependent on specialization and division of labor, freedom is at a low level because the conceptualization and execution of action are separated. The individual is denied conscious control of her or his participation and comprehension of purpose in acting; the gap between theory and execution is widened and as a result one's consciousness and freedom diminishes. Society consumes itself through its own oppression. The least oppressive societies in history have been the least economically and technologically advanced because economic effectiveness supposedly began with the division of labor. Until then each person had faced independently hunger, disease and death. Pain and pleasure were experienced entirely and independently by each being in her or his contact with natural forces. In higher economic forms of life, the very essence of production is different. The qualitative transformation appears to be a liberation from nature. Through the early forms of subsistance, hunting, gathering, fishing, one was in direct contact with nature. It is interesting that Weil does not describe early economic forms of life in terms of dominance, or subservience to nature. Instead she viewed human life in terms of its fusion with nature; there was a sense of participation of the human effort with nature; action was not merely a reflection of an indomitable will, nor a degrading reaction to an unpredictable force; human action and life were fused with and participated with nature.

At this stage, one's freedom is not impeded by the existence of other people because of one's own direct contact with the elements determining one's existence; one is not degraded nor threatened by the presence of the other because one has not yet created one's own mechanism of oppression, that is, the transfer of force from nature to society. This perhaps idyllic stage of human life fulfills Weil's ideal of perfect liberty where freedom with regard to others accompanies a sense of participation with nature. In higher forms of economic production, nature continues to restrain but less apparently. The transformation seems to give greater free will as natural forces are felt less directly, with less immediacy. As the transformation progresses, economic life and production are increasingly estranged from nature and give us the illusion of having passed from subservience to mastery. At the same time, the personification of natural forces increase correspondingly and gradually lose their attributes of divinity. Obviously the original forces of nature persist elusively but the former sense of freedom and participation has disappeared and other people have become our enemies. The reciprocity between oneself and nature is supplanted by the principle of collective existence, that is, the opposition between the components of the master/slave duality.

The Other: The only true obstacle to our freedom is the existence of others. Nature would not have subjugated primitive peoples if it had not been symbolized by beings in human form. Without the human symbol of divine will, or the personification of natural forces, nature can break but not humiliate us. Matter offers resistance but by its inertness is permeable and open to manipulation and control. It is penetrable to our thought because it has none, and is objectifiable. The existence of the other threatens one's own by the impenetrability of thought. Division of labor in a society of specialized professions creates dependency. In so far as one is dependent upon the thought of others, one ceases to exist. There is no further purpose for judgment or decision. This dependency on others nourishes the mechanism of oppression, the dual structure of the powerful and the oppressed. This structure constitutes two opposing yet dependent elements. The members of society alternate between the two extremes that these terms represent. The structure perpetuates itself by the dependency of each term upon the other, a dependency strengthened by mutual resistance and antagonism. The reflected image of ourselves that we see in the power of the Other alienates us; it threatens to separate us further from ourselves. Furthermore, in the power of the Other's thought we see a judgment of ourselves. As the object of another's thought, one is negated; one's own power and control is negated because one is objectified. The main obstacle to our freedom, in Weil's view, is the conceptual power of the Other which threatens to or succeeds in polarizing even further the antagonistic dual elements of mind and body. By our fear of the Other we seek the power to overcome and become the object of the Other's fear. We thus create and maintain our own oppression. Whereas our freedom draws its strength from the natural resistance of matter, perfect freedom can never exist unless we cease to find in others an image of ourselves. the opposition of subject-object that defines the mechanism of oppression is an extension of our natural being, the mind-body dualism; the master/slave struggle is an exteriorization of our inner conflict. The forces of 'déracinement/enracinement' assume even greater complexity as our own being is composed of dual forces whose conflict and tension we displace or exteriorize into our own physical reality. Within ourselves this tension between opposing yet complementary forces is an intrinsic essential element of our being because the forces within us continually seek balance, mediation. Exterior to ourselves, outside of ourselves, a way of life must exist as well to mediate the forces of mind and body so that an oppressive polarization of these opposing forces does not manifest itself and thereby eternally bind the human spirit. Thus one can comprehend Weil's strong belief in the need for a way of life that integrates mind and body, that allows cohesiveness among the members of society without an individual loss of dignity and power.

> On ne pourrait se représenter la possibilité d'un progrès quelconque au seul vrai sens du mot . . . que si l'on pouvait concevoir à titre de limite idéale une société qui armerait l'homme contre le monde sans l'en séparer. . . .[6]

Again one encounters in Weil's writings the recurring image of cohesiveness with detachment and displacement, a symbolic evocation of "déracinement/enracinement". Weil gives an effective description of the instability of power and "la course au pouvoir."[7] The continual displacement of power and the polarization of society into the dual realms of the powerful and the powerless is the fatality and mystery of collective existence. The fact that power can never be permanently possessed or stabilized hinders its

demystification.
Power is unstable by nature.

> Ainsi il y a, dans l'essence même de la puissance, une contradiction fondamentale, qui l'empêche de jamais exister. . . .[8]

The unacceptability of human relationships based on unwilling submission or domination is the source of social disequilibrium. The division of labor by which we have displaced power from its original source in nature triggers a fatal dispersion and displacement of force among ourselves. the result is the infamous "course au pouvoir."

> . . . il n' a jamais pouvoir, mais seulement course au pouvoir. . . .[9]

Our inability to understand power prevents us from controlling its abuse. Power is continually destabilized; the centers of freedom and violence are continually displaced and never contained. The individuals comprising the dual realms of power are instruments of the fatal nature of force; as such they are potential victims of a dehumanizing situation where the purpose and reason of their action is subordinated to the demands of power itself. This is the reversal of Kantian priorities brought about by unnatural force and violence; the means, power, have become the end and the human being has become the means. At last Weil's definition of oppression is complete. Specialization, centrality of power, and the race for power are the conditions of existence of an oppressive society. Oppression, as Weil has proven, is the most evident form of uprootal or "déracinement." Its resolution, in Weil's eyes, is progressively but never fully attained; ironically the symbolic power of "déracinement" evokes not only the negative force of alienation but the positive force of uprootal, that is, uprootal of oneself against one's own entrenchment in a lifestyle pervaded by alienating or oppressive forces, yet, as history has proven, uprootal must be complemented by its opposite "enracinement." The combined effect of these opposing yet complementary forces is the farthest point possible from oppression.

It is important, however, to cite the change in Weil's view of oppression that occurred in the latter years of her life. There is a significant difference in perspective between her *Analysis of Oppression*, written in 1934 and published in 1937, and the memoranda written for Free France in 1943, published posthumously in 1949 under the title *Enracinement*. In Weil's earlier work, specialization, centrality of power and the race for power are objectively conceived as the conditions of existence for an oppressive society. In Weil's later essays, however, included in *Ecrits de Londres* as well as *Enracinement* she defends a more hierarchical structure of power whose legitimacy is based on public consent.

Roy Pierce points out Weil's distinction between legitimate subordination and oppression based on whether or not the subordinates can comprehend and justify their obedience. Weil stated in this later essay that if the subordinates do comprehend, their action is still methodical and they remain conscious, free beings. If their obedience is not comprehended as necessary to their own well being, directly or indirectly, it is oppressive.

> ... les luttes entre concitoyens ne viennent pas d'un manque de compréhension ni de bonne volonté; elles tiennent à la nature des choses.[10]

Thus, the tension of the struggle between the two opposing elements is an equalizer, evidence of mutual resistance which stimulates and invites challenge. The danger exists, however, in the potential violence of the struggle, violence of any form. Violence triggers a reversal of the natural relationship between the means and the end as human ideals degenerate into a race for power.

Centrality of Power and Knowledge: Centralization is the main feature of an oppressive political system. To uphold this centralized power, there must be a class of elites. This class depends on the existence of privilege in the form of a monopoly of knowledge and force. The complexity of religious rites in early society was understood only by the priests to whom the people entrusted authority and power. Technocrats and scientists, in Weil's estimation, are analogous to the priests because they possess the privileged monopoly and complexity of knowledge which justifies their authority. Military strength in all ages is the privilege of the strong. In modern society's divided form of labor, the organization of gold and money exchange has become the privileged domain and specialty of a parasitical class. In labor, the conceptualization of process and design is determined by a handful of individuals. These are the principal forms of privilege in every oppressive society. The degree of power and rapport between these factors is different with each society. In his study of Weil's political and social theories, Roy Pierce describes this general phenomenon as "the complexity of knowledge," which allows people to mystify their own specialized knowledge and thereby create a sense of dependency upon themselves.

> ... as long as the others regard this knowledge as essential, they are dependent upon the people who alone have it. . . .[11]

Power: "La Course au Pouvoir": Oppression is not an inevitable consequence of specialization and privilege, nor of the resulting social structure based on the master/slave duality. The opposing duality between those who command and those who obey is the vitalizing force and structural determinant of all societies. Tension between the two poles brings society closer to a stage of equilibrium of balanced distribution of power.

> ... la lutte de ceux qui commandent . . . est ce qu'il y a au monde de plus légitime . . . il s'établit entre la pression d'en bas et la résistance d'en haut, un équilibre instable qui définit à chaque instant la structure d'une société. . . .[12]

In the latter period of her life, Weil views the centralization of power and specialization of tasks and knowledge as justified and legitimized in a political order where power is understood and consented to. The reader tends to wonder, however, if this consent reflects true understanding, if it is really a form of methodical action. An imporant point of both Weil's early and later writings on power is that true understanding is based on both experience and objectification of that experience. In a political hierarchial order, experience is by necessity narrowed and specialized. Therefore it is impossible that popular consent to that political order be based on a true and complete understanding of all the elements and levels of power consented to in such a political system.

Weil's changing viewpoint, however, led her to emphasize the beneficial as well as the harmful features of the power struggle. She maintained in her later writings that the opposing duality between those who obey and those who command is the vitalizing force and structural determinant of all societies. The opposing pair "déracinement/enracinement" contain a necessary tension.

Thus the tension of the struggle between the two opposing elements is an equalizer, evidence of mutual resistance which stimulates and invites challenge. Participation in social struggle, in the tension between those who obey and those who command, involves and unavoidable implication with violence and the ephemeral possession of power.

> Participer . . . au jeu des forces qui meuvent l'histoire n'est guère possible sans se souiller ou sans se condamner d'avance à la

défaite.[13]

The nature of human force, even at its most humane level is such that the equilibrium of power can never be maintained; "le je" and "le moi" can never be in perfect balance nor can they be assimilated, fused permanently with society. The removal of power from nature has polarized the subject/object duality within and among us.

Simone Weil's theory of oppression, her conception of freedom as conscious action, and her analysis of the natural instability of power, provide the principles upon which are based her decontruction of power. The social structures of power are built upon certain cultural myths which Weil attempted to demystify. The following sections of this chapter study Weil's attack on each of these myths. In this chapter, discussion of 'déracinement' has taken on another dimension of meaning. The first two chapters have shown the phenomenological development of Weil's philosophy and, consequently, of the theme of "déracinement/enracinement," from inextricable involvement to a state of flexible, detached integration with the world. In this chapter, 'déracinement' also describes the absence of freedom.

MYTH AND THE DECONSTRUCTION OF POWER

Jean Giraudoux concludes his 1935 play, *La Guerre de Troie N'Aura Pas Lieu*, with a discussion between Hector and Ulysses on the fatality of war.[14] Both characters are portrayed as rational lucid leaders: Hector perhaps is the more idealistic because of his certainty that war between Troy and Greece could be prevented, whereas Ulysses is portrayed as more realistic, experienced and more mature because of his certainty that war is inevitable; like Weil, Giraudoux believed that the danger of German aggression came from France's own weakness, not from Hitler's strength. Although Giraudoux denied that the play had been written as a political allegory, it is obvious that his mythological presentation of events did effectively illustrate the conflict between France and Germany.[15] His artistic realism and profundity of character reinforced the thesis of the inevitability of war resulting from the weakness of human character. As a young teacher of philosophy Weil had been recently impressed by this play. Giraudoux's influence on Weil had obviously encouraged her to pursue a deeper comprehension of war and violence through a study of myth, as Giraudoux had done. Weil's most significant essays on pacifism were based on a use of Greek myth and legend. The nature of Weil's response to Giraudoux's view of war and destiny in "L'Iliade ou le Poème de la Force" and "Ne Recommençons Pas la Guerre de Troie" are in effect the affirmation of an Existentialist ethic. Essentially she is demonstrating the need for lucid, clear reasoning as the most effective instrument in confronting the vicissitudes of war and peace. Certainly, as Giraudoux points out in his plays, violence is contagious and war is a chance manifestation of basic elements in nature and human character; but Weil responds, there is still within us the capacity to resist and minimize the presence of force, power, and violence. Weil effectively uses myth and Greek legend to illustrate this point. In fact, the entire history of Greek and Roman civilization provides an allegorical base for Weil in her writings on power.

In these two essays, Weil forms the analysis by which all of her statements on war, pacifism and nationalism can be interpreted. She analyzes the concretization of ideals and symbols, and the danger incurred when these concretized ideals became absolute. In the context of Weil's own philosophy, this is a negative form of "enracinement." In her mythological and political discussions of pacifism, the ideal of freedom is concretized either within the framework of the nation or of violent revolution. "Nation" and "revolution" become symbols of freedom, but the symbols themselves become the absolutes; symbol consumes its meaning; the survival of a particular form of concretized meaning, that is, a particular symbol, becomes all important. Representation has been so closely associated with the ideal it expresses that the symbol, even in its most degenerate form, is conceived as the only possible expression of that ideal, at least in the public mind.

As social and political transformations take place, symbols lose their true meaning but remain as absolutes. The cultivation of these false absolutes transcends the limit of private moral action and an immoral code of public action is legitimized. The result is a dual sense of morality, and the inability to orient oneself and one's society to a true sense of justice. The legitimacy accorded immoral public action and its contradiction with the code of private morality disorients the individual. Symbols and action, formerly the means, now become the purpose. One's loyalty to false absolutes and symbols allows the symbol to consume the ideal it formerly expressed. The violence one justifies in pursuit of a constantly displaced ideal uproots and dehumanizes one further. In the contagion and displacement of violence one loses sight of the ideal that had originally motivated action.

The unbending pursuit of freedom through loyalty to the State or through loyalty to a revolutionary cause leads to war and a greater loss of freedom. Weil's implied superimposition of myth and modern history is a powerfully evocative expression of this dislocation of ideals and truth. By her discussion of ancient legend and epic, Weil shows that myth provides the most effective illustration of this tendency. Here again, a review of Weil's thought evokes the symbolic pair "déracinement/enracinement." The reversal of priorities is a negative form of "déracinement," and a violent uprootal from truth. The cultivation of false absolutes and entrenchment in a vacuum of symbols without meaning is a negative form of "enracinement." The reassociation of symbol with meaning is a positive form of "enracinement" achieved through uprootal from falsehood and flexible reintegration with truth.

MYTH AND HEROISM

Force is the source of centrality, the true subject of the *Iliad*, claims Weil in her analysis of the epic poem. Throughout her essay Weil portrays the reverberation of force upon the perpetrators of violent crimes. The violence of Hector's death reverberates upon Achilles whom the Trojans destroy in vengence, upon the Trojans who are annihilated by the Acheans, upon the Acheans who fall prey to violence and defeat.

> Ainsi la violence écrase ceux qu'elle touche. Elle finit par apparaître extérieure à celui qui la souffre[16]

Shortly before this article was written in 1939-1940, Hitler had violated the Munich Compromise of 1938 by his invasion of Czechoslovakia and Poland in 1939. France had declared war on Germany and was close to capitulation. The essay was published at Marseilles in *Les Cahiers du Sud* during the beginning of the German Occupation of northern France. In her preparation of the article, Weil had addressed herself to two types of readers—those who cringed in disbelief at the contagion of terror and violence they had attributed to an earlier age of human development were those who would most probably regard the *Iliad* as an historical document of the past; those who recognized the recurrence of force throughout history would comprehend the Greek epic's comparative value for modern civilization, an analysis of a recurring tendency to uproot ourselves.

Weil maintains that the fatality of life's brevity and the vicissitudes of peace and war are, essentially, displacements of violence. In the midst of these displacements of force and violence, the identities of both the vanquished and the victorious are brutalized. Both become the objects of power.

> ... la force ... pétrifie différemment, mais également, les âmes de ceux qui la manient. ... (*La Source Grecque*, 32)

Weil shows in her essay various forms of enslavement and objectification by force, the various forms of "déracinement"; the weak are destroyed by physical violence or by the prolonged threat of death, whereas the powerful are objectified by their abuse of force and by the natural instability of power which reverses the roles of the master/slave duality. Force uproots and destroys both. Weil describes Priam as he begs for mercy from Achilles; she translates from Greek depicting young women and children terrorized by their impending death; her description of slaves provides the strange spectacle of people whose identity had become so obliterated by force that they were only capable of lamenting the suffering of those who had destroyed them.

> Qu'un être humain soit une chose, il y a là, du point de vue logique, contradiction; mais quand l'impossible est devenue une réalité, la contradiction devient dans l'âme déchirement. (*La Source Grecque*, 16)

The analysis of epic poetry lends itself particularly well to the deconstruction of the myth of heroism. In his psychoanalytic study of this myth in the major epics of Oriental and Western culture, *Le Triomphe du Héros*, Charles Baudoin indicates that epic poetry lends itself particularly to heroic myth; an understanding of heroic myth helps to clarify epic structure.[17]

Classical or Greek and Roman epic was often valued as the beginning of the narrative tradition of the hero; Weil departs from this tradition when she rejects the presence of the archetypal figures of hero and villain or anti-hero. She establishes this at the very beginning, when she maintains that the only central figure or protagonist in the *Iliad* is force. It is force which commands, and manipulates. The human spirit is continually diminished by relationships with force.

Badouin cites three major tendencies which had formerly dominated the critique of the heroic myth in epic literature—historical, naturalistic, and moral. The historic interpretation presents the myth as a fabulated consolidation of legend and historic exploits accomplished by several different individuals; this interpretation justifies the creative function of a cultural or national archetype. McCoy and Hutson note in their study, *Epics of the Western World*, that whether or not an epic is written before the establishment of a nation, the hero demonstrates the spirit of a national culture; therefore the heros of epics such as Achilles, Roland, and Beowulf are national heros, predating the establishment of the Greek, French, and English nations just as Aeneas and Vasco da Gama are epic heroes exalting the virture of already founded nations.[18] In Weil's writings there is an obvious revolt against that form of mythical interpretation. The naturalistic interpretations cited by Baudouin are closer to Weil's own view of the epic; according to the naturalistic interpretation, the human struggles are portrayed as an expression of nature's perpetual circular movement between resurrection and death; the hero is the incarnation of the sun, forever in combat with the darkness. The vestiges of Weil's pantheistic beliefs of early days as a student and young teacher of philosophy engrossed in Spinoza account in part for her particular emphasis on human transmutations of nature in Homer's *Iliad* and for her view of force as an equalizer. The moral interpretation also cited by Baudouin explains in part Weil's interest in the Greek epic as a political allegory. Baudouin indentifies this interpretation as a meditation on inner human conflict and immortality, conveyed in imagery.[19]

The didactic tradition of interpretation of the mythical element of Greek epic emphasizes the hero's victory against the Other and against himself as reflected in the uniformity between the Other and himself; the hero's struggles are complex because they reflect inner conflict, conflict with the Other who threatens one's own freedom, and struggle against divine law by defiance of limits blocking one's own aspiration for immortality and absolute freedom. Weil appears to agree with this same type of analysis but rejects the idea of victory.

The historic interpretation is completely rejected by Weil, whereas the didactic and naturalistic interpretations encompass certain dimensions of Weil's analysis, but not all. Her essay on the *Iliad* presents a new and unusual approach because of her pacifist perspective; her concepts of force, power, and violence enrich her interpretations. They provide the means for the deconstruction of myths of heroism and power.

Although this approach obviously facilitates Weil's own philosophy and political convictions, this break with the concept of a hero came at a critical time in literary and philosophical development. In the late 30's and early 40's when this essay was composed and published, the traditional concept of the hero had already begun to be challenged. Freud had given a psychoanalytical critique of the myth of the hero in *Interpretations of Dreams* at the beginning of the century; his theories had been developed by Otto Rank and by Carl Jung who studied the complexity and origins of cultural and religious myths and archetypes. Political and social violence had disrupted European tradition and stability. In modern philosophy, developing concepts of Existentialism, Psychoanalytical theory, and Materialism were on the rise, toppling the traditional structure of belief. This disruption of cultural tradition had begun to affect literature and literary criticism. Weil's ideas on force and displacement appear at this time as others besides herself challenge narrative tradition.

The continuity of narration had been achieved in great part by the presence of a central figure or protagonist; the epic had traditionally been considered his story, a poetic narration of his adventures as either victim, hero, or both. Despite the centralizing presence of power or force, Weil revealed a major element of discontinuity in the Greek epic. This favor shown discontinuity corresponds to her belief in the necessary presence of discontinuous elements within the scheme of universal continuity. This is a Greek idea, an aspect of Greek aesthetics and literature which Weil valued all her life. Despite the unifying presence of force, however, the immediate effect of Weil's analysis on Greek epic narrative is discontinuity and fragmentation; characters are no longer consistently identifiable with a certain trait or value, except for those who have kept themselves well beyond the reach of power. The master/slave roles imposed by violence are continually reversed; there are no victors nor vanquished; even the centralizing presence of force and power break with the traditional continuity of narration because in Weil's analysis force is continually displaced. The continual decentering of unity breaks with the tradition of structural continuity in narration. Weil's analysis of a Greek epic based on the instability of power and the displacement of structure and unity evoke certain Derridean ideas on the force and displacement of symbol. Weil's analysis of power closely parallels that of René Girard in his book, *La Violence et le Sacré* (cf. Note 20). The destruction of war and violence is communicated by the structural effect of displacement and fragmentation, and the disintegration of former symbols. Weil's description reveals a view of war not unlike that found in several more recent ones in the novels of Bernanos, Celine, and Simon. The binary pair "déracinement/enracinement," so very prevalent in Weil's later works, contains the symbolic volatility of power, perpetually moving between dispersion and synthesis.

Thus, Weil uses the centrality of force to deconstruct the myth of heroism. The deconstruction of this myth, the leveling of all human character, serves to react against the reversal of Kantian priorities and to deconstruct the myth of power and false absolutes.

Her interpretations point out the absence of a heroic figure in this epic. Hector, who in victorious battle demonstrates strength and valor, confronts the terror and expectation of death ignominiously, a death that reduces a mythical figure to the level of others. Weil traces the vicissitudes of Achilles, whose historical image is that of a strong, heroic protagonist; Achilles is portrayed throughout the poem as a grieving, humiliated man, powerless to prevent Helen's seizure. Weil perceives constantly in her description of the *Iliad*, the dual experiences of victory and defeat, of pride and shame, that structure the action and characterization of the main personalities, including Hector, Agamemnon, Achilles and Ajax. A quality of Greek myth and legend is revealed by this discussion, built upon a dual, antithetical structure of alternating power and weakness. The characters are amoral, neither profound nor shallow. What draws is not the complexity of their personalities, but the complexity of their experiences, a continual series of disequilibriums. Heroism and courage are constantly contested by scenes where the formerly stoical and courageous are humiliated or pathetic in their pleas for mercy. Weil was correct in her claim that force and violence was the source of movement and the centrality of concern in this epic poem.

> ... la force ... est faite avant tout de la superbe indifférence du fort pour les faibles, indifférence si contagieuse qu'elle se communique à ceux qui en sont l'objet. ... (*La Source Grecque*, 26-27)

Equally as mercilessly, those who possess force are crushed by the illusion of momentary possession. In this context, Weil makes a very important point about myth and legend.

She suggests that because violence crushes everyone, it is an equalizer. It fuses together the powerful and the powerless; violence, which is by its own nature continually displaced, breaks the antithetical structure of the master/slave duality and fuses together subject and object. Weil's interest in myth and legend becomes increasingly significant because an original understanding of violence can be traced back to Greek civilization and their legends and myths; violence acts as a source of fusion between the opposing dual elements of the social structure. Violence is a negative source of unification. Weil, like other philosophers, had vainly tried to resolve the dualities characterizing our existence, dualities that in certain social conditions left the individual vulnerable to self-estrangement. Despite the sense of tragedy and destruction that violence implies, its potential as an equalizer, a source of fusion and solidarity attracted Weil, and was an important revelation for her in the course of her studies of primitive and classical civilization.[20] Again the symbolic power and volatility of "déracinement/enracinement" manifests itself, but in this case, violence, a form of "déracinement," functions as a force of synthesis and integration.

Violence determines the narrative structure because it is a central feature of the human experience. The awareness of this common experience and potential shown in classical poetry, myth and legend accounts for the emphasis placed on the Greek and Oriental values of equilibrium, moderation, expressed by the term 'metaxu.'

This is one of many indications Weil makes in her writing of the great value she attributes to the Greek cultural idea of mediation, equilibrium, and harmony. Beyond its punitive value, the displacement of power and force is the leveler of individuals. It is a form of geometrical symmetry which reduces us all to a common denominator. This rigorous form of geometrical retribution is the dominant theme of what Weil considers the only true epic. The *Iliad* is the only true epic of Western literature whose reductive equalizing force is the pivot determining both its structure and its deconstruction. It is significant that the most important structural element of the epic, in Weil's opinion, is that which determines its own deconstruction. It is this essential structural element which Weil extends not only to the epic but to tragedy as well, a genre with an equally strong mythological base.

> La tragédie attique, du moins celle d'Eschyle et de Sophocle, est la vraie continuation de l'épopée. . . .(*La Source Grecque*, 39)

Weil considers Attic tragedy an extension of Greek epic because of the same reductive element of force providing for both the structure and deconstruction of tragedy.

> Ce châtiment . . . constitue l'âme de l'épopée; sous le nom de Nemesis, il est le ressort des tragédies d'Eschyle. . . . (*La Source Grecque*, 22)[21]

The term 'nemesis' captures the problem of co-existence with the Other, of freedom and power. The Other is both the reflection and estrangement of oneself, both one's friend and one's enemy. Weil notes that Homer, the composer of the *Iliad*, was Greek not Trojan. According to Thucydides, eighty years after the fall of Troy, the Achaeans or Greeks were also defeated and conquered. Weil suggests that the *Iliad* was actually the lamentation of a conquered people; their comprehension of exile was accentuated by their own conquest of the Trojans in whom they saw their own image as both conquerors and victims; again the ironic complementarity and displacement of the forces of integration and uprootal. This contributed to the ambiguity of their rapports, tinged with both fraternity and enmity. Her remarks concerning epic and tragedy imply that extension of the mythological conflict between the two parts of oneself or between oneself and one's reflection. The conflict, however, has manifested itself differently; in Western culture, concretized symbols and absolutes have caused an abandonment of the ideal balance of forces within the individual and society; in Oriental culture, mediation is still present as a valued principle.

Weil praises the bitter lyricism throughout the *Iliad* that expresses the leveling, reductive effect of force. Her interpretation displaces scenes and creates the effect of fragmentation by her juxaposition of scenes of peace with those portraying war. Scenes from the battlefield interrupted by discussion of portrayals of family life render the narration ironic and tense. In this contrast between peace and war, there is a symbolic juxtaposition of objects evoking absence, the awaiting of life or death. The idea of 'attente' was the mood of contemporary France, and Weil's emphasis on it was no doubt related to her continual reference throughout her political and historical essays to France's period of 'attente'; it expressed for modern France the expectation of war, the expectation of defeat, invasion and occupation, and finally, the expectation of deliverance.

> cette periode d'attente douloureuse est la plus importante pour la destinée de la France. L'avenir de la France sera celui qu'auront forgé ces années d'apparente passivité. . . .[22]

In her juxtaposition of scenes of peace and war, Weil contrasts the expectation of life and death, and the varying effects of warfare or violence on the perpetrator as well as the victim. She accomplishes this through a metaphoric use of 'house.' One's home is one's source of peace, shelter and individuality. One's body is the worthy or unworthy containment of the soul or spirituality. Hector's house evokes his individualizing bond of emotion to Andromache. His house symbolizes the await of Hector and all the expectations of life. The house contains Andromache who awaits Hector, the visual arousal of bright-haired maids and the hot bath they draw in anticipation of his arrival wait for Hector. In contrast, far from hot baths and in the absence of symbols evoking life, Hector has awaited death; during the moments he spent in expectation of Achilles's blow, the fear and terror of the expectation of death turned him into an object. The objectified body in which the soul resides is contrasted to one's home; the two frameworks within which the soul resides contrast obviously and the varying forms of 'attente' contribute to Weil's commentary.

There is also the juxtaposition of games. Hector's memory of his youth is evoked by the fountain at the gates of Troy where as a young boy he raced with other youths and where now he raced to escape Achilles. One game is superimposed on another; war is likened to a game; throughout this tension between scenes of peace and war, Weil creates the effect of an illusion, of play, a game disrupted by violence. Yet the violence of the actual game serves as both an element of unity and disruption; it bridges the expanse of time separating one game from another. At the same time, it disrupts and detaches one even further from one's past.

The tension created by this disruption and fragmentation of chronological experience is even more effective because of the contrast in style noted by

Weil. There is a significant difference in the styles of language used to describe peace and war. Pathos lends itself to poetical lyricism whereas a more realistic abrupt style creates the effect of fragmentation, disruption, and violence associated with war.

Weil interprets the final revelation of war through Homer's use of similes; both Greek and Trojan warriors undergo transmutations in their exposure to violence which liken them to beasts, elements of nature or catastrophe in the verses of the *Iliad*. The petrifactive quality of force and violence determines these transmutations. Weil believed that in animalizing the human being, Homer had described the art of warfare and indicated the difference between spontaneous and methodical action. Only brief moments of the soul's illumination interrupt the poem's evocation of war.

> la force en est le seul héros. Il en résulterait une morne monotonie, s'il n'y avait, parsemés ça et là, des moments lumineux; moments brefs et divins où les hommes ont une âme. L'ame qui s'éveille ainsi, un instant, pour se perdre bientôt après par l'empire de la force, s'éveille pure et intacte. . . . (*La Source Grecque*, 33)

These moments are attained through either deliberation or through a feeling of personal affection such as parental, filial, conjugal love. The one form of emotional bond which Weil underlines as an essential element of the epic is friendship, a bond that exists between comrades as well as between enemies. Yet force as the dominant theme of the epic weakens and dismantles this bond itself. Force, in Weil's eyes, is the determinant of total uprootal of unmediated displacement.

There is also in Weil's commentary, her perception of the complexity of one's immersion in violence.

> l'âme que l'existence d'un ennemi a contrainte de détruire en soi ce qu'y avait mis la nature ne croit pouvoir se guérir que [par] la destruction de l'ennemi. . . . (*La Source Grecque*, 30)[23]

The destruction which becomes one's objective is a form of blind self-defense from violence and its memories; it also responds to the lure, the attraction of death. The desperation that possesses one immersed in violence arouses a two-fold need for slaughter and self-destruction, the murder of oneself and of one's reflection in the Other, total, absolute "déracinement."

Weil's existential view of life as a progression, a projection towards death and nothingness uncovers a source of desperation for the soldier, for all those involved with war. That war is not a game but a reality which enfolds one's own death is insupportable knowledge. For the common individual, death exists as a future. The human being cannot support the idea that death is one's future; that reality estranges one from oneself, adding to the dehumanization caused by one's own immersion in violence. It is the final irony of unmediated 'déracinement.'

For such individuals, the only tolerable solution is deliverance through violence, a view explored by other existentialist writers, Malraux in particular. It is preferable to choose deliverance through destruction rather than master the memories and awareness of violence itself and the suffering it causes. Weil assumes, of course, the point of view of the person who seeks survival. The alternative choice for the soldier, that of complete retreat from violence, is also an acceptance of immediate physical death.

At the end of the first day of battle the Greeks had lost sight of their objective. They had begun by battling for Helen and in the contagion and exaltation of violence were instead driven by a lust for destruction and domination. Displacement determines this entire discussion, displacement of symbol and displacement of violence. Weil's ironic observation on the uncertainty of Helen's actual geographic location is appropriate, since the geographical displacement expresses metaphorically the Greeks' loss of objective. But even in the beginning, when the symbolic persona of Helen drove them into battle, the objective incarnated by Helen was ambiguous; its ambiguity renders it all the more volatile. This is a theme Weil effectively develops in her essay, "Ne Recommençons Pas la Guerre de Troie."

> Les Grecs et les Troyens s'entremassacrerent autrefois pendant dix ans à cause d'Hélène. . . . Sa personne était si évidemment hors de proportion avec cette gigantesque bataille qu'aux yeux de tous elle constituait simplement le symbole du véritable enjeu; mais le véritable enjeu, personne ne le définissait et il ne pouvait être défini, car il n'existait pas. . . .[24]

Weil thus deconstructed the myth of the hero, using the symbolic duality of 'déracinement/enracinement' to evoke the instability of power.

THE MYTH OF THE GREAT BEAST

> L'Enracinement est autre chose que le social. . . .
> (*La Pesanteur et la Grâce*)[25]

There are three myths from Plato's *Republic* that relate to Weil's writings on power; the myths of the Cave, the Great Beast, and the Ring of Gyges. Forever seeking the origin of myth and belief, she uses metaphorically the concept of the Great Beast to describe the power of the Social, that is, the psychological power of the collective over the individual in determining value, thought, and morality. The first myth is that of the Cave and the spiritual and intellectual vacuum it symbolizes. For Weil, our own concept of time is our compensation, our initiation of eternity. To emerge from the cave is to aspire towards eternity beyond human conceptions of past, present, and future. To remain within the darkness of the cave is to remain obediently and passively under the domination of the collective mind, cultivating the idolatry of the Social and of false absolutes.

> The only real things for them would be the shadows of the puppets. . . .[26]

The myth of the Great Beast appears in Book VI of the *Republic*. The myth of the cave follows almost immediately in Book VII of the same work. Socrates had compared the power of the masses to that of a Great Beast, deploring the human tendency to define truth, virtue and morality according to the impulse of the collective whole, that is, the mythical Great Beast. This is Socrates', or rather Plato's, comment:

> It is as if a man were learning the impulses and desires of some great strong beast.[27]

This metaphor has a significant application throughout Weil's writings, particularly in her essays on nationalism, social revolution, and power. The concepts of 'nation' and 'revolution' are false absolutes imposed by the collective on the individual mind and communicate most effectively the tyranny of the Social. Weil's discussion of the state and social revolution are attempts to deconstruct the myth of "la bête sociale" and the substitution of the relative or the absolute. According to Weil, the collective animal is the object of all idolatry; it is the force which chains us to the earth. George Panichas has commented that the Great Beast symbolizes for Weil "a transcendent social idolatry" essential to those who still dwell in the cave; when the force of the collective takes the place of the divine in the individual soul, "the collective soul is ascendant."[28]

C'est le social qui jette sur le relatif la couleur de l'absolu. Le

> rémède est dans l'idée de relation. La relation sort violemment du social. Elle est le monopole de l'individu. La société est la caverne, la sortie est la solitude. . . .[29]

The collective forces reinforces the illusion of equivalency between the relative and the absolute, that is, between meaning and its representative forms relative to each society and era.

The third myth also appears in the *Republic*, Book II; this is the myth of the Ring of Gyges, the story of a shepherd whose discovery of a ring gives him unlimited power by making him invisible.

> We will come on the just man in the very act of becoming unjust. . . . Because every . . . being . . . desires . . . more, . . .[30]

The shepherd misuses his power, slays the king, marries the Queen and becomes the unscrupulous ruler of an ill-gotten kingdom. In her commentary on this myth in *La Pesanteur et la Grâce*, Weil describes it as the mythical illustration of the dual sense of morality she attributes to western culture. Possession of the ring of Gyges is the key to invisibility and detachment from one's own crimes; she refers to it as "la faculté de mettre à part."

> L'anneau de Gyges devenu invisible, c'est précisément l'acte de mettre à part. Mettre à part soi et le crime que l'on commet. . . .[31]

She describes the ring as the key to absolute license and immorality in the realm of public action. The ring of Gyges grants legitimacy to all actions of the Social.

> (Guerre, haines de nations et de classes, patriotisme d'un parti, d'une Eglise, etc.). Tout ce qui est couvert de la chose sociale est mis dans un autre lieu que le reste et soustrait à certains rapports. . . .[32]

The ring also provides a distance and space where one can withdraw from one's own moral failure and crime.

> J'en use lorsque je remets de jour en jour l'accomplissement d'une obligation. Je sépare l'obligation et l'écoulement du temps. . . .[33]

Possession of the ring symbolizes the inconsistencies in our application of moral criteria, judging other civilization by moral standards that we do not impose on ourselves, from which the collective mind releases us. Even when such detachment is consciously achieved, even when one affirms it by one's own act of will, one eventually becomes unaware of one's own withdrawal and detachment; one lives in an ambivalent state where one obeys without understanding the criteria of public morality. The action of throwing away the key, the ring of Gyges would be a refusal of the Social and of the alienating contradiction between public and private morality. The refusal of the ring of Gyges would be a lucid affirmation of the relation between our actions and those of the other. Justice is the establishment of such a relation in our minds and in ourselves. In Weil's view, it is the point of contact between reason and will, the human point of accessibility to the divine.

> l'acte de jeter la clef, de jeter l'anneau de Gyges, c'est l'effort propre de la volonté, c'est la marche douloureuse et aveugle hors de la caverne. . . .[34]

Together the myths of the Cavern, the Social Beast and the Ring of Gyges form a coherent structural foundation for an understanding of Weil's critique of the mythical value associated with the concept of "the State" and "Revolution," the major forms of the power of the Social. The mythical value of the Social and its associated absolutes is an evidently negative manifestation of "déracinement," obedience to signifiers estranged from their original meaning. In the following sections on the myth of the State and the myth of Revolution, there will be a discussion of the various ways in which Weil sought to deconstruct the mythical power of the Social. Deconstruction is, in this case, a positive form of "déracinement" because of the importance of reintegration retrieving for the individual a valid form of regrounding. Weil's discussion of the State as a manifestation of the Great Social Beast concerns problems of language, history, and politics. For the first part, her essay on "Réflexions sur les Origines de l'Hitlérisme" will form the basis of the discussion of displacement of popular images and historical roles, and the attempt to localize violence. The second part will discuss the notion of patriotism, the departure from its former capacity for equilibrium through flexibility and displacement, and the uprootal and loss of identity that has resulted from France's break with the past; this second part will be based primarily on *L'Enracinement*, her final political work. The third section treats Weil's various statements on Colonialism, providing another perspective to the deconstruction of the myth of the State. Her discussion of Revolution will also be approached as the second major manifestation of the power of the Social. The myth of revolution also has its basis in language, history and politics; it will be discussed in sections entitled, "Revolution and History," "Critique of Marxism," "Militarism," "Bureaucratic Rule," and "Technocracy and Mechanization."

THE MYTH OF THE STATE

> But a nation ... cannot be the object of supernatural love. It has no soul. It is a Great Beast.
>
> (*Gravity and Grace*)[35]

Introduction. Less than a year prior to France's final capitulation to Germany, Weil began a series of essays and studies that she continued writing through her period of service in London up until her death in 1943. These were reflections examining and challenging the bulwark of beliefs, values and historical interpretations supporting French and German nationalism and ethnocentrism.

The nation state had become the ultimate value, not the welfare of individuals within or outside its bounds. With the reversal of values, the permanence of the nation state became the objective of all political action. "La France Eternelle" and "L'Eternelle Allemagne" were falsely-chosen absolutes, claimed Weil, that were at the heart of the true reasons for the rise of Hitler and Nazism. As each person's nation became a symbol, it also became the measure of public morality, thereby condoning acts normally unjustifiable for the private individual. This led to further alienation of the individual torn between the demands of private and public action. "La France Eternelle" and "L'Eternelle Allemagne" became determinants of war, peace, and morality.

During this pre-war period of alienation and irreality, these terms reflected an uncertain attempt to get a hold on good and evil. By viewing different nation states as the incarnation of good or evil, the source of difficulty would be localized and banished, as was the scapegoat driven into the wilderness in ancient times in an effort to contain and banish misfortune. This eased the uncertainty of collective existence and simplified morality by denying the complexity of individual and collective identities. Politics between nations were determined by the moral superiority and permanence attributed to one's own country, and by the point on the spectrum of permanence and morality that defined one's image of the country and civilization with which one was dealing. One's own nation had become a moral absolute, and a determinant of war and peace.

The true objective of politics is stability and peace. The greater the equilibrium of power between nations, the greater would be stability and freedom. In the face of the rising extremes of French and German nationalism of the pre-world war II era, a reaffirmation of the true objective of politics and of all collective and representative action was badly needed. A return to this objective of peace was hindered by the devaluation and subordination of all other forms of human collectivities to that of the nation state. The guardianship of the Nation had become the objective of public action and war.

Weil dismantles the myth of permanence and morality associated with the concept of the nation state. She takes as prime examples, France and Germany, arch-rivals of the period. A study of European history denies their infallibility and permanence. The reaction to Hitler's rise within France had been a surge of generalizations that stereotyped Germany as a permanent threat to mankind, and France as a historic symbol of freedom and individualism. The public national image within each of the two nations was, in turn, associated with strength, permanence, and moral righteousness. But Weil points out that each country's history presented a tableau of temporality and transformation, not of permanence and stability. The different vicissitudes of history experienced by the two cultures could not be reduced to a single principle of morality or dominance. If generalizations about France and Germany were to be made from historical experience, they would be exactly the opposite from the popular, yet falsely generalized images evoked in the public mind.

Weil denied that Germany had ever posed the threat of world domination until the twentieth century. The threat of world domination had existed before Hitler but not by any German people. Before Hitler, Charles V and Philippe II of Spain, Louis XIV and Napoleon had attempted to dominate Europe militarily. Ironically, the greatest threat to European peace and civilization had more frequently come from France than from any other power.

> Ni l'Espagne ni la France n'ont été, à la suite de leurs défaites, anéanties, démembrées, ou même désarmées. . . .[36]

Weil implies a certain prejudice against Germany on the part of France. Neither Spain nor France were reduced following their defeats as was Germany following the First World War and the Treaty of Versailles. In the case of Spain and France, the danger displaced itself, stated Weil (cf. note 37 below), with the change of circumstances; but for Germany, the danger appeared embedded and localized, associated closely with the Germanic identity; Weil commented on this in a letter to Bernanos following her return from participation in the Republican struggle in Spain:

> La volonté d'humilier l'ennemi vaincu, . . . me guérit une fois pour

toutes de ce patriotisme naïf. Les humiliations infligées par mon pays me sont plus douloureuses que celles qu'il peut subir....[37]

As the object of bitterness and humiliation, Germany was the scapegoat driven into the wilderness and as such became all the more dangerous. In both her historical and political writings, Weil points out the contagion of alienation; those who became victims of our fears are rendered all the more dangerous by the humiliations we heap upon them. The danger appears defined and localized by the exile and isolation of the Other; but, in reality, its containment is a sign of contagion and impending displacement, a dangerously aggravated form of "déracinement."

LA FRANCE ETERNELLE

Weil traces her country's history to invalidate the sense of immortality and immutability of France as a symbol of unity and freedom. In doing so, Weil was not trying to deny the French people a source of hope in such a difficult time of demoralization. Rather she was trying to find a more lasting basis for freedom and patriotism.

France is not eternal, not in terms of its guardianship of liberty and peace. Napoleon was at least as terrible as Hitler, Weil maintains, by his campaign against Holland, Switzerland, and Spain and his plundering of poor communities along the Tyrol. Richelieu, Louis XIV, and Napoleon embedded within French tradition the notion of the State; they all contributed to its evolution and refinement through suppressive centralization. In Weil's description of the Restoration, the pacifism of the period under Louis Philippe is viewed as a parenthetical phase during which time the memory of France's threat to world peace continued to haunt other nations. In the same way, France would continue to fear and alienate Germany after 1918 as she had been exiled following the final Napoleonic defeat. The memory of national glory had begun to haunt the French themselves after 1815 and pushed them towards a desire for further military conquests. This nostalgic feeling of a natural right to conquest was reinforced by literature of the period. Weil cites the popular poetry of Barthélemy and Hugo's glorification of French conquests and military victories through his elegies and epic poetry. The chauvinist spirit was exalted and justified by the literature of the time.

Weil describes the irony of the stereotyped images of freedom and tyranny respectively attributed to modern-day France and Germany as a reversal of historical roles. For the last four centuries from the death of Charles V to the Revolution overthrowing the Bourbon Kings, France had been a symbol of domination and a threat to European peace; in the same period,

Germany was an example of freedom.

According to Weil's account, the reign of Charles VI was the beginning of several hundred years of tyranny for the French. It also foreshadowed the tradition of oppressive centralization for much of Europe.[38]

Weil believed that Richelieu was the closest historical precedent to Hitler.[39] It was Richelieu who invented the centralized, all consuming entity of absolute rule, the State. This is a judgement shared by most historians, that Richelieu was the methodical, amoral theoretician of state rule who lay the groundwork for centralization of power in France.

Many writers describe the period of the late 1930s and the early 1940s by the terms "ambivalence," "incoherence," "irreality," and "estrangement." The comparison Weil makes between the era of Richelieu and that of Hitler illustrates the suitability of such terms. The norms determining and justifying private and national action were so contradictory that it was difficult to decide what was right or wrong, what was real or false. Treaties and pacts were agreed upon but violated; war and violence were prolonged by madmen; there were no limits to the satisfaction of national prestige.

The Machiavellian principle applied by Richelieu that a government owes complete loyalty to the State, rather than to its citizens or to its King is the methodical separation of morality from politics that Maurras paraphrased three centuries later by the phrase "La Politique d'abord" (cf. note 40). Weil considered Cardinal Richelieu more dangerous than the atheist, Charles Maurras, however, despite the latter's championing of "L'Action Française." Richelieu as a religious leader performed a worse sacrilege in Weil's eyes because his worship of the State alone was a form of idolatry.[40]

The increasing difference of public and private morality characterizing the period of Richelieu's absolute service to the State left France uprooted; he had destroyed much of the moral foundation of French society. France sustained this experience, however, because it offered stability and escape from devastating civil wars between noble families.

> son devouement à l'Etat a déraciné la France. Sa politique était de tuer systématiquement toute vie spontanée dans le pays, pour empêcher que quoi que ce soit put s'opposer à l'Etat. . . .[41]

Evidence of the mood of servility during this era appears in what Weil considers Corneille's servile and ingratiating language and forms of address. These extreme expressions of humility and politeness characterizing the literature of preciosity and Pre-Classicism were not typical of everyday speech. Weil finds proof of this in Théophile de Viau's writings.[42]

Louis XIV continued Richelieu's policies of absolute obedience to the State of which he became the symbol. The Sun King was all the more powerful and formidable because he incarnated the State itself. During his reign, the State reached its height in destruction. Weil retraced the events of the Sun King's youth and the building of paranoia which made him an intractable model for modern dictators. His was truly a totalitarian regime whose depths of cruelty and abasement are discussed in the writings of Saint-Simon and Liselotte. But, as Weil points out, adulation of royal patronage demanded of all literary figures of the time would be more analogous to Stalin's imposition of a moral and intellectual vacuum than to Hitler's own brand of terrorizing tactics.

The one outstanding similarity between Hitler and Louis XIV was the subservience each of them obtained through the humiliation of their adversaries.

Hitler broke several treaties as had Louis XIV, in particular his isolation of the Munich Compromise broken in March 1939 when Hitler overran Czechoslovakia; this was his first truly devastating blow to European stability. According to Weil, Hitler's aggression against Czechoslovakia, Poland, the Low Countries and his expected attack on France and England had their parallel in Louis XIV's devastation of Italy and Holland among others; but Weil considered the havoc caused by the Sun King far worse because it was arbitrarily and recklessly carried out without the pretext of war. There is some doubt as to the validity of Weil's assumption that Hitler's actions were entirely methodical by contrast; but the comparison between Hitler and Louis XIV still remains credible.

> . . . l'aggression non-motivée contre la Hollande faillit anéantir un peuple libre et fier de l'être, et dont la civilisation à ce moment était plus brillante encore que celle de la France, comme les noms de Rembrandt, Spinoza, Huyghens le montrent assez. . . .[43]

Thus, the recently acquired term "La France Eternelle" is an evocative image that contradicts history. Not until the time of Richelieu and Louis XIV did the nation concept truly exist. Not until the Revolution did the French nation state represent a framework by which freedom could be safeguarded. France as a symbol of freedom and sovereignty dates only from the Revolution and the associated struggles for worker emancipation and national sovereignty during the nineteenth century. "La France Eternelle" was thus a false absolute, a negative form of "déracinement" deconstructed by Weil.

L'ETERNELLE ALLEMAGNE

"L'Eternelle Allemagne" is no more legitimate nor accurate in its implication of the historical permanence of the German state. There is complete dissimilarity between the period preceding Frederick II and that which started with his reign. The absolute extremes of command, obedience, and imposed terror by arms did not exist in Prussia before his accession onto the throne. Weil claims that the creation of a new concept of the Prussian state was France's responsibility. Not only did Richelieu and Louis XIV provide the examples of absolute rule for Frederick II, not only did the greatest French writers of the period sing his praises, but Napoleon's destruction of the remaining vestiges of the Holy Roman (Germanic) Empire, and his conquests of Prussian territories continued on a smaller scale by Napoleon III in 1870 inspired the consolidation of an embittered sense of German nationalism.

Weil interprets German Romanticism as the natural reaction to the depression and violence caused by Napoleon's aggressive campaigns. The adoration of force is an aspect of German Romanticism that Weil notes particularly and associates with the dominant presence of Napoleonic Occupation and military force. Hitler was the heir to this Germanic Romantic tradition inspired by France's invasions and oppression of Prussian territory. He was the incarnation of force in the Napoleonic tradition. The German romantic tradition was also a reaction to Kant and the rational spirit imbued in his works. Ironically Kant figures predominantly in the revival of French rationalism. The modernist rise of German phenomenology that began with Hegel did not penetrate France until Kojeve's translation of the *Phenomenology of the Mind* in the early part of this century; until then the image of cultural opposition persisted in the form of French rationalism vs. German Romanticism. Obviously these images were inaccurate and all the more disorienting by the uprooted and displaced traditions they represented.

There was no precedent for Hitler in Medieval German History. On the contrary, the small German communities of the Middle Ages were models of later free, prospering France, and Italy. The Holy Roman Empire (Germanic) was of no great threat, having failed in its attempt to conquer a weak and divided Italy. In fact, Weil praises the Empire's association with Marlborough's coalition at the time of Louis XIV's accession to the throne.

The tradition of force and military might is so alien to Germanic experience that the closest ancestral precedent to Frederick II that Hitler could claim was that of the early Germanic tribes described by Caesar and Tacitus two thousand years ago.

Weil questions Hitler's interpretation of history and his claim regarding the racial propensity of Germanic peoples for dominance and absolute rule.

The spread and consolidation of the Roman Empire provides the framework of historical accounts revealing qualities of the two cultures, Germanic and Roman. Weil finds upon examination of these accounts that the cultural characteristics of the early Germanic peoples were vastly different from those claimed by Hitler. In fact, the traits of Hitler's modern Germany resembled most closely those of the Ancient Romans

> Entre les peuplades décrites par César et Tacite et les Allemands actuels, il n'y a aucune ressemblance. . . .[44]

The German people enjoyed warfare and relished the challenge of combat, but their goal was security, not domination. Caesar relates that these people avoided aggressive enemy attacks by the devastation and emptying of surrounding territory. Weil asserts that this differed essentially from the Roman's and Hitler's goal of suppression and enslavement of opposing cultures. Weil seems to regard Hitler as a methodical ruler who distastefully sought war as a means to an end; ironically Weil regards the early Germanic Tribes' enjoyment of battle less harmful than the goal fo warfare projected by the Romans and by Hitler.

Weil's comparison of Hitler to a Roman Emperor is strengthened by the supposed similarity of their methods. The key to diplomatic relations for both, in Weil's view, was pretense, to compromise and pledge friendship and allegiance until the potential victims were completely vulnerable and all the more demoralized and confused by a defeat they were not psychologically prepared to sustain.

> On pourrait analysér en détail chaque action des Romains, à partir de la victoire de Zama, pour y retrouver l'application de cet art. Hitler, dans une conversation, a parfaitement bien formulé à cet égard la règle à suivre, en disant qu'il ne faut jamais traiter quelqu'un en ennemi jusqu'au moment précis òu on est en train de l'écraser.[45]

Weil is not just referring to the crushing Roman reaction to Persia's preparation of war, to the conquests of Antiochus nor to the Acheans' rebellion. She is evidently describing the disbelief and feeling of unreality that characterized the French reaction to war with Germany and eventual capitulation. However, Weil does not apply her previous effective analysis of the contagion of violence to her commentary on early Germanic culture; despite Weil's serious attempt at clearheadedness and lucidity in deconstructing the myth of force and power in our culture, she unconsciously shows a breach of objectivity by her reduction of Roman civilization to an absolute, to an image of ultimate cruelty and force. She thus denies the complexity of Roman society and regards it with a certain closemindedness. Weil portrayed effectively the uprootal and displacement of opposing values and had shown how neither good nor evil, strength nor weakness, could consistently define a single national collectivity. Still, she was prone to stereotype, justly or unjustly, her contemporary situation in Europe. Hitler's Germany is defined by association with the Roman Empire and reduced to the absolute of evil. In disqualifying Hitler's claim to the Germanic tradition of domination and supreme rule, she provided a reverse stereotype whereby the qualities of the Romans correspond particularly to Hitler's Modern Germany; the early Germanic tribes were lazy, she insists. Therefore modern Germans, who are industrious and hardworking like the Romans were, are not reflecting an inherited trait of their race; a common trait of industriousness is implied and links contemporary German civilization to the hated Romans. Weil shows that Hitler's claim is all the more invalid by the fact that the early Germanic tribes possessed a sense of honor, candour, and simplicity; she substantiates this by quoting Tacitus. She contrasts these good qualities with the perfidious conduct of Caesar and other Romans, enumerating instances that she presents with intensive detailed description. She repeatedly compares Hitler's perfidy and cruelty to that of Caesar and to other Roman rulers. This stereotyping or categorization does not invalidate Weil's analysis; on the contrary, despite her struggle for fairness and objectivity in searching out the true causes of violence and force and in trying to overcome the prejudices perpetuated in language and false values, the fact that she herself was subject to such stereotyping makes one all the more aware of the importance of her inquiries. The concept of "L'Eternelle Allemagne" is thus another false absolute, a form of "déracinement" uprooted and deconstructed by Weil.

LA PATRIE ET LA NATION

> ... je devrai rompre avec l'arôme de ces années essentielles. ...
> notre héritage n'est précédé d'aucun testament. ... (*Feuillets d'Hypnos*, Rene Char)[46]

During the year before her death in 1943 in Ashford, Kent, Weil worked in London for De Gaulle's Free French organization. The book published posthumously in 1949, *Enracinement*, contains memoranda which she wrote and submitted as recommendations on the policy to be pursued after the Liberation. In *Enracinement*, Weil gives a more detailed analysis of the extremes of French nationalism. The nation remains as the absolute form of a human collectivity; she shows how, in the past few centuries, all other forms of collectivity and association have become subordinated to the concept of nation. She leads to the conclusion that this has estranged the French people from a former sense of true patriotism and uprooted them from their past and a sense of cultural identity. She poses this as the fundamental cause of France's involvement with war and its eventual defeat. She is fearful that as France emerges from the ravages of the German Occupation the French people will once again depend entirely on their sense of national identity to determine the foundations of moral action and individual sovereignty. She is afraid that individual morality and identity will once again be consumed by the State in a reversal of priorities and a loss of objectives and purpose. For this reason she retraces the history of patriotic feeling in France, its original purpose and the transformations it underwent in the course of history.

> La nation seule, depuis déjà longtemps joue le rôle qui constitue par excellence la mission de la collectivité à l'égard de l'être humain, à savoir assurer à travers le présent une liaison entre le passé et l'avenir. . . .[47]

The decomposition of the nation coincides with the same period in which nationalism had become the main value. The family had become a less vital social unit. One's culture was less defined by an awareness of ancestry and personal heritage than by one's participation with a national identity. The life of the village, the province, the city and the region were subordinated to the demands of, and to the cultural prestige of the nation state. Even before Germany invaded, defeated, and occupied France, France had already lost herself. Even before the war, there was already pervasive incoherence and ambivalency in French society.

> Le peuple français, en juin et juillet 1940, n'a pas été un peuple à qui des escrocs cachés dans l'ombre, ont soudain par surprise volé sa patrie. C'est un peuple qui a ouvert la main et laissé la patrie tomber par terre. . . . (*L'Enracinement*, 131)

The Occupation was only a more violent manifestation of this decomposition. At the time of Weil's writing in 1943, there was a new rise in nationalism and a consolidation of resistance to the Axis Powers. Weil, however, like some, distrusted the new hope and value placed again on the nation.

> . . . la patrie n'est jamais si belle que sous l'oppression d'un conquérant, si l'on a l'espoir de la revoir intacte. C'est pourquoi on ne doit pas juger, par l'intensité actuelle du sentiment national, de l'éfficacité réelle qu'il possèdera, après la libération, pour la stabilité de la vie publique. . . . (*L'Enracinement*, 132)

The concept of the nation is a comparatively recent phenomenon in Europe, whereas patriotism has always existed in one form or another. But the object of patriotism was undefinable, diffuse. In medieval times, loyalty was shown toward the feudal lord, to the city, to both, or to territorial environs whose boundaries were not distinctly drawn. Weil considered earlier forms of patriotism as a flexible concept whose object was easily displaced according to one's own sense of social and economic identity. These were purer forms of patriotism because of their capacity for displacement and flexibility. Gradually, the Kingdom of France developed into a distinct entity; still, in Weil's view, the consciousness of being French did not deter from the flexibility of a dual sense of patriotism towards one's king and towards one's country. Weil is somewhat idealistic in her consideration of the period of French national history that ended with the death of Charles V. She associates greater legitimacy and purity with the patriotism and obedience of the French people prior to the beginning of the centralization of power and methodical construction of the French State that followed. In her eyes, this dual form of patriotism provided in the individual consciousness a greater sense of equilibrium between individual and collective interests; it also allowed for a purer form of obedience, legitimized by one's sense of willful and reasoned participation in the hierarchy of power. Although self-acknowledged and self-willed subordination is an essential concept in developing a framework where the demands of both freedom and order are met, Weil overlooked a great deal of history. Her major point concerning the transformation of the notion of patriotism is valid, however. In more recent times, a different form of patriotism took hold which supplanted the former dual loyalty to one's country and to one's king. The development of this new form of patriotism accompanied the increasing centralization of power. Weil cites two reasons for this; the first was the degeneration of monarchy under Charles VI and the subsequent despotism of French rule which continued until the end of the eighteenth century; the second reason was that throughout French history, provinces were regarded and treated as conquered territories rather than as part of a Kingdom thereby discouraging the loyalty and respect of new subjects. For example the territory south of the Loire, before its conquest in the thirteenth century, was a prospering, fine civilization with a strong regional sense of patriotism and solidarity. The entire city of Béziers was razed by the French conqueror who brought with him the Inquisition. A general revolt took place in the form of widespread conversion to Protestantism in the area. D'Aubigné himself attributes the powerful growth of Protestantism to the reaction against what had taken place, the annihilation of the Albigensian civilization. The obstinacy of the Huguenots was a form of revolt against the centralized power.

Other regions of France whose assimilation had begun by an uprootal of regional culture and authority was Burgundy, the Franche-Comté, Corsica, and Brittany. Weil discusses in detail the history of these regional struggles as well as French cruelties towards Flemish cities and citizens. Some of her remarks concerning the Bretons' struggle for autonomy has particular relevance in recent years.

> Si discrédité que soit l'autonomisme breton. . . . Il y a des trésors latents dans ce peuple, que n'ont pas pu sortir. La culture française ne lui convient pas. La sienne ne peut pas germer; dès lors il est maintenu tout entier dans les bas-fonds des catégories sociales inférieures.

All of these and other French territories were not bound together until the Revolution. The hope for a sovereign nation provided the force of consolidation. Weil points out the paradox of this new form of patriotism based on a violent rupture with the past and tradition, not on a love nor identification with it. But this supposed past from which the Revolutionaries broke away had really begun only with Charles VI, evolving into a centralized system of rule under Richelieu's iron hand; its traits of centralization and despotism particularly accentuated under Louis XIV. Weil condemns in particular the philosophers of the Enlightenment who, she believed, reinforced in their progressive ideas and influence the conception of progress and revolution as an intellectual break with the past, not as a return nor as a revalorization of it. The revolutionary spirit was part of every social struggle through French history beginning with the emancipation of the serfs.

> les révoltes du XIVe siècle, le début du mouvement des Bourguignons, la Fronde, des écrivains comme d'Aubigné, Théophile de Viau, Retz. Sous François Ier un projet de milice populaire fut écarté, parce que les seigneurs objectèrent que si on le réalisait les petits-fils des miliciens seraient seigneurs et leurs propres petits-fils seraient serfs. Si grande était la force ascendante

qui soulevait souterrainement ce peuple.... (*L'Enracinement*, 143)

The interruption of this tradition by the cold and long, centralized reign of the Sun King as well as the Enlightenment's approach to history left the Revolutionaries with no sense of a past, of a cultural identification. Weil sees an existentialist dimension in this new sense of patriotism which, having no apparent link or determination by historical tradition, was a choice, an affirmation of will revolting against what was seemingly the obstacles of historical tradition and destiny. In this way a new sense of patriotism was born, estranged from history; its foundation was the present and its projection into the future.

At first the hope for national sovereignty was the objective of this new sense of patriotism. La patrie was at this time a tremendous ideal of individual freedom through the nation concept. As history has shown, the Revolution's objective of national sovereignty was diluted and lost as power displaced itself in a series of reversals. Royalty became an uprooted concept as it lost its historical justification. Patriotism had to attach itself to another objective when the ideal of national sovereignty seemed incompatible with national rule. This new objective became the guardianship of the State. The dual loyalty to one's king and one's people had ended with Charles V, as French monarchy took on a despotic form. As the centuries passed, the two terms became increasingly contradictory and incompatible in definition. The two senses of the term "patriotism" disappeared, substituted by loyalty to the State.

The events that most definitely marked the demise of the form of patriotism born with the Revolution took place in 1871 following the establishment of the Commune and beginning of the Third Republic. This was the final year of Revolutionary patriotism. As Weil sees it, 1871 marked the clash between two incompatible forms of glory: freedom and conquest.

The motif of Roman rule reappears throughout her description as a symbol of the failure of national sovereignty. She claims that under the Third Republic, the French state closely resembled the Roman Empire by its structure. The vestiges of Roman influence survived the revolution, in the centralized dominance of the State. Fouché is another symbol for her of this continuum of Roman influence. Contempt for politics, for the police and the State it symbolized became a tradition. Weil refers to this tradition of disobedience and contempt for authority as "le rebours de l'idolâtrie." As the deterioration of the Third Republic followed its course, citizens became accustomed to unfulfilled expectations; disdain for political authority became a tradition and the French people, including those who participated in its leadership, lost a sense of obedience and became what Weil called "le mendiant insolent." (*L'Enracinement*, 199)

Weil believed that, up until the last years of the Third Republic, no institution nor any aspect of public life had evoked affection or loyalty. The mood of intellectual and moral constraint initiated by Richelieu persisted up until the Second World War. The vacuum of love or respect for the State made the Frenchman's military sacrifice all the more difficult. This was Weil's explanation for the wave of pacifism, anti-pacifism, and anti-patriotism after 1918, particularly in France; the war veterans' intense patriotism and the pacifist disillusionment coexisted as opposite reactions to this moral vacuum.

Schooling in France before the war reinforced the incoherency and ambivalency of modern morality that has resulted from this recent form of patriotism. Instructors communicated to their students moral principles of personal behavior based on a sense of justice, and consideration of others. But this code of private morality according to Weil was contradicted by the approach to teaching history; the students' knowledge of world history was centered around the history of France's development and growth. Weil criticizes this ethnocentric approach to teaching by which a justification of one's own nation or civilization is the determining principle. In this way a prejudiced view of one's past is perpetuated. The extreme ideologies of Maurras and l'Action Française as well as the extreme view of certain French and German National Socialists resulted from such a prejudiced view of history.

The dual sense of morality manifests itself in the daily actions and lifestyle of the French citizen who had been conditioned, in Weil's opinion, to judge and discuss events and their consequences from the point of view of France's greatest national interest. Weil contrasts this dual sense of morality—the Roman legacy—with the forgotten value of humility associated most closely in her culture with the Christian religion, which, in turn, she carefully distinguishes from the ingratiating humility of the Vichy government. She reminds the reader of the unfortunate misassociation of humility with duplicitous subservience that was caused by the Vichy Collaborationists. This only strengthened the association of force with good, and weakness with evil. The perspective of each side, the Collaborationists and the 'Resistants' centered around the refusal of defeat for France. The French of both political camps identified strongly with the Roman value of victory. Those who were the strongest resistors to occupied forces were polarized from and disdainful of those who accepted defeat whether or not they collaborated with German forces. This explains, also, in great part, the willingness of the French Collaborationists to associate their country with the conquerors of Western Europe.

Weil draws an interesting parallel between the Vichy Collaborationist government and France during its most glorious period of conquest. Both were impelled by the same moral contradiction justifying the unification of territory. The measures of historical conquest used to consolidate the French nation were no different from those of Weil's contemporaries who sought to unify Europe by the same means.

However, patriotism maintained its continuity. There were two reasons for this: the first primary reason for the continuance of patriotism, even in its new form, was that there was nothing else left as a basis for solidarity, nothing besides nationalism. Later, the French consequently clung to a patriotic love for France as the symbol of national sovereignty. But as Weil indicates several times in her historical discussion, sovereignty and nation have never truly co-existed in French history as equally strong concepts in a political framework. In adversity, the word "France" become dissassociated from its actual meaning; in peace, this evocation of France reinforces the State as the supreme value, the only value and source of identity left in the process of uprootal and centralization.

> La perte du passé, collective ou individuelle, est la grande tragédie humaine, et nous avons jeté le nôtre comme un enfant déchire une rose.... (*L'Enracinement*, 154)

The second reason was the inability of the French people to accept defeat, to be among the vanquished.

The greatest shock for France was defeat because France, in its perhaps unconscious emulation of Rome, had traditionally been on the side of the victorious and strong. Within Western culture the most damaging legacy left by the Roman civilization was contempt for the vanquished and humiliated and our inability to sustain defeat. Weil goes so far as to suggest that this was probably one of the main reasons for the collaboration of the Vichy government, the notion that France must be among the victorious and strong.

> L'idée du héros méprisé et humilié, si commune chez les Grecs, et qui forme le sujet même des Evangiles, est presque étrangère à notre tradition; la culte de la grandeur conçue selon le modèle romain nous a été transmis par une chaîne presque ininterrompue d'écrivains célèbres.... (*Ecrits historiques et politiques*)[48]

Before the glorious era of the French state, among the major writers in France were philosophers and poets whose compassion and purity of style was due, in great part, to their respect for the weak. Writers such as Montaigne, La Boétie, Rabelais, Villon, Maurice Scève, Agrippa d'Aubigné, Théophile De Viau, Retz, Descartes and Pascal are mentioned particularly by Weil as writers "qui n'ont été ni les serviteurs ni les adorateurs de la force." Weil implies by this that these writers lived in the pre-Classical period before the completion of the French State, when humility and willful obedience were primary cultural values. But in future generations, the Roman idea of force was the cultural value principally retained in literature.

> La seule chanson de geste connue dans les lycées célèbre Charlemagne, c'est-à-dire une entreprise de domination universelle. Les héros des trágedies nonreligieuses de Corneille mettent au-dessus de tout leur gloire, qui consiste à vaincre, à conquérir, à dominer, et ne songeraient jamais à subordonner cette gloire à la justice ou au bien public.[49]

Weil emphasizes the influence on French culture of Roman methods of rule and conquest, particularly evident in the proud defense of a colonial empire; even the Revolutionaries were inspired by the Roman mentality; the purity of their action was diminished when the Revolution became a war of conquest: the notion of a Republic was lost in the violent reversal of power. By the attitude of conquest ingrained in them by their own culture, the Revolutionaries' action proved self-defeating. The example of Augustus and of other Roman emperors had virtually obsessed both Louis XIV and Napoleon; it was only for their lack of ability and circumstance that they were not able to maintain the same system and duration of hegemony. Subsequently, the same Roman tradition became Hitler's inspiration.

It is thus that Weil deconstructs the mythical association of the terms "La Patrie" (homeland) and "Nation," a false construct that uprooted identity, value, and individualism. Weil deconstructs the historical basis for the rise of nationalism in a vacuum of spirit and justice. Both the deconstruction of a symbol and its prior alienation from an historical basis and meaning are complementary forms of "déracinement." Because the deconstruction of myth leads to reintegration, each movement of uprootal assumes the respective powers of the binary pair "déracinement/enracinement," each term in this case functioning as the other.

THE COLONIAL EMPIRE

> Quand je songe à une guerre éventuelle, il se mêle, je l'avoue, à l'éffroi et à l'horreur que me cause une pareille perspective, une pensée quelque peu réconfortante. C'est qu'une guerre européenne pourrait servir de signal à la grande revanche des peuples coloniaux

pour punir notre insouciance, notre indifférence, et notre cruauté.
. . . (*Feuilles libres*, mars 1937, Simone Weil)[50]

War and Colonialism. Péguy was one of the writers and philosophers of the early twentieth century who admired greatly the Roman empire. This, and his claim that World War I was a "just" war that men were happy to die for, shocked Weil. Her negative reaction was caused not only by the absurdity of sanctifying war by calling it "just," but she was also disturbed by the evident contradiction: admiration of the Romans' rule by force in the consolidation of an empire on the one hand and France's bitter, vengeful determination to prevent Germany from achieving a similar expansion of power. Vercingétorix is praised in French history; yet the value placed by French tradition on force and the State is part of the French emulation of the Romans who conquered Vercingétorix. Péguy and others died despite this contradiction, or rather, because of it.

> Donner comme critérium que la conquête est un bien lorsqu'elle accroît la nation dont on est membre par le hasard de la naissance, un mal lorsqu'elle la diminue, cela est tellement contraire à la raison.[51]

In her critical essays on colonialism, Weil shows the existence of a colonial empire to have been one of the main reasons for the two World Wars. Competitive claims on foreign territory was a source of great antagonism and chauvinist rivalry between Germany and France. The Indochinese conquest had been an act of revenge against the Germans when the latter had dared to defeat the French in 1870.

> N'ayant pas su résister aux Allemands, nous sommes allés en compensation priver de sa patrie, en profitant de troubles passagers, un peuple de civilisation millénaire, paisible et bien organisé. Mais le gouvernement de Jules Ferry a accompli cet acte abusant de ses pouvoirs et en bravant ouvertement l'opinion publique française. . . .[52]

Morocco. In February 1937, the publication *Vigilance* published one of Weil's first statements on colonialism. Earlier that year, the French had reacted with great moral indignation to Germany's expressed intentions to take over the French colony of Morocco. As far as the French were concerned, Morocco had always been French; the French nationalists felt they had a moral claim to

Moroccan territory. The historical detail Weil provides contests that claim. French domination in Morocco dates only from 1911. She retraces events as far back as 1880 when the Treaty of Madrid recognized the special trading privileges of the main European powers with Morocco which was, until 1904, officially independent. In 1904, France was defeated by England at Fashoda; in exchange for Morocco, the French abandoned their guardianship over Egyptian independence, and Egypt was taken over by the English. Germany, however, demanded a part of Moroccan territory which it did not obtain. Following the French military take-over in Morocco in 1911, there were disputes over Moroccan territory between Germany and France. Germany sent a warship to Agadir on the Moroccan coast, threatening war but Caillaux instigated negotiations. Germany recognized the French protectorate in Morocco and in return a section of the French Congo was added to the German territory of Cameroun. Weil considered this treaty unfair and interpreted it as one of the causal events leading to the First World War.

> Le plus beau, c'est qu'après la victoire on a repris le morceau du Congo cédé en 1911, et on a pris le Cameroun, et on a gardé le Maroc. . . .[53]

Weil approaches the question satirically, reproducing the mood of defensiveness and alert that had spread a few weeks earlier in France.

> Le Maroc est pour la France en quelque sorte une seconde Lorraine.
> . .[54]

She seems to mock the readers themselves in describing the German threat of takeover in Morocco as a menace to French sovereignty. She compares Morocco to Alsace-Lorraine in a style reminiscent of Daudet's description of the German takeover of Alsace after the Franco-Prussian war (cf. *Les Contes du Lundi*, 1873), a style of mordant sarcasm.

In 1906, the Treaty of Algésiras had granted France very limited rights on Morocco; the equality of trading rights with Morocco and all European powers was to continue; there was to have been no French military presence in Morocco except for a few instructors for the Moroccan police force. In 1911 there was a French military takeover in Morocco under pretext of internal disorder threatening the welfare of Europeans. That was the end of the Treaty of Algésiras. Yet the violation of this treaty was considered unrelated to the Versailles treaty which Germany threatened to violate. The latter act was met with moral indignation by the French whereas the former was not.

Thus the French colonial empire, maintained and strengthened by the violation of treaties and a deeply-ingrained sense of natural, moral right to power, led to a World War. One form of uprootal, colonialism, led to another, the catastrophe of utter destruction. For all the cathartic power of war, releasing and liberating vengence and bitterness, war and colonialism were forms of "déracinement" with no complementary function or symbolic power for reintegration or "enracinement."

Xenophobia. One of the tendencies pervading western culture since the Greeks is that which leads us to search outside of ourselves for the causes of violence. That is one of Weil's main points in her essay on power; it is the basis of her explanation of the inevitable instability and temporality of power. The unacceptable image of ourselves that we see in the other is what provokes fear. Xenophobia is the clearest example of this and the scapegoat theory permitting the transfer of guilt. In Giraudoux's play, *La Folle de Chaillot*, the leading character rids the world of evil by localizing it, incarnating it in the form of three unscrupulous figures, a stockbroker, an enterprising minister, and an oil dealer, all representative of the superficial values that degrade the modern individual. Although it is a fantastical dream to purify ourselves through the localization of evil, Giraudoux unconsciously reinforces in our minds the mythical power of that phenomenon. Much of the play's power centers around that myth; and ideals of freedom and good are dangerously dependent on the concept of a purge. This fantasy or myth has vastly influenced our ideas on crime, punishment and social order. The Dreyfus case at the end of the last century was an extreme example, not simply because in that instance the individuals responsible within the French military were conscious of their own guilt, but because others besides the perpetrators recognized it as a lie but still went along with it in the name of national good. However, in most instances in modern society, mythical cultural barriers have become so strong that we are usually not aware of our own guilt or responsibility in our interpretation of violence.

Weil had great admiration for Giraudoux's artistry and idealism. Her main biographers, Cabaud and Pétrement, describe in detail Weil's exultant and enthusiastic reactions to performances of his plays. *Electre* appealed to Weil and inspired her to write her own version of the play, interpreting the character and symbol of Electre differently; it also led her to write poetry, a sample of which she sent to Valéry who responded with encouragement and interest for her skill and control in versification. Despite the creative inspiration received directly from Giraudoux, Weil responded critically to a radio broadcast made by Giraudoux during the first year of war, on the duties of French women. Her controlled indignation was fueled by the perception that Giraudoux, a writer normally sensitive to the fatality and frailty of human nature, still thought and wrote in terms of absolutes. The French nation, especially in wartime, was one such absolute. Having skillfully poeticized the fatality of war in *La guerre de Troie n'aura pas lieu* and the fatality of revolution in *Electre*, Giraudoux still does not present an understanding of the true origins of violence. Absolutes are most obvious, in *La Folle de Chaillot*, when Josephine describes Charles Martel's execution of his Arab enemies in Poitiers as an illustration of the necessary elimination by death of the individuals incarnating evil. Even in a recent revival of this play in Spring 1980 by la Comédie Française, the audience was captivated by the fire and chauvinist idealism of Josephine's representation of evil by the word 'Arabe'; the public within the theater, as well as those who watched a television film of the play demanded by public acclaim, were entranced by the fantastical localization of evil as well. They seemed unaware of the dangerous manifestation of cultural prejudice in attempts to concretize and contain evil. Weil's criticism of Giraudoux's inaccurate affirmation that the French Empire's cohesiveness was based on bonds of fraternity and tolerance was, however, a criticism of the French public's ignorance and indifference to the true nature of power. Her defense of Algerian and North African immigrant laborers is still relevant to modern French life. Even during the 1979-1980 theatrical season, as audiences listened intently to Giraudoux's fantasy, the strike of the dark-skinned, pitifully-paid Algerian and North African street cleaners continued, and piles of garbage obstructed traffic and passenger walkways in the métro. Giraudoux's analysis of evil and power had not helped. Weil's might have made more of a difference.

In March 1937, Weil reacted to a violent labor confrontation in Tunisia in an article which appeared in *Feuilles Libres* under the title "Le Sang Coule en Tunisie." Weil wrote it shortly after her return from service in Spain to the Republican cause where she had gone after voicing deep criticism of Blum's neutralist policy towards the Spanish Civil War. For the same reasons she criticized the apparent indifferences of the Left towards the French Empire's repression of laborers in the colonies. Tunisians and Indochinese were, at that time, the main objects of mistreatment. Weil and others considered the indifferent attitude towards colonial repression of leaders championing the workers' cause within metropolitan France an abandonment of worker solidarity. Even the progressive liberals and socialists of the 'Rassemblement Populaire' were unconcerned with the contradiction characterizing their struggle for social and economic rights within France and the repressive treatment of foreign workers abroad by the French themselves.

There were, in her estimation, the usual reasons for this contradiction. First of all, of course, was the element of distance; one's lack of perception and identification with those experiencing pain is dulled by the physical distance separating the sufferer from the spectator. Then, of course, was the culturally devaluating argument that these people were accustomed to pain. If such people were not accustomed and destined for such servility, they would resist. But the struggle of those who did in fact resist was devalued by the assumed association with Hitler or Franco. This was the justification made when the Algerian national organization l'Etoile Nord-Africaine' was dissolved.

Following the dissolution of 'L'Etoile Nord-Africaine,' Messali Hadj was sentenced to prison for two years.[55] Weil had regarded Messali's condemnation and the disbanding of 'Etoile Nord-Africaine' the French public's attempt to vindicate itself by a localization of guilt. She considered the effort to find those guilty of 'menées antifrancaises' a futile witchhunt and a vindication of public responsibility for the true causes of l'Etoile's insurgency. In her article "Qui est Coupable de Menées Antifrançaises?" dated 1938, Weil describes the continued displacement of culpability that frustrated the French government and finally necessitated their unconscious self-vindication through Messali's condemnation. Her discussion is in the form of an indictment reminiscent of Zola's famous "J'accuse" address to the French military.

> J'accuse l'Etat français et les gouvernements successifs qui l'ont représenté jusqu'à ce jour, y compris les deux gouvernements de Front Populaire; j'accuse les administrations d'Algérie, de Tunisie, du Maroc; j'accuse le général Noguès, j'accuse une grande partie des colons et des fonctionnaires français de menées antifrançaises en Afrique du Nord. Tous ceux à qui il est arrivé de traiter un Arabe avec mépris. . . .[56]

In her review of parallels between the labor movement within France and colonial politics, Weil shows that the same vindication of blame occurred in June 1936 when France was polarized into two social and political camps. Factory owners, industrialists, and most of the upper and middle classes blamed those of the Left, including the worker and militant activists of the working class for the disorder and violence; the Left, in particular those leading and supporting the Popular Front, responded that tradition and order inspires revolt when it perpetuates itself by force. Ironically, although Weil felt that the Left had arrived at an exact articulation of the problem of violence and power, the Left's indifference to the colonial situation was evidence that power and oppression had been displaced. What was not recognized by the Left and the Right was that both labor and colonial struggles were different forms of the same problem.

In spite of the contact between North African workers and French laborers and in spite of support the former provided the latter in 1936, the French worker did not give reciprocal support during the time of the dissolution of 'L'Etoile Nord-Africaine' and Messali's condemnation. As a result, the North African became increasingly estranged from the antifascist struggle.

Weil's article "Ces membres palpitants de la patrie" which appeared in the March 10 issue of *Vigilance* in 1938 was one of the first public statements exposing France's treatment of Algerian immigrant workers in France. It was also an extensive discussion of the ideology of L'Etoile and the precise events leading to its dissolvement, including a description of the manipulation of L'Etoile's supporters by the *Rassemblement Populaire*. Petrément described Weil's friendship with Messali Hadj and their conversations together.

> Simone avait parlé longuement avec lui et il s'était rendu compte qu'elle accueillait ses idées avec sympathie. . . .[57]

Messali related in a television interview in 1968 how during one of their conversations together, Weil had promised to speak to Blum to intercede for Messali. This was done successfully during the first government of the Popular Front; it was the second government under Chautemps that finally did arrest Messali and disbanded L'Etoile. Weil did her best to help him and her article "Qui est coupable de menées antifrançaises?" had been written during this time. She prepared a motion of protest accepted by the Saint Quentin sectin of the "Comité de Vigilance des intellectuels antifascistes," published in *Vigilance*, January 10, 1938. But Messali Hadj was sent to prison anyway, and the disbanding of 'L'Etoile Nord-Africaine' remained official.

The arguments she used reflect those in her commentary on power written in the same year. The existence of the Other is the rein on one's own power; by the fact we so closely identify with the Other, the Other's freedom is both a threat to and an affirmation of one's own. The Other is one's mirror and, as such, arouses either fear or conscience, because the Other's yearning and capacity for violence reminds one of one's own like potentialities and frustrations. Only at a complete stage of identification of oneself with the Other is one capable of humane action. At that moment, neither party is objectified nor dehumanized by the predominance of one person's freedom and power over another. If the fusion and mediation is ideally maintained one acts humanely, with conscience. If the tension created by such an identification is disrupted it degenerates into fear and an abuse of freedom. It is the concept explored by Weil in her essay on the *Iliad*, used in later years to develop her concept of 'attente,' an intense state of concentration of will, intellect, and spirit by which one refuses to relinquish a momentary bond of trust and oneness with the Other. This concept itself is the source of Weil's great appeal to many of those who have become acquainted with her philosophy.

By an abdication of will and concentration, one leads oneself to justify the predominance of one's own freedom over that of the other. The wall of power built into the traditions of Western culture prevents its members from a conscious, permanent identification with those whom they overpower, economically and politically.

The clash in Tunisia was of great significance in bringing to public attention the immorality of France's colonial policy. When starved and overworked children perished in the mines of Indochina, there had been little attention given, since there had been no bloodshed associated with their deaths, as visible signs of violence. But in the Tunisian workers' revolt, the French finally began to perceive a crisis because blood had been shed, the most comprehensible and understandable symbol of violence. That is a problem that Weil evokes; our dependence on symbols and entities is symptomatic of our inability to function and relate to each other on other levels; to reach beyond the cultural barriers we build between ourselves, and arouse social conscience, we are dependent upon the most debilitating of all symbols—the rich, colorful effusion of violence.

Weil's major study on colonialism and its possible solution through a suspension of colonial power and commitment to a plan for progressive emancipation was written during her period of service for Free France in London. Published as an article, it was, however, for unknown reasons, not included in the 1949 publication of *Enracinement*, the collection of her recommendations made during her period of service in London for De Gaulle's Free France, received enthusiastically by the public at the time of publication. This little known paper on colonial policy was again published in 1960 as one of her several essays and studies collected under the title, *Les Ecrits historiques et politiques*. It is paradoxical that Weil's most significant recommendations on colonial policy were not truly accepted until France was immersed in the violent struggle for Algerian independence.

The localization of evil, our dependency on symbols and entities, and an abdication of will and consciousness are all elements of Weil's analysis of xenophobia. All constitute a debilitating form of "déracinement", and all, translating an essential fear of one's own reflection in another, contain the seed of violence and war.

THE MYTH OF REVOLUTION AND THE SOCIAL

Introduction: In August 1933, the publication *Révolution Prolétarienne* published the article "Perspectives—Allons-nous vers la Revolution Prolétarienne?"[58] This was Weil's first major critique of the Socialist movement and the ideological transformations that had taken place since Marx found his materialist conception of history and later collaborated with Engels to systematize a theory of scientific socialism. Some of the ideas expressed in this article were reiterated in a more extensive analysis of power begun in 1934 and published in 1937 under the title "Reflexions sur les causes de la liberté et de l'oppression sociale."[59] Earlier in 1933 and during the preceding summer of 1932, she had written and had published a series of penetrating articles on political developments observed in Germany, examining the ideologies and politics of the National Socialists, the Communists and the Social Democrats, as well as the debilitating effect of unemployment, depression and torpor experienced acutely by Germans during the early years of the economic crises prior to Hitler's rise to power.[60] Her writings during and following the Spanish Civil War (1936-1938) are also an important part of her critique of the revolutionary ideal, documenting her experience with revolution and war.[61] In the publication, *La Condition Ouvrière*, are compiled her factory journal of 1934-1935, her discussion of her experience and labor problems of the period which appear in the form of letters and articles written throughout the years 1934-1941.[62] All of these writings reflect her general conclusion that the Marxist vision of an impending, spontaneous revolutionary transformation of society was a cruel empty hope.

Entrenched in ideological dogma, the work 'revolution' had taken on mythical proportions. Revolution had become a mythical concept because of the absence of the element of participation and of lucid, methodical reasoning in the conceptualization of social change. Weil believed that Revolution needed to be redefined as involvement and conscious participation in a self-determining progression (Praxis) towards freedom and constructive social change. Social action had to be conceived methodically and lucidly in terms of its means and end with a clear understanding as to conditions and effects of change in actuality. Until the meaning of 'revolution' had been grasped in terms of its realistic possibilities, it would retain its mystique, ambiguity, and remain an empty dream in a vacuum of possibilities.

Until its mythical aura is expunged, 'revolution' enhances the ideological power of the Social, threatening individual rationality and identity. Understanding and control of the notions of reform, social transformation and revolution is the individual's duty in protecting herself or himself against the domination of the Social while at the same time meeting the responsibility of social participation and commitment. In the context of Weil's writing, 'enracinement' is the retention of both individual and social consciousness; it provides an equilibrium between the individual's fusion with and detachment from nature and society (déracinement/enracinement). To master the notions of social change is to confront and control the social mechanisms of power and oppression.

The Anonymous Social extends its power not only through ideology, through the mystique of ceremony and tradition. The Power of the Collective Social Animal also moves against the individual in the form of machines which absorb and determine human movement and initiative and in the form of bureaucratic rule which filters and limits the development of individual intelligence. The era of machinism and bureaucracy endow science and the media with control over formation of individual consciousness. The Great Beast's power is magnified through this deformation of revolutionary struggle. Only by conceiving revolution and social change lucidly in terms of reality and individual dignity can one understand and orient the power of social transformation and avoid the tyranny of the Great Beast.

Through her political and historical essays Weil sought to deconstruct what had become a mythical concept of Revolution. This demystification will be described in three stages. First is a rapid overview of the three forms revolution has taken in history: spontaneous mass action, revisionism, and the combination of both legal and illegal action represented by the October Revolution in Russia. This reflects the viewpoint expressed in Weil's earlier discussion of revolution in her article "Perspectives" in 1933. Second is an examination of the theoretical basis of Marxism to see if it is capable of fulfilling the objective of revolution. Third is a discussion of reasons for the failure of the modern application of Marxist Socialism during Weil's lifetime. Weil, the only French Socialist before the Second World War to examine methodically the shortcomings of Marxism, saw three main reasons for this failure: war and militarism, centralized bureaucratization, and machinism, all forces of "déracinement."

REVOLUTION AND HISTORY: THE FAILURE OF LIBERATION

Spontaneous Mass Action: Weil's commentary underlines the historical failure of Revolution defined as spontaneous mass action. Through her critical assessment of the authoritarian centralized rule of terror that dominated France after 1789, Weil defined the tendency of such revolutionary movements to deteriorate into a state of militarism and political terror. In late eighteenth-century France, the general revolutionary struggle had deteriorated following the

Girondins' declaration of war with Austria, the invasion of France by German armies and involvement in European war against the English, Spanish and Dutch coalition.[63] Following the final blow to French monarchy when in August 1792, the royal family was officially overthrown by the National Assembly, the September massacres began the Reign of Terror under the government of the Convention led by Robespierre, Danton and their Committee of Public Safety. Louis XVI was executed in January 1793.[64] What had begun as a revolutionary struggle had deteriorated into international war and political terror. The First Republic was declared but lost in the violence of political turmoil preceding Napoleon's rise to power. The energy of the lower working classes was sapped and exploited in the consolidation of economic and military power by the bourgeoisie and by Napoleon's military caste. Weil's disillusionment with this era was an implied criticism of Idealist philosophy, of Hegel's romantic vision of the transformation of slavery into mastery through history and through the development of the state.

Weil specifically states that one must avoid the disillusionment of those who having fought for Liberty, Equality, Fraternity in 1792, 1793, found under subsequent governments only "Infantry, Cavalry and Artillery," a phrase borrowed from Marx's commentary on the failure of the Paris Commune in his work, *The Civil War in France*.[65]

The Paris Commune and the St. Petersburg uprising particularly illustrated the inefficacy of spontaneous mass action. The 'fédérés' of 1871, unfortunately, did not organize themselves effectively enough against the Versailles government. Government troops entered an undefended area of Paris and in the following week approximately 20,000 insurrectionists and 750 government troops were killed; following the defeat of the Commune was a period of harsh repressive government action: 38,000 were imprisoned and more than 7,000 deported.[66] In Weil's opinion the lack of methodical planning of action and dependency on the strength of spontaneous mass movement was the reason for this devastating failure. Weil thus questions the paradoxical description of the Commune as a historical symbol of social revolution; the strength of spontaneous mass action was momentary and valueless because it was unmethodical and uncomprehended; Weil considered dangerous the use of prior revolutionary struggles that failed as historical symbols of impending liberation.

The St. Petersburg uprising on January 9, 1905, marked the beginning of the Revolution of 1905. It had been the first threat to Russian autocracy since the Decembrist uprising of 1825 against Nikolai the First. It became known historically as Bloody Sunday during which time the troops fired on unarmed workers gathered at the Winter Palace, killing one hundred people. It led to mutinies, strikes, and finally to the October Manifesto in which the Emperor agreed to the formation of Soviets, or workers councils, and of a national legislative body–the Duma.[67] This began a period of constitutional government in which participated the parties of the Socialist Revolutionaries (later responsible for the surge of terror and the assassination of 4,100 officials), some Constitutional Democrats, and the Social Democrats who had split in 1903 into the factions of Bolsheviks and Mensheviks.[68] The St. Petersburg revolt was, for Weil, an example of an ineffective, aborted, spontaneous mass action. Weil does overlook the changes it led to; it was the first blow against an autocratic government, which resulted in the formation of constitutional government. Her general assessment is accurate, however; although the uprising did lead to changes, it marks a period of reformism which was compromising and slow. It was a revolutionary act that ended in no clear victory either for the government or for the Russian people. It had only the cathartic release of violence and the certainty of further destruction, of further 'déracinement.'[69] It was also a prelude to the terror of the Socialist Revolutionaries, the conservatism and punitive hangings imposed by Stolypin who was premier of the Second Duma from February to June 1907.

Revisionism: Weil expressed a particular disillusionment with revisionism, with parliamentarianism as a means of revolutionary transformation. This is one of the main parallels between Weil and Rosa Luxemburg. Weil stated that, in Germany, August 1941 "marked the bankruptcy of proletarian mass organizations, both on the political and trade-union levels, within the framework of the system."[70] The reformists solution had not been successful. In August 1914, the Social Democratic delegation to the Reichstag had voted in favor of the war credits.

> Dès ce moment, il a fallu abandonner une fois pour toutes l'espérance placée dans ce mode d'organisation, non seulement par les réformistes, mais par Engels. . . .[71]

This was a final blow to the anti-militarist, international solidarity which Rosa Luxemburg had helped to build through the Second International; the cause of international worker solidarity and pacifism was lost when more powerful voting members of the Left accepted the argument that the war was a defense of the Fatherland against czarist reaction.[72] Luxemburg had called this "the capitulation of Social Democracy."[73]

Engels would have been the first to protest against the debauch of parliamentarism. . . . The 4th of August. . . .[74]

The October Revolution: Weil states in her article "Perspectives" that the Russian Revolution of October 1917 had brought new hope and prospects; disciplined militants had effectively oriented the spontaneous energy of the masses; from this rare combination of legal and illegal movement, methodical and spontaneous action had fused to bring about change and well-founded hope. Bolshevism was to replace "the stinking corpse" of German and Russian Social Democracy, so named by Rosa Luxemburg; communist and socialist parties throughout the world would help the proletariat realize its aspirations. But Weil points out that in the fifteen years between the October 1917 Revolution and the date of her own writing no viable changes had taken place towards the true realization of Marx's ideal. There were no soviets. Social Democracy had survived until the thirties in Germany, swept away only by the effects of Fascism, not Communism. "The October regime" did not seek to internationalize effectively the original movement for a proletarian state; instead, it abandoned principles of worker solidarity and worked to stifle revolutionary activities abroad.

Throughout history, action defined as revolutionary had failed. Prior spontaneous mass movements of revolt ended in either defeat or in the establishment of new forms of oppression. Revolutionary change pursued through revisionism or parliamentary legality ended in compromise and submission to militarism and political terror, in alienation from oneself. The combination of legal and illegal action of the October Revolution in Russia had had momentary success, ending in a perversion of revolutionary ideals through a bureaucratization of power and authority. The past forms of revolution had failed, and in Weil's eyes, could provide no basis of hope. Even at the time of Weil's writing, Europe had no valid prospects for revolutionary transformation. Socialism had already given way to bureaucratic deformation in Russia and the Socialist struggle and reform initiative among the German working classes was deteriorating, demoralized by high employment; in Spain, the Republican struggle had become an international war. Despite all this, there were still hopes for the socialist struggle in this brief period of four years between the date of Weil's first major article, "Perspectives," in 1933 and that of the major essay containing her Marxist critique, "Réflexions sur les causes de la liberté et de l'oppression sociale" in 1937. Weil was both a participant in this struggle and a skeptical critic of those whose hopes she shared. But these hopes were vague, undefined and threatened by their own ambiguity.

MARXIST CRITIQUE

Weil believed that Marx had given an effective account of the mechanism of capitalist oppression, so well-conceived that one finds it difficult to visualize how this mechanism could stop functioning. Of major importance in this analysis is the economic explanation of the extortion of surplus value. According to Marx, this extortion is causally linked to the demands of competition which in turn relates to the principle of private property. Marx contends that since private property is the cause of the economic exploitation of the worker, it should be eliminated; all property should be made collective. Weil cites what she considers consequent difficulties resulting from this theory. She believed that Marx's analysis of the true reason for the exploitation of the workers did not go far enough. Every nation was bound by the unspoken rules of economic competition and power struggles. Every nation or every type of working collectivity had to restrain the consumption of its individual laborers so that maximum energy and time could be utilized to meet the demands of economic and military competition against rival nations or collective bodies. This is the key statement of Weil's critique of Marx's theory by which she contests Marx's claim that private property is the cause of social exploitation within the capitalist system.

Weil establishes that Marx knew that during the period of development of big industry the primary characteristic of capitalism, the sale and purchase of labor, had become a minor determinant of the industrialized system of labor. She proves that although Marx comprehended the mechanics of bureaucracy and recognized it as an oppressive force, he failed to separate it from the question of private property; he thereby failed to deal with the danger contained in the administrative function, which led to the emergence of a new form of oppression. Weil thus believed that Marx had erred in reducing the problem to a question of private property. The problem lies in the game of power, the inevitable master/slave duality and displacement of force manifesting itself within the industrial, scientific structure of our society. The power that crushes the workers is not that alone which is wielded by a propertied middle class, but is that which functions within the framework of an industrially centralized economy. Weil criticized Marx's claim that the struggle for power would end when socialism existed everywhere. The claim contradicted what he maintained later, that socialist revolution could not occur simultaneously in different countries. The effects of a transformation of power in one country would inevitably meet with the economic presures exerted by countries of opposing ideologies; in meeting these pressures, it would be necessary to exploit and consume the energy of the working masses and the original objective of equal distribution of power, knowledge, and resources would disappear under the pressures of international competition.

Weil believed that the Marxist concept of productive forces had its mythological aspects. Marx does not explain why the development of productive forces was inevitable. The absence of this rational basis of materialist theory likens him to Lamarck, in Weil's opinion. Weil significantly challenges the usual comparison of Marx to Darwin; dialectical materialism and Darwin's evolutionary theory based on the survival of the fittest through the adaptation of organic functions to the demands of the environment were both deterministic concepts that reflected the social being's increased faith in the beneficient powers of matter. Weil indicates, however, by her refusal to consider Marx and Darwin comparable, her belief tht the Marxist theory of dialectical materialism did not have the objective scientific basis of Darwinian theory. Instead, Weil compares Marx to Lamarck, the biologist propounding the theory of spontaneous generation. Lamarck had based his entire biological system on the principal of adaptation but had never explained the mystery of this tendency of living creatures to adapt. It was Darwin who explored and demystified the principal of adaptation and gave it scientific, rational basis. In the same way, Weil believed that Marx's theory was lacking in scientific, rational objectivity when it left unexplained the increasing the development of production and material resources. Weil believed that Marx was assuming, without strong basis, that material forces possessed a mysterious virtue that would eventually vanquish the opposition of social institutions. This implies another very significant difference between Marx and Darwin. The evolutionary principle of the survival of the fittest, although based on the concept that exteriority demands adaptation to its own conditions, contains an existentialist element. Insofar as the forces of determinism are comprehended and confronted, an element of self-determination is inevitably involved in the formation of life and in the successful adaptation to the environment. Darwin's demystification of the principle of adaptation, unlike Lamarck's, consequently involved both determinism and free will. Weil obviously respects and identifies with this combination. The absence of this balance between the two forces of self-determination and pre-determination weakens Marxist theory and renders it mythological.

Weil searches for a basis to Marx's belief in the unlimited development of productive forces. Recognizing the Hegelian origins of Marx's thought, Weil was critical of Marx's attribution to matter that which in Hegel's dialectic had been the role of the mind or spirit.

Hegel croyait en un esprit caché à l'oeuvre dans l'univers, et que

> l'histoire du monde est simplement l'histoire de cet esprit du monde, lequel, comme tout ce qui est spirituel, tend indéfiniment à la perfection. . . .[75]

By substitution of matter for mind as the motive power of history, Marx had claimed to restore the Hegelian dialectic which had been reversed. Weil believed that the most dangerous aspect of this reversal was not in recognizing the strength of determination by matter, but rather the assumption that this determinism would take a moral and beneficent direction, that the development of material and productive forces would take on moral consciousness in its domination over the human spirit.

> . . . par un paradoxe extraordinaire, il a conçu l'histoire, à partir de cette rectification, comme s'il attribuait à la matière ce qui est l'essence même de l'esprit, une perpetuelle aspiration au mieux. . . .[76]

Weil thus believed that the transferral of the principal of progress from the mind to matter was the influence of the capitalist and materialist spirit. The purpose of the dialectic is to mediate and synthesize the forces of Materialism and Idealism; and elimination of either term or a refusal to recognize the forces of both mind and matter was unrealistic. The substitution of one extreme by another reversed the relationship between the means and the end, and rendered Socialist thought utopian and mythological.

Weil was disillusioned with what she considered Marx's capitulation to the superstitions of his time. She believed that he had given in to the superstitions of the age of industrial and capitalist expansion and to the cult of progress and scientism, thus legitimizing the highest spiritual expression of the bourgeoise.

By his faith in material, scientific force, Weil considered Marx to be in conformity with the general current of capitalist thought. Dujardin criticized Weil for her supposed failure to recognize the value of many of the principles of dialectical and historical materialism. But he as well recognized that Weil was most hostile to Marx's efforts to legitimize our moral dependency on the scientific concept of progress.[77]

The religion of industrial might reduced the individual and the Socialist movement into instruments of historical or productive progress; the dignity of the individual was no longer the objective of social action.

> . . . la tâche des révolutions (devient) . . . l'émancipation non pas des

hommes mais des forces productives. . . .[78]

Weil also criticizes the utopian belief in an eventual liberation from necessity by the development of material forces.

Weil saw no evidence supporting Marx's belief that modern technology, as perceived during the prewar years of the thirties, could assure that the personal development of each individual would cease to be hampered by modern working conditions. Profits would be taken away from the workers, under any system, for reinvestment in industrial production. Even calculation of the total amount of labor that could be dispensed with at the cost of transformation of the property system would not resolve the problem. Weil believed that an unlimited increase in productivity was inconceivable, only the supposition of those reacting to the unprecedented speed of technical progress since the beginning of the Industrial Era. The perpetual motion machine, which would go on producing work without consuming or creating more work, notes Weil, was disproved by scientific application of the law of conservation of energy. She believed that Marx had not fully considered the transformation by human labor of energy extracted from natural resources. At the time of Weil's writing even, extraction and conversion of coal and petroleum were becoming more costly and unprofitable. The discovery of new energy sources was only a possibility; there was no assurance that the utilization of such new energy sources would call for less labor than that of heavy oils or coal. The abolition of private property, underlined Weil, would be far from sufficient in itself to prevent work in mines and factories from continuing to weigh as a servitude on those subjected to it.

In her challenge to Marx's belief in the potential of unlimited development, she notes the absence of preliminary studies as a basis of documentation for this assumption. She utilizes this example to attribute to our scientific culture the fatal habit of generalizing, of extrapolating, instead of studying conditions of a given phenomena and the limits implied by them. The factors that combine to increase productivity do not develop separately, although each must be analyzed separately. Weil believed that Marx neglected to consider all the economic and social relations which combine to achieve a given form of technical achievement and thereby advocated a political philosophy that contained the probability of further repression or 'déracinement.'

MILITARISM

Weil maintained in an article published in November 1933 in *La Critique Sociale* that the revolutionary movement had led to a justification of increased militarism and war.[79] Up until August 1914, revolution and pacifism were unrelated. France's misguided involvement in European war in 1792 had glorified the concept of revolutionary war; it was a paradoxical symbol that confused conquest with liberation and thereby lost sight of the true objective of revolutionary struggle. The promotion of war as a tool of liberation is one of the basic reasons for Weil's disillusionment with the popularized concept of Revolution. In addition she is distrustful of the inconsistent positions taken by Socialist theoreticians towards pacifism and war. In the early nineteenth century, she states, Louis Philippe had been criticized by revolutionaries for his pacifist position. Later Proudhon lauded war and thereby helped to cultivate the image of war as a form of liberation.[80] Weil refers to Marx's involvement with proletarian organizations during the war of 1870;[81] in the course of the First International he had encouraged the workers of both countries to distinguish between offensive and defensive military confrontation in order to justify their own participation.

> Marx . . . invita les ouvriers des deux pays en lutte à s'opposer à toute tentative de conquête, mais à prendre part résolumment à la défense de leurs pays contre l'attaque de l'adversaire. . . .[82]

She denounces Engels's attempt to bring Germany to war with France and Russia in 1892.[83] She was critical of Engels's willingness to provoke bloodshed and violence in an attempt to consolidate the workers' movement in Germany. She noted the inconsistency of Socialist positions towards pacifism which hindered the consolidation of the German workers movement in the early part of the century. The Spartacus organization in 1914 and the Bolsheviks in 1917 considered war an instrument of imperialism;[84] war was valuable only in so far as it crushed the forces of tyranny within one's own country; the proletariat's role, therefore, was to abstain from participation or support of such war and even work towards the defeat of one's own country. Weil was sympathetic to the position that had been taken by Luxemburg and Liebknecht and their perception of the displacement of the true dangers to the workers movement, that is, their realization that war would only perpetuate the economic and political strength of capitalist interests. However, encouraging the workers to support the defeat of their own country and thereby risk replacement of one form of oppression by another was, in Weil's opinion, a source of disagreement among members of the German proletariat and a basic cause of disunity: Weil perceived within the Marxist tradition an ambiguous, inconsistent position concerning war and militarism. She believed that this was the major reason for the lack of unity and clarification of Marxism and the workers' movement it has represented in modern times.

> Un point du moins était commun à toutes les théories, à savoir le refus catégorique de condamner la guerre comme telle. Les marxistes, et notamment Kautsky et Lénine, paraphrasaient volontiers la formule de Clausewitz selon laquelle la guerre ne fait que continuer la politique du temps de paix, mais par d'autres moyens, la conclusion étant qu'il faut juger une guerre non par le caractère violent des procédés employés, mais par les objectifs poursuivis au travers de ces procédés. . . .[85]

Weil maintained that Marxism in the last fifteen years following the Russian Revolution had been falsely associated with pacifism. She was critical of the fact that the pacifist position of the Bolsheviks in 1918 was undertaken for reasons of strategy unrelated to possible moral convictions concerning war. Her critique extended to a basic distrust of the association of Marxism with Pacifism that had taken place in most European countries following World War I. The devastation of land, cities, and the death of millions had led to a deeper awareness of the interrelation of pacifism and socialism. Weil insisted that Marxist propagandists had simply reacted to and exploited the mood of the times. There was still, within Marxist doctrine, no theoretical basis that would have justified a pacifist position. Marxist ideology could not claim a propensity for peace.

Weil was shocked by the association of Marxist revolution with militarism. She indicated the contradiction by showing that Marx's portrayal of the social structure by which the individual became the tool of a vast economic machine reproduced itself on the battlefield; the same factors of economic and industrial competition crushed the worker-turned soldier and determined the outcome of military confrontation. Weil claims that the major error of Socialists is to consider war a consequence of international politics, of foreign policy; it is more an indictment of domestic policy. Consequently the absence of a position against militarism within Marxist ideology is self-defeating; rule by force ultimately transforms revolution into a form of political oppression.

> . . . il s'agit d'une remarque bien simple, à savoir que le massacre est la forme la plus radicale de l'oppression. . . .[86]

Weil uses the examples of the French, Russian and Spanish Revolutions to show how immersion in war led to the establishment of a despotic state government. She indicates the parallels between the Russian and French

Revolutions to show that revolutionary war, even in the service of a modern Marxist state, leads to a despotic centralized government. Lenin is compared to Robespierre for his eventual abandonment of democratic principles; just as Robespierre's consolidation of centralized state power facilitated Napoleon I, Lenin provided the same advantage for Stalin. The war question is of greater centrality in the history of the Russian Revolution. Weil agrees with Trotsky's perception that war was the tool of the bourgeoisie who were using it to reaffirm their political strength and dissolve, or at least exhaust, the revolutionary spirit within Russia. The Revolution was initially a blow delivered by Russian soldiers against the war they had been compelled to fight under the disintegrating authority of an anachronistic military and political hierarchy. Despite the Bolcheviks' subsequent dismantling of the military in obedience to Marx's declaration that the dictatorship of the proletariat precludes the presence of a police force and of armies, the military was reconstituted as the Soviet Union became involved in Civil War between the Bolcheviks and the White Russians and as the threat of foreign intervention increased.

The same view is reflected in Weil's writings on the Civil War in Spain including short manuscripts, the journal she kept while accompanying Durruti's anarchist guerrilla forces, and the well-known letter she wrote to George Bernanos. Her observations and reactions to the deterioration of the Republican struggle in Spain are an essential part of her critique of Marxism, of the modern concept of revolution and its ambiguous association with civil and international war. She criticizes the appraisal and frequent glorification of events in Spain by journalists and writers, who, after a brief visit and exposure to 'revolution,' return with a superficial comprehension of the effects of social transformation and war in Spain. She provides brief but penetrating observations on the psychological effects of revolution on the Spanish people.

> . . . chaque jour amène du nouveau. Et puis la contrainte et la spontanéité, la nécessité et l'idéal se mêlent de manière à apporter une confusion inextricable non seulement dans les faits, mais encore dans la conscience même des acteurs et spectateurs du drame.[87]

Weil insisted upon the parallels between the Spanish and Russian revolutions. The goals of revolution in both cases had included the elimination of a military, of a police force, and of involuntary labor; all of these reappeared following both the Spanish and Russian revolutions. Weil was particularly shocked by the measures taken by the Spanish Popular Front government to institute a system of forced labor in Spain, in particular, the use of the death penalty.

Weil's letter to Bernanos is the most complete testimony she provided concerning her experience in Spain and what she perceived as the failure of the Spanish Revolution. She wrote the letter in 1938, almost two years after her return from Spain in September 1936. It was written in reaction to Bernanos's *Les Grands Cimetières sous la lune*.

> J'ai reconnu cette odeur de guerre civile, de sang et de terreur que dégage votre livre; je l'avais respirée. . . .[88]

Bernanos's book had unleashed memories for Weil of the violence she had observed in Spain. She recounts her own horror stories, which she claimed did not match the magnitude perceived and portrayed by Bernanos following his own experience with the Spanish Civil War as a supporter of the Royalists and a witness to the executions of Franco's forces; but they still enabled her to comprehend the contagion of violence reversing the priorities of human dignity and power. This comprehension provided a bond between Weil and Bernanos, members of two directly opposed ideological camps. The movement towards liberation disappeared in the confusion between the ideal and the reality, in the ambiguous spontaneity of political terror. In such an atmosphere of violence, the original objective of the socialist struggle was lost. Weil wrote in 1936.

> Dans la tourmente de la guerre civile, les principes perdent toute commune mesure avec les réalités, toute espèce de critérium en fonction duquel on puisse juger les actes et les institutions disparaît, et la transformation sociale est livrée au hasard. . . .[89]

Weil wrote also in her letter to Bernanos two years later:

> On part en volontaire, avec des idées de sacrifice, et on tombe dans une guerre qui ressemble à une guerre de mercenaires, avec beaucoup de cruautés en plus et le sens des égards dus à l'ennemi en moins. . . .[90]

The impending war against Hitler was misconstrued, as part of the proletariat's struggle against Fascism. Germany was equated with Fascism. Weil noted that the German workers and others supporting National Socialism, Communism, and Social Democracy supported Hitler at one time or another directly or indirectly in the course of what they had believed to be a revolutionary struggle against capitalism within and without Germany. Ironically German aristocrats and capitalists were also manipulated by Hitler and temporarily indulged in their hatred of Communists. Weil reported during her stay in Germany that Socialists who were among both proponents and adversaries of Hitler had mistakenly believed themselves engaged in a revolutionary struggle, but in the end found themselves mere ploys of political exploitation. The political camps of capitalists and communists were manipulated and polarized in the wake of Hitler's rise to power, and the fight against Germany was dangerously equated with the proletarian struggle; the impending war against Germany was misconstrued as a revolutionary war. The Marxist position towards war remained ambiguous, disoriented even further from its original objective by the political incoherency of the post-revolutionary period in Germany and the devastating effects of the economic crisis.

The French, Russian, Spanish and German examples prove, in Weil's judgment, that involvement in war and violence results in the loss of objective and in an oppressive perversion of the revolutionary cause. It is one of the main reasons for her disillusionment with Marxism and for the belief that the notion of revolution had to be rethought and conceived in terms of its true meaning. Thus Weil effectively deconstructed a further form of "déracinement", a falsely conceived notion of revolution.

BUREAUCRATIC RULE

With the advent of bureaucratization in the modern age in all domains of economic and political life, conscious individual action essential for constructive social transformation had disappeared. There is one function which dominates over all others, Weil showed; that is the bureaucratic function of coordination. Bureaucratization is present in every realm of life. Weil believed that the purest form of bureaucratic domination existed in the deformation of the workers' state, in the state bureaucracy of the Soviet Union, but that there was still within capitalistic societies an equally dangerous, more diffuse form of bureaucracy.

In capitalist countries, bureaucracy remained diffuse, not yet consolidated into a coherent system as in the U.S.S.R. It existed in three principal branches: 1) state bureaucracy, 2) industrial bureaucracy, and 3) union bureaucracy. Weil's identification of these three forms was based particularly on her detailed observations of events in Germany during her visit in the summer of 1932. Weil had also been very impressed by Fried's book which explained the system of state and industrial bureaucracy in Germany. The rise of technocracy and state capitalism was a phenomenon unrecognized by members of the workers' movement in Germany. Each one of these three forms of bureaucracy (state, industrial, and labor) could be replaced by any of the others, according to the theoreticians of the German publication, *Die Tat*. The three branches tend to unite and become one vast system. Weil proved, however, that this consolidation of forces has taken place only in the U.S.S.R., where a single bureaucracy controls the state, the economy, and labor unions, because in the U.S.S.R. the legalized expropriation of private investors and property owners allowed for a central consolidation of authority and force. Weil disagreed with Fried, that this could possibly take place in Germany. Although constructive social transformation was as great an impossibility in the U.S.S.R. as in Germany and Italy, the presence of private property owners within fascist states prevented a consolidation of the three bureaucratic branches into one unified central system in Germany; in other words, Germany's present political situation prevented her from envisioning the same centralized development of the Soviet Union.

Although these three bureaucratic structures were not fused into one central system, they were so interrelated that each lost its political independence and effectiveness. This diffuse form of bureaucracy paralyzed the labor movement in Germany, according to Weil's observations on German reformism, social democracy, and national socialism.

German Reformism. The workers' movement had displaced itself and found a new homeland in Germany following 1871 where it became more methodical, organized and legal. During Germany's colonizing period in the late nineteenth century, the German workers had shared in the era of economic expansion; the workers' movement had made considerable progress through domestic policies improving labor conditions. The First World War and the German Revolution of 1918 had interrupted the progress of the workers movement.[91] This movement regained its impetus only in October 1923.[92] The period from 1924 to 1929 were years of increasing prosperity for Germany and great gains for German workers.[93] These were also the years of extensive organizational development of German labor and their integration within the system of German parliamentarianism. In an article written in Germany in 1932, Weil traced the development of union bureaucracy from post-war years of German prosperity to the election of Hitler as chancellor in 1932.[94] The prosperity of the twenties had provided lasting benefits for the German worker but had also resulted in the consolidation of power for the labor unions.

> En ce moment, malgré plus de quatre ans de crise, la Conféderation Générale du Travail compte . . . plus de quatre millions de

membres;

Weil believed, however, that these advances were nonessential in view of the fact that the unions were dominated by the State and capitalist interest. The strength of the union had developed within the framework of a capitalist economy and state bureaucracy and was dependent on the system within which it had developed; the union itself, because of its dependency on the system of state and industrial bureaucracy, had no real power of its own. The main recent historical example that Weil uses to illustrate the harmful effects of this bureaucratized labor movement and its domination by the state is the acceptance by German labor unions of the principle of tariffs. By this law, every work contract was legally binding; unless the employer involved failed to meet the terms of the work contract, a strike was declared illegal and labor unions were legally bound to oppose it, by the new law of "Friedenspflicht."

Weil affirms that the unions did support "Friedenspflicht" in October 1932. Following the passage of the law allowing the lowering of wages below the amount contracted with workers, there was a general strike. At first the labor unions supported these strikes because they were legal according to the "Friedenspflicht" law; but after the measure of lowering salaries was approved by the courts, the unions themselves broke the strikes. Weil criticized the passive reaction of labor when Von Papen's regime ousted the Social Democrats from the government during the coup d'Etat of July 20, 1932.[95] The Social Democrats and labor unions had been partners in German Reformism, the parliamentary legal form the workers' movement had taken in the last half-century. Weil had defined Social Democracy in Germany as "l'expression parlementaire des relations qui existent entre l'appareil syndical et l'appareil d'Etat."[96] In 1920, the Social Democratic Party had reacted vigorously to Kapp's coup d'etat.[97] Weil attributed their contrasting passivity during Von Papen's action in 1932 to the paralyzing bureaucratic relations between labor and government.

The events of July 20 triggered a confrontation and an estrangement between the leaders of the Social Democratic Party bureaucracy and the other members. But the movement of revolt aroused by this confrontation was ineffective against the entrenchment of power wielded by the unions' bureaucratic structure.

National Socialism: In her discussion of National Socialism in Germany, Weil indicates that the deterioration of the workers' movement and its increasing ambiguity and incoherency had led to the rise of fascism. A great portion of an exasperated proletariat was drawn by Hitler and became part of the anonymous masses supporting National Socialism. The Communists, by their refusal to form a common front with the Social Democrats in 1933 following the fall of the Weimar coalition, had contributed to the deterioration of the socialist struggle. Hitler, Weil demonstrated, was a manipulator of the masses par excellence.[98] His rise was due, however, not only to his own demagoguery and charismatic appeal as a political leader, but also to the lack of consolidation among those of the Left favoring constructive, social change. This led to the emergency of the dangerous psychological power of the social, the blind, fanaticized masses. The result of such incoherency was the establishment of a bureaucratic dictatorship violating promises made to capitalists as well as to socialists.

German Communist Party: During her stay in Germany, Weil was able to comprehend the domination of the German Communist Party by the Russian Communist Party bureaucracy. This was the reason for the German Communist Party's abandonment of the Social Democrats in July 1932, and for their sabotage of the Social Democratic Party's efforts to form a common front against Hitler's National Socialists. There had been a formal order issued by the Komintern to the German Communist party to align with Hitler's party at the time of the Plebicite organized by Hitler's followers against the Social Democratic Landtag. During the ascendance and parliamentary successes of the National Socialist Party, Communist efforts were directed continually against the Social Democrats. Despite the support of the Trotskyists and Brandler's followers who justified every act of the Russian Communist Party, the Soviet bureaucracy proved to be a paralyzing influence in an incoherent situation dominated by volatile mass movements.[99] Finally, when Hitler's followers turned against the Communists, attacking them publicly in the street and privately in their homes, the German Communist Party felt compelled to turn against the Fascist regime, despite the resolutions of the XIe Plenum. Their common interests with the Social Democrats became evident when Hitler's forces attacked indiscriminately Communists and Social Democrats. This led to the creation of a Marxist bloc. The Communist Party at that time organized a common front. Weil claimed, however, that they failed to strengthen it by enlarging and relocating it onto the industrial scene. Although there was a certain amount of consolidation between the Social Democrats and the Communists, resulting in the formation of anti-fascist committees, it took place too late; Hitler had already consolidated his position.

The Soviet Union: Weil was among the many critics of the Russian deformation of the workers' state and Marxist ideal, many of whom like Victor Serge, Boris Souveraine, wrote for the publication, *Revolution Proletarienne* and belonged to Souveraine's organization, "Cercle Democratique."[100] In other articles written a year later, Weil reiterated her criticism of the situation in the Soviet Union. In the summer of 1933, an article by Weil was published in *Révolution Prolétarienne*, constituting an urgent appeal to the syndicat members to perceive the dangerous aspects of the political evolution of the C.G.T.U. which was becoming more and more subservient to the Soviet Union. The article was a challenge to the union workers to confront this situation. "L'appareil est en train d'installer un regime de dictature administrative."[101] It seemed to her that democratic trade unionism of the C.G.T.U. was being destroyed. Much of the controversy was a reaction to the position taken by the Soviet government in regard to German immigrants of the Left who had been refused entrance to the Soviet Union. The immediate result in France was to cause serious divisions among French Syndicalists.

At the Congress held at Reims in August 1933, Weil, after several rejected requests, was finally granted the opportunity to speak on the situation of the German Communist immigrants. She provided proof of the situation by discussing an article from *Neue Weltbuhne*, a German newspaper, in which the author expressed his concern about the U.S.S.R. and the terror provoked by Hitler. She discussed in addition another article written in response to the first, that had appeared in *Gegaenangriff*, the newspaper of German immigrants. In this response the closing of Russian borders to Communist immigrants had been confirmed. German militants, having vainly sought entrance to Soviet Russia, had been emprisoned in Hitler's concentration camps. Following Weil's presentation of this information, there were threats and violent physical attacks attempted against her. She considered this proof of the degeneration of the C.G.T.U. into a mere extension of the Russian state machine.[102]

Weil's article, "Perspectives," contained a particularly vituperative attack against the administrative machine that had replaced a consolidated movement of free, conscious revolutionaries.

Through Souveraine, Weil had met and conversed with Trotsky; she had even provided him refuge in her parents' home during his stay in Paris.[103] Gustave Thibon and Simone Pétrement both related how Weil interrogated him on his violent repressive measures in 1921.[104] The divergency of opinion between the two is reflected in Weil's article, "Perspectives." Trotsky, she wrote in an exasperated tone, persists in his claim that the Soviet Union provides the fulfillment of Marx's idea of the dictatorship of the proletariat, of a workers' state, despite the presence of certain bureaucratic deformations. He also insisted that the expansion of this workers' state would eventually take place; he and Lenin had erred only, he claimed, in their prediction of how long such an expansion would take place. But she replied in her article that their mistake had stemmed rather from a confusion between quantity and quality.

> ... quand une erreur de quantité atteint de telles proportions, il est permis de croire qu'il s'agit d'une erreur portant sur la qualité, autrement dit sur la nature même du régime. . . .[105]

Weil was also critical of the belief that the situation in the Soviet Union was part of a general transition, either towards socialism or capitalism; she considered irrational the idea that the oppression of the workers could possibly be a stage in beneficial social transformation. Marx himself, she reminded her readers, had stated that the bureaucratic and military administrative machine is one of the greatest obstacles to a transition towards Socialism.

Thus Weil effectively deconstructed another form of "déracinement" and its various manifestations, that is, bureaucracy inrooted in German Reformism, in National Socialism, and in the Stalinian state. All three were manifestations of "déracinement" by their suppression of conscious individual action.

TECHNOCRACY AND MACHINISM

Weil demonstrates how, even during Marx's lifetime, the mechanism of oppression had been transformed by changes within the capitalist system. The changes had been caused by increased machinism accompanied by an evolving technocracy or industrial bureaucracy. Weil repeatedly indicates passages from Marx's writings which reveal an awareness of this transformation. The major factor determining the oppression of workers was the structure of the factory and the industrial hierarchy which it reflected. The oppression of salaried workers was no longer a consequence of the economic relationships of property and exchange; machinism had reduced this to a minor factor. The opposing relationship between the seller and buyer of labor was only one of several relationships contained within the evolving system of production dominated by machinism.

> A l'opposition créée par l'argent . . . s'est ajoutée une autre opposition, créée par le moyen même de la production, entre ceux qui disposent de la machine et ceux dont la machine dispose. . . .[106]

Weil points out that, contrary to Marx's claim, these two opposing relationships are not interdependent. One form of opposition can continue to exist after the other has been eliminated as in the case of the Russian experience where the elimination of private property proved to have no negative effect on the formation of the industrial hierarchy and the intensification of machinism. She is primarily concerned, however, with the capitalist system where the coexistence of these two opposing relationships has led to greater confusion.

> ... les mêmes hommes se vendent au capital et servent la machine; au contraire, ce ne sont pas toujours les mêmes hommes qui disposent des capitaux et qui dirigent l'entreprise. . . .[107]

The system of rationalization and the growth of a technocratic class contributed to a system where the machine became an insurmountable barrier between the workers' thought and action. Before the establishment of Taylor's system of rationalization, it was possible for skilled workers to execute their work as artisans, with intelligence and an independent sense of creativity and judgment. Later, following Taylor's influence and the advent of mass production, salaries were determined by quantity, not quality. Workers were paid according to the number of uniform objects produced within a particular period of time. This led to a greater specialization of tasks and the rise of foremen and a managerial class. The specialization of labor led to a monotonous repetition of uniform tasks which estranged thought from action.

As the growth of the technocratic class expands the barrier between worker and owner, 'sociétés anonymes' replace the ownership and control of industry formerly run by capitalist entrepreneurs. Weil displays a familiarity with the writings of contemporary economists such as Pound, Palewski, and Laurat,[108] whose opinions reinforce her own on the transformation of capitalism, and the emergency of a bureaucratically-run, technocratic society. Weil and others believed, perhaps prophetically that a new social class had arisen from the expansion of technocracy–a new managerial class of technicians. Weil disagrees with the conclusion drawn by Laurat based on a comparative study of the financial mechanisms supporting bureaucratic, administrataive classes within the U.S.S.R. and capitalist countries. Laurat had concluded that the U.S.S.R.'s system was more supportive of their administrators by the fact that their salaries or dividends, were determined before the estimation of profits. Weil maintains that the capitalist or rather evolving technocratic system in Western countries works the same way; despite a decrease in profits the administration receives the same amount in financial compensation. The technocrats or administrators remain untouched, protected by the intermediary position of their own class.

Deconstruction of Power 141

The rise of bureaucracy and technocratic class was indicative of a trend towards an increasingly specialized society. The transition results in an intensification of the master/slave duality, a relationship rendered all the more volatile by an increasing degree of interdependency and estrangement. Roy Pierce has been the first to coin the useful term "complexity of knowledge" in his discussion of Weil's views on the mechanics of power.[109] The term "complexity of knowledge" in Weil's discussion of technocracy can be used more specifically to refer not only to the simple dehumanizing separation of action from thought, but also to the fact that no member of the production team has a full, comprehensive grasp of the process; workers are ignorant of technical knowledge; technicians like the industrial engineers whom Weil portrays are without an understanding of theoretical foundations and practical experience; scientists and theoreticians have neither practical nor technical knowledge. Scientists, in their own right, have become so specialized that they do not have a grasp of the process by which their own studies are applied; they lack also an understanding of the relationships between their field of science and others. In all realms of life one is engulfed by a system whose structure prevents full comprehension, a system which by its nature disorients and alienates the individual. In this system the bureaucratic administrative function predominates and survives all others. As Weil indicates, the relegation of the coordinating function to an intermediary bureaucratic class has endangered and complicated the problems of culture and society; the source of alienation becomes indefinable when one's own knowledge and comprehension is too limited and specialized to establish the needed sense of relation and contact.

The machine is a mystery for the worker because the latter lacks the technical and mathematical background to perceive in it an equilibrium between forces. The engineer, however, through use of differential equations applied to the study of material resistance, is able to understand this displacement and equilibrium of force. Weil's year in factory work was an attempt to demystify, to understand the powerful mechanisms of machinery and industrial processes of production; her goal was to comprehend the intensity and specialization of factory labor that stilted the expansion of knowledge and skill that comes from conscious participation. The determination of action and process by minds and forces other than one's own had led to the mystification of work and life in the developing age of automation, machinism, and specialization. It is one of the many forms of 'déracinement' analyzed by Weil, seeking demystification and the restoration of conscious participation.

Factory Life; The Effects of Machinism and Rationalisation: In *La Condition Ouvrière*, published in 1951, are gathered her observations and reactions to

142 Deconstruction of Power

experiences in the munitions and automobile factories where she worked, and her reflections and opinions on the labor strife of the period between 1933-1937. Weil had spent approximately a year in factory labor, 1934-1935; she had worked mainly for Alsthom Electrical Works in Paris and two other companies in Boulogne-Billancourt: J. J. Carnaud & Forges de Basse-Indre, and Renault.[110] In her letters to Albertine Thévenon, to Boris Souvarine and in her factory journal, she recorded impressions and experiences that describe the working conditions in French factories of the 1930s. These conditions had been determined by machinism and by the monetary interests of maximum production which had led to the development of Taylorisation and assembly-line production.[111]

The first effect of unhappiness was reflected by the mind itself which sought to flee from the mechanism in which the worker loses identity and becomes a cog in the entire piecework of productive and collective work. The complexity of this mechanism takes on mystical proportions. Weil compares her experience to those recounted by Jules Romains in his work, *Hommes de Bonne Volonte*;[112] for both writers, the combined force of workers and machine had evoked the mysterious psychological power of the collective unconscious.

Because the worker is not free she or he is unable to receive joy from a task. One is a spectator playing the role of intermediary between machines and the product. Consciousness of this estranged role invisibly affects the worker, both in body and soul; this is why Weil underlines this "repliement sur le présent . . . la retraction de la pensée" that occurred in such great intensity among workers as a way to escape the present reality.[113] The mind cannot escape because it must constantly follow the monotonous series of action perpetually repeated, and must be prepared to find in itself the solution to any unexpected breakdown or difficulty. "Rien n'est pire," observed Weil, than this "mélange de la monotonie et du hasard."[114] Weil describes a working schedule determined by the necessities of maximum speed and rule by a detached managerial class. The individual feels alone in a place where one concerns oneself solely with what one has done, not in the manner or skill with which it is accomplished. It is natural and appropriate for one to stop after having created something, even for an instant, to be aware of it "comme Dieu dans la Génèse."[115] It is exactly this moment of creative consciousness which is suppressed in factory work. The machinery workers would not attain the required speed if moments of reflection interrupted rapid consecutive actions, leaving no true space to distinguish a beginning from an end. The result, of course, is an inescapable state of passivity followed often by the brutalization of the worker.

In a letter to a former student, included in this collection, Weil describes the minimal chances for work within the factory that allows for the freedom of initiative, thought and intelligence. She did on occasion discover teams of men allowed to work on technical projects.[116] But for the most part production was too specialized to allow the worker a reasonable amount of creative participation. Domination of machines and the inflexible belief that only specialized or assembly-line labor would lead to a maximal degree of production eliminated most possibilities for individual initiative. Emergence from this system was rendered even more difficult by the determination of job assignments according to sex.

> Les femmes, elles sont parquées dans un travail tout à fait machinal, où on ne demande que de la rapidité, . . . le tragique de cette situation, c'est que le travail est trop machinal pour offrir matière à la pensée.[117]

Before the series of labor reforms of the late thirties and forties following the mass strikes and factory occupations of June 1936, the system of mass production and machinism subjected the individual laborer to an extremely hazardous working environment. Weil's experiences exposed her to some of these dangerous conditions.

Approximately a month after Weil began work at the Lecourbe factories of Alsthom Electrical Works at 90 centimes an hour (plus 25% commission, based on the number of uniform objects produced each hour), the hair of a female worker was removed by a drilling machine. There were at regular intervals, breakdowns in electricity which resulted in poor lighting. Despite these breakdowns, workers were expected to produce as usual at maximum speed. Even night teams working when lights were regularly dimmed were expected to work at maximum capacity. Frequently, temperature varied from machine to machine. The amount of production demanded did not take into account the difficulties of working in poorly heated or ventilated areas. In the fabrication of spools or reels for the subway and trolley cars, Weil also discovered the danger of working in the furnace area where the spools of copper have to be passed through the fire. Evidently, there was little or no precautions provided to protect the worker from severe burns.

Workers were literally driven towards maximum speed and production. In her letter to Souveraine and in her factory journal, Weil described her experience at the Gautier factories, following her termination at Alsthom factories. She began working with a stamp press. After producing 400 pieces an hour for a consecutive period of four hours the foreman threatened to fire her if she did not double her rate of production. She managed to bring it up to 600 an hour and was kept on because there was a shortage of labor.[118] She described the pace and environment of the factory where people worked nine hours straight without any break. They were women workers who literally ran from one job to another so as not to be paid less. Besides presses, there was assembly-line production where the expected production rate had recently doubled.

> une ouvrière qui est à la chaîne, et avec qui je suis rentrée en tram, m'a dit qu'au bout de quelques années, ou même d'un an, on arrive à ne plus souffrir, bien qu'on continue à se sentir abrutie. C'est à ce qu'il me semble le dernier degré de l'avilissement. . . .[119]

This final degree of abasement, the estrangement of mind and body was the form of uprootal ("déracinement") both analyzed and experienced by Weil.

CONCLUSION

Weil thus concludes that our conception of revolution has failed; it has failed as a historical symbol of liberation because of the inefficacy and ambiguity of our own thought in perceiving a realistic basis for action. The emergency of a technological society produced new forms of oppression, new forms of 'déracinement', unaccounted for within the vast compendium of Marxist writings. Weil's commentaries on Marxism, state and industrial bureaucracy, technocracy and machinism preceded the revisionist attempt of the French New Left in readapting the Marxist ideological basis to the changing realities of culture and technology. Her commentaries on Militarism and its contamination of the revolutionary ideal throughout the history of Socialist and Marxist struggle have not been echoed by the New Left and have been underestimated as an integral part of her Critique of Marxism and of the Myth of Revolution.

War and militarism, centralizing bureaucratization, and machinism, immersed the individual in an age of alienation. The subsequent loss of the revolutionary ideal was a manifestation of the reversal of Kantian priorities. The means of power has drowned its end, individual dignity, in a sea of violence; the human being has thus become the tool of matter and destruction, manipulated by the Anonymous Social. Weil sought to demystify these forces of uprootal constituting the Power of the Social over the individual. Her commentaries do so and thereby encourage the exercise of individual intelligence and will for the realization of true 'enracinement,' the reintegration of the self.

TRADITIONAL RELIGION AND THE SOCIAL

> ... le bien central pour tout homme est la libre disposition de soi.
> ... (*Attente de Dieu*)[120]

A discussion of Simone Weil's critique of the Social and the forces of uprootal and alienation therein would be incomplete without consideration of the religious writings produced during the last years of her life 1940-1943.[121]

This was a period of spiritual and religious exploration for Weil. In 1935 she had begun to feel an identification with Christianity. Her spiritual autobiography, in the form of a letter addressed to Father Perrin shortly before her departure for America in May 1942, recounts her main religious experiences which had oriented her towards Catholicism. Her visits to a small Portuguese village, to the Chapel of Santa Maria degli Angeli in Assisi, Italy, and her study of the metaphysical poetry of George Herbert, had definitively consolidated her adhesion to Catholic belief. But by the time she began to meet and converse with Father Perrin in June 1941, she had already decided not to become an official member of the Church. His encouragement and discussion with her motivated the body of Weil's writing which discusses the danger of the Church as an expression of the Social and its role in the estrangement of the individual. These writings are in the form of letters written to Father Perrin during the period of January to May 1942, later called "Hésitations devant le baptême" by Perrin himself who published the main body of Weil's correspondence to him in 1950, seven years after Weil's death, in a collection entitled, *Attente de Dieu*.

> Pourtant des obstacles restent.... Ce qui me fait peur, c'est l'Eglise en tant que chose sociale. ... .[122]

Weil was sensitive to her own vulnerability to the domination of the Social, reflected in the Church; this manifests itself particularly in the psychological power of ceremony. Weil's decision to remain outside of the Church stems from a comprehension of her vulnerability to the power of the collective element within institutionalized religion, Jewish and Christian; it also reflects the individual's need to retain distance and disciplined intelligence for the discernment of true faith and of the difference between participation and social idolatry.

> J'ai en moi un fort penchant grégaire. Je suis par disposition naturelle extrêmement influençable, ... et surtout aux choses collectives.[123]

146 *Deconstruction of Power*

In the course of Weil's transition toward Catholicism, she sought to safeguard carefully the authenticity and purity of belief by the retention of individual conscience and intelligence. In her first letter to Perrin, she delineates three domains of power: that governed entirely by divine will; that determined entirely by individual autonomy or will, and an ambiguous domain where the human capacity for attention and intelligence fuses with divine power. The major importance of 'attention' in Weil's religious philosophy is alone indicative of the existential nature of the decreation process discussed in her writings; the value she places on individual will and intelligence is retained throughout every point in her philosophical transition; even the abnegation of self was an expression of individual will and depended on the individual's disciplined sense of intelligence expressed through 'attention' by which one eventually merged with and became one with the Divine Spirit.

Weil felt that the collective element of the Church was a trap limiting the individual's capacity for true faith and discernment of the true meaning of liturgical symbols and images.

> ... une certaine formation de l'intelligence pour ... ne contempler dans l'Eucharistie que ce qui y est enfermé par définition....[124]

Weil affirms the value of these liturgical, ceremonial symbols and images, but she fears the domination of the Social over individual intelligence which renders one unable to relate to their true meaning. The presense of the Social obscures in her mind the difference between faith and its social imitation.

Weil elaborates on the limits preventing an accurate perception of the meaning of the sacraments. The sacraments are symbols which have two levels of meaning. In the presence of the Social, it is difficult, almost impossible, to grasp the specificity of meaning of the sacraments. Weil maintains that most members of a congregation comprehend only the second level of meaning, in so far as the sacraments constitute ceremonial symbols of a religion to which they adhere. Although Weil rejects Durkheim's complete reduction of religion to an expression of the Social, she perceives that the misperception of religious symbol is caused by the confusion of individual belief with the Social.

> ... le sentiment social ressemble à s'y méprendre au sentiment religieux.[125]

However, Weil does not deny the value of the Congregation. Adherence to a synagogue or church is possible for those who can distinguish between the two levels of meaning associated with the sacraments or other religious symbols; it is possible and valuable but only for those who can master the equilibrium between participation and individual belief. It is for those whose strength of spirituality will prevent them from relinquishing the conscious specificity of their own experience while belonging to and identifying with a group. It refers again to the essential problem of true 'enracinement' sought by Weil in philosophy, politics, science and spirituality; it expresses the ideal balance between collective and individual freedom, of integration tempered by intellectual objectivity and detachment. Weil considered herself among those whose spirituality was not strong enough to retain individual belief while immersed in the presence of the Social. Weil indicated her apprehension that in adhering to the church she would not have the strength of objectivity to resist commiting crimes on its behalf. If saints who had participated in the crusades and in the Inquisition could have condoned bloodshed for the sake of their church, Weil believed that much weaker individuals such as herself would be even more inclined to such nationalistic support of the Catholic Church.

The congregation has the guardianship of dogma; but because dogma or theology is the demonstration and object of contemplation for the individual faculties of faith, love, and intelligence, Weil believed that there was an inevitable incompatibility between the individual and the Congregation (in the form of a synagogue or church). This is demonstrated particularly in Weil's criticism of the Church's power of censure and excommunication, the abuse of the power of the Social through 'anathema sit.' J. Patricia Little has commented in her article, "Le Refus de l'Idolatrie dans l'Oeuvre de Simone Weil" that Weil considered the idolatry of the Church to be the most dangerous forms of social idolatry because of its presumed divine authority; operating on both the temporal and spiritual level, the Church's use of excommunication and anathema was a form of spiritual persecution abhorred by Weil because it negated the Church's true function as the guardian of the sacraments and the Holy Scriptures.[126]

What Weil believed contributed most of all to the presence of the Social within the Church was the combination of nation and religion. The fusion of nationalist sentiment and religious ideology was the true basis of power of the Social within the Church and Synagogue. According to Weil, Rome and Israel provided the historical precedents for the later fusion of national and ecclesiastical power. Weil's discussion of this danger appears in later letters to Father Perrin, in an essay entitled, "Israel et les Gentils."[127] It also appears in a letter written by Weil to Father Couturier in New York with whom she had pursued a discussion of her doubts concerning official conversion, a letter later published as *Lettre a un religieux*.[128] Similar commentary appears also in *La Pesanteur et la Grâce*[129] and in *La Connaissance Surnaturelle*.[130]

Weil believed that Christianity lost its purity following the conversion of Constantine I in the third century, B.C., and the spread of Christianity throughout the Roman Empire. The medieval church's abuse of temporal power was a demonstration of its romanization and impurity, according to Weil. She believed that the danger of the Social represented by the Church was in great part a consequence of this fusion of Roman and Christian values. She thought that the Roman spirit of empire and power had contaminated the spirit of Christian love and justice. For this reason she nurtured a disdain for medieval Christianity and consequently for its spokesmen, Saint Thomas d'Aquinas and Saint Augustine.

Weil believed also that the importance of the community and the congregation emphasized in Jewish theology and traditional belief reflected a historical propensity for religious nationalism. Weil nurtured a total, unequivocal aversion for Judaic theology. This is unfortunate because her lack of objectivity concerning Judaism detracts from the credibility of her critique. Father Perrin attributes her disdain for Judaism to the influence of Marcion;[131] Petrément claims, however, that it was the similarity between Marcion's views concerning the Old Testament and Weil's own opinions which drew her to study him further.[132] Weil's comments are, indeed, at times shocking and extreme.

> Israel. Tout est souillé et atroce. . . . Les Juifs, cette poignée de déracinés a causé le déracinement de tout le globe terrestre.[133] (*La Pesanteur et la Grâce*, 167)

It is unfortunate that Weil, having distinguished between fanatical Christianity and true Christian belief in love and justice, did not also seek to distinguish between elements of truth and fanaticism in Judaic theology. Evidently, Weil was unaware of the existence of Talmudic texts of oral and written interpretive value which had been of equal, if not greater, determination of Judaic belief following the destruction of the Second Temple. There is, nevertheless, validity in her examination of certain aspects of the Old Testament. It is right that she questioned certain aspects of Judaism which she felt reinforced a dogmatic spirit and an idolatry of the Social, in particular the notion of history and the idea of the chosen people emphasized in the Old Testament as well as the value placed on community and solaridity. J. P. Little interpreted Weil's critique of Judaism as a refusal of the adoration of history. In Judaism and in the Christian notion of revelation, time is conceived as linear; time is becoming, progression. Little compares this view to Weil's own belief in time as circular. This is a valuable observation which can be supported by a reading of Weil's *Cahiers* and final spiritual writings. Weil's increasing adherence to hellenic concepts of aesthetics and morality had led her to identify more closely and integrate into her own religious philosophy the Greek notions of circularity, harmony, and balance. Little contrasts the Judaic consciousness of historical progress through which divine will is revealed and the consciousness of being of the Greeks with their cyclical conception of history; she affirms that Weil was deeply hostile to the notion of a people serving as the instrument of a God manifesting his will through history and thus Weil was unable to perceive the *transition* of this people from being chosen to serving a universal God.

> ... le témoignage d'un peuple qui perd peu à peu son exclusivité nationale à l'égard de son Dieu, et qui se rend compte peu à peu que le Dieu d'Israel est aussi le Dieu universel. . . .[134]

Weil's refusal to join the Church was an attempt to retain and dignify individual intelligence. She was seeking particularly to avoid the domination of the Social that was manifesting itself at that time in the form of extreme fanaticism and loyalty towards the Catholic Church in France. Such sentiment had raised the Church to the level of a sanctified national entity. Although Weil does not specifically allude to certain individuals or movements, one thinks automatically of Maurrassian traditionalism, L'Action Française, La Jeunesse Ouvrière, and the extremes of nationalistic sentiments evoked by the right-wing association of church and state that nourished the prejudices of the Collaborationist government. Tragically, Weil's association with the term 'enracinement' was misunderstood for years after her death and inadequately distinguished from the political and religious position she had warned against. Beyond the controversy and shock caused by the details of her discussion, beyond the possible inaccuracies of her statements concerning Christian and Judaic theology, her defense of individual intelligence and belief is of primary importance in her religious writings; it is her major contribution to twentieth-century thought and raises her above the baseness of collaboration and hatred.

Conclusion: The deconstruction of power is thus complete. Simone Weil's theory of oppression, her conception of freedom as conscious action and her analysis of the natural instability of power, provide the principles upon which are based her deconstruction of power. Weil thus sought to dismantle, to uproot the cultural myths upon which are built the social structures of power.

In her analysis, the forces of alienation and uprootal, of "déracinement" are most evident. The binary pair "déracinement/enracinement" describes the diversely opposed conditions and movements in Weil's analysis. Uprootal of oneself from conscious action or participation is, at the same time, entrenchment and mystification. Uprootal, "deracinement" describes as well the refusal of an alienating condition. It serves as the initial movement towards true "enracinement", integration with capacities of displacement, difference and flexibility. Both dialectical elements have negative and positive symbolic power. Deconstruction, in essence, provides reconstruction, the total philosophical construct of Weil's thought.

Notes to Chapter 3

[1] Simone Weil, *Réflexions sur les Causes de la liberté et de l'Oppression Sociale* (Paris: Editions Gallimard, 1955), 89-90.

[2] Ibid.

[3] Ibid., 93.

[4] *Knowledge and Value, Introductory Readings in Philosophy*, ed. Elmer Sprague and Paul W. Taylor (New York: Harcourt, Brace & Co., 1959), 698-707.

[5] "Education in Action–The Story of John Dewey," *The World Tomorrow*, 14 (no. 4, April 1931): 106-9.

[6] Weil, *Réflexions sur les Causes de la liberté et de l'Oppression Sociale*, 91.

[7] Ibid.

[8] Ibid., 57. In her political essay "On Violence," H.Arendt's description of the phenomenon of violence is very close to Weil's: *Crises of the Republic* (New York: Harcourt, Brace & Jovanovich, 1969) 106. Weil's influence on Arendt in other domains has been documented by Arendt herself in her discussion of science, labor and language in *The Human Condition* (Chicago: University of Chicago Press, 1970), 131, 287.

[9] Weil, *Réflexions sur les Causes de la liberté et de l'Oppression Sociale*, 59.

[10] Simone Weil, "Obéissance et Liberté." *Oppression et Liberté* (Paris: Editions Gallimard, 1955), 192.

[11] Roy Pierce, "Simone Weil: Sociology, Utopia and Faith," *Contemporary French Political Thought* (London: Oxford University Press, 1966), 99.

[12] Simone Weil, "Lutte des Classes," *Oppression et Liberté*, 170-71.

[13] Weil, "Obéissance et Liberté," ibid., 192.

[14] Jean Giraudoux, *La Guerre de Troie N'Aura Pas Lieu*.

[15] Roy Lewis, *Giraudoux: La Guerre de Troie N'Aura Pas Lieu* (London: Camelot Press Ltd., 1971), 6, 9. "Giraudoux was appointed Minister of Information in 1939. . . . When France fell, he refused to cooperate with the occupying powers. . . ." Of the play, *La Guerre de Troie N'Aura Pas Lieu*, Lewis comments, "The desire to give the play contemporary significance has led to its being treated more or less as a political allegory."

[16] Simone Weil, "L'Iliade ou Le Poème de la Force," *La Source Grecque* (Paris: Editions Gallimard, 1953), 26.

[17] Charles Baudouin, *Le Triomphe du Héros* (Paris: Librairie Plon, 1952), xlll.

[18] Arthur Hutson and Patricia McCoy, *Epics of the Western World* (Philadelphia: Lippincott, 1954), 8.

[19] Baudouin, *Le Triomphe du Héros*, 111.

[20] Similar conclusions on violence were made by René Girard, *La Violence et le Sacré* (Paris: Editions Bernard Grasset, 1971), 31, 46.

[21] Ibid., 70-72. In Girard's discussion of the common mythological basis of epic and tragedy, he indicates the transferral of violent action to violent debate. The symmetrical exchange of combat manifests itself verbally in tragedy. "Le débat tragique est une substitution de la parole au fer dans le combat singulier." The contagion of violence expresses itself through unresolved, perpetual verbal exchange.

[22] Simone Weil, "Fragment," *Ecrits historiques et politiques* (Paris: Editions Gallimard, 1960),

315.

[23]Ibid., 45. "On ne peut pas se passer de la violence pour mettre fin à la violence... la violence est interminable. . . ." (Girard).

[24]Simone Weil, "Ne Recommençons Pas la Guerre de Troie," *Ecrits historiques et politiques*, 256-57.

[25]Simone Weil, *La Pesanteur et la Grâce* (Paris: Librairie Plon, 1948), 165.

[26]Plato *The Republic: A New Version founded on Basic English*, ed. Ivor Armstrong Richards. (New York: Norton, 1942), 132. Subsequent references will refer to this edition.

[27]Ibid., 115-16.

[28]Simone Weil, *The Simone Weil Reader*, ed. George A. Panichas (New York: David McKay co., 1977), 391.

[29]Weil, *La Pesanteur et la Grâce*, 161.

[30]Plato *Republic*, 40-41.

[31]Weil, *La Pesanteur et la Grâce*, 139.

[32]Ibid.

[33]Ibid.

[34]Ibid.

[35]Simone Weil, *Gravity and Grace*, tr. Arthur Wills (New York: Putnam's Sons, 1952), 221.

[36]Simone Weil, "Réflexions Sur Les Origines de l'Hitlérisme," *Ecrits historiques et politiques*, 13.

[37]Simone Weil, "Lettre à Georges Bernanos," *Ecrits historiques et politiques*, 224.

[38]Simone Weil, *L'Enracinement—Prélude à une Déclaration des Devoirs Envers l'Etre Humain* (Paris: Editions Gallimard, 1949), 136.

[39]Weil. "Réflexions Sur les Origines de l'Hitlérisme," 16.

[40]Simone Weil, "Ebauches de Lettres," *Ecrits historiques et politiques*. Weil criticizes Richelieu's skill in manipulatory statesmanship in the excerpt of a letter where she asserts that Richelieu's methods of domination were in part based on the political strategies of Charles d'Albert, Duc de Luynes, whom Weil describes as ordinary, mediocre. Desmond Seward, *The Bourbon Kings of France* (New York: Harper & Row, 1976), 41, states that Luynes was the first real friend of Louis XIII; the two men used to hunt falcons together. He also described Luynes as a mediocrity whose role as trusted friend and confidante to Louis XIII was the means to his successful rise to power.

Weil accurately described Luyne's manipulaton of the royal family's paranoiac fear of assassination that began with Henri IV's death. Marie de Médicis and her young sons, King Louis XIII and Gaston d'Orléans, all feared a similar end. As Weil correctly points out, Luynes exploited this fear and nurtured a sense of mutual distrust between members of the royal family, particularly Louis XIII's fears of his mother and brother who had shown himself to be far more capable as a ruler. Richelieu imitated Luyne's cultivation of these fears, by which method he eventually overthrew Luynes himself when his (Luynes's) followers had begun to support Gaston d'Orléans. Richelieu then used the same tactics to alienate the king from the Queen Mother. It was also Louis' basic sense of fear and distrust that Richelieu exploited by his provocation of civil war, disorder, and a feeling of peril for the King's own person.

[41]Weil, *L'Enracinement*, 150.

[42]Weil, "Ebauches de Lettres," 110-11.

[43]Weil, "Réflexions sur les Origines de l'Hitlérisme," 15.

⁴⁴Ibid., 18.

⁴⁵Ibid., 39.

⁴⁶René Char, *Feuillets D'Hypnos* (Paris: Editions Gallimard, 1946).

⁴⁷Weil, *L'Enracinement*, 129-30.

⁴⁸Weil, "Réflexions Sur les Origines de l'Hitlérisme," Conor Cruise O'Brien also comments in his article, "The Antipolitics of Simone Weil," *Simone Weil: Interpretations of a Life*, ed. George Abbot White, (Amherst: University of Massachusetts Press, 1981), 106-7. She wrote, ". . . [France's] natural place was on the side of the victors; therefore . . . the easiest . . . least painful method of bringing about the indispensable rectification was to change ideas."

⁴⁹Weil, "Réflexions Sur les Origines de l'Hitlérisme." The cruelty of Roman domination is reflected in the vacuum of feeling and sensitivity that Weil attributes to Roman literature. In contrast, Greek verse and tragedy give proof of a more humanistic, compassionate society, moderate in its engulfment of power.

⁵⁰Simone Weil, "Le Sang Coule en Tunisie," *Ecrits historiques et politiques*, 338.

⁵¹Weil, *L'Enracinement*, 186-87.

⁵²Simone Weil, "A Propos de la Question Coloniale," *Ecrits historiques et politiques*, 367.

⁵³Simone Weil, "Le Maroc ou de la Prescription en Matière de Vol," *Ecrits historiques et politiques*, 333.

⁵⁴Ibid., 331.

⁵⁵Ahmed Messali Hadj was an Algerian nationalist leader. Following participation in the First World War, he remained in France and in 1924 founded the Algerian nationalist organization, "L'Etoile Nord-Africaine." He was imprisoned several times for his political activities. In 1929 he reorganized "L'Etoile." This organization became the Parti Populaire Algérien in 1937, shortly before Messali's imprisonment by Chautemps' government, the second government of the Popular Front. Later the PA was replaced by the MTLD–Le Mouvement pour le Triomphe des libertés démocratiques which in 1946 elected five representatives to the National Assembly. In 1954, however, the MTLD split into two groups–Le Mouvement nationaliste algérien and Le comite révolutionnaire d'unité et d'action. The latter one was responsible for the establishemnt of the Front de Libération Nationale. Messali, following several periods of imprisonment, did not fully recover his freedom until 1962, the year of Algerian independence.

⁵⁶Simone Weil, "Qui est coupable de menées antifrançaise?" *Ecrits historiques et politiques*, 339-40.

⁵⁷Simone Pétrement, *La Vie de Simone Weil*, vol. I (Paris: Librairie Fayard, 1973), 174-75.

⁵⁸Reproduced in Simone Weil, *Oppression et Liberté*, 11-38.

⁵⁹Weil, *Réflexions sur les Causes de la liberté et de l'Oppression Sociale*.

⁶⁰Reference is made to the following articles reproduced in *Ecrits historiques et politiques*: "Premières Impressions d'Allemagne–1932," "La grève des transports à Berlin–1932," "La situation en Allemagne–1932-1933," "Sur la situation en Allemagne–1933."

⁶²Simone Weil, *La Condition Ouvrière* (Paris: Gallimard, 1951).

⁶³*Encyclopedia Britannica*, 14th ed., s.v. "French Revolution."

⁶⁴"The Girondins (1791-1793)," *The French Revolution: Conflicting Interpretations*, ed. Frank A. Kafner and James M. Laux (New York: Random House, 1968).

⁶⁵Karl Marx and V. I. Lenin, *The Civil War in France: The Paris Commune* (New York: International Publishers, 1940).

The actual history of the Paris Commune of 1871 describes the whole period of Parisian history from March 18 to May 28, 1871, often nicknamed the Insurrection of the 18th of March because the proletarian insurrection officially began on that day of battle in the wake of France's defeat in the Franco-Prussian War and the collapse of Napoleon III's Second Empire. The French, demoralized by the four-month siege of German troops from September 1870 to January 1871 deeply resented the presence of German troops stationed outside Paris and were not enthusiastic about peace negotiations. There had been a royalist majority in the National Assembly elected in February 1871 to conclude a peace with Germany. the Republic Parisians were afraid of the conservative spirit of this new body of legislators who would, they thought, possibly try to restore the monarchy. Antagonism increased when the assembly eliminated the salaries of the National Guard who were mostly workers who had served during the siege. The Assembly also terminated the moratorium on debt and rent payment and placed the government center in Versailles where the Bourbon Kings had reigned in isolated luxury. Thiers, executive head of the provisional government, had decided to disarm the National Guard. Their arms were gathered on the Butte Montmarte. Among both parties, there was a mutual fear that the relinquished weapons would fall into the hands of the Prussians. On March 18 the unplanned insurrection began when resistance occurred during the government's attempt to remove the arms (*Encyclopedia Britannica*, vol. 69, s.v. "Commune of Paris, 1871"). The National Guard took over Paris and Thiers's government fled to Versailles; municipal elections were held in Paris resulting in the victory of the revolutionary commune government. Similar communes arose in Lyons, Marseilles, Saint-Etienne. The Jacobins were among the Commune leaders; they wanted tight centralized control by the Paris Commune government in the tradition of 1793; there were also the Proudhonists who were in favor of a decentralized power based in a federation of communes throughout France, and the Blanquists who insisted on violent action (Marx, *The Civil War in France: The Paris Commune*, 18). Weil's own political positions and philosophy indicate her aversion to Jacobin and Blanquist positions emphasizing violence and centralization of power. Philippe Dujardin has accurately stated that Weil's own emphasis on decentralization and her respect for individual and private property puts her in the lineage of Proudhonist philosophers (Philippe Dujardin and Simone Weil, Idéologie et Politique [Grenoble: Presses Universitaires de Grenoble, 1975], 130). "Simone Weil est l'héritère du proudhonnisme mutualliste, expression d'une France encore largement artisanale et paysanne mais déjà ménacée par le machinisme, et du radicalisme d'Alain, idéologie de la bourgeoisie, et notamment de la petite bourgeoisie provinciale. . . ."

[66]*Encyclopedia Britannica*, vol. 6, s.v. "Commune of Paris, 1871."

[67]Ibid., s.v. "Revolution of 1905 and the First and Second Duma." [68]Ibid.

[69]Ibid.

[70]Simone Weil, "Prospects," *Oppression and Liberty*, tr. Arthur Wills and John Petrie (Amherst: University of Massachusetts Press, 1958), 2.

[71]Simone Weil, "Perspectives-Allons-nous vers une Revolution Prolétarienne?" *Oppression et Liberté*, 12.

[72]Rosa Luxemburg, "Beginnings of the German Revolution," *Selected Poltical Writings*, ed. Dick Howard (New York: Monthly Review Press, 1971), 359.

[73]Rosa Luxemburg, "The Crisis in German Social Democracy," ibid., 324.

[74]Rosa Luxemburg, "Our Program and the Political Situation," ibid., 384-85.

[75]Simone Weil, "Critique du Marxisme," *Réflexions sur les Causes de la liberté et de l'Oppression Sociale* (Paris: Gallimard, 1955), 20.

[76]Simone Weil, "Y a-t-il une Doctrine Marxiste?" *Oppression et Liberté*, 240.

[77]Philippe Dujardin, *Simone Weil–Idéologie et Politique* (Grenoble: Presses Universitaires de Grenoble, 1975), 122-23.

[78]Weil, "Critique du Marxisme," 18.

[79]Simone Weil, "Réflexions sur la Guerre–1933," *Ecrits historiques et politiques*, 229-39.

[80]Pierre-Joseph Proudhon, *Les Confessions d'un Révolutionnaire pour servir à l'histoire de la Révolution de Février* (Paris: La Voix du Peuple, 1849). This was Proudhon's explanation of his revolutionary and anarchist politics and his participation in the insurrection of February 1848, which reinforces the public image of Proudhon as a terrorist. See Alan Ritter's study, *The Political Thought of Pierre-Joseph Proudhon* (Princeton: Princeton University Press, 1969). Despite the negative historical image both conservatives and Marxists have attributed to Proudhon, Weil was justified in pointing out the inconsistency of his attitude towards war; his justification of violence as a tool of revolution was demonstrated by his participation in the February insurrection and by his sympathy for mid-nineteenth century social revolutionary movements. The following is an excerpt from Proudhon's writings where he expresses sympathy for the involvement of English aristocracy: "Tandis que le matérialisme . . . dévore . . . le peuple russe est entraîné au champ de bataille par tous les sentiments qui ennoblissent . . . ." "Correspondance," *La Guerre et la Paix–Recherches sur le Principe et la Constitution du Droit des Gens* (Paris: Librairie des Sciences politiques et sociales, 1927), vii-viii.

[81]Again Weil is referring to Marx's zealous efforts to distinquish between a defensive and offensive war; he credits the French and German workers battling each other with awareness of that distinction, but criticizes the German Emperor, Wilhelm, whom she felt had used the pretense of a defensive war to invade Alsace and bombard the city of Strasbourg. (Marx, *The Civil War in France*, 26, 28).

[82]Weil, "Réflexions sur la Guerre-1933," 230.

[83]Weil is referring to the anarchist crisis of 1892-94 in France, and Engels' involvement with the Social Democratic Movement in Germany. France had concluded an alliance with Russia, and Engels' political leadership was considered dangerous to a supposedly peaceful, stable era of colonial expansion.

[84]Following the vote of August 4, 1914, Rosa Luxemburg and Karl Liebknecht held a meeting attended by a group which eventually became known as the Spartacus League, formed to begin oppositional action. Following Rosa Luxemburg's release from prison in February 1916, there was another meeting of the group, now calling itself "Spartacus." Howard, *Selected Political Writings*, 359. There was a left-wing rising, known as the Spartacist Revolt, on January 5, 1919, two months after the German Revolution of 1918. The Spartacist Revolt was crushed by the so-called Free Corps (*Freikorps*), volunteer units condoned by Gustav Noske. Noske was responsible for military affairs within the government. The Free Corps troops used this chance to arrest and murder Luxemburg and Liebnecht, the Spartacus leaders. (*Encyclopedia Americana*, vol. 2, s.v. "Spartacist Revolt")

Liebknecht, was a parliamentary representative in the Reichstag from 1912 to death; Luxemburg and Liebknecht were the leaders of the Spartacus movement, the left-wing section of the German Social Democratic Party. Luxemburg along with Liebknecht had organized the Second International and had led protest against the August 1914 vote for war credits. See related reference: Karl Liebknecht, "Le Vote contre les crédits de Guerre (Déclaration au Reichstag du 2 décembre 1914)," "Que veut dire La Ligue Spartacus? Discours prononcé à Berlin fin décembre 1918," *Militarisme guerre, révolution* (Paris: François Maspero, 1970), 239-48, 131-33.

[85]Weil, "Réflexions sur la Guerre–1933," 231.

[86]Ibid., 234.

[87]Weil, "Fragment–1936," 217.

[88]Weil, "Lettre à Georges Bernanos–1938," 221.

[89]Weil, "Fragment-1936," 217.

[90]Weil, "Lettre à Georges Bernanos," 224.

[91]Following the last year of the German Empire, the transition to constitutional monarchy

had been carried through peacefully at the order of the high command. On November 7, revolt broke out at Kiel and spread to Berlin, and soon to the interior. Workers' and soldiers' councils were established and the officers disarmed. On November 9, Prince Max of Baden resigned and transferred his powers as chancellor to the leader of the SDP, Friedrich Ebert. Another important Social Democrat, Philipp Scheidemann, proclaimed the German Republic and a new government was set up—Council of People's Commissars, formed of SDP and independent Social Democrats with their two leaders, Ebert and Hugo Haase, as co-chairmen. The Spartacus League was not represented. An alliance between Ebert and the army took place to prevent the spread of Bolshevism. An armistice was signed with the Allies. In the elections held on January 19, 1919 (two weeks following the murder of the Spartacus leaders) the SDP polled the largest vote. In February, the Assembly elected Ebert as president of the Republic and Scheidemann formed a coalition government of the SDP, the Catholic Center and the Democrats, a new party formed from progressives and liberals. The new government was called the Weimar Coalition because it met at Weimar. The Weimar Coalition, in June 1920, lost its majority never to regain it. The government became "middle class" in character and the strongest party, the SDP, was usually in opposition. The Weimar Republic continued until 1933. (*Encyclopedia Americana*, vol. 12, s.v. "Germany: History")

[92] 1923 was a year of great crises for the Weimar Republic: The Reparations Commission concluded that Germany had not fulfilled its treaty obligations and French divisions marched into the Ruhr. The Free Corps organized armed resistance. The right-wing government of Wilhelm Cuno claimed a policy of passive resistance which cost so much in payments to strikers that the mark became valueless. The Free Corps promoted a separatist movement in the Rhineland. In Saxony and Thuringia left-wing socialist governments were formed. Right-wing extremism flourished in Bavaria of which one group was the National Socialist German Workers Party, the Nazi Party; its leader was Adolf Hitler. However, in October and November, Stresemann, a moderate conservative, led the new German government on the road to recovery by a series of financial reforms. By the end of 1923, the main danger had passed. However, the great crisis had a lasting political effect: the middle classes, who had lost all their financial security, had lost their trust in republican institutions. (*Encyclopedia Americana*, vol. 12, s.v. "Germany: History")

[93] The years 1924 to 1929 were the best years of the Weimar Republic. Stabilization and prosperity were brought about by large U. S. loans. Following the Dawes plan and the treaties of Locarno, large foreign investments were made in Germany. German industry was re-equipped, production boomed, wages were high, and in 1927, unemployment fell to 1,000,000. Public works projects were undertaken and reparation payments were met. Marx, chancellor from 1923 to 1924, was responsible for two of the major achievements of the Weimar Republic in social legislation, a comprehensive scheme of unemployment insurance covering 16,000,000 people and the extension of state arbitration in labor disputes. (*Encyclopedia Americana*, vol. 12, s.v. "Germany: History"; *Encyclopeida Britannica*, vol. 10, s.v. "Germany.")

[94] Weil, "La Situation en Allemagne," 146-94.

[95] This "coup d'état" was the action of the government of barons, led by Von Papen, who immediately following his accession to power as chancellor deposed the coalition government of the Social Democrats. This destroyed the last Social Democratic bastion in Germany; after the elections of July and November, 1932, Schleicher became Chancellor, but his resignation was forced by Hindenburg, the president. Hindenburg had been infulenced by Von Papen who had joined political forces with Hitler in 1933. By the end of January 1933, Hitler had been appointed chancellor by Hindenburg, with Von Papen as vice-chancellor. Later Hitler discarded both men. (*Encyclopedia Americana*, vol. 12, s.v. "Germany: History.")

[96] Weil, "La Situation en Allemagne," 160.

[97] Weil is referring at this point to the Kapp putsch attempted in March 1920. As a result of the increasing political radicalization of Germany, there was an attempt by the government to disband the most extreme of the Free Corps. The Free Corps responded by a mutiny and a march on Berlin. Following the frightened departure of the government from Berlin, Wolfgang Kapp and

Gen. Walther von Luttwitz set up a counterrevolutionary government. But the Kapp putsch was defeated after a few days when the trade unions came to the support of the legitimate government by proclaiming a general strike. (*Encyclopedia Americana*, vol. 12, s.v. "Germany: History.")

[98]*Ecrits historiques et politiques*, 152, 154-55.

[99]Heinrich Brandler, one of the main leaders of the German Communist Party. By trade a construction worker, he had become active in the SPD and the trade union movement before the war. During the war he joined the Spartacus League, and became respected in labor circles during the Kapp putsch, when he occupied and held the city of Chemnitz without bloodshed until after the collapse of the proletarian uprising in the Ruhr and central Germany. He later became party chairman, a position he kept until April 18, 1921, when he was arrested in connection with the uprising of the German Communist Party in March of that same year. Although sentenced to prison for treason, he was released and was sent to Moscow as the representative of the German Communist Party (Kommunistische Partei Deutschlands). Later in August 1922 he returned, and in February 1923 he was reelected into the leadership of the party. (Werner T. Angress, *Stillborn Revolution—The Communist Bid for Power in Germany*[Princeton: Princeton University Press, 1962], 102.)

[103]Pétrement, *La Vie de Simone Weil*, 1: 383-87. "La réunion devait avoir lieu le 31 décembre 1933. Trotsky arriva dès le 29 ou le 30, avec sa femme, Nathalie Sédov, et ses deux gardes du corps. . . . Simone profita de la présence de Trotsky pour discuter avec lui. La discussion devint rapidement une dispute; de la piece voisine, ou se tenaient les parents Weil, on entendait des éclats de voix. (Les éclats de voix devaient être ceux de Trotsky. Simone parlait toujours avec calme; elle ne s'échauffait pas dans les discussions.) Nathalie Sédov, qui était avec les parents, disait avec étonnement: 'Cette enfant qui tient tête à Trotsky!' 384-386.) 'Jacques de Kadt, qui participa à cette réunion, a raconté le départ de Trotsky et le sien: "Quand nous pénétrâmes dans l'antichambre pour prendre nos vêtements, une jeune fille, ou jeune garçon, vint nous aider. Trotsky lui demanda, sur un ton badin, si elle persévérait toujours dans ses idées contre-revolutionnaires. Elle répondit, ayant l'air de ne pas remarquer le persiflage, par une définition qui éstablissait une sorte d'identité entre les termes 'révolutionnaire' et 'contre-révolutionnaire', soutenant qu'il fallait, en recherchant la vérité, restreindre les limites de cette terminologie. Je connaissais cette maniere sérieuse de raisonner par quelques articles que j'avais lus dans *La Révolution prolétarienne*. . . ., articles qui m'avaient fait impression. Cette femme, c'était Simone Weil. . . ., 386.

[104]Thibon made this comment in conversation with me, summer of 1980 in Saint Marcel d'Ardèche, his home. Pétrement also indicated this in *La Vie de Simone Weil*, 1: 384: "Simone lui reprocha en particulier sa conduite à l'égard des marins de Cronstadt. Trotsky lui dit: 'Si vous pensez ainsi, pourquoi nous recevez-vous? Etes-vous de l'Armée du Salut?'"

[105]Weil, "Perspectives," 15. Philippe Dujardin, in his study *Simone Weil–Idéologie et Politique*, gave a negative interpretation of Weil's critique of Marxism. He affirmed that it was indicative of an increasingly conservative philosophy. He seemed to believe that her challenge of terminology used by Marxists and Leninists was a rejection of Socialist principles. The cautious detachment she maintained in later years from organizations was interpreted by Dujardin as an abandonment of principles of solidarity and a retreat into individualism and classical idealism. I disagree with him that this examination of Socialist principles and terminology is indicative of a supposed loss of interest in reform or an abandonment of Socialist principles, but his study is one possible interpretation. Of particular relevance to Weil's study of Soviet bureaucracy based in part on her encounter with Trotsky, is Dujardin's use of a quote by Trotsky to support his own claim that Weil's Marxist critique is indicative of the ambiguity and inconsistency of her philosophy. (Dujardin, *Simone Weil-Idéologie et politique*, 129-30.)

[106]Weil, "Perspectives," 22.

[107]Ibid.

[108] Ibid., 23, 24.

[109] Roy Pierce, "Simone Weil: Sociology, Utopia, and Faith," *Contemporary French Political Thought* (London: Oxford University Press, 1966), 99.

[110] Weil, *La Condition Ouvrière*.

[111] Weil's study on rationalization completed in 1937 is among the articles included in the collection *La Condition Ouvrière*. It is based on a lecture that she gave on February 23, 1937 ("La Rationalisation," 289-315).

[112] Simone Weil, "Expérience de la Vie d'Usine–Marseille, 1941-1942," *La Condition Ouvrière*, 328-30.

[113] Ibid., 335.

[114] Simone Weil, "Journal d'Usine," *La Condition Ouvrière*, 67-68.

[115] Simone Weil, "Trois Lettres à Mme. Albertine Thévenon," *La Condition Ouvrière*, 28.

[116] Weil, "Journal d'Usine," 57, 26, 15, 148-49.

[117] Simone Weil, "Lettre à une élève," *La Condition Ouvrière*, 32.

[118] Jacques Cabaud, L'Expérience Vécue de Simone Weil, 106-8.

[119] Simone Weil, "Lettre à Boris Souvarine–1935," *La Condition Ouvrière*, 39.

[120] Simone Weil, "Formes de l'Amour Implicite de Dieu," *Attente de Dieu* (Paris: Fayard, 1966), 200.

[121] Weil's opinions on Christian and Judaic theology are among the most controversial aspects of her writings of this period. As a result, much bitter dissension has taken place among critics examining her work in depth. There are those such as l'Abbé Charles Moëller who attributes her decision to remain outside of the Church as an unofficially declared but faithful Catholic, a reflection of the supposed manichean direction of her own misguided philosophy (Charles Moëller, "Simone Weil et l'incroyance des croyants," in *Silence de Dieu*, vol. 1 of *Littérature du XXe siècle et christianisme* [Tournai-Paris: Casterman, 1953], 220-25). In 1963 Father Perrin published a collection of critical essays written by himself and other priests refuting Weil's critiques as a general defense of Catholic theology (J. M. Perrin, et al., *Réponses aux questions de Simone Weil*, [Marseille: Aubier-Editions Montaigne, 1964]). There are others, such as Paul Giniewski whose book *Simone weil ou la Haine de Soi* (Paris: Berg International, 1978) expresses the anger of Holocaust survivors against Weil's condemnation of Judaic theology and against the phenomenon of dispersion and assimilation within European society which she incarnated. Weil was the grandchild of Russian and German Jewish orthodox immigrants; she had been raised in a family and intellectual environment of agnostic, Hellenistic, and free-thinking Jews; eventually she became an undeclared convert to Catholicism. This experience was typical of many Jewish intellectuals of her time, products of the diaspora and assimilation. "Il avait voulu lui faire le procès du juif assimilié, déraciné," declared Blum, the husband of Marie-Louis Blum-David (called Malou). Malou Blum had directed and testified to Simone Weil's participation in the resistance; she stated that Weil had assisted in the distribution of an underground publication, "Les Cahiers du Témoignage Chrétien." This publication was founded by Father Joseph-Marie Perrin, a former volunteer Dominican priest in the German concentration camps. At the time, Perrin was providing Weil with the counsel needed to decide whether or not she would finally join the Church. Wladamir Rabi and Emmanuel Lévinas, however, in contrast to Giniewski, have given more objective balance to their interpretaion of Weil, despite the conflict between their ethnic background and Weil's views on Judaic theology. Lévinas stated in speaking of Weil: ". . . abime franchissable est l'amour de Dieu. . . . Les fossés infranchissables sont sa haine de la Bible et son horreur du peuple juif. . . ." (Revue *Evidences* no. 24, 1952, repris dans *Difficile liberté* [Albin Michel, 1963], 160), remarks repeated by Rabi in "La Conception weilienne de la création, Rencontre avec la Kabbale juive," *Simone Weil: Philosophe, historienne et mystique* Colloque de

Cérisy-la Salle, du 21 juillet au 1er août 1974 (Paris: Aubier Montaigne, 1978).

[122]Simone Weil, "Hésitations devant le baptême–Deuxième Lettre," *Attente de Dieu*, 23.

[123]Ibid., 24.

[124]Weil, "Formes de l'Amour Implicite," 195.

[125]Weil,"Hésitations devant le baptême," 16-17.

[126]Janet Patricia Little, "Le Refus de l'Idolâtrie dans l'oeuvre de Simone Weil," *Cahiers Simone Weil*, Tome II, no. 4 (Paris: l'Association pour l'Etude de la Pensée de Simone Weil, 1979), 208.

[127]Simone Weil, "Israel et les Gentils," *Pensées sans ordre concernant l'amour de Dieu* (Paris: Gallimard, 1962), 47-62.

[128]Simone Weil, *Lettre à un religieux* (Paris: Gallimard, 1951).

[129]Weil, *La Pesanteur et la Grâce*.

[130]Simone Weil, *La Connaissance surnaturelle* (Paris: Gallimard, 1950).

[131]Marcion, the leader of a "heretical" movement in early Christianity during the second century A.D. An important teacher of gnosticism, he also influenced the development of early Christianity by his adherence to the writings of St. Paul. At that time, his teachings were considered a dangerous perversion of the Gospel. He believed in the teachings of St. Paul in whom he saw the antithesis between Law (Old Testament) and Gospel. (*Encyclopedia Britannica*, vol. 14, s.v. "Marcion") This is very similar to Weil's own attempt to resolve the dual roles of the divine–*Necessity* and *Love*–through her concept of creation/decreation (discussed in the chapter on Deconstruction and Self and in depth by Miklos Vëto in his study *La Métaphysique Religieuse de Simone Weil* [Paris: Librairie Philosophique J. Vrin, 1971]). Marcion's gnosticism is revealed by his attitude to matter and to the flesh; matter is treated as the principle of evil; the flesh was unworthy of redemption. Both Marcion and Weil emphasized the importance of the cross and suffering. Marcionite churches spread rapidly through the empire, but the movement lost strength and probably merged into Manichaeism (*Encyclopedia Britannica*, vol. 14, s.v. "Marcion"). Weil's own interest in the Cathars and Gnosticism ("Lettre à Déodat Roché," *Cahiers d'études cathares*, no. 2, reprinted in *Pensées sans ordre concernant l'amour de Dieu* [Paris: Gallimard, 1962]) must have reinforced her study of Marcion.

[132]Pétrement, *La Vie de Simone Weil*, vol. 2 (Paris: Fayard, 1973).

[133]Weil, "Israel," 168.

[134]Little, "Le Refus de l'Idolâtrie dans l'Oeuvre de Simone Weil," 201-2.

[135]Maurice Barrès, *Les déracinés* (Paris: Plon, 1935).

Chapter 4
Science and Uprootal

INTRODUCTION

As Weil had stated as a young student in 1929, it has been a human tendency since the beginning of time to distrust one's own senses and power of reasoning and to submit oneself to the authority of others, the primal form of 'déracinement'.[1]

From the beginning the human creature possessed the perception and consciousness by which the chaos of the universe would be transformed into order conceptualized and imposed by the self. Beyond consciousness of oneself and an infinite capacity for perception of the world, a human being possesses no inherent knowledge or talent. Following the primal stage of human ignorance humanity never stagnated; it always pushed forward in a continuous pursuit of understanding; the pursuit was pushed to the point of distrust and eventual challenge of information related by the senses, to the point of questioning the legitimacy of one's conceptualization of reality.

This had two major consequences in Weil's opinion: First, an *abnegation* of the self—one's distrust of one's own spiritual and intellectual capacities for a comprehension of reality was so great that obedience and submission, was, in large part, self-imposed; a helplessness and uncertainty led one to relinquish power and responsibility. Second—*dependence* upon some greater authority. The consolation found in submission to a higher spiritual order conditioned the human being to obedience, and submission extended to the realms of political and economic power. Science, the base from which the power of nations is determined becomes in Weil's essays, the realm of intellectual power and priesthood. Her perception of contemporary historical events was formed by this understanding of the relation between science and power.

Weil perceived a certain historical irony in the plight of Western Europe, in the physical and economic devastation of her homeland at the time of her writing. In this somewhat harsh judgement she saw her contemporaries as having willed their own dilemma by obedience to and participation in an evolution towards a valueless society. The same moral vacuum recognized by Adorno and Horkheimer of the Frankfurt school led individuals to grant authority to a force whose basis and direction they did not understand, resulting in the estrangement of science from reason and morality. George Friedman in his book, *The Political Philosophy of the Frankfurt School*, underlines the refusal of the modern scientist and individual to comprehend the potential danger of equating science and morality; since the Enlightenment, science and reason had led us towards a more progressive human condition but in our own times we have seen "the darker side of reason" when the methodologies and procedures of social scientists and philosophers did not permit their personal sense of morality to influence scientific principle.[2]

> Modernity's reason led into an unreasonable condition in which the common sense of the humane tradition had to be denied. . . .[3]

The destruction of the Second World War was only one of the many more violent consequences of this crisis of uprootal and of the need for reintegration and equilibrium between the demands of liberty and necessity.

> . . . la tempête qui nous entoure a déraciné les valeurs, et les met toutes en question pour les peser sur la balance, toujours fausse de la force. Nous, du moins, pendant ce temps, mettons-les toutes en question, nous aussi, chacun de nous pour son compte, pesons-les en nous-memes dans le silence de l'attention et souhaitons qu'il nous soit accordé de notre conscience une balance juste. . . .[4]

These lines written to a student in 1937 have proven themselves valuable as the basis for Weil's future studies on science. They clarify strongly the importance of 'déracinement', and 'enracinement' as dominant themes in Weil's writings on science. In the context of this chapter, Weil's usage of these terms shows how we have become strangers to ourselves, by spiritual and intellectual abnegation and dependence. By our obedience to power and symbol we have driven ourselves to extremes and have become ruled by absolutes—be it determinism, free will, or a blind and covetous search for mastery. As a result we have become separated from ourselves. For Weil, the key is reintegration through review, re-evaluation, and mediation. For this reason, she attempts to help bring about a conscious understanding of science through the analysis and teaching of its history and development. This chapter discusses the objectives and success of this endeavor.

Weil's writings on science include her early thesis, "Science et Perception dans Descartes." Her major essays on science were written during the period following France's capitulation to Germany and its subjection to occupying forces. Her historical study in Greek, Classical and Modern Sciences, "La Science et Nous" was written in Marseilles in 1941. Her article, "L'Avenir de la Science," a review of a scientific publication by the same title, was written in early 1942, appearing in the April 1942 issue of *Cahiers du Sud* under the anagrammic pseudonym, "Emile Novis." Her long essay, "Réflexions à

Propos de la Théorie des Quanta" appeared in the December 1942 issue of the same review *Cahiers de Sud* under the same pseudonym, its content directed particularly as a response to Max Planck's *Initiations à la Physique*, which was translated into French in February 1941. In addition most of her additional commentary on science, in the form of letters for the most part, was written in the early forties before her death, either at Paris or at Marseilles.[5]

EARLY WRITINGS–REINTEGRATION OF THEORY WITH ACTION

In 1929, with "Science et Perception dans Descartes," Weil compares modern science to Greek science. Gone are the mechanical models of physical phenomena like the mechanical construction the first astronomers used to reproduce the paths of the stars. Science, she wrote, which at the time of the Greeks, was the science of numbers, figures and machines, seems to be no longer anything more than that of pure relationships. In this light, Weil imagined the resuscitation of Thales and his reaction to the forms of modern science. Whereas the Greeks of the sixth and fifth centuries B.C. expressed the fundamental principles of physics through geometry, modern scientists have converted physics to algebraic language whose principles are used to express and manipulate physical phenomena–"la science des purs rapports." The resuscitated Thales would see the realm of intuition, of common sense, abandoned.

Thales would lament the demise of Greek mathematics, Weil indicates, as a source of knowledge and meaning in itself and would disdain the reduction of mathematics in modern times to a mere functionary role, to a language.[6] Repeatedly she refers in this essay to Poincaré's assertion that mathematics is to be conceived primarily as a language. Thus, according to Poincare whom many considered the greatest mathematician of our century, mathematics is no more than a language of convenience.

In this early essay, much of what Weil says concerning mathematics and science in undeveloped, and in certain respects, naive. In later writings she will examine in greater depth her idealization of Greek science and the slow polarization of science from culture proceeding from the Renaissance, sharply accelerated by the scientific developments of the early twentieth century. In this early essay on Descartes, the reversal of the role of mathematics and its reduction to language expresses the early awareness on Weil's part, of the reversal of the human role in the course of history; whereas Thales, Descartes, Alain, and Weil conceived mathematics, like human existence, as ends in themselves, both have been reduced to tools. Both have become tools in the scientific and political media, the power they formerly contained having become the end and themselves the means. In view of this simultaneous devaluation of mathematics, and human existence, Weil's concern for the changed role of mathematics has unsettling validity. The manipulation of symbols has been vital to the advancement of science but its effects on culture have been costly.

Weil points out the gap the resuscitated Thales would perceive between theory and application. Weil was to later criticize Roman culture for its priorities of use and mastery; she considered this a complete defamation of Greek science and culture. Weil praised the Greeks' balance between theory and application. In this early period, she felt that this was the needed priority of modern science.

Although the second part of this thesis is effective as an analysis of Perception, the first part's intended exploration of the gap separating "la pensée commune" from "la pensée scientifique" is less successful. Her initial arguments are striking but insufficiently developed. Descartes is considered the founder of modern science whose analysis of geometry was as critical for the development of classical and modern science as were Thales' geometrical discoveries for Greek science; Weil's orientation at this time was very strongly Cartesian. Her remarks on Thales and Greek science serve merely as an introduction to her commentary on the value and orientation of Descartes and his contribution to modern science.

> C'est... à l'origine de la science moderne qu'il nous faut remonter, à la double révolution par laquelle la physique est devenue une application de la mathématique et la géométrie est devenue algèbre, autrement dit à Descartes....[7]

Weil does review in depth Descartes' contributions to these two transformations and what dimensions of his analysis influenced both the Empiricist and Idealist Schools of thought. She shows also how Descartes maintained the valuable rapport between theory and application, and kept intact the original purpose and meaning of mathematical science despite its determination of other realms of scientific knowledge, such as physics.

But only in later essays did Weil effectively respond to her original question—that is, what are the reasons for the divergencies between science and culture.

As a philosophy instructor at the Lycée de Jeunes Filles of Le Puy, she put forth plans for a continuation of this effort through the teaching of the history of science and mathematics. She had just received from the friend the results of a study on the teaching of the history of the sciences and was apparently moved to share in this pedagological venture. The letter is valuable, not only because it discusses the success of a particular teaching experience, not only because it outlines the basic priorities of Weil's future studies on science, but most particularly because it is her most succinct expression of the ignorance and misunderstanding alienating the sciences and the humanities. Much of the responsibility for this lies in teaching, in education. It is interesting that Weil recognizes that the fault lies with the humanist as well as with the scientist.

> Mes élèves. . . . n'avaient aucune idée, ni de la liaison entre les sciences ni des méthodes qui ont permis de les créer. . . .[8]

Her main interest is the unification of abstract theory with its physical application, the reestablishment of individual contact with physical reality.

In a letter to Alain in 1935, Weil expressed particular interest in the methodology of Langevin for the teaching of the history of the sciences.[9] One can see the influence this philosopher had on Weil's ideas on science and its interpretation through pedagogy. Three stages should be stressed in the teaching of scientific history: 1) theory, 2) application of theory, and 3) work experience in the field of applied theory.[10]

Weil's views on pedagogy and the teaching of sciences were also influenced in part by Alain. As both Alain and Weil believed, it was only by analogy that one could find a common meeting point between abstraction and concrete analysis by projecting thought upon particular examples. She suggests the possible format of a physics manual for primary schools, where the interpretation of natural phenomena would be presented in the form of analogies, perception necessarily conceived as a stage in the acquisition of scientific knowledge.

These projects conceived by Alain and Weil, remind one of the initial efforts of eighteenth century philosophers of the Enlightenment, to record not only the scientific achievements of their time, but to recognize and explain through diagrams and pictures the dignity and intricacies of scientific application through craft, métier, and various forms of labor. The philosophers and rationalists of the early part of the century, significantly enough, had recognized the need for a renewed attempt for a synthesis of science and culture, for an elimination of the gap alienating theory from application. The vast work of the Encyclopédists had begun with the attempt to translate a much smaller work. If time and circumstance had allowed, perhaps Alain, Weil, Langevin, and others would have produced more credible results in that direction. Bergson, Alfred Binet, Paul Langevin, Leon Brunschvicg, Bachelard, Husserl, Meyerson and Milhaud were only a few among many involved in this effort.

I believe that Weil's reflections on science at the end of this second year of teaching contributed to the turn her views took concerning necessity and freedom. Her subsequent experiences in the factories and in the Spanish Civil War intensified her interest in the need to reintegrate theory and application, but her experiences with death, war and labor left her more resigned, and hardened. Her youth had been that of an incredibly energetic activist; yet she would continue her participation and commitment in later years with more detachment from particular social and political structures. As one reads works written after 1938 following her adventure in Spain and the months of work with Renault and other industries, the reader notices a greater emphasis on necessity, obedience, and a deeper, almost anguished awareness of the dependence of freedom on the contingencies of nature and technology. One wonders what would have occurred had Weil's own ambitions and the antisemitic policies of the Vichy government not prevented her from returning to teaching, had the war and the Occupation not scattered or destroyed theoreticians like Brunschvicg, Bergson, Langevin, or Bachelard. Perhaps, the sense of domination and destruction that ended that era would have been corrected or reoriented in part by the realization of pedagogical projects and the work of respected philosophers and scientists in closing the gap between theory and application, between science and culture, between morality and progress.[11] The demands of war, unfortunately, interrupted the remedial transition towards reintegration, towards true "enracinement."

A COMPARATIVE VIEW OF THE PERIODS OF SCIENTIFIC DEVELOPMENT

GREEK SCIENCE

> beau–enracinement--pacte entre soi et ses propres conditions d'existence–cercle du temps–faire que le temps soit un cercle et non pas une ligne....[1]

Weil's respect for Ancient Greece was based on the fact that Greek culture, philosophy, science and religion were determined by principles of order, necessity, harmony, balance and renewal. These principles resembled most closely Weil's conception of true "enracinement".

The goal of Greek science was an understanding of the relation between order and the conditions determining its presence, as opposed to what Weil and others define as the goal of Classical and Modern science, that is, the rapport between desire and the conditions determining the satisfaction of its demands. In Weil's view, the Greek conceptualization of order relates more effectively to the universe than does the idea of desire, project, effort.

Yet there are parallels between both concepts. The relations of each order to its object or goal contain identical conditions. The same necessities of space and time constitute both obstruction and support for the creators of order and project. Reflecting upon the conditions of an order is to conceive it as already established. This order relates reciprocally to those resulting from work and project. Every act presupposes an order within the universe along with certain proportional relationships.

But the spirit of each of the two sciences differs essentially. Wherever order was perceived, the Greeks reproduced an image of it, submitting to its laws or principles as an expression of universal necessity. Their concept of natural law was rigorous, but its finality and discipline reinforced poetical balance and harmony.

She relates "les jeux mathématiques des Babyloniens où on se donnerait la solution avant les données. . . ."[13] to modern mathematical sciences. One works through axioms as did the Greeks, but our choice of axioms is arbitrary. Her brother evidently maintained that modern mathematics still had its basis in reality, "la matière dure."

". . . tu parles d'art et de matière dure, mais je ne puis concevoir en quoi consiste cette matière. . . ."

For Weil, mathematical symbol has no material basis. As Weil implies, it is a metaphor diminished in meaning because of loss of contact with the reality it expresses.

The Greeks believed that the harmony and order of the universe was governed by mathematical laws. Perhaps this accounts for their major interest in and development of the science of geometry. The essential difference between Babylonian and Greek mathematics, writes Weil in a letter to her brother, is that the Greeks refused to exercise mathematics for its own sake. She believed that this was most probably the reason for the delay in translating the algebraic treatises they had inherited from the Babylonians,[14] the transcription of these treatises into Greek geometry by Diophantus could have taken place much earlier, along with the major developments in Greek mathematics of the 6th and 5th centuries, B.C. Their interest was in relating theory to concrete examples, not only for the sake of technical applications but for an understanding of their place in the world and for an identification with the structure of the universe. Their study of mathematics helped them to develop a conception of the workings of natural law. Greek mathematics and art had this common purpose. The Greeks' order is more justifiable to Weil than that of the Babylonians because the latter relates to concrete matter transformed by geometrical laws.

It is generally assumed that the Egyptians discovered geometry through the practice of land measurement. The seasonal overflow of the Nile would destroy the boundary of everyone's land. This discovery, as others, came about for utilitarian purposes; in the same way the knowledge of numbers originated with the Phoenicians' commerce and business dealings. In the seventh century, B.C., Miletus maintained political independence, and kept up a prosperous commercial connection with Egypt and Babylon. This is the town where Thales lived (624-548 B.C.);the legend is that he earned his living by selling salt for which he seems to have traveled in Egypt and in Chaldea. Thales supposedly imported into Ionia the methods of surveying that he discovered in use in Egypt.[15] The discovery of rational geometry is generally attributed to him. He arrived at the theorem of proportions by which he calculated the height of the pyramids and the theorem of the triangle inscribed in a semi-circle.[16]

As Weil discusses the history involved with the development of geometry she considers Thales's discovery of similarity between triangles ("à l'heure où l'ombre de l'homme est égale à l'homme, l'ombre de la pyramide est égale à la pyramide") to be an example of the Greeks' transposition of the inherited Babylonian art of algebra into geometry.[17]

Weil's belief that most of the Greeks' discoveries stem from the principle of proportion, expressed through their search either for the proportional average of two numbers or that of two such proportional means,[18] is shown in her discussion of developments in Greek geometry following Thales. She offers a hypothetical rendering of the properties of a rectangular triangle which history attributes to Pythagoras; the details and justification of this discover had hitherto been unknown

> C'est que cette découverte a pour origine le problème d'une moyenne proportionnelle entre deux quantités connues. Deux triangles semblables ayant deux côtés non homologues . . . représentent une proportion à trois termes.[19]

In further illustration of the dominant theme of proportion, Weil also analyzes closely Menaechmus's discoveries on the properties of cones, and his solution of the duplication of the cube.[20] As Weil mentions, Menaechmus was the student of Plato and one of the two geometricians who solved the mystery about the duplication of the cube.[21] The other was Archytas, who vulgarized many of Pythagoras's original discoveries, who, according to Weil, solved it through the use of a torus. Menaechmus solved the problem by his work with cones (two parabolas, or one parabola and hyperbola).[22]

Thus proves Weil, there is a continuous series of problems whose solution was based on the principle of proportion referring respectively to Thales's initial discovery in geometry through proportional measurement, to Pythagoras's discovery of the triangle rectangle, and to Menaechmus's discovery of the duplication of the cube.

The chief extant sources of our knowledge of Greek arithmetic are Books VII-X of Euclid's *Elements*, the *Introduction of Arithmetic* (of Nicomachus—end of first century, A.D.), and the *Arithmetic* of Diophantus (third century, A.D.). It should be pointed out that, while Euclid shows a purely mathematical interest in the rigorous demonstration of the theorems about numbers, Nicomachus and Iamblichus are very largely influenced by the mystic numerology of the earlier Pythagoreans and Plato.[23]

In the Hellenic period (650 to 300 B.C.), Greek philosophical thought offered diverse explanations of the origin and the purpose of the universe. There were three main tendencies—The Ionian, The Pythagorean and the Eleatic Schools: the Ionian school was represented by Heraclitus who defined existence as an unstable becoming. This was the final reality which could be understood not through intelligence, but through intuition. The Pythagorean school sought this final explanation in number, an abstract principle not directly available through the senses. The Ionian philosophers as did Heraclitus recognized spiritual properties in matter. The Pythagoreans attributed physical and even moral qualities to numbers. The divergencies as well as similarities of these schools provide the basis for the development of the principles of continuity and discontinuity, and the opposing philosophies of Idealism and Materialism. The Eleatic School to whom belonged Leucippus and Democritus prepared the development of materialism through their atomic theories.[24]

Pythagoras was a philosopher of the sixth century B.C., whose ideas were revived in the first centuries of the Christian era. What is important in his influence is his discovery that phenomena which appear heterogeneous through sensation, may nevertheless indicate a definite numerical relationship. Figures varying in shape may have the same surface. Musical sounds are produced according to intervals (octave, fifth, fourth), which follow a numerical law. Imbued with this idea Pythagoras extended his study of arithmetic beyond commercial needs (*Stobaeus*, I, p. 20, I). He and his school came to the conclusion that number and its properties constitute the basis of all things. Hence number is not an abstraction; it is a concrete reality, although our senses cannot directly apprehend it. Numbers for each spatial, physical and even spiritual property are clearly defined. By their combinations they give birth to the beings and the things which we see. The contributions which the Pythagorean school made to arithmetic, geometry and astronomy were very remarkable. They definitely directed Greek science along rational paths.[25] This is a reflection of the spirit of the times, the conceptualization of the universe in terms of harmonic regularly ordered relationships, concretized through mathematical units. The notion of proportion is a reflection of this order and harmony.

The legend about Thales and the pyramids was important because the geometricians of Antiquity reasoned obscurely upon the triangle, the circle, without a methodological means of judging the structure and its proportional change in terms of a geometrical image.[26] Even more illustrative of this sense of necessity, rigor and balance is Thales's initial discovery when he realized the infinite number of proportions varying with the strength of sun and shadow, thus introducing the theory of variable proportion, that is, function.[27]

Proportion is a dominant theme in Greek mathematics, particularly evident in the Pythagorean theorem and the discoveries involved with commensurable and incommensurable numbers that have been analyzed by Weil.

Weil associates the discovery of incommensurables to the principle of proportional means, relating in turn to the Greeks' conclusion that the diagonal of a square is incommensurable. For this end, she reviews Socrates' interrogation of a slave, in a passage of *Menon*, on the subject of the duplication of a square. Socrates did so to prove that the capacity for rational understanding is common to all. He leads the slave to conclude that it is possible to duplicate a square by use of the diagonal. This understanding of the diagonal, insists Weil, must stem from a knowledge of incommensurables.[28] She also discusses an unidentified text by Aristotle in which he demonstrates the incommensurability of a diagonal "par l'absurde," because if the diagonal were commensurable, the even number would be equal to the odd number. The number that is composed of both even and odd number factors is evidently the one that measures the diagonal. Since the Pythagorians, who discovered incommensurable numbers, consider Arithmetic the study of even and odd numbers, they could be credited with the discovery, also, of the diagonal as the means to duplication of a square. Weil believed the Greeks' reaction to the discovery of incommensurables must have been very favorable.

The discovery of incommensurables served to reassure the Greeks that everything can be conceived in terms of "rapport" or "proportion"; the system of number theory and the discovery of commensurable and incommensurable units is an expression of this. Proportion, as the Greeks conceived it, provided the means for retaining in a single point of thought the diversity of time and space. Without proportion, thought would be impossible. Paradoxically, the principles of regularity (or proportion) and diversity must work together so that thought is constantly on the point of destruction by the diversity of space and time, but always retrieved by the presence of regularity or proportion. As thought and physical being are dispersed through time, physical and conceptual existence are unified throughout the diversity of its experience by a sense of proportion. In equating the observer's view of the diversity of the world of art in terms of the harmonic proportions originally put forth by a creator or artist, Weil expresses her sympathy for the omniscient viewpoint held by Greek tradition, of logos and continuum and unity. Her distrust of an evolving relativist position was evident, but the complexity of her views on structure and difference in her writings relating to science and culture have been underestimated. Thus Greek science, with its concepts of logos, harmony, continuum and discontinuum expresses the ideal philosophy of a healthy society. In Weil's view, their's was the path towards true "enracinement."

Algebra—Symbol and Meaning. In her writings on relativity and Quantum Theory, Weil attributes to the rupture between Classical and Modern science not only the emergence of the discontinuum principle but also the different role of Algebra, or mathematical symbols. In Physics algebra became no more than a means to summarize established relationships between concepts of Physics accumulated through experimentation.

As Weil proves in "L'Enseignement des Mathématiques," Descartes considered mathematics as a principle of explanation, the sole means of human control over nature; it was not yet reduced to the role of a language, that of a system of signs and signifiers. The use of letters to represent proportional relationships was used by the Renaissance scholars to preserve the original equations transmitted through the Greeks, Hindus and Arabs. The algebraic equation communicates the idea of function. The algebraic forms of the Renaissance are the modern equivalent of Greek geometry; both represent combinations of continuous quantities analogous to distances. The Fourier series on heat are an example of the effectiveness of Algebra in such an analogy.[29]

Since the major break at the end of the nineteenth century, the role of algebra has progressively grown in importance to the point that physicists have come to regard it as signified material in itself communicable only through itself.

But the demands of algebraic formulae and ordinary language are different, evidently. Relationships between ideas cannot be totally grasped by relationships between letters as symbols. The attempt to express relationships between ideas in equations, which are handled according to algebraic laws and numerical data from the experiment, can lead to results which, once translated into spoken language, violently oppose common sense. In such cases, there may be a false appearance of profundity, states Weil, because even profound philosophical and mystical meditations constitute contradictions and untranslatable concepts for ordinary, communicable language. However, for algebraic formulae, it is totally different.

Through the devaluation of symbols and mathematical formulae, science expresses a general social phenomenon. Through the multiplicity of signs and symbols, we have estranged ourselves from the patterns of our own thoughts and minds.

Weil's formula to describe the devaluation of contemporary civilization is "l'argent, le machinisme, l'algèbre."[30] By algebra she means that referents are replaced by their signs. Things are totally consumed by the presence of symbols which represent them.[31]

Weil was especially critical of contemporary science, describing it as unintelligible to ordinary people, obscure even to the scholars themselves whose specialization left them ignorant of domains beyond their own field of expertise. Science, has lost its initial purpose which was the search for Truth and the Good and has been become oppressed, overwhelmed by signs that engendered themselves. The more scientific progress accumulated combinations of signs, the more thought was estranged, unable to comprehend the notions dealt with.

In "Réflexions à propos de la Théorie des Quanta," later cited and commented by Arendt in *The Human Condition*,[32] Weil warns against the rapidly increasing specialization of science which renders control and verification of scientific theories more and more difficult. Since science is concerned with physical phenomena it ought to function consequently as representation. Weil believes that scientific explanations or formulae fail in their symbolic function because they do not communicate meanings translatable into human speech and thought.

The estrangement through dependence on signs and formulae, which in itself is a reversal of the relationship between the means and the end, becomes the symbol of law to which all oppressive society subjects individual thought, a negative form of 'déracinement.' Signs, words, and algebraic formulae in the field of learning, money, and credit in economics are all the function of realities;[33] that is, signs and symbols constitute the substance of social relationships. This indicates the extent to which signs and symbols, originally the means to expression and understanding, have themselves usurped the place of reality in a movement of uprootal, 'déracinement'. Individual estrangement from reality conceived in terms of symbols and signs reflects the absence of thought and conscious reflection as a mediating, integrating force between the individual and that person's social and physical reality.

CLASSICAL SCIENCE

There are three main principles that characterize the period of Classical Science according to Weil: 1) Work, 2) Necessity, and 3) Entropy.

Work:
> Entre le désir et la satisfaction de ce désir il y a pour nous une distance qui est le monde même. . . .[34]

There was a rebirth of scientific culture during the Renaissance, considered by Weil as the dawning of the capitalist regime. During this period the liaison between theory and application was recognized for the first time. From the era of Descartes and Newton in the late Renaissance to the end of the 19th century, Weil defines this period in terms of the aspirations and the goals of its philosophers and scientists. This was the period of Classical Science.

Classical science attempted to show all phenomena as a manifestation of the principle of labor. Thus the universe was defined by the classical scientists' representation of the relationship between sovereign human act and the limiting conditions imposed by certain inevitable laws of natural necessity, mechanical and geometrical laws, limiting human action, which Weil refers to as "la malédiction du travail," more specifically as "la malédiction originelle."[35]

The law defining work is that of indirect action. According to this principle each simple step involved in the execution of work is independent of all others and only indirectly related to the desired objective.

An important step took place when the classical scientists derived from the principle of work the concept of energy, which henceforth formed the basis of studies of natural phenomena. From the support LaGrange found in work previously done by Bernouilli and d'Alembert,[36] and by means of differential equations, he arrived at the single formula defining all possible states of equilibrium or movement of any system of bodies affected by the forces of mass and/or speed. Maxwell discovered the "valeur explicative," that is, the infinite application of a mechanical model designed to describe a particular phenomenon.[37] At the heart of these revelations was the concept of energy derived from the principle of work.

By the formulation of mechanical models, it is understood, maintains Weil, that the relations between two successive conditions of matter is equivalent to the relationship between the initial step and the final point of completion of a project of human labor. For each type of phenomena are noted numeric equivalencies between measurements taken in the course of observed experiments as well as a common rate or equivalency in weight and distance. The concept of work is perpetually present.

Necessity and Entropy: Weil accepts the Manichean notion that the spirit is destroyed by the expansion of time and space; as expressed through the symbol of the cross, human effort extends itself across the superimposed structures of time and space, perpendicularly joined. The symbol of crucifixion appropriately is representative of eternity as the human effort which extends itself, is endlessly dispersed in the perpetuity of space and time. Time separates one from oneself by the temporal distance put between what the thinking creature is and what one aspires to be. A fusion of aspiration with reality, if at all possible, is momentary and absorbed into the past. Time and space constitute the sources of necessity in Classical Science, invariable, separate entities which limit human existence. Although Weil was deeply religious, it is safe to regard her use of the cross in this context as an objective image of eternity. Certainly the crucifixion symbol conveys vividly the estrangement by inevitable finitude and submission to nature. It is an image particularly fitting for the understanding of necessity and determinism in the Classical period.

Time expresses not only the power of natural necessity but the superior force of destruction over those who build. Nature's law of necessity directs time by the gradual imposition of old age, by the rapid erasure and opposition entailed in slow painful efforts in daily life.

In the contest between human life and time, the latter has the advantage. The rapidity with which fields can be burned and human life extinguished, in contrast to the time needed to plant, grow and nurture, gives the creator the disadvantage. On the other hand, neither creation nor destruction gains the advantage in terms of space and mass, both expressions of natural necessity. Space, states Weil, "est indifférent à toutes les directions...(et) les poids de la dynamique sont des poids élastiques qui ne tombent jamais sans rebondir. . . ."[38]

They are both, however, obstacles which necessitate labor. The principle of work and the notion of energy involved therein are defined by these two basic sources of limitation and power. In addition, Weil states, "toute transformation a un sens qui n'est pas indifférent."[39] That is, every change is governed by the law of entropy, expressed in the mathematical language of physics.

Entropy is the name for the function mathematically formulated by Clausius in which an amount of heat is provided to a system at the time of a reversible change or transformation. This quantity of heat was yielded at a certain absolute temperature. The entropic level of a system indicates its level of order. If the system gives off heat, the amount of heat is negative and the entropic level goes down. When it receives heat, the heat is positive and entropy increases. Entropy remains constant during a reversible transformation or cycle bringing it back to its initial state. In the case of irreversible change or transformation, entropy increases; the entropic level of a system increases which determines its energy degradation.[40] This phenomenon is described by Weil as "une transformation de l'énergie, telle qu'il ne se trouve aucun moyen quoiqu'il arrive . . . de rétablir . . . l'état initial . . . la grandeur qui augmente toujours sauf intervention de facteurs exterieurs. . . ."[41] This is the crowning achievement of Classical Science. The increase in entropy reflects an increase in energy.

Because of this major discovery, the classical scientist was able to interpret all phenomena in terms of simple variations of energy, as expressions of the simple law of entropy. Weil recognizes the law of entropy as an expression of natural necessity, of the total indifference of the universe to our desires and needs.

The impersonal constraints of natural necessity provide us with a view of ourselves. Indifferent nature imposes on us this objectifying view which serves as a rein on ourselves, a means of control or self-discipline. With these elements of limit: time, space, distance, work, energy, entropy, with this essential contact with impersonal necessity, one's ignorance and illusions give way lucidly to reality and knowledge. Necessity is not only a source of constraint and limit, but also the means of contact, of revelation as one understands the systematized involvement of oneself with the world.

Finally, Weil sees in Classical Science the refinement of the concept of necessity as a purifying force. Classical Science led to an interpretation of all phenomena in terms of work; energy is an attempt to systematize, to reduce the workings of the universe to a single principle, a single expression of necessity.

Weil recognized the inevitable end to the era of Classical Science, its own limits enclosed within itself. Weil was right to do so. Beyond the analogy of the most simple form of labor with events and natural phenomena, Classical Science had little more to offer. Discoveries and facts have accumulated in the course of scientific history without possible integration into the scope of the human mind. The amount of unsynthesized scientific data surpasses our grasp. Consequently, there is even greater distance between conceptualization and reality by the alienation of original thought from the facts it interprets. The failure to renew, maintain and grow in contact with the true scale of reality hindered further contributions of Classical Science.

Yet, it is significant that Weil rejected the limitations of the Classical vision of the world and the human being, a vision reflecting the positivistic belief in determinism and natural necessity. Even if a single human mind could synthesize vast data and experimentation, even if Classical Science could provide one with the means for expanding the conceptual capabilities of the human mind, there would still be an essential limitation.

Weil identified with the main premises of Classical Science; yet she challenged the extremes of Positivism and deterministic beliefs. In the works of Balzac, Zola, and Dickens, the energetic spirit of the industrial and technological age of Western Europe in the nineteenth century manifested itself. In the works of these writers representative of Realism and Naturalism there is deterministic interpretation of events (*La Grandeur et la Décadence de César Birotteau, Great Expectations, L'Assommoir, Le Travail, Le Bête Humaine*, etc.). The cultural and scientific tendency of the time was to define in terms of work, production, and energy. Carried to extremes, it produced the later works of Zola, Barrès, and Taine. It was such an extreme vision of blind necessity, Weil claimed, that paralyzed science at the peak of its Classical period. The world is certainly that which alienates desire from satisfaction; it is also more than that, Weil insists, that is, we possess an element of free will without which we could not exist. This independent moral judgement with which we are endowed, which defines us partially, is unaccounted for by Classical Science, in Weil's view; in fact it is contradicted or acted against. Defining a human life by the necessary limits of its action, is to disregard the element of independent will and morality. This is, evidently, counter to Greek science, whose goal was that of Truth in terms of harmony, equilibrium, proportion, beauty, as expressions of Good. Thus in Weil's view, in the period of Classical Science the drive of mastery and desire often became confused with the search for Truth, for Good. Power became the equivalence of Truth.

Weil's objection to such a paralyzing deterministic scheme of the human creature's relation to the world shows also a reaction against the idea of causality held by the Positivists and its defense through the rationalist explanations of Brunschvicg. This reaction was of an intuitive and spiritualistic order. It is another indication of how difficult it is to categorize Weil's thought in any particular domain as it contains so many elements associated with opposing camps or schools of thought in philosophy, literary and scientific history. She deplores the rejection of determinist belief, yet in her own recognition of the necessary element of free will and freedom, she approaches arguments of the advocates of relativity such as Bergson and Bachelard.

"Déracinement/Enracinement" are opposing yet complementary forces in the form of free will, necessity, discontinuity, continuity, harmony, dissonance, etc. It is very significant that in Weil's perception of Classical Science, she perceives the necessary complementarity of opposing forces within the principle of work. She is critical of the extreme deterministic vision unbalanced by the opposing force of free will.

MODERN SCIENCE

The main consequence of Modern Science was that the concept of work, project had become irrelevant.

> ... on en a retiré l'analogie entre les lois de la nature et les conditions du travail, c'est-à-dire, le principe même....[42]

According to Classical physics the path of a stone rising outlines a straight vertical line. The stone is considered as a single point, a single atom, and it is more complicated, combining movements of particles of stone and of air. The conditions or laws of necessity governing these units or atoms of movement are different from those of Classical physics.

Two main ideas separate Classical and Modern Sciences: 1) the theory of Relativity, 2) Quantum theory.[43]

The theory of Relativity mentioned here and developed in the era of Modern Science was not the generalized one which extends to all conceivable movement the idea of relativity that Classical mechanics applied only to straight and uniform movement. It relates rather to Special Relativity. Through a series of experiments, a particular measure of the speed of light was obtained. The findings of experiments in the late nineteenth century led to conceiving the speed of light as constant in every direction. Weil believed there was a contradiction between these two main sources of findings; a limited or finite speed cannot be constant in every direction if one measures it in terms of a system which is itself moving in a certain direction.[44] Translated into algebraic formulae, these two findings appeared irreconcilable.

Weil criticized but did not ever develop an effective analysis of the Relativity theory. However, her remarks on time and space in addition to the brief comments here are indicative of her views on relativity.

The Quantum Theory established by Planck centers on the main principle of science, that is, the concept of energy. It is the theory that energy of action generates further energy during the course of time; however, the production of energy does not take place in a regular, constant and continuous progression. The factor of discontinuity determines this major scientific theory, that is, the energy which is produced manifests itself in uneven, discontinuous quantities, in successive bonds, and these bonds, are called quanta. The Quanta Theory destroyed and removed from the realm of Modern Science the principle of work, labor, Weil stated, by the element of discontinuity.

Planck introduced the concept of discontinuity into the study of energy. Weil discussed at length the association of discontinuity with irreversibility, a concept closely linked to the analysis of black ray. The principle of the degradation of energy, the second principle of thermodynamics, called–Clausius's principle, brought the idea of irreversibility into the study of energy. A transition from a more probable state to a loss probable one is almost irreversible.

> ... si on balaie de la main des caractères d'imprimerie qui formaient un vers de Valéry, on les mettra en désordre, et si on les balaie encore de la main un grand nombre de fois, on ne reformera pas un vers de Valéry. . . .[45]

In this manner, Boltzmann, physicist and a contemporary of Planck, had explained the irreversible transformation of mechanical energy in heat energy involved with friction. Through the use of probability, Planck reproduced the phenomenon of black ray. Discontinuity was found through his study of these probability formulae. Since these probability formulae reflected the workings of energy, the principle of discontinuity was inevitably related.

> ... le plus singulier est que, lorsque Planck affirma: 'la matière ne peut émettre l'énergie radiante que par quantités finies proportionnelles à la fréquence', il ne fut pas conduit à cette proposition par l'étude des phénomènes microscopiques où l'expérience permet de mesurer des seuils, mais par celles d'un phénomène macroscopique–principe de la dégradation de l'énergie....[46]

This finding was applied to all transformation of energy. Consequently, the concept of project or work, of continuous movement expressed by the geometrical image of the straight line, no longer provided the means to understanding the physical change.

Weil was critical of the fact that what brought the principle of discontinuity to the forefront, was not experimentation, but probability formulae, what Weil termed more specifically as "une transition naturelle entre la notion d'entropie et celle de probabilité. . . ."[47] (Cf. Section on *Discontinuity and Continuity*).

Significantly at this time, chance was linked to the movement and interaction of atomic particles. Brownian movement showed that matter seemingly in equilibrium was not in such a homogeneous state at the microscopic level. Weil discusses in depth the assimilation accomplished by Boltzmann of probability factors involved in entropy and in atomic particle movement.

> ... un mouvement naturel de la pensée amena à rapprocher les deux probabilités surgies simultanément dans les esprits, celle qui est liée à l'entropie et celle qui est liée aux atomes, et à les regarder comme une seule et même probabilité. . . .[48]

The break-off point between Classical Science and Modern Science occurred when entropy, formerly defined as a function of energy which increases in the form of heat, is redefined as a numerical calculation of probability in the combination and movement of atoms.[49] This was, Weil believed, "un désaccord entre la raison et la science. . . ."[50] The error, in her view, was in believing that a mere change of level brings a radical transformation to the laws of Nature. Rationally, however, a change in scale constitutes an increase or decrease in the distribution of energy, but no change in the relationship governing the transformation.

As one goes from the immediately perceivable physical world to that of atomic particles, heat becomes movement, a change which, according to our perception, would be not merely quantitative but qualitative, a difference in the nature of movement and heat. This essential difference applies to the conditions of work. The principle of the conservation of energy allows results only proportional to effort exerted. Yet one does not always profit from the full extent of the original effort exerted.

Entropy has no meaning for a theoretical world of atomic particles where there is only movement; but it is a relevant concept previously defined by Classical physics, an immediately perceivable world in terms of physical phenomena, that is, in terms of work, and energy. It had to be interpreted so as to relate to both the physical and the theoretical worlds. Consequently it was assimilated into a formula of probability.

The presence of discontinuity came about through this problematic "changement d'échelle" as well as through the basic premise of the Quantum theory, that is, energy produced in uneven, discontinuous quantities.

It is significant that acausality and antideterministic views have given way in recent years to a new sense of determinism, that is, a recognition of a minimal element of predetermination present in the workings of relativity, fragmentation, and displacement. It is interesting that the midway point Weil arrived at in her acceptance and challenge of contemporary science, is reflective of the self-questioning taking place in the early years of the modern scientific era, by such figures as Einstein and Schrödinger. Weil lacked, perhaps, technical expertise, although in the later years of her life, she made a very serious study of the natural sciences and their historical development. But the correspondence of her conclusions to those of contemporary scientists and philosophers as well as respected writers of our period shows the significance of her perceptions. The point in reviewing her seemingly contradictory ideas about discontinuity, determinism, the invariability of space and time is not to prove or disprove their validity, but to show once again, how Weil's conclusions were so much a reflection of the tensions of her time. It is, however, striking that philosophers and scientists like Ilya Prigogine and Isabelle Stengers, have recently concluded the necessity for a reintegration of technology with nature, thus articulating the need for a new alliance, an inevitable compromise between the forces of determinism and freedom, of permanence and instability, of continuity and discontinuity, of relativity and invariability, of time and space, of chance and necessity[51]—in other words, the need for a new "enracinement" as envisioned by Weil. As general and prejudicial as her perceptions were at times, the judgments to be discussed here were significantly accurate in perceiving this need for reintegration and the necessary bringing together of culture and science.

THE CRISIS OF DETERMINISM AND ACAUSALITY

> ... la vie, le destin, la liberté, la spontanéité, devenaient les émanations de profondeurs enfouies, qui se voulaient inaccessibles à la raison. . . .(Prigogine and Stengers, *La Nouvelle Alliance*)[52]

Philosophical Climate: In examining Weil's views on science, particularly Classical science, it is useful to consider her in the context of her own time. In the first few decades of the twentieth century, the thoughts and writings of philosophers, sociologists, physicists, mathematicians and psychologists both reflected and influenced the general public's attitude towards science. The philosophy of the early twentieth century, which deeply affected the formation of young rationalists such as Weil, can be divided into three main movements—Empiric Positivism, Epistemological Idealism, and Spiritual Positivism.[53] The main personalities representative of each movement are well known. Comte, Taine, Renouvier, Brunschvicg, Bachelard, and Bergson are central figures of French philosophy.

Empiric Positivism developed slowly from the beliefs and writings of

Auguste Comte, former secretary to the utopian philosopher, Saint-Simon. A reaction against traditional metaphysics and Eclecticism, Empiric Positivism assumes a strict fixity and immutability in the laws of nature.[54] Taine is well known as a typical representative of Empirical Positivism. He applied to all realms of knowledge the empirical principles of natural science and subjected art to the same determinism he saw in nature. Based on eighteenth century French sensualism reinforced by Mill and Spencer, Taine's determinism appeared as a very strong although pessimistic doctrine which left little room for mysticism and free will.[55]

Among the critics of Empiricism and Positivism were many belonging to the Idealist and Epistemological schools. They formed the reaction against the exaggerated belief in the omnipotence and self-sufficiency of exact science. The beginnings of this movement was almost contemporary to that of Empirical Positivism. Kant, the founder of this movement, claimed that the existence of that knowledge was dependent on the human creature's conceptual capacity to bring things into relation with each other. Kant is considered the founder of the synthetic conception of knowledge by which knowledge is an act of reciprocal penetration from within and without, of the individual and the world.[56] In Weil's lifetime, this still formed the basis for a "critique des sciences." The adherents of this critical school consisted of scientists, mathematicians, and Epistemologists. Among these were the mathematician and astronomer, Henri Poincaré; Emile Borel, a mathematician who worked extensively on statistical probability; the physicist, Pierre Duhem; the chemist, Meyerson;[57] Gaston Milhaud, a writer on mathematics and philosophy. Among the Epistemologists were Hannequin, Hamelin, Couturat, Liard, Naville, Parodi, and particularly, the dominant figures of Brunschvicg and Bachelard.

In opposition to this rationalist movement represented by Idealists and Epistemologists like Poincaré, Brunschvicg and Bachelard, there was a general movement of anti-rationalism of which the early Existentialists and spiritual positivists were a part. Antirationalist existentialism dates from much farther back in time, in the writings of Montaigne, of Pascal in so far as he was opposed to Cartesian Rationalism, in Rousseau's opposition to the Encyclopédists.[58] The beginning of existentialism as an antirationalist movement is most usually recognized in Kierkegaard's revolt against Hegel, and his belief in the individual's power and mystery. The beginnings of spiritual positivism were inspired by the theories of Maine de Biran. Among its representatives were Ravaisson who emphasized the concept of Habit as evidence that freedom had penetrated into the necessity of Nature, that beauty was the Mind made manifest in Matter;[59] Lachelier, Ravaisson and Bergson were considered the founders of this renaissance of spiritual metaphysical positivism in France.[60]

There was, in addition, the influence on scientists of the ideas of the Vienna Circle and of logical positivism or empiricism that Brunschvicg criticized in his work, *Les Etapes de la Philosophie Mathématique*.[61] These movements suited rational analysis and modern science. The Vienna Circle, aspiring towards "Weltauffassung," based upon empiricism and logical atomistic analysis, was very receptive to physical sciences and mathematics. H. S. Hughes describes the movement as fully developed in the early 1920's. Ludwig Wittgenstein's *Tractatus Logico-Philosophicus*(1921) was

> ... the most influential philosophical work of the post-war years ... neopositivists were able to rehabilitate the scientific method in philosophy....[62]

Max Jammer indicated that, in Germany, the philosophical movements of the later nineteenth and early twentieth centuries prepared the intellectual climate for the formation and development of the modern quantum theory.

> .... contingentism, existentialism, pragmatism, and logical empirism rose in reaction to traditional rationalism and conventional metaphysics.....
> [63]

German physicists were often pressured into conforming with these new philosophical directions. This is significant because scientists of German nationality were responsible for most of the major developments in modern physics. To a certain extent, extrinsic factors led German physicists to seek and accept acausal quantum mechanics. Following Germany's defeat, the predominant intellectual environment of the Weimar intelligentsia was that of neoromanticism and antagonism towards the sciences and their applications of analytical rationality.[64] It is paradoxical that this period of deep hostility to physics and mathematics was one of its most creative. Following the German defeat in 1918, the self-assurance and confidence of scientists had to confront a drastically altered scale of public values and valuation of their own field. The pressure of German Idealism, irrationalism, and mysticism characteristic of the post-war mood was felt by scientists such as Wilhelm Wien, Freidrich Poske, Max Born, and Max Planck.[65]

In the Weimar intellectual milieu, there was a rejection of reason as an epistemological instrument because it was considered inseparable from positivism, mechanism, and materialism. This Life philosophy based on intuition, on the hunger for unmediated and unanalyzed experience affirmed the immediate apprehension of values and not causality as the proper object of scholarly or scientific activity. During this same period Oswald Spengler's *Decline of the West* appeared, the great statement of relativistic pessimism, expressing the general intellectual mood in Germany following its defeat. It was a major indictment of Classical physics and its principle of causality or determinism:

> ... the principle of causality, ... a "late" manifestation of the hatred of the powers of destiny, of the incomprehensible. . . .[66]

The wave of conversions to acausality in the latter part of 1921 prompted a series of public demonstrations in support of causality by major physicists. Planck on June 29, 1922, as secretary of the Prussian Academy used the opportunity of a special session honoring Leibnitz to affirm the transcendental character of the law of causality. Later, in the same year, he gave an entire lecture at the Prussian Academy reaffirming allegiance to the principle of causality:

> ... the assumption of a causality without exception, of a complete determinism, forms the presupposition and the precondition for scientific cognition. . . .[67]

It is significant that despite the contributions of Planck, De Broglie and Einstein to modern advances in physics towards the acceptance of indeterminacy, they themselves were caught in the transition.

Planck remained faithful to Classical Determinism up until his death in 1947. Yet the classical concept of determinism was menaced at the quantum level he introduced. Planck admitted that the world view based on causality was no longer entirely explanatory but that it remained along with statistical laws and indeterminacy a truthful and applicable concept.[68]

De Broglie converted twice to determinism, once in 1927, after which he adopted the indeterminist view of Heisenberg, Bohr, and others, and again in 1951, following the work of Jean-Pierre Vigier and David Bohm. It should be noted that such physicists as Einstein, De Broglie, Bohm, and Vigier had hoped to reduce the uncertainty relations of Heisenberg to a causal model.[69]

Einstein searched for a supercausal solution to the quantum problem by means of over-determined systems of differential equations.[70] It is somewhat ironic that Weil did not recognize Einstein's own struggle against the surge of indeterminacy. The complexity of his life and his involvement in science and politics is a demonstration of that, as shown by Ronald Clark in his biography of Einstein.[71] His own refusal of absolute determinism reflected, as did the opinions of Weil and others, the profundity of the crisis. Einstein believed that his fellow physicists were seeking a failure of causality without attempting to find possibilities for a causal solution.

Even before his technical paper was printed on the Uncertainty Principle Heisenberg declared in 1927:

> ... quantum mechanics establishes definitely the fact that the law of causality is not valid. . . .[72]

The impact of this final blow against determinism left philosophical thought in a state of flux and uncertainty. This doubt and unsureness led in great part to the early beginnings of twentieth century existentialist philosophy in the works of Husserl, Marcel, Weil, and Sartre, reflected by their confrontation of the inextricable involvement of the autonomous self with the powers of nature. The involvement of self with the world is inevitable as is that of free will with deterministic processes. Only two years following Heisenberg's declaration, Weil expressed in her thesis on perception the uncertainty and disorientation of self wavering between power and nature. In the years following, Weil progressed toward a more deterministic outlook; this can be attributed, certainly, to her own eventual conversion and evolving religious beliefs; but her changing viewpoint also deeply reflected the general evolution of philosophical and scientific attitudes towards an acceptance of both elements of determinism and indeterminacy (in the form of free will or in that of a self-governing autonomous process) as a fusion of forces inevitably involved with each other.

These were the influences and environment of Western Europe at the time of Weil's development and writing on science. She was in the middle of the vast crisis of determinism consuming the energy of philosophers and scientists; people were only beginning to understand the consequences of Planck's Quantum Theory (1905), the introduction of the Copenhagen School of Probability he represented, and Einstein's Relativity Theories of 1905 and 1916. Her commentaries reflect the uncertainty of her age. Weil's understanding of the recent advances in physics is exacting. The studies she undertook in the sciences must have been extensive in view of the concepts and ideas she handles with ease. One could not challenge nor devalue her views on the sciences by assuming her ideas had no credible basis of knowledge.

In her essays on science written after 1937, it seems evident that Weil was also experiencing a major shift in her philosophy. What is particularly striking is the combination of recognizable rationalist and anti-rationalist elements in this part of her work on science; it seems evident that she was at the crossroads of the two movements.[73] In her doctoral thesis and essays on science, the influence of Alain is extensive, particularly her development of the theme of "travail" and the needed link between theory and application. It is interesting, however, that, although these two above-mentioned themes persist in her work, the influence of Brunschvicg later becomes more dominant, as shown by her deep interest in Pythagorism, in Mathematics, in contemporary and recent scientific developments. These were themes touched upon by Alain, but developed extensively by Brunschvicg.

Determinism: Determinism is a scientific principle according to which every action and fact has a cause, and in the same conditions, the same causes always produce the same results. Consequently, facts are determined by necessary and universal laws. In philosophy it expresses the interdependence of phenomena noted throughout the ages, even those of which we are ultimately ignorant.[23] In 1814 LaPlace, in his *Essai Philosophique sur les Probabilités*, explained the concept in the following way:

> Nous devons envisager l'état présent de l'univers comme l'effet de son état antérieur et comme la cause de ce qui va suivre. Une intelligence qui, pour un instant donné, connaîtrait toutes les forces dont la nature est animée et la situation respective des êtres qui la composent, si d'ailleurs elle était assez vaste pour soumettre ces données à l'analyse, embrasserait dans la même formule le mouvement des plus grands corps de l'univers et ceux du plus léger atome; rien ne serait incertain pour elle, et l'avenir comme le passé serait présent à ses yeux. . . .[75]

Scientists and philosophers perceived in LaPlace's hypothesis the true definition of determinism. But it is only an ideal determinism; it is a subjective, abstract concept arrived at through a mathematician's reasoning. From an epistemological point of view, determinism has two main aspects: determinism of facts, which postulates efficient cause, and determinism of laws which determine statistical regularity and probability.[76] In other words there are two levels of determinism—the cosmic level of natural determinism and the experimental level of scientific determinism. In Weil's time, there was still a certain amount of doubt among those who protested the distinction between universal necessity or determinism, and scientific determinism. To a certain extent the latter implies the former and is an expression or manifestation of it. Weil herself comments on this and sees a certain absurdity in distinguishing between the two. Weil's ideas on determinism reflect an identification with the classical vision of philosophy and science expressed in LaPlace's definition. In Classical Science, it was accepted that the universe possessed the character of an isolated system, and therefore scientific determinism was an expression of universal necessity; the fact that this view was accepted by proponents of both infinitist philosophy (Giordan Brun, Descartes, Spinoza, for example, and of finitism such as Dühring and Nietzsche,[77] all of whom adhered to rigorous determinism) demonstrates how deeply ingrained this classical belief was.

The complexity of the struggle between deterministic and non-deterministic beliefs explain in part the contradictions found in Weil's ideas on determinism, probability, and discontinuity. Determinism, necessity, finality are dominant features of Weil's writings on science. Particularly in her later works, her deterministic view of the world became stronger and stronger. The influence of Platonic philosophy became more dominant, and a reinforced Christian monotheism emerged from the slightly pantheistic view of her earlier days. Spinoza's influence on Weil's deterministic views was enormous. It is important to understand her discussion of necessity and the difference in cultural representation of the concept by societies affected by the transitions from Greek to Classical and from Classical to Modern Science. In Greek science, necessity was a source of unity and harmony expressed through circular images, providing security and consolation through the social, religious and scientific identification with harmony, balance, and moderation. In the period of Classical Science marked by Cartesian mathematics and Newton's gravitational theories, the circle gave way to the symbolic and geometrical image of the straight line. Necessity or the forces of both scientific and universal determinism were expressed by the straight line as an expression of praxis (of spiritual transcendency).[78] Paradoxically, at the same time, the straight line became a symbol also of the human effort, the project for the affirmation of free will and power as societies began to understand the implications of expanding economic and technological power. The straight line expressed both Necessity and Freedom, where exteriority and individual will were represented by the collision of two straight lines pushing in directly opposite directions, neither giving way.[79] The straight line symbolizes all the deterministic forces of finality, necessity, causality. Weil perceives in the straight line the necessity of labor on the levels of science, perception, and universal law. The principle of work expressed through the straight line becomes both a humbling, limiting force as well as a means of deliverance from the limitations it symbolizes. In Weil's picture of Classical Science, the presence of phenomena such as energy, entropy, are expressions of necessity, of universal laws of expansion expressed by the image of the straight line.

As Weil sees Modern Science, there are no images beyond that of mathematical formulae which can capture the transitional changes affecting concepts of determinism (or necessity), free will, and relativity. In all fairness it should be recognized that although the crisis of determinism began with Planck's theory in the early twentieth century, concepts of scientific determinism were still in a state of flux at the time Weil was writing on science, that is, in the late thirties and early forties. Scientific developments had led many to reject traditional principles of determinism at both the scientific and universal levels. Many, on the other hand, reacted to the challenge in the other extreme, by clinging to the absolute forces of necessity in all realms, discounting any element of free will. Then there was the crisis of determinism within science itself, that is, scientists who, though not disputing necessity as a universal force, identified a different set of factors and laws determining scientific activity. Probability and change played greater roles in the interpretation of data and phenomena. Still there were scientists like Einstein who questioned the validity of rejection of scientific determinism on the atomic or microscopic level and doubted the greater emphasis on chance and probability.[80] It is interesting that in Weil's discussions of modern science, it is not the presence of discontinuity as a major concept that she questioned. Discontinuity is not a new force; it was particularly important in Greek mathematics and science, although its strength lay dormant for some time during the period of classical science. In fact she seems to evoke it as a force of vitalization and renewal with the idea that destruction and displacement lead to creation.[81] She arrives at the conclusion that because of the structure of classical scientific conceptions, they could progress no further without some radical change. They had imposed their own limits, their own source of stagnation. Classical science had to transform itself. Planck's Quantum Theory, based on the principle of discontinuity, provided the means of transformation. Weil and others feared the implications of dependency upon probability and chance as the means of applying discontinuity. This is an enriching feature of science and philosophy but its application through manipulation of probability formulae may be questioned. Strangely enough, however, it has been verified time and again though application to experimental situations. The bottom line becomes the measure of trust we attribute to progress based on formulae untranslatable in terms of logical thought. What is the danger in dependency upon concepts foreign to patterns of human thought processes?

Quantum Theory and Quantum Mechanics: The crisis of determinism was indirectly caused by the Quantum Theory of Max Planck (1900). Weil identified the crisis of determinism provoked by this theory as the beginning of the modern scientific era. Louis de Broglie, like most physicists and scientists of the time, also considered Planck's Quantum Theory as the dividing mark between Classical and Modern Science.

> ... as long as the physicists were unaware of quanta, they were unable to comprehend the profound nature of physical phenomena. ... [82]

Progress in Optics is intimately connected with recent advances in physics, particularly associated with the Quantum Theory and the later development of Quantum Mechanics. In *Continu et Discontinu en Physique Moderne*, Louis de Broglie explains the historic dilemma of undulatory and rectilinear propagation of light. It was a complicated controversy, involving a choice between traditional adherence to Cartesian concepts of geometry, that is, movement necessarily conceived through the structure of a straight line, and the scientific advances of interference and diffraction leading to the necessary structural description of light as a series of waves. It involved an even greater source of conflict, a dispute between those who conceived light as a series of continuous waves, and those who viewed it in the discontinuous structural form of corpuscular particles, that is, a choice between a predictable continuous structure and an unpredictable, discontinuous group of moving particles.[83] The vestiges of the rejected Cartesian image of geometrical movement remained central in the minds of early twentieth century rationalists. Weil herself found difficulty in accepting the concept of the wave, that is, movement conceived as a curve instead of in a straight line in the image of "praxis." Weil's own position reveals how complicated a controversy it was. Weil was among the rationalists who conceived movement in the traditional sense as a straight line. Yet by supporting Descartes' view of rectilinear propagation they were, by assoication with the development of that traditional viewpoint, supporting a view that light consisted of unpredictable discontinuous movement. It is significant that Weil, whose writings place such value on continuum, balance, and equilibrium, positioned herself with the rationalist point of view. As she wrote to a student in 1937:

> Quant à considérer la notion d'onde comme une notion *première* concernant la structure de la matière, ne serait-ce pas absurde? l'on ne pense une onde qu'au moyen des notions de choc et de poussée, appliquées aux fluides.[84]

De Broglie explained the main conflict between the corpuscular and wave theories as that of two antigonistic conceptions of the nature of light; according to one, light must be formed by corpuscular movement through space; according to the other, light manifests itself by the movements of waves.[85] In the nineteenth century, the results of experiments carried on by Young, and Fresnel supported the wave theory. Fresnel seemed to have found in wave concepts all the aspects of diffraction and interference known in his time; he succeeded in proving that the undulatory nature of light is not in contradiction with rectilinear propagation in homogeneous media. As De Broglie wrote:

> Fresnel comble cette lacune en montrant que la propagation rectiligne, est aussi une conséquence de la progagation des ondes. ...[86]

By 1900, the work and testing of the wave structure of light seemed incontestable. Yet the particular physical nature of the wave was unknown. The contributions of Vjolta, Coulomb, Oersted, Davy, Biot, Laplace, Gauss, Ampere, Faraday and others led to the development of electricity and John Clerk Maxwell's eventual creation of the general electromagnetic theory. Maxwell's discovery is significant for this discussion of De Broglie's wave theory because Maxwell saw in his general equations of electric phenomena, the possibility of light considered as an electromagnetic disturbance. He thereby caused the whole science of optics to be included in the framework of electromagnetism, thus uniting two domains which had seemed entirely Not In Dictionary ? Photoelectronics showed the limits of the wave theory that had not been known before the discovery of electromagnetic theory and the corpuscular concept returned, expecially with the development of Planck's Quanta Theory:

> ... la matière ne peut émettre et absorber cette lumière que par quantités finies et égales à hv . . . par "quanta". . . .[88]

According to De Broglie in his essay, *Continu et Discontinu en Physique Moderne*, all further developments on light theories confirmed Planck's hypothesis.[89] In 1905, Einstein interpreted this hypothesis by affirming that all light frequency is made up of corpuscular particles of energy hv. Yet despite this proof of the corpuscular nature of light, it was impossible to return to former concepts affirming its absolute nature because the science of interference and diffraction gave solid arguments of support to the wave theory.[90] The problem was to reconcile the two structures, both conceived as necessarily present and vital to the understanding of light.⁹¹.

Bohr, through his complementarity theory approached this reconciliation. By the complementarity of corpuscules and waves, he emphasized that since both of these concepts are useful for the description of phenomena, they must be employed alternately, depending on the situation, despite the fact that the images they provide are irreconcilable and can never be simultaneously applied to a description of reality.⁹² De Broglie developed the idea of complementarity even further. In 1923, he had formulated the hypothesis of the wave character of material particles. In 1924, he submitted his doctoral thesis, *Investigations into the Quantum Theory*, in which he tried to bridge the gap between the corpuscular and wave theories. With any moving particle he associated a wave of definite wave length; in the case of particles with a significant mass the corpuscular properties predominate, but in the atomic scale, wave properties become prominent with corpuscles. He tried by various hypotheses to preserve the traditional deterministic interpretations of classical physics. Because of the mathematical difficulties he encountered he had to agree with the probabalistic and indeterminist interpretation.⁹³ Both waves and corpuscles were recognized as properties of discontinuum. In 1927, following the discovery of Heisenberg's Uncertainty Principle, Schrödinger and De Broglie developed a more precise formulation of wave mechanics. Also, in the same year, their hypothesis and formulae were confirmed by the experiments of Davisson and Germer proving electron diffraction and the wave character of material particles.⁹⁴ In 1937, Weil wrote of Louis De Broglie:

> Son intuition de génie consiste, il me semble, essentiellement à avoir aperçu que, l'apparition de nombres entiers dans les phénomènes atomiques, depuis la découverte sensationnelle de Planck sur les mouvements stables des électrons, implique quelque chose d'analogue à des interférences d'ondes.⁹⁵

Weil wrote this only ten years after the development of Quantum Mechanics in the 1920s, the period of progressive experimentation during which De Broglie, Bohr, Heisenberg, Einstein, and others developed and revised Planck's unnoticed Quanta Theory. The crisis of determinism had really began with the development of Quantum Mechanics during which time the implications of Planck's theory had become clear. The consequence was a rejection of Classical Determinism and the reinforcement of discontinuum, instability as creative forces. In the quotations given here, Weil is obviously referring to De Broglie's participation in this movement during its peak years,

1923-1927.
> Par ailleurs, la mécanique quantique aboutit à des formules où se trouvent des termes ne satisfaisant pas à la règle de commutativité de la multiplication. Dans l'imagerie de la mecanique ondulatoire, ce phénomène mathématique bizarre apparaît comme correspondant à la dualité entre l'aspect 'l'ondes' et l'aspect 'corpuscles' de la matière. De toute manière, on admet que cette noncommutativité correspond à l'impossibilité de mesurer simultanément et d'une manière exacte deux grandeurs.[96]

Heisenberg's Uncertainty Relations challenged the validity of determinism at the microscopic level because they show that it is impossible to measure exactly in an infinitesimal system both the position and speed of an elementary entity. The statistical information of the system prevents extensive understanding of its dynamic forces and tendencies. Heisenberg's theory indicates an unavoidable imprecision. Whereas in classical physics and in the world of perception, the interference of the observer is considered negligible; in quantum physics, the undivided whole formed by the observed system and the instruments of observation define the phenomena. Consequently Heisenberg's relations of incertitude had tremendous impact for the concept of determinism. Yet, there is one tautological difficulty: speed suggesting a displacement of position, how would it be possible to grasp position and speed at the same level?[97]

Weil refuses the idea that the experimentation on Quantum Mechanics of the 1920s endangered Classical views on Determinism. That is the main idea she is communicating to the student to whom she addresses this letter in 1937.

> . . . Je cherche en vain ce qui, dans tout cela, porte atteinte au déterminisme. Que nous soyons incapables de déterminer par des mesures deux grandeurs à la fois, est-ce à dire que ces grandeurs soient *en soi* indéterminées? La question même n'a pas de sens.[98]

It is evident that Weil, in recognizing Heisenberg's conclusions, does not agree as to their implications for the principle of determinism. A certain degree of incomprehensibility is inevitable, because of the finite nature of our existence and our liited intellectual capacities. It is not an indication that the process is not predetermined. Furthermore one is already aware that the process of experimentation inevitably modifies the measured phenomena. This is callled the 'negligible factor'. As one descends in magnitudes from the macroscopic to the microscopic and further on, a limit is reached where the factor is no longer negligible."⁹⁹ Weil points out in the above quotation Heisenberg's attempts to measure the extent of imprecision involved in Quantum Mechanics. Weil understood that Quantum Mechanics eliminated certain confusion about "la notion de négligeable." In pursuing a particular goal, one neglects to a certain degree a minor factor in the experiment. Physicists such as Heisenberg tried to legitimize this room for error by an infinitely small mathematical unit. The smoother a plate of metal becomes the less is hindered the speed of a marble rolling horizontally upon it. One can't make the metal plate as smooth as one desires, but one can be sure of progression towards perfect smoothness in the course of time and further technical development. Yet, total, perfect smoothness will never be attained. The quantity of error, assumed by mathematicians as infinitely small, can be reduced by mathematical calculation, as shown above. Yet, in physics, the reduction of error is limited. It can be only lessened or reduced to the extent permitted by the current development of technology. The negligible factor in physics is, therefore, not infinitely small. But with the vast technological developments of the past century, this had been forgotten. Weil indicates that it was the Quantum theory that reminded us again of this limiting reality.

Even if science were to overcome this irreducible error, the procedures of observation and measurement unavoidably affect the phenomenon under observation. We will never grasp the total reality of physical phenomena because of the irreducible factor of error, and because of the unavoidable disturbances of our means of observation.

Determinism is still in her view and in that of many others living in the precarious years prior to and during the Second World War a necessary concept. Despite the value of probability and its application to modern physics, probability cannot replace causality.

> DeBroglie introduit la probabilité dans sa description des phénomènes, mais cela n'implique nullement que nous devions substituer la probabilité à la nécessité dans notre conception des phénomènes. . . . Je cherche en vain ce que les 'relations d'incertitude' . . . peuvent avoir de révolutionnaire. . . .¹⁰⁰

It should be emphasized at this point that Weil was not criticizing the necessary development of Quantum Mechanics, of the Uncertainty Principle nor of the involvement of probability in modern physics. What she was challenging was the general conclusion that the processes discovered were contradictions of what she and others conceived as a universal principle—that is, causality, determinism, necessity.

Needless to say, contemporary physicists could not agree with the deterministic view. With a few exceptions, physicists deny the presence of hidden, strictly determined processes which would underlie the apparent contingency of the observed phenomena. They believe that observed statistical laws of macrophysics cannot be reduced to classical causal models but are, instead, irreducible features of an objective physical reality. This attitude, in Milec Capek's view, author of *Philosophical Impact of Contemporary Physics*, is explained by the strong spirit of positivism prevailing among contemporary physicists who eliminate all unobservable factors.[101] Einstein finally acknowledges the influence of Hume and Mach[102] in his rejection of the absolute frame of reference after several failures to detect its existence through mechanical, optical, or electromagnetic experimentation. A similar positivistic motive is present, states Capek, in the minds of physicists dealing with the problem of determinism in quantum mechanics. Empirically unattainable determinism is considered useless.[103]

There were certain features in the language of physicists insisting on the inadequacy of classical determinism which inevitably led to confusion and misinterpretation. This must have occurred when philosophers or philosophically-minded physicists read or heard discussions about the "uncertain position" or "uncertain velocity of an electron" or about the "probability of the occurrence of an electron" or "the impossibility of determining simultaneously both the position and momentum of a particle."[104] It was natural for nonscientists to interpret this in a subjective sense whereby the indeterminacy of the microphysical event was only the human uncertainty resulting from our technical inability to understand *all* determining factors of an observed phenomenon.[105] The indeterminacy would be instead a result of the interference caused by the physicist's observation which changes the conditions of the observed phenomenon.[106]

Contemporary physicists may be right in their claim that the elements of indeterminacy are in nature, rather than in the limitations of our mental and physical capacities. Whatever may be the final conclusions on this matter, it is clear that philosophers and physicists hardly exaggerated when they spoke of the crisis of determinism triggered by the Quantum Theory. There were those who, understandably, hesitated before passing completely from one simplifying view to another, that is from absolute laws of causality to a system of complete indeterminacy. The views of such people would not be devalued. Weil was among them, insisting on the compatibility of necessity and chance, thereby recognizing the co-existence of probability and causality, of a certain element of indeterminacy within the sphere of predictability.

There was a struggle in Weil's attempt to resolve the conflicting powers of necessity and liberty. During the late thirties and beginning years of France's subservience to the German Occupation, she affirmed the inadequacy of the classical scientific view in its failure to take into account the element of free will we all possess. Surely she adhered to the dominance and more powerful presence of determinism; but still, she believed, this does not explain everything. She affirmed that we are more than slaves to necessity, to the universe; there is an element of spiritual power within us all, however minimal. Recognition of the opposing yet complementary forces within us and in the universe would lead to true "enracinement". Obviously Weil also sees in this independent element of will, moral potentiality.

In order to understand fully the Crisis of Determinism evoked and reacted to in Weil's commentaries on science, the following sections will discuss Weil's ideas on Irreversibility, Continuity and Discontinuity, Probability and Chance, Space and Time.

DISCONTINUITY AND CONTINUITY

During and particularly towards the end of the nineteenth century, discontinuity became a dominant concept in every branch of science: in the consequential effects of mathematical grouping, in the kinetic theory of gas, in the atomic theories of physics, in chemistry, in the biological discoveries of mutations. Weil considered all of these developments as part of a natural return to discontinuity, originally introduced in the number theories of the Pythagoreans. Even Bohr's theory of complementarity in reference to waves and corpuscles as a physico-chemical description of our metabolism is an application, in Weil's view, of the ancient idea of the correlation of opposites, an idea which corresponds to Weil's own belief in the complementarity of opposites ("déracinement/enracinement").

But for science, it was a new concept. From the Renaissance there had been vain attempts to impose a unity to science. Finally the introduction of the correlation of opposites recognized the necessary subsistance of continuity and discontinuity. In light of this, Weil outlined for her students of philosophy and for the general teaching of philosophy, instruction in the history of mathematics oriented toward a fundamental resolution of continuum and discontinuum.

What isn't understandable, in her view, is the usage of discontinuity in contemporary physics, in the Quantum Theory. That is, the idea that energy manifests itself in uneven discontinuous quantities, called quanta. This introduces the concept of discontinuity into the study of energy through probability formulae and the dubious assimilation of entropy into probability formulae.

Weil's defense of continuity as the basic principle in nature corresponds to the Classical scientists' and philosophers' point of view, a view still persisting during Weil's lifetime. In his book, *The Philosophical Impact of Contemporary Physics*, Milic Capek explains this mechanical scheme of nature, classical corpuscular-kinetic mechanics. Matter, which is discontinuous in its structure, that is, made of absolutely rigid and compact units, moves through space according to the strict laws of mechanics. There are no actual changes in quality. All seemingly qualitative differences in nature are only differences in configuration or movement of these elementary units. Qualitative changes are only surface effects of the displacement of these units; they are no more than 'psychic additions of the perceiving human mind'; they are not really in the nature of things.[107]

This corpuscular-kinetic view of matter first appeared in early Greek atomism. Its premises were supported since the time of Gassendi and Newton, and have been a persistent influence on physics until the end of the nineteenth century.[108] In modern times, its appeal has diminished but has not altogether disappeared.

Two basic senses, sight and touch, constitute the classical view of matter, which did not transcend the limits of our sensory imagination. All other senses were subordinated to sight and touch. The subordination of these secondary to primary qualities facilitated the classical vision. The world of atoms in which all qualitative diversity is reduced to differences in configuration and motion of the homogeneous and permanent elements simplifies and systematizes the confusing realm of heterogenous sensory qualities.[109]

The universe was regarded as an enormous aggregate of bits of homogenous material whose quantity remained constant.[110] It was for this reason that the evolving principle of irreversibility, challenging as it did the constancy of matter and energy, was an uncomfortable one. The classical concepts of space, time, matter, motion, and causality, appearing in this corpuscular-kinetic explanation are what Weil thinks of as science itself.

Energy is a concept dependent upon that of space. Space cannot be conceived other than in terms of continuity—"il est la continuité même; il est le monde pensé du point de vue de la continuité. . . ."[111] From the time of Galileo, science has interpreted all phenomena in terms of chance in the relationship of space and time; only distance, speed, and acceleration have been recognized as variable factors. In the light of this scientific tradition, Weil maintains these two basic premises, that time and space can only be conceived as continuous quantities.[112]

In order for a mass to reach a certain height, it must pass through intermediate stages towards the projected height or depth. Thus distance is a reflection of this continuity; all forms of geometry express this. Time is expressed by physicists in the same terms; that is, as straight, uniform, mere units of continuous movement. As a result, speed is necessarily conceived in the same way, as it constitutes the relation of distance to time; and in turn acceleration as the relation of speed to time must also be conceived similarly, in the realm of continuous movement.[113] Weil thus maintains what she sees as the inconsistency of the use of the principle of discontinuity by the Quantum theorists to describe the creation of energy and movement. All elements involved in the process of action reflecting a change upon matter (time, space, speed, acceleration) are fueled by the concept of continuous movement.

At this time, Classical Physics confronted the remergence and development of atomic science. It became necessary to conceive of microscopic nondivisible particles, governed and mobilized by necessity, that is, by the deterministic, corpuscular-kinetic view of matter. As Weil pointed out, these movements had to be regular and united by observable laws of necessity and probability, to render them observable at the human level. The form of probability is what she seems to criticize, that is, the difference between "probabilité discontinue" and "probabilité continue";[114]

Classical Physics considers a raised stone as a single atom and unit of energy, outlining a vertical straight line. With the advent of atomic science, energy movement is no longer conceived in terms of order and continuity but as complex combinations of movement. A link must be made between the two levels of physical science.

Weil reviewed carefully Planck's attempt to establish such a link through the study of energy. As already stated, he sought to express the relationship between energy and temperature and decided on the use of black ray where the exchanges of energy between bodies depended solely upon their temperature. He reproduced mathematically such a particular case of black ray where energy was determined by the temperature level, the oscillators of Hertz.[115] Planck discovered a secondary relation between energy and entropy instead of the direct one between temperature and energy.

Planck sought to reconstruct formulae that would envelope these two relations; he adopted Boltzmann's view that entropy at the atomic level is the measure of a probability factor. Such a constant (H) had no possible relation to Classical Science, insisted Weil, although Planck claimed that "... grâce à elle qu'on pouvait connaître les domaines ou intervalles indispensables pour le calcul des probabilités (car) le calcul de la probabilité d'un état physique repose sur le dénombrement du nombre fini de cas particuliers également probables par lesquels l'état considéré est réalisé."[116]

There are other forms of probability based on the principle of continuity instead of discontinuity, which could have been applied to this experimentation in Weil's view. Yet as she points out, no allusion to such a possibility was made in Planck's book explaining his discoveries.[117]

In reviewing the history of probability, the experiment proposed by Weil corresponds to that performed by Buffon in the seventeenth century, "le problème de l'aiguille;" this experiment was developed into the concept of "les probabilités continues" by Daniel Bernouilli in the eighteenth century; subsequently some of Europe's most famous mathematicians developed the science of probability, Lagrange, Laplace and Gauss, for example.[118] In her notebooks, Weil's notes on Gauss's studies show what must have been an extensive study of the question.[119]

Pétrement cites Weil's questioning of the probability calculation in the *Quantum Theory*:

> . . . Il contient, dit-on, une erreur au sujet du fondement de la théorie des quanta. Simone croit que c'est parce que Planck utilisait la probabilité numérique, discontinue. . . .[120]

Among the correspondance exchanged between Simone Weil and her brother André in 1941-1942 during Weil's stay in Marseille, fragments of letters to her brother indicate that there was an exchange regarding this question. Weil asks her brother what prevented the usage of a continuous form of probability.[121] Fragments of her following letter indicate that she had received an answer from her brother but it had not satisfied her. The content of the passage gives no clue as to the exact nature of his response except the general impression that Weil's brother felt that she was mistaken in her analysis. Pétrement, in mentioning this correspondance, did not indicate the exact nature of his answer.[122]

It would be interesting to know just to what point Weil's views were scientifically accurate or invalid. Yet, it is enough to understand the depth of her perceptions regarding the revolutionizing force of discontinuity without challenging the scientific precision of her analysis. Her fears reflected the limited and threatened classical perspective of her times, yet the only aspects of discontinuity that she challenged in the course of modern science, were its use as a means of conversion of entropy into a probability factor and as a means of transforming the immutable, invariable nature of time and space. This resulted in a revolt against previous conceptions of determinism. Both formulae developed in the relativity and quantum theories relating to these questions of discontinuity, time and space, were, in her view, factors in the propagation of symbols and formulae increasingly distanced from their original meaning.

Whatever may or may not have been Weil's error in her understanding of these symbols and formulae, she accurately analyzed the danger of our increased dependence upon them, and our increasing distance from an understandable, communicable meaning of their complexity. Necessary or not, the rejection of classical science marked the beginnings of a symbol-oriented society, and the gulf distancing science from culture in a vast movement of 'déracinement'.

IRREVERSIBILITY

The concept of irreversibility expresses for Weil the ultimate point of the Classical scientific belief in determinism. Irreversibility is manifest in an order based on a series of disorders leading toward a state of equilibrium; as explained by Zemansky, professor *emeritus* of physics in New York:

> As a system proceeds toward its equilibrium state, it goes through states of greater and greater disorder. . . .[123]

This order based on instability and disorder is logical, in Weil's opinion; each disequilibrium in invalidated by another until a final state of order, of equilibrium is reached.[124] She also recognized it to be a purifying source.

The concept of irreversibility aggravated the Crisis of Determinism by attributing to our view of necessity an even greater measure of incomprehensibility. Necessity and determinism in their incomprehensible path toward equilibrium and order, alienated us even further from ourselves. As irreversibility implies a series of disorders in the form of molecular instability and heat dissipation which eventually leads to a new state of equilibrium, separate acts comprising work are in themselves indifferent and unrelated to the final state of accomplished goal, to the desire finally satisfied.

Weil's discussion of entropy, irreversibility, and energy shows her reognition and respect for an Anti-Newtonian viewpoint. Heat or Energy and Gravitation coexist in the physical universe; yet, although expressive of the predetermined process toward equilibrium, they are forces which oppose each other, as affirmed by Prigogine and Stengers.

> La chaleur et la gravitation, . . . coexistent en physique, et pire, comme va le reconnaître Auguste Comte, ils sont antagnistes. . .
> .[125]

This is the opposition also underlined by many Anti-newtonian chemists of the eighteenth century and others who had insisted on the difference between the essentially spatio-temporal behavior characteristic of mass and the specificity of matter.[126]

Matter took on its own specificity, its own power. It becomes, in a way, representative of an autonomous universe. The law of gravity had expressed in the minds of most a divine or cosmic determinism. With the advancement of scientific theories supporting the energy potential in matter, both the coexistence and the opposition of the two theories seemed to represent the ambiguous confrontation of necessity and free will. Their coexistence alternates in history between a predominance of Kantian, Hegelian Idealism, followed by Marx's reversal in Dialectic Materialism. Neither proves satisfactory and many strive towards a balance between the two. Among those searching for this balance were Weil and members of the Frankfurt School. *La Pesanteur et la Grâce* uses the opposition between gravity and energy as the basis of her work. The encounter of the ascending and descending forces of gravitation and energy take on religious and spiritual dimensions, as it did in the work of seventeenth century moralists. Weil's analysis of each of these forces is very complex. What is significant in the present context, however, is her use of opposing scientific phenomena—gravity and energy, to convey the complexity of the involvement of determinism with autonomy, two opposing yet complementary movements of the natural universe, and of the human spirit, the unrecognized strength of "déracinement/enracinement."

PROBABILITY AND CHANCE

Sommes-nous, ô hasard, l'oeuvre de tes caprices?[127]

Probability is the nature of an assertion which has the greatest chances of corresponding to reality, that is, at the perceptible level of physical phenomena. In mathematics, it is the relationship of the total number of possible instances or occurrences of a possible event, given that all variables are equal. The calculation of probability has been developed in a wide range of applications such as actuarial sciences, demographics, manufacturing, marketing, and statistics.[128] There is difficulty in defining chance because of the alternate domination of determinable and indeterminable consequences and factors. Both materialists and finalists confuse chance with determinism. As Goblot put it: "La négation de la causalité, c'est la contingence et non le hasard."[129] Chance is actually an accidental and unpredictable interference between two or more causal series whose reciprocal relations are rigorously determined.[130] The inseparable factors of probability and chance are involved closely with the question of determinism, as discussed by Weil. Thus involved are the forms of necessity or determinism tempered with the forces of chance and probability. The affirmation of factors other than necessity involved in the final results affirms the role of chance. All of the categories ruled by chance have an equal possibility for realization. Weil's notion of continuity and invariability is tied in with the concept of probability, defined as distribution of equal forces of possibility.

Weil's concern with this question reveals a certain interesting stage of development; although she disagreed with the absolute revolt against determinism, she was keenly sympathetic with the modern scientists' belief in the dual forces of chance and necessity. As so often in other matters, she found herself in a situation of crisis. Clinging to beliefs in causality and continuum, she was nevertheless receptive to assimilation of chance and probability, and factors of determinism that were typical of the period of transition between Classical and Modern Science.

She was receptive to the reappearance of chance in science through modern atomic theories.

> L'apparîtion du hasard dans la science a fait scandale; on s'est demandé d'òu il venait; on n'a pas réflechi que l'atome l'avait amené; on ne s'est pas souvenue que déjà dans 'antiquité le hasard accompagnait l'atome, et l'on n'a pas songé qu'il n'en peut être autrement . . . .[131]

She seemed to be very deeply influenced by Hegel's thesis concerning chance and necessity. Chance is not incompatible with necessity, she maintained. On the contrary, they always appear as combined factors. There are only six categories, for instance, that a single dice may fall into, six categories which have between themselves numeric relationships. Yet there are countless ways of throwing dice which cannot be similarly categorized.

Research and discovery relating to irreversibility, chance and determinism came to a climax in the study of the molecular composition of genetic codes, the fundamental base of biology. One of the leaders in this field was Jacques Monod. In his book *Hasard et Nécessité,* Monod affirmed the predominance of chance over determinism in natural processes. In recent years the balance sought between necessity and chance has fallen in the direction of those espousing, like Monod, acausality, which, mysterious and incomprehensible has increased the alienation of self from environment.

> . . . ancienne alliance est rompue; l'homme sait enfin qu'il est seul dans l'immensité indifférente de l'Univers. . . .[132]

The study of "accidental" alterations involved in molecular genetics (that is, the molecular disorders resulting in genetic makeup) led Monod to the following audacious conclusion:

> Le hasard pur, le seul hasard, liberté absolue mais aveugle, à la racine même du prodigieux édifice de l'évolution. . . .[133]

Monod's discovery marked the complete rejection of causality or determinism. With the toppling of causality comes also a revolt against religion and God, a total rejection not only of anthropocentrism but of the teleological design, the logos by which we have defined ourselves for so many centuries. Weil had progressed beyond LaPlace's vision from which chance had been excluded entirely; she had considered necessity and chance compatible forces, both contributing to a final determined point of equilibrium. In her analysis of Monod's study, *L'Idéologie du Hasard et de la Necessite,* Madeleine Barthélemy-Madaule criticized Monod's exploration of mutation and defended the same compatibility of chance and necessity as did Weil.

> . . .comme le fortuit, l'exceptionnel, dans un systeme soumis à la nécessité, le fait du hasard devient nécessaire. . . .[134]

The crisis continues, unresolved, despite the favor with which Monod's views have been considered in recent years. There is still strong belief, however, in the possible reintegration of the living creature with nature, within a scheme where determinist and nondeterminist forces coexist. Through one or the other extreme we have been led historically to "déracinement", to an alienation from nature and from ourselves. For this reason, Weil feared both the blind belief in absolute determinism and the complete rejection of causality. The dark, pessimistic tone with which Monod concludes his study underlines our solitude and alienation from an indifferent and incomprehensible world. What is needed and hoped for is 'enracinement' as described by Weil, "une nouvelle alliance" as forecast by Prigogine and Stengers, where reintegration with nature would allow for both necessity and nondeterminist forces, namely chance and free will.

SPACE AND TIME

Space: Space and Time are invariable in relation to matter and life. They are expressions of necessity, of determinism. Weil was influenced by the Manichean image of the torn, abused mind. The mind's dispersal throughout space and time is expressed through the symbol of crucifixion.

The thinking creature is dispersed or alienated from itself through the passing of time. The multiplicity of identities of the self with the passing of time alienating the individual from a consoidation of one's own being, is an idea inherited from Hume[135] which also affected Bergson's and Proust's conception of "le Moi" through the multiplicity of moments in Time. In Weil's view, time and space are deterministic, invariable forces which prevent a consolidation of the self.

Although time and space as expressions of necessity oppose the affirmation of free will and sovereignty, the material universe subject to sense perception reinforces the individual's feeling of having the right and capacity for power. The juxtaposition of objects in space reinforce one's image of lost and forbidden sovereignty, in Weil's view. Without this hope and intuition one could not live because one can only reflect upon what is perceived.

Weil identifies with the classical scientific conception of space and time established by Galileo which consists in interpreting all change in phenomena in terms of the relationship of space to time, associated so closely with the presence of energy; no variability is admitted except that of speed, acceleration, and distance.

This is one reason for Weil's negative comments concerning Einstein's Theory of Relativity in which time slows down and is assimilated as a fourth dimension of space. It should be noted that she carefully distinguishes between the general theory of relativity that is closer to the classical conception of space and time and the Special Theory of Relativity. Although Weil writes only briefly on both, she was more critical of the latter, as would be expected, given her own orientation to philosophy and science.

The Relativity theory is an important branch of modern physics which draws its name from the fact that it is a continuation of the theory brought out by Galileo. In 1638, Galileo proved parabolic movement of projectiles in a vacuum; he declared also the principle of inertia and the law of variations of speeds.[136]

> . . .n'est-ce pas dès lors un paradoxe très audacieux d'affirmer que le mouvement parfait soustrait aux actions extérieures, indéfinimment durable, est un mouvement uniforme rectiligne?. . .[137]

Relativity brings to physics the laws which must combine measures of time, length, mass, energy, in order to explain physical phenomena. Classical Determinism is based on spatiotemporal continuum or infinite divisibility of nature in space and time. Einstein and De Broglie were among those who belonged to the Cartesian tradition in physics and the philosophy of science. In the Cartesian tradition there is a tendency to eliminate distinctions between material bodies and their surrounding space. Because of their adherence to the Euclidean form of space which by its own homogeneous nature cannot fuse with its changing physical content. Descartes and his followers came to an impasse. Einstein in his general theory of relativity continued the Cartesian tradition of fusing space and physical reality into a single entity, even though the Euclidean homogeneity of space was rejected, and space was fused with time.[138] Weil and others had great difficulty in confronting this rejection of Euclidean space as well as the reduction of time to a fourth coordinate of space.

General Relativity consists in extending to all possible movements the notion of relativity that Classical mechanics attributed to straight and uniform movements. This was the result of the investigations of Copernicus, Kepler, Galileo and Newton, which led them to attribute certain regular movements in the astronomical world, particularly that of earth and celestial bodies. There were the forces of speed, and inertia. Weil and others were not uncomfortable with Einstein's articulation of General Relativity.

It was the theory of Special Relativity that Weil criticized, badly named in her view, because she felt it had very little relation to relativity of movement. She notes a series of experiments that led to the measurement of the speed of light and other experimentation at the end of the nineteenth century that resulted in viewing the speed of this light as constant in all directions.[139]

Weil considered these conclusions that were translated into algebraic formulae by Einstein, as irreconcilable. She questioned not only the relativity of time, that is, time considered as a dimension of space, but also the application of non-euclidean geometry, the curving of space, and speed considered both infinite and measurable.

"Le vide" used in many of Weil's religious writings is that element of purity and abstraction whose very presence is contrary to the natural law of entropy. In the beginning was "le vide," emptiness, non-being. Weil refers to the creation as the filling up of space, the beginning of autonomy and identity. Through the presence of spiritual grace and self-willed abnegation of self, "le vide" reappears.

> ... ne pas exercer tout le pouvoir dont on dispose, c'est supporter le vide. Cela est contraire à toutes les lois de la nature; la grâce seule le peut.[140]

It is well known that Henry More's divinization of space influenced

Newton's philosophy of nature in which absolute space is considered a divine attribute, by which divine omnipresence as well as divine knowledge was made possible.[141] Newton merely confused the logical priority of space with an ontological priority. The logical priority of space to its physical content was a dogma which few questioned. For Newton as for Gassendi and More, this priority was temporal as well; absolute space, as a divine attribute, had to have existed before the creation.[142] Newton's insistence on the independence of space from its material content was summarized by Bertrand Russell in his *Principles of Mathematics*:

> It does not follow, merely because there is space, that therefore there are things in it.[143]

There is a similarity between Russell's and Weil's ideas on determinism, time and space in a scientific context. Russell, in Part VII of the above-mentioned work, presented an accurate systematization of the basic principles of Classical Science, much of which coincided with Weil's views. But most significantly, the works of both authors shows how Newton's philosophy dominated minds as late as the beginning and first half of this century. The rapport between classical space and classical matter has its counterpart in philosophy in the relationship of non-being to the solidity of being. The relationship between abstract being and non-being was the same as that between matter and void. Void precedes matter which fills it, as non-being is logically antecedent to being. There is a striking correspondence between this theory and the religious metaphysical views of Weil on creation and decreation. In Weil's last religious writings, particularly *La Pesanteur et la Grâce*, and *La Connaissance Surnaturelle*, Weil indicates a gradual progression through the stages of creation, autonomy, 'attente', and 'décréation' through a rejection of identity, a transcendence of the self towards non-being, non-identity. By an abnegation of the self one decreates oneself and merges with a harmonious, eternal divine presence. The parallels with Saint Augustine and Malebranche are evident. What is most interesting, however, is the interplay of science and philosophy in this first half-century and its manifestation in writings of philosophers. In Paul Valéry's collection of poetry, *Charmes*, the aspiration towards non-being as a means of purification expresses an idea very close to Weil's who, incidentally, greatly admired Valery.[144]

Que l'univers n'est qu'un défaut
Dans la pureté du Non-être[145]

The modifications and expansion of the Classical scientific concept of void preceding matter coincided with philosophical speculation on the relationship between non-being and being. It clashed, however, with the development of modern philosophy. Bergson was among those philosophers questioning the self-sufficiency and logical, temporal priority of non-being.[146] The beginnings of Existentialism were marked by a similar challenge made by Heidegger—"Why does any being exist and not just nothing?"[147] The traditional belief adhered to by Weil and others in the immutability, the logical and temporal priority of space was challenged in the course of modern scientific and philosophical development.

Weil, as did Classical physicists, believed in two other features of space—infinity and mathematical continuity (infinite divisibility).[148] The infinity of space is clearly supported by Kant in his concept of the transcendental aesthetic.[149] Bertrand Russell also defends the view of space as homogeneous and infinite at a time when revolutionary discoveries were modifying the concept of space.[150] The infinite divisibility of space, as seen previously, is a concept found in Greek thought. It is implied in the first postulate of Euclid stating that it is possible to draw a straight line between any pair of points.[151] It is also seen in the tenth book of Euclid, which proves the possibility of bisecting any straight line segment.[152]

Geometrical similarity between various layers of spatial magnitudes was also a concept of Classical physics that Weil adhered to.[153] The invention of the microscope by Jansen in 1590, and that of the telescope by Féry and later Mersenne and Newton in 1671, allowed new unlimited possibilities to be opened concurrently in the direction of the infinitesimal and in the opposite direction of unlimited volume and vastness. The theme of Gulliver developed in Swift's fantasy was invented in a time of significant advancement for Classical Science on both microscopic and astronomical levels; in the same period Pascal evoked the anxiety of the human condition, overwhelmed by its enigmatic nature by which one floats between two chasms of infinity unable to grasp either the infinitely large nor the infinitely small and thus unable to define oneself.[154] There are parallels between Pascal and Weil to be examined, but the one that concerns us here is not the image of purgatory evoked by Pascal's floating indecisively in a Dantesque-type universe. Weil, as did Pascal, reacted with amazement and with irony to the classical discovery of the relativity of magnitude. But unlike Pascal, she viewed it as and expression of harmony and predetermined order; the analogy between structures was an expression of a unified whole. This obviously conflicted with modern scientific theories which challenged the applicability of macroscopic, determinist laws on the microscopic or even atomic level. Even in our century, following the discovery of the Quantum Theory which served to invalidate scientifically the application of laws of the macroscopic world to phenomena perceived at the microscopic level, there were scientists and philosophers of great stature and prominence, who adhered also to the classical idea of relativity of magnitude, such as Bohr, and Whitehead.[155]

Both Russell and Weil affirm the independence of space with respect to time. Both refuse the relativity of space and time.[156]

Yet there is in Weil's beliefs on space this inconsistency between the immutability of space and her view of the disintegration or multiplicity of beings through space and time. This is derived from Augustinian philosophy but it still creates an inconsistency in Weil's writings. It is a contradiction most probably reinforced by Hume's influence, his view of the disintegrated parts of one's being united in space and time by the imagination, forming one's personality, what Hume contemptuously considers a fictional entity created by one's imaginative powers. This accounts in part for Weil's later idea of imagination as a force comparable to entropy, consolidating and filling up the vacuum of empty space and non-being.

... l'imagination combleuse de vides est essentiellement menteuse....[157]

In any case the inconsistency is there. If one adheres to the idea of immutability of space, place or change in place would have no causal effect. It should be noted that Weil's belief in the homogeneity of both space and time, both independent of one another, leaves one with very rigid spatial and temporal structures. Change of space would necessarily have to allow for heterogeneity in time. Bergson's philosophy responded to this necessary flexibility in the coexistence of homogeneous space with a heterogeneous concept of time. Admittedly Weil's concept of space as representative of a certain inflexibility in classical physics and philosophy helps understand why the crisis of determinism she and others confronted was inevitable, the crisis of determinism, the clash of the forces "déracinement/enracinement."

It is interesting that Weil defends space as absolute, a representation of eternity as her image of the crucifixion would suggest. Her conscious or unconscious adherence to the idea of space as eternal and prior to the contingency of its material content is a reflection of her identification with Classical Physics, and of a choice between the Idealist and Materialist philosophies, the foundations of both found in Descartes' philosophy, Descartes insisted on the inseparability of space from matter. He thus contested the logical priority of space affirmed by Newton. But Descartes' argument was weakened by the fact that his philosophy of nature retained only the geometrical properties of matter. There was therefore difficulty in retaining space as 'plenum', particularly if impenetrability was a subjective *secondary* quality. There was a further inconsistency: Descartes' insistence upon the inseparability of space from matter contradicted his view of space as the only true reality of the physical world. This inconsistency led in part to the dual foundation of two opposing schools of Idealist and Materialist philosophies. The Idealist tradition influenced by Descartes affected Weil more deeply than the Materialist School. The latter tradition has been associated with the Encyclopédists, later, the Utopian reformers such as Owen, Fourrier, Saint Simon. The influence of Saint Simon's utopian, progressive ideas is reflected in the Positivistic philosophy initiated later by Auguste Comte. The extremes of scientific positivism became associated later with persistent elements of scientism and dialectical materialism during the first part of this century.

Although Weil strives for detachment from both schools of Idealism and Materialism, she is associated more closely with the Idealist tradition, along with most Rationalists of her time whose identification of Idealism with Cartesian philosophy was a deeply ingrained part of their culture.

Time: The independence and absolute nature of time, particularly in regard to change, was explained by Newton:

> ... Absolute time and mathematical time, of itself, and by its own nature, flows uniformly, without regard to anything external.[158]

Classical Physics very clearly distinguished between time and concrete becoming. Like space, time is empty and is prior to the changes that fill it. Because of its emptiness as a receptacle for change and motion, time takes on spatial dimensions which explains the close analogy between space and time in science.[159] According to many major philosophers, time existed even before the creation of the world. It was regarded as a divine attribute, as was space.[160]

Weil's refusal of the causal action of time on space again underlines the closeness of her views to Classical Pysics. The structure of space was necessarily rigid, independent of time. The homogeneity of time was retarded as the basis for the unity of nature in time by logical induction, and the laws of conservation, inertia, were thought to be based on the assumed causal inefficacy of time. Thus time was necessarily kept separate and independent of space.[161]

Saint Augustine questioned in his *Confessions* the possible existence of two times, past and future; the present does not remain the present but continually merges into the past, thus proving existence and time continually passes into that which ceases to be.[162]

> Thus, can we not truly say that time *is* only as it tends toward non-being?[163]

The influence of Saint Augustine on Weil was considerable. Weil reflects particularly in her religious works on the temporal movement towards non-being. Reality is nonexistence. In her scientific essays, time is one of the two expressions of necessity. Her use of the cross illustrates her view of space and time as universal coordinates, divine expressions of coeternity. her description of the disintegration of human personality through space and time expands the image of the crucifixion, as human limits are juxtaposed upon and surpassed by the infinite expansion of space and time. For Saint Augustine and for Weil, time is destructive.

Yet there is still an unresolved contradiction between Weil's above mentioned description of time as an illusion, "une irréalité" in later spiritual works, *i.e., La Pesanteur et la Grâce*. It may be a significant indication of Weil's departure from the Classical conception of Time, refusing temporality as a purely divine expression of determinism since she views it as a creation of our minds. The temporal chains with which we have enslaved ourselves are illusions. Time does not exist, but the determinism which it expresses does.

> ... le temps, à proprement parler, n'existe pas (sinon le présent comme limite), et pourtant c'est à cela que nous sommes soumis. Telle est notre condition. Nous sommes soumis à ce qui n'existe pas.[164]

Saint Augustine believed in the finiteness of physical world process contrary to the classical infinitism.[165] He, and later Weil, anticipated the reversibility of time, that is, the lack of distinction between past and present, the "cheminement" of being towards non-being. In spite of Weil's expression of the temporal and spatial infinitude present in her use of the cross as an image or representation of the universe, the ideas of finitude, the obliteration of temporal distinctions and the the aspiration towards non-being reveal what must have been an acceptance of the modern scientific theory of reversibility of time.

This may, but not necessarily, be viewed as a contradiction of her affirmation of time as continuous or absolute in her scientific essays. It should be understood, however, that the challenge to determinism was difficult because of the complexity of the issues and scientific advances involved. Weil may not have related her final belief in reversibility of time to the Relativity Theory or to Planck's Quantum Theory. She may not have been aware of the scientific implications of her rejection of the classical conception of time. Her ideas on time were most probably determined in great part by Renouvier, who was among the very few influenced by Saint Augustine.[166]

It is somewhat ironic that Weil, who so heartily criticized Nietzsche for his praise of Callicles and for other influential ideas on Greek culture, should share his concept of the reversibility of time, of eternal reoccurrence that appear in *Also Sprach Zarathustra*, and the *Birth of Tragedy*.[167] Temporal reversibility was also defended by Poincaré, the mathematician whom Weil criticizes for his defense of the reduction of mathematics to the role of a language in modern times.

By the image of the cross, Weil has consciously or unconsciously revealed another contradiction inherent in the Classical view of space and time and in her own. The point of fusion of the two linear images contradicts the classical conception of space and time as unrelated and independent. Capek explains the three-dimensional model of Classical space-time. A Euclidean plane, vertical or horizontal represents space, while time is symbolized by a straight line perpendicular to the plane. There is an infinite number of successive spaces represented by parallel planes, each perpendicular to the time axis. Each cross section contains points which represent simultaneous events.[168] Thus space is inevitably related to simultaneity, a temporal concept. By the fusion of the two coordinates, a process is created by which all points are simultaneously affected by their temporal and spatial structures. Weil accepts the simultaneous involvement of space (or movement through space) and time. The determination of motion by time is a classical conception developed by Galileo, containing an implicit clue as to the eventual evolution of relativity of space and time in Modern Science.[169]

The impossibility of separating space from time was formulated by H. Minkowski, following Einstein's development of the Special Relativity Theory. The spatialization of time, however, was a distortion, a misrepresentation of Einstein's relativity theory by the reduction of time to a mere fourth dimension of space.[170] This was a point that Weil rejected and seemed to be the basic reason for her criticism of Einstein's relativity theory. This misrepresentation led to much controversy. Emile Meyerson in his discussion, *La Déduction Relativiste* lists many philosophers and scientists who had also interpreted the proposed fusion as a spatialization of time.[171] Even in the literary realm, H.G. Wells described the movement of his main character of *The Time Machine*,[172] as progression through the fourth dimension of space, that is, time, as well as through the other three.

Yet there were others who, like Weil, refused this spatialization of time. Paul Langevin was one of these.[173] Meyerson also underlined the necessary distinction between space and time even in the relativity theory. The ironic and crowning point of support came from Einstein himself who in 1928 stated that the spatialization of time was a misinterpretation of the relativity theory. The misinterpretation, he wrote, was made by scientists as well as by philosophers.[174]

CONCLUSION

Weil sought in her commentaries on science to show the disintegration of value in Western civilization brought about by the extremes of Modern Science and by the disassociation of symbol from meaning. Through her comparisons of Greek, Classical, and Modern Science, she reflected upon how our technological advancement has alienated us from our universe, and from knowledge about ourselves. This is also a point made by Meyerson, that the disappearance of truth is an intrinsic consequence of modern scientific development.[175]

Weil uses her comparison with Greek science and culture to underline the contrast or separation between theory and application bred by Sophism which has reached exaggerated proportions in modern times. The destruction of Greece, and the defeat and capitulation of France followed by the collaboration of the Vichy government, led to a cynical and demoralizing acquiescence to the Right of the Stronger; this was an inheritance from the Sophists reinforced by Hobbes's *Leviathan* and the independent spirit of Nietzsche's *Zarathustra*. It led to the 'natural necessity' that those who have power have the creative right to determine what is justice. The estrangement of theory from application, of thought from labor characteristic of both highly developed cultures, ancient and modern, indicates the need to pass through a period of review of the application and direction of science so as to reorient technology and scientific advancement towards the replenishment of resources and the welfare of society. The politics of domination have already made us subservient to matter, to symbols and to our technological creations, so that we have lost the notion of truth. Twenty years later Arendt would express the same idea—the danger of disassociated meaning.[176]

The loss of meaning in action and speech is a consequence of the crisis of uprootal and the need for reintegration, for an equilibrium between the demands of necessity and free will. For this reason Weil speaks in admiration of the values of Greek science, whose discoveries as she pointed out, stem from the principle of proportion, and order. This necessary fusion of theory with application stemmed from and was reflected in their belief in proportion, equivalence, and harmony. The valorization of proportion led to Thales's invention of geometry, the duplication of the cube, the discovery of incommensurability, the subsequent discovery of the diagonal as the means to the duplication of a square. It was also the reason for the Greeks' delay in translating the Babylonian art of algebra into geometry, a fear of such dependence on symbols.

The presence of diversity, difference, discontinuity, discentering and displacement in Weil's perception of the Greek idea of proportion complicates Weil's involvement in the later Crisis of Determinism when the Classical world view is challenged by the consequences of enolving Quantum Mechanics and Einstein's Relativity theory. Weil's views represent the difficulties of many in facing this rejection of determinism.

Espousal of both Classical and Modern world views give rise to many contradictions: the view that the modern concepts of energy, entropy, irreversibility, and work were expressive of a universe ruled by laws of determinism or necessity; the apparent recognition of both discontinuity and continuity as participating forces in the physical workd, yet the refusal of energy conceived as discontinuous particles, as anything other than continuous movement; doubt as to the necessary application of discontinuous probability instead of a continuous form of probability; her belief that the possibilities of continuous probability were insufficiently explored by Planck before turning to discontinuity. Although Planck's image of a discontinuous form of probability could, without doubt, be justified by modern physicists, the question Weil raises is a significant one. She raised it for the same reason De Broglie, Einstein, and Schrödinger fougnt against the complete rejection of causality, of deterministic forces of nature. Weil's commentaries reflect the early modernist struggle between absolutes—that of an exaggerated belief in a universe governed rigidly by mathematical laws of continuum and causality, and that of a world completely unstable, and unpredictable. The apparent contradictions in Weil's essays relate significantly to the compromise that evolved from this crisis. Space and time were conceived as continuous yet the classical concept of time as continuous and irreversible was contradicted by her acceptance of temporal reversibility bringing her closer to Bergson's and Einstein's beliefs in relativity. In addition there were other valuable observations noted in her writings, such as her discussion of the doubt and uncertainty left us by the marginal error or negligible factor Heisenberg interpreted in his Uncertainty Principle.[177] There was also her rejection of time as a fourth dimension of space, the spatialization of time later recognized as a misrepresentation of Einstein's theory of Special Relativity.

The 'je' emerging in Weil's doctoral thesis has grown in its power and autonomy until its inextricable involvement with the world comes to a crisis point. Both the extremes, that of empirical positivism and that of free will were forces, extreme points of alienation, of "déracinement," which Weil refused in her essays on science.

"Déracinement/Enracinement" expresses continually the complementarity and opposition of dual forces of determinism and non-determinism, necessity and free will, continuum and discontinuum, dissonance and harmony. Each element of these dualities function both negatively and positively. Each movement contains both the cause and the solution which is, in essence, the tension and balance between the two forces of "déracinement/enracinement."

Notes to Chapter 4

[1] Simone Weil, "Science et Perception Dans Descartes," in *Sur la Science* (Paris: Editions Gallimard, 1966), 11.

[2] George Friedman, *The Political Philosophy of the Frankfurt School* (Ithaca: Cornell University Press, 1981), 15-16.

[3] Ibid.

[4] Simone Weil, "Réflexions à Propos de la Théorie des Quanta," in *Sur la Science*, 208-9.

[5] All essays mentioned constitute the collection of pieces in *Sur la Science*.

[6] Weil, "Science et Perception dans Descartes," 14-15.

[7] Ibid., 17.

[8] Simone Weil, "Lettre à un Camarade," *Sur la Science*, 103.

[9] Weil referred in this context specifically to the pedagogical value of a study done by the French physicist, Paul Langevin, on the history of the Sciences. His studies had influenced her orientation to the teaching of the sciences and had determined her projects and class outlines. She was most probably referring to lectures given by Langevin: "La Valeur Educative de l'histoire des Sciences" in December 1926 before the Conseil d'Administration de la Société Française de Pédagogie. This lecture was published in *Bulletin de la Société de Pédagogie* 22 (December 1926), and in *Revue de Synthèse* 1 (April 1933). Langevin delivered another lecture on June 11, 1931, at the Musée Pédagogique entitled "La contribution de l'enseignement des sciences physiques à la culture générale." Information on Langevin's close involvement with pedagogical reform can be found in his biography, *Paul Langevin, Mon Père*, by André Langevin (Paris: Les Editeurs Français Réunis, 1971).

[10] Simone Weil, "L'Enseignement des Mathématiques," 108-9.

[11] Other sources which review in depth the individual work and concern of philosophers and scientists for pedagogical reform in the years prior to World War II:
1. Guy Avanzina, *La Contribution de Binet à l'Elaboration d'une Pédagogie Scientifique* (Paris: Librairie Philosophique J. Vrin, 1969).
2. Gaston Bachelard, *Le Nouvel Esprit Scientifique* (Paris: Librairie Felix Alcan, 1934).
3. Paul Langevin, *La Pensée et l'Action*, textes recueillies et presentés par Paul Labérenne (Paris: Editions Sociales, 1964).
4. Léon Brunschvicg, "L'Actualité des Problèmes Platoniciens," *Actualités Scientifiques et Industrielles*, no. 575 Conférences du centre Universitaire Méditerranéen de Nice publiés sous la direction de M. Paul Valéry (Paris: Herman et Cde. Editeurs, 1937).
5. ———. "La Physique du Vingtième Siècle et la Philosophie," *Actualités Scientifiques et Industrielles*, no. 445 (1936).
6. Edmond Husserl, *The Crisis of European Sciences and Transcendental Phenomenology*, trans. David Carr (Evanston, Il.: Northwestern University Press, 1970).
7. Léon Brunschvicg, *Les Etapes de la Philosophie Mathématique* (Premier Tirage, 1912), Nouveau Tirage augmenté d'une préface de M. Jean-Toussaint Desanti (Paris: Librairie Scientifiue et Technique, 1972).
8. Martin Heidegger, "La Question de la Technique," Essais et Conférences, traduction française de "Die Frage nach der Technik," in *Vortrage und Aufsatze*, (Neske Verlag, 1954).
9. Rose Marte Mosse-Bastide, *Bergson Educateur* (Paris: P.U.F., 1955).
10. Henri Bergson, "Lettre à Léon Brunschvicg," *Ecrits et Paroles* 3 (Paris: P.U.F., 1957-59), 588..

[12] Simone Weil, *Cahiers* 1 (Paris: Plon, 1951), 11.

[13] Simone Weil, "Extraits de Lettres et Brouillons de Lettres à André Weil (janvier-avril 1940)," in *Sur la Science*, 220.

[14] Ibid., 219.

[15] Morris Cohen and I. E. Drabkin, *A Source Book in Greek Science* (Cambridge, Mass.: Harvard University Press, 1948), 34.

[16] Arnold Reymond, *History of the Sciences in Greco-Roman Antiquity* (New York: Biblo and Tannen, 1963), 24-25.

[17] Weil, "Extraits de Lettres," 213-14.

[18] Weil, "La Science et Nous," in *Sur la Science*, 123.

[19] Weil, "Extraits de Lettres," 214.

[20] Ibid., 215. Verification of this can be found in Eratothenes' "Letter to Ptolemy-Euergetes," *Commentary on Archimedes' Sphere and Cylinder*, 89-96. Eratothenes, however, wrote that there were three geometricians of Plato's School who tackled this problem presented by the Delians who were seeking to double an altar by order of the oracle. These three were Archytas, Menaechmus, and Eudoxus. (Cohen and Drabkin, *Sourcebook in Greek Science*, 62-64, consider the nature of the whole solution of Eudoxus through "curved lines" as doubtful.)

[21] Ibid., 215. "The solutions of Menaechmus involve the determination of the intersection of two conics." (*Source Book*, 64.)

[22] Ibid., 215.

[23] Cohen and Drabkin, *Source Book in Greek Science*, 5-6.

[24] Reymond, *History of the Sciences*, 21-22.

[25] Ibid., 35-36.

[26] Weil, "Science et Perception," 23-25. According to legend Thales found the basic theorem of mathematics by seeking to measure pyramids, comparing them to their shadows, measuring the human figures in proportion to their shadows. (See note 22.)

[27] Ibid., 12.

[28] Weil, "Extraits de Lettres," 244.

[29] Weil, "La Science et Nous," 124.

[30] Simone Weil, *La Pesanteur et la Grâce* (Paris: Librairie Plon, 1948), 153.

[31] Marcel De Corte, "La Pensée Sociale de Simone Weil," *Synthèses* 9 (1947): 309-20.

[32] Hannah Arendt, *The Human Condition* (Chicago: University of Chicago Press, 1958), 287-88.

[33] De Corte, "Le Pensée Sociale de Simone Weil."

[34] Weil, "La Science et Nous," 125.

[35] Ibid.

[36] Ibid.

[37] Ibid.

[38] Ibid., 129.

[39] Ibid.

[40] *Grand Larousse Encyclopédique*, vol. 4, s.v. "Entropy."

[41] Weil, "La Science et Nous, 129.

[42] Ibid., 147

[43] Weil, "Théorie des Quanta," 187.

[44] Ibid., 187-88.

⁴⁵Ibid., 192-93.
⁴⁶Ibid., 192.
⁴⁷Weil, "La Science et Nous," 155.
⁴⁸Ibid., 156.
⁴⁹Ibid., 157.
⁵⁰Ibid., 157-58.
⁵¹Ilya Prigogine and Isabelle Stengers, *La Nouvelle Alliance—Métamorphose de la Science*.
⁵²Ibid., 17.
⁵³Isaac Benrubi, *Contemporary Thought of France* (New York: Alfred A. Knopf, 1926), 13-14.
⁵⁴Ibid., 19.
⁵⁵Régis Michaud, *Modern Thought and Literature in France* (New York: Funk & Wagnall, 1934), 25.
⁵⁶Benrubi, *Contemporary Thought of France*, 85.
⁵⁷Ibid., 103-13.
⁵⁸André Vergez and Dénis Huisman, *Histoire des Philosophes Illustrée par des Textes* (Paris: Fernand Nathan, 1966), 395.
⁵⁹Benrubi, *Contemporary Thought*, 141.
⁶⁰Ibid., 143.
⁶¹Léon Brunschvicg, *Les Etapes de la Philosophie Mathématique* (Paris: Librairie Blanchard,1972).
⁶²H. S. Hughes, *Consciousness and Society: The Reorientation of European Social Thought, 1890-1930* (New York: Knopf, 1958), 399-401.
⁶³Max Jammer, *The Conceptual Development of Quantum Mechanics* (New York: McGraw-Hill, 1966), 166-67.
⁶⁴Paul Forman, "Weimar Culture, Causality, and Quantum Theory," 1918-1927. Adaptation by German Physicists and Mathemeticians to a Hostile Intellectual Environment," *Historical Studies in the Physical Sciences*, vol. 3 (Philadelphia: University of Pennsylvania Press, 1971), 4.
⁶⁵Ibid., 1-115.
⁶⁶O. Spengler, *The Decline of the West*, vol. 1, *Form and Actuality* (New York: Knopf, 1926), 120.
⁶⁷Forman, "Weimar Culture, Causality and Quantum Theory,: 92-93.
⁶⁸Max Planck, *The Philosophy of Physics* (New York: Norton, 1936).
⁶⁹Capek, *The Philosophical Impact of Contemporary Physics*, 320-21.
⁷⁰Ibid., 94-95.
⁷¹Ronald Clark, *Einstein: The Life and Times* (New York: World Publishing Co., Avon Books, 1971) 11.
⁷²Ibid., 104-5.
⁷³It is undeniable that her writings completed a year or two before her death in 1943 reflect her recent personal conversion, as seen in her close association between Platonic and Christian philosophies, her increasing emphasis on Determinism, and gradual refusal of free will.
⁷⁴*Grand Larousse Encyclopédique*, vol. 4, s.v. "Déterminisme."
⁷⁵M. Le Comte Laplace, *Essai Philosophique sur les Probabilités* (Paris: Mme. Ve. Courcier,

tionary ? Libraire pour les Mathématiques et la Marine, 1814), 3-4.

[76] Grand Larousse Encyclopédique, vol. 4, s.v. "Déterminisme."

[77] Milic Capek, *The Philosophical Impact of Contemporary Physics* (Princeton: Van Nostrand, 1961), 121.

[78] In Weil's religious philosophy, contact with necessity (in the form of work, beauty, or pain) is the passage to spiritual transcendency.

[79] Weil, "Science et Perception," Deuxieme Partie.

[80] Forman, "Weimar Culture, Causality, and Quantum Theory".

[81] Weil, "La Science et Nous," 137-43.

[82] Louis De Broglie, *The Revolution in Physics* (New York: Noonday Press, 1953), 14.

[83] Louis De Broglie, *Continu et Discontinu en Physique Moderne* (Paris: Editions Albin Michel, 1941), 16.

[84] Weil, "Fragment d'Une Lettre à un Etudiant," *Sur la Science*, 117.

[85] De Broglie, *Continu et Discontinu*, 16.

[86] Ibid., 20.

[87] De Broglie, *The Revolution in Physics*, 51-53.

[88] De Broglie, *Continu et Discontinu*, 28.

[89] Ibid.

[90] Ibid., 30-32.

[91] Ibid., 33.

[92] Ibid.

[93] De Broglie, *The Revolution in Physics*, 298.

[94] Ibid., 302.

[95] Weil, "Fragment d'Une Lettre," 117.

[96] Ibid., 117-118.

[97] *Grand Larousse Encyclopédique*, vol. 4, s.v. "Déterminisme."

[98] Weil, "Fragment d'une Lettre," 118-19. also from Léon Brunschvicg, "La Physique du Vingtième Siècle et la Philosophie," *Actualités Scientifiques et Industrielles*, No. 445 (1936): 26-27.

[99] Weil, "La Science et Nous," 160-61.

[100] Weil, "Lettre à un Etudiant," 119.

[101] Capek, *Philosophical Impact of Contemporary Physics*, 295-96. It is significant that a prominent scientist-philosopher such as Thompson retains up until the last quarter of our century such an opinion on determinism. It underlines the importance of reflections voiced during the critical years of struggle between determinism and indeterminacy. Thompson maintains ironically that indeterminacy will prevail, not because it is physically impossible to discover all the factors and consequences of a physical event, even at the microscopic level, but because such exhaustive research would conflict with the status quo. This is an argument somewhat different from that of Weil's but it does echo the same claim that predictability, though beyond the willingness of our physical efforts, is possible on *all* levels, both macroscopic and microscopic, that determinism remains a primary concept. This belief, though tinged with cynicism, persists in modern times. It may be scientifically simplistic and inaccurate, but the fact that such a view still persists proves its relevance, that there is doubt and a feeling of incompatibility with the complete rejection of causality and determinism.

[102] Ibid., 297.
[103] Ibid.
[104] Capek, *Philosophical Impact of Contemporary Physics*, 295.
[105] Ibid., 295-96, 297.
[106] Ibid.
[107] Capek, *The Philosophical Impact of Contemporary Physics*, 79-80.
[108] Ibid., 5.
[109] Ibid., 5-6.
[110] Ibid., 6.
[111] Weil, "La Science et Nous," 192.
[112] Ibid.
[113] Weil, "Théorie des Quanta," 192.
[114] Weil, "La Science et Nous," 153.
[115] Ibid., 154.
[116] Ibid., 154-55.
[117] Ibid., 157-58.
[118] Grand Larousse Encyclopédique, Vol. 8, s.v. "Probabilité."
[119] Weil, *Cahiers* I: 108.
[120] Simone Pétrement, *La Vie de Simone Weil–II, 1934-1943* (Paris: Librairie Fayard, 1973), 386.
[121] Weil, "Extraits de Lettres," 254.
[122] Pétrement, *La Vie de Simone Weil*, 386.
[123] Mark W. Zemansky, *Temperatures Very Low and Very High* (New York: Dover Publications, 1964), 32. Reversibility is defined as a process in which the system and its environment are stable without complications such as acceleration, waves, friction, etc. "Every property like pressure, temperature, magnetization, etc., is *uniform throughout the entire system*. . . . very close to equilibrium at all times," 26. In her essay, "Réflexions sur la Théorie de Quanta," Weil also discusses irreversibility and the transition towards recognition of probable states on the microscopic level, 192-93.
[124] Weil, "La science et Nous," 137.
[125] Prigogine and Stengers, *La Nouvelle Alliance*, 119.
[126] Ibid.
[127] A. de Lamartine, "Le Désespoir," *Premières et Nouvelles Méditations Poétiques* (Paris: Pagnerre-Furne-Hachette, 1870), 49.
[128] See note 116.
[129] Edmond Goblot, *Le Vocabulaire Philosophique* (Paris: Librairie Armand Colin, 1920), 175.
[130] See note 116.
[131] Weil, "La Science et Nous," 150.
[132] Jacques Monod, *Le Hasard et la Nécessité, essai sur la philosophie naturelle de la Biologie Moderne* (Paris: Editions du Seuil, 1970), 194-95.
[133] Ibid., 127.

[134] Madeleine Barthélemy-Madaule, *L'Idéologie du Hasard et de la Nécessité* (Paris: Editions de Seuil, 1972), 39.

[135] It is interesting that Weil is influenced by Hume's teaching, especially in view of his criticism of Berkeley's Idealism; his claim that causality was a creation of the mind is in direct opposition to Weil's affirmation of Necessity, Determinism. Hume, however, did to a certain extent, influence Weil's criticism of French Epistemologists and Idealists such as Brunschvicg.

[136] *Grand Larousse Encyclopédique*, Vol. 5, s.v. "Galilée."

[137] Weil, "Fragments," 272-73.

[138] Capek, *The Philosophical Impact of Contemporary Physics*, 318.

[139] Ibid., 188.

[140] Weil, *La Pesanteur et la Grâce* 20.

[141] Jammer, *Concepts*, 111.

[142] . A. Burtt, *The Metaphysical Foundations of Modern Physical Science* (New York: Humanities Press, 1951), 257.

[143] Bertrand Rssell, *Principles of Mathematics* (New York: Norton, 1903), 465.

[144] Pétrement, *La Vie de Simone Weil*, II: 164-65.

[145] Paul Valéry, "Ebauche d'un Serpent," *Les Charmes, Oeuvres* I (Paris: Bibliothèque de la Pléiade-Gallimard, 1957), 139.

[146] Henri Bergson, *Creative Evolution*, tr. A. Mitchell (New York: Modern Librar, 1944), 299-300.

[147] Capek, *The Philosophical Impact of Contemporary Physics*, 14.

[148] Weil, "Science et Perception," Deuxième Partie.

[149] Immanuel Kant, *Critique of Pure Reason*, tr. Norman Kemp Smith (New York: Humanities Press, 1950), 69-70.

[150] Bertrand Russell, *An Essay on the Foundations of Geometry* (New York: Dover, 1897), 49.

[151] Cohen and Drabkin, *Source Book*, 44, 50.

[152] Ibid., 50.

[153] Weil, "La Science et Nous," 155-56.

[154] Blaise Pascal, *Pensées* (Paris: Editions Garnier-Frères, 1958), 87-92.

[155] Capek, *The Philosophical Impact of Contemporary Physics*, 25.

[156] Russell, *Essay*, 112-13.

[157] Weil, *La Pesanteur et la Grâce*, 26.

[158] Ibid., 36.

[159] Ibid., 51, 121-25, 353.

[160] Ibid., 49.

[161] Ibid, 49-51.

[162] Augustine *Confessions and Enchiridion*, Vol. 7, tr. and ed. Albert C. Cutler (Philadelphia: Westminster).

[163] Ibid., 255.

[164] Weil, *La Pesanteur et la Grâce*, 59.

[165] Augustine *Confessions and Enchiridion*, 7: 253.

[166] Capek, *Philosophical Impact of Contemporary Physics*, 354, "Very few thinkers of the Classical period adopted St. Augustine's "finitist" attitude towards the cosmic past. Renouvier and his school in France, F. C. S. Schiller in England, DeWitt Parker in the United States, and a few others dared to challenge the official dogma of infinitism which has been accepted almost exclusively."

[167] Ibid., 125-26. See also Weil, "Extraits de Lettres," 240-43, 247-52.

[168] Capek, *Philosophical Impact of Contemporary Physics*, 153.

[169] Weil, "Fragments," 272-73.

[170] Capek, *Philosophical Impact of Contemporary Physics*, 158-59.

[171] Emile Meyerson, *La Déduction relativiste*, (Paris: Payot, 1925), 89-101.

[172] H. G. Wells, *The Time Machine: An Invention* (London: Heinemann, 1894).

[173] Paul Langevin, "L'aspect général de la théorie de la relativité," *Bulletin scientifique des étudiants de Paris*, No. 2 (1922): 6.

[174] Capek, *Philosophical Impact of Contemporary Physics*, 160.

[175] Benrubi, *Contemporary Thought of France*, 106-113.

[176] Hannah Arendt, *The Human Condition* (Chicago, University of Chicago Press, 1958), 3-4.

[177] See note 32; also simliarity of Arendt's view, *The Human Condition*, 287.

Chapter 5
Deconstruction of Self

In the religious works of Simone Weil, the concept of 'déracinement' takes on a greater complexity of meaning. This meaning is expressed through Weil's usage of the term 'décréation.' 'Décréation' has three functions in Weil's philosophy: it provides the spiritual detachment necessary for effective social participation; as such it forms the bridge between the human and the divine; it satisfies a personal need for purification through spiritual anonymity, retreat and total detachment. Each of these functions is fulfilled as Weil progresses further in the decreation process.

The first of these functions is most carefully described in one of Weil's last essays, "La Personne et le Sacré" included in the publication, *Ecrits de Londres*.[1] It had originally been published as "La personnalité humaine, le juste et l'injuste," *La Table Ronde*, December 1950. Here Weil describes the reduction of the Personal to the Impersonal Self. The essay was initially a reaction to the growing popularity of Mounier's theory of Personalism.

Mounier had been involved in the restoration of religion to the center of national life in France under Pétain's "national revolution." Pétainist Catholicism had preached obedience, order and compromise with the enemy. The Church, seeking favors from the Vichy government, had shown itself to be inflexible and dogmatic. Mounier, eventually became disillusioned by the prostitution of religious ideals by the Collaborationists. His publication, *Esprit*, was banned in August 1941 following difficulty with the Vichy censors. After his organization of clandestine studies in the southern zone and the liaison he established between his group and the leaders of Combat,[2] he was arrested by the Vichy government and kept in confinement until the summer of 1942.[3] By the time Weil had arrived in London in December 1942 to work for Free France, Mounier was already living in exile in the Drome where he was beginning his reappraisal of true Christian spirituality and purity. His apocalyptic vision of a new Christendom, and his "tragic optimism" took form during the early forties.[4] By the late forties and early fifties, Mounier's New Personalism had become considerably popular yet controversial, particularly in the ranks of the Communist and Catholic Left. The publication of Weil's article in 1950 was, in part, utilized as a reaction against the revival of religious reformism initiated by Mounier. Mounier's prime means of reforming Christianity was based on his concern for the human person.[5] But not all Christian beliefs could be transposed into Personalism. It is interesting that Weil's religious beliefs led her to the same conclusion of the need for spiritual renewal through "a balanced sense of contemplation and action, deep religiosity and political commitment" that John Hellman, the most recent biographer of Mounier, attributes to his subject.[6] Weil, however, retained the principles of sin and redemption whereas Mounier discarded them. Weil feared particularly the possible return to the idolatry of the self and of the Social through the elevation of the Human Person; she considered it a false imitation of spirituality and a dangerous basis for social commitment; she feared particularly a return to the egotism and social idolatry that had begun the war. Her article offers an alternative path to the social involvement and realization of individual value, through a detachment of the self and reduction to the Impersonal.

> . . .l'être humain n'échappe au collectif qu'en s'élevant au-dessus du personnel, pour pénétrer dans l'impersonnel. A ce moment il y a quelque chose en lui; une parcelle de son âme, sur quoi rien de collectif ne peut avoir aucune prise. S'il peut s'enraciner dans le bien impersonnel. . . .[7]

The Human Person does not contain the essential element of individual identity.

Personality is a dressing needed to be shed so as to discover the true sanctified core of the self. The human personality is not the vital sanctified element of the self which provides the spiritual detachment necessary for a comprehension and pursuit of truth. This is found only in the reduction of the self to its impersonal core. The Impersonal, the sanctified core of the self, is that part of us which is vulnerable to injustice. The Impersonal equates truth with good and nourishes within us the expectation of justice. The Impersonal is that primal sense of purity awakened by the incomprehensibility of affliction. It is, therefore, for Weil, the only state wherein one may truly comprehend and achieve absolute justice. In his study of Weil, Michel Narcy accurately states that contact with the Impersonal is achieved through one of two possible ways: through exposure to pain or beauty.[8] Beauty in the Greek and neo-classical sense refers naturally to all manifestations of Truth. Weil's views on the Impersonal confirm the validity of Narcy's interpretation.

Weil specifically describes labor or work as an indirect form of suffering; therefore, by the physical affliction it imposes it provides contact with injustice which in turn evokes the Impersonal. However, it would be inaccurate to qualify Weil's experiences with and comprehension of work so simply; in the factories, working without proper safeguard from individual bodily harm under the pressure of production quotas and terrible periods of sinusitis, Weil judged work objectively and subjectively as a negative experience,[9] in the fields of Le Rhône and l'Ardèche, however, Weil viewed labor as a positive, consciously creative act.[10] In both cases, however, it exposed her to ultimate necessity, the law by which one can only achieve and comprehend the interrelationship between oneself and one's environment indirectly. This distance and the resulting dispersion of oneself and one's desires through space and time provide the necessary contact with affliction for the passage of the personal to the Impersonal.

Weil's articulation of work as an essential experience of necessity was cited particularly by Hannah Arendt in her book, *The Human Condition*. Arendt used it in support of her challenge to the Marxist contention that a higher development of technology could liberate the individual from the necessity of labor. This refers back to an argument presented by Weil herself in her "Critique du Marxisme." Arendt states: "Weil's *La Condition Ouvrière* (1951) is the only book which deals with the problem without prejudice and sentimentality."[11]

Janet Patricia Little has also written an extensive study on the function of labor as essential contact with necessity in the passage of the Personal to the Impersonal. Little analyzed the importance of necessity and obedience in an article entitled, "Action et Travail chez Simone Weil" by saying, "Le travail est . . . une condition . . . de la nécessité, mais c'est ce par quoi j'ai une certaine emprise sur le monde." Little views Weil's religious metaphysics as an extension of her philosophy of action whereby the satisfaction of individual desire gives way to obedience and consent to the law of necessity.[13]

Weil establishes that contact with injustice or necessity and our vulnerability to affliction reduces the individual to a state of intense, impersonal awareness; it removes the impurity of the ego and renders the individual more sensitive and more effective in her or his social participation. One can conceive justice truthfully only by a rediscovery of the Impersonal.

This essential contact with necessity or affliction for passage to the ultimate state of awareness transposes Weil's earlier reference to violence as an equalizer in her commentary on the *Iliad* and in her political essays on colonialism. Two recurring themes have been shown in her political and historical writings: the absence of true power, and violence and force as the common denominator reducing both the powerful and the powerless to the same level. When Weil became deeply immersed in religious questions, she interpreted the exposure to the equalizing force of violence as contact with necessity and affliction and reduction of the Personal to the Impersonal. In the section on power and violence above, I have already noted that the concepts of the contagion of violence and the instability of power appearing in Weil's prewar essays reappear in Girard's study on violence and myth, published in 1972.[14] Equally as striking is the resemblance between the two titles—Weil's "La Personne et le Sacré," and Girard's *La Violence et le Sacré*.[15] In each of these works, violence is discussed as the means towards purification.

However, it should be recognized that in her later religious works, Weil distinguishes between violence and destruction; the principle violence, is used in Weil's religious philosophy to describe the experience of moral and psychological affliction, not physical death. Contact with necessity is the transposed equalizing force.

This points to a distinction between the notions of 'le droit' and 'la justice'. Inherited from the Romans, the notion of "le droit" relates to force. Love, not force, is what Weil believes to be the true basis of divine justice; therefore 'le droit' as the basis of human justice renders it impure. She believes that this association with the idea of force is the basis of falsely conceived relations in human society.

Detachment, within the realm of the Impersonal becomes for Weil the only path towards an understanding of Truth. "Enracinement" within the realms of politics, labor, and science, involves "déracinement," uprootal, detachment from false absolutes and illusions of power; in the spiritual realm also, Weil seeks to uproot herself from a dependency on the false vanity of the human person reflected in the predominance of the Ego and the Social to reorient herself towards the absolutes of truth, beauty, and justice.

The passage from the Personal to the Impersonal fulfills the need for spiritual detachment necessary for effective social participation. Weil describes this passage through the separate stages of dispersion and the abandonment of personal identity. Yet throughout this process, the will is retained and imposed as the essential instrument of the gradual intensification of intelligence and attention leading to the culminating stage of impersonal awareness. As stated, the first stage is dispersion, a loosening of the hold of a collectivity on its individual members.

The second stage is the abandonment of one's dependency on personal identity. This serves both as a final, absolute renunciation of self and as simply, a detachment from the trappings of the self for a greater comprehension of truth. In the context of Weil's writing, this second stage, the passage from the Personal to the Impersonal is called "le processus décréateur."

Le Processus décréateur—The Deconstruction of Self: In notes and commentary appearing throughout her works, decreation is given particular emphasis as a central principle.

> Décréation: Faire passer du créé dans l'incréé.
> Destruction: faire passer du créé dans le néant.
> Ersatz coupable de la décréation. . . .[16]

Miklos Vëto in his book, *La Métaphysique religieuse de Simone Weil* notes that the term "décréation" had originally been Péguy's neologism, diametrically opposed in meaning to Weil's usage of the term.[17] Vëto, whose book is the deepest analysis of the process of 'décréation' in the context of Weil's writings, defines it in the following way:

> . . . c'est le seul terme qui puisse exprimer adéquatement son intention fondamentale, celle de la vocation auto-annihilatrice des êtres humains. . . .[18]

Weil describes throughout her writings the separate stages of the decreation process: creation, autonomy, anguish, and final detachment.

Creation: Decreation and Creation are both complementary and opposing actions. The creation is, in Weil's analysis, a movement of withdrawal, abdication by God, who in an expansive act of love, provides the space and absence for the human presence. The creation was for the Divine a denial of presence and self out of love for the object of the Creation. But for the human creature, the creation was the expansion of power and sin; existence is defined as the absence of God, whose act of love paradoxically created an essentially sinful condition for the human person. By the creation, the human being is condemned to a state of autonomy. Creation is a dispersion of power; although it is a sacrifice, a retreat conceived by Weil as an act of love, it imposes on the human creature a state of impurity and sin. Decreation allows one to imitate the creation of one's own abdication and reduction of self. In Weil's final religious writings, completed moments before her death, the term 'abandon' replaces that of 'abdication'.[19] This corresponds to the feeling of wrenching and anguish which she relates at this final point accompanying the necessary reduction of self. What she conceived as her own impurity and worthlessness intensifies her own unwilling passage towards death.

Both critics, Miklos Vëto and Wladimir Rabi, have noted in studies on Weil's concept of decreation the parallel in Jewish mysticism concerning the withdrawal or abandonment by God.

> . . .l'étrange similarité de ces vues avec la notion Kabbaliste du Tzimtzum, ce retrait de Dieu dans la Création.[20]

Autonomy: The divine movement of retreat and abdication imposes an abundancy of freedom and presence. The imposition of autonomy is compensation for the state of impurity in which we are plunged. The creation was the imposition of absence and non-being. It is the vacuum, created by the abdication of divine power and presence, filled up by the plenitude of being rendered possible by the abdication of human power and presence; autonomy is conceived as absence and sin, the appearance or imitation of true being and existence; renunciation of the self and fusion with the divine spirit is presence and true existence. But total, complete fusion does not seem to have been Weil's objective. It was more the purifying strength contained in the act of renunciation and in the harmony and balance of the opposing movement of tension between creature and creator. Here again recurs Weil's ideal of 'enracinement', where unity is based on mediation between the forces of integration and detachment. Weil finds in the concept of the Trinity, mediation between the forces of 'déracinement' and 'enracinement', between 'creation' and 'decreation'.

Weil wrote in *La Pesanteur et la Grâce* that necessity, affliction, the burden of need and the exhaustion of work are all expressions of divine love, just as the creation was also. Necessity is the "screen" between ourselves and the divine permitting us to be.[21] Without the protective illusion of time, matter and space, there would have been no development of the self or of personality to eventually be rejected. Being is thus achieved through the total circularity of movement between creation and decreation. Without the creation we would not have been abandoned to our own freedom and responsibility. Without autonomy, we would not have developed the strength to distance ourselves from the illusions of being that exist in time, matter and space. Through decreation, we are able to essentiate ourselves. The total experience of being is centered around the autonomy which is granted us and which we willfully reject.

> Il a été donné à l'homme une divinité imaginaire pour qu'il puisse s'en dépouiller comme le Christ de sa divinité réelle. . . . Nous participons à la création du monde en nous décréant nous-mêmes. . . .[22]

The physical law discovered by Pascal, the tendency of liquid or gas to distribute itself evenly over a given area is a metaphor in Weil's analysis for the state of autonomy following the creation. As matter tends to extend its mass the self tends to extend its power and presence. Acceptance of vacuum or emptiness is renunciation of the extension of one's own power.

> Comme du gaz, l'âme tend à occuper la totalité de l'espace qui lui est accordé. Un gaz qui se retracterait et laisserait du vide, ce serait contraire à la loi d'entropie. . . .²³

Pascal had denounced the human tendency to avoid confrontation with the ambiguity and uncertainty of one's own condition as the human creature wavers between the infinitudes of power and servitude, of life and death. He had criticized the tendency of most individuals to divert themselves from this uncertainty, instead of facing it squarely. Weil's comments on 'L'imagination combleuse' are Pascal's. In the state of autonomy following the creation, the imagination gives the illusion of a plenitude of being and thus enables the individual to avoid confronting the ambiguity and emptiness of existence. Weil also believed that imagination prevented suffering from becoming a means of purification. A rejection of one's dependency on imagination was the passage towards anguish, awareness and total detachment.

> . . .si on arrête l'imagination combleuse, il y a vide. . .si on accepte, n'importe quel vide, quel coup du sort, peut empêcher d'aimer l'univers. . . .²⁴

The renunciation of the illusion of temporality is also part of this emergence from autonomy. Time is an imitation of eternity. The imagination provides the illusion of past and future as an escape from nothingness. Weil believed that our assumption of structural temporality indicated our desire for escape from infinities described by Pascal. Acceptance of nothingness is an acceptance of our finality and a rediscovery of eternity. Separation of desire from its object is also part of this gradual renunciation. Following the removal of its object, the energy of desire is increased, intensified.

Anguish and Total Detachment: In her essay "Amour de Dieu et le Malheur," Weil describes the stage of affliction through which the self must pass to reach the final point of the decreation process.²⁵ Vëto coined the term 'la souffrance redemptrice' to describe this process.²⁶

Weil distinguishes between "la souffrance," and "le malheur." "Le malheur" is the irreducible element of suffering, that part of physical and emotional affliction which cannot be erased by the mind. "Le malheur" is an uprootal of spiritual life, a form of living death imposed on the soul through the experience or apprehension of physical pain. Weil describes it as the nail penetrating the soul and joining together the decomposing effects of physical pain and social degradation. She builds an analogy as we have seen earlier between the nail intersecting the cross and the force of necessity dispersed throughout the totality of time and space. For Weil, both provide the point of juncture between the Creation and the Creator.

> La distance . . . qui sépare Dieu de la créature se rassemble . . . en un point pour percer une âme en son centre. . . .[27]

Both the biblical figures of Job and Jesus represent the experience of affliction. For Weil, the story of Job particularly expressed the human confrontation with absence and darkness, and the despair which is caused by the revelation of divine indifference. Thus the passage through anguish towards detachment is a revelation and acceptance of absence. It is also a profound sense of abandonment and condemnation. Weil describes Job's cry of innocence as a revolt against his subsequent loss of self.

For this reason, the cross has important symbolic value in Weil's philosophy. Apart from its association with the crucifixion, the cross has always been a powerful symbol, evoking the mere geometrical strength and order of the universe. For Weil it is the absolute expression of necessity. The final uprootal of the soul from the illusion of autonomy and free will parallels the movement of the nail driven into the flesh, both contacts with necessity. The cross is the symbol in Weil's work of abandon. The Passion of the abandoned son has double meaning for Weil: it is both the literal martyrdom of the divine on the cross and the abandonment of the human to sin and suffering. Both the movements of creation and decreation receive fulfillment on the cross.

The cross thus also communicates fusion, reintegration. Weil considers this as "the circular movement of grace." By one's contact with necessity one achieves the same point of fusion, one reconstructs the cross and its intersection between the two coordinates of eternity.

The cross thus symbolizes for Weil eternity, necessity and beauty, abandon and martyrdom, fusion and purification. Its symbolic power contains within it all the dimensions of affliction as a stage in spiritual renunciation. But most interesting of all is its value as the symbol of the tension by which one moves upwards in the antithetical movement against pain and sin. This brings us to what, in my opinion, is the most valuable and interesting aspect of her religious philosophy—the concept of attention.

Attention—the Mediating Power of Intelligence: Weil explains her concept of 'attente' and the power of attention in an essay entited, "Réflexions sur le bon usage des études scolaires en vue de l'Amour de Dieu," which was included in the collection, *Attente de Dieu*.[28]

She distinguishes attention from the physical, muscular effort usually associated with an expression of will. Intelligence is maintained by the intensity of desire. She describes attention as a negative effort. The physically imposed effort that leads to fatigue and exhaustion diminishes one's power of attention; it hinders the state of disponibility, of abandon and 'détente' through which the power of attention or intelligence is developed.

> L'attention consiste à suspendre sa pensée, à la laisser disponible, vide et pénétrable à l'objet. . . .[29]

In a state of true attention, thought waits in openness as a vacuum waiting to be filled. Thought waits and provides an opening for the expansion of desire. Intelligence or attention is this imposed sense of flexibility maintained by the intensificiation of desire.

Study is for Weil preparation for a higher sense of spiritual awareness because it is the realm of life where the power of attention first begins to develop. She attributes all shortcomings and mistakes in academic work to the absence of this flexibility and openness. Understanding and intelligence works not in the form of an active search but in that of receptivity and openness. This emphasis on 'attente' should not be misconstrued as an absence of will. It is the highest expression of personal will and effort. "L'attention est un effort, le plus grand des efforts peut-être, mais c'est un effort négatif."[30] One's awareness increases by a self-imposed state of openness and detachment; in the realm of spirituality, disciplined, self-willed passivity leads to the abnegation of the self. This provides for the tension by which one moves upwards, by moving willfully towards slavery and self-denial; this tension of paradoxical movement is symbolized by the cross. The intensity of desire leads one to impose upon oneself a state of flexibility and passivity; one chooses to combat one's own tendency for action to fill up the vacuum of ignorance and uncertainty. Through the tension of this antithetical movement, the duality of the master/slave relationship is finally overcome.

However, Weil's conception of "attente" and the power of attention provides not only the anchor controlling and directing the passage towards total abnegation and detachment; it is not only the bridge between the human and the divine. It functions also as the source of spiritual receptivity between individuals.

Weil had begun to conceive this concept in her essay on the *Iliad* (cf. "Iliade ou Le Poème de la Force," and the section on the Myth of Heroism above) which she had written earlier in 1939, the year that war had begun. The essay reflects a still understandably pessimistic view of human relationships. In her discussion of the *Iliad*, she referred to fraternal contact as something rare and momentary, a brief and occasional interruption into the monotony of violence. Her concept of attention evidently developed in conjunction with her religious ideas, although the concept of affliction changes somewhat and acquires value as a source of redemptive violence.

> C'est savoir poser sur lui . . . un regard attentif . . . òu l'âme se vide . . . pour recevoir en elle-même l'être. . . .[31]

In a completely nonreligious sense, the power of attention makes room for the receptivity that bridges the gap between oneself and the other. For a layperson, it is the most optimistic aspect of her philosophy. This has been the greatest source of appeal for Weil's writing in the last twenty years. A simplistic, perhaps naive concept in appearance, it expressed the intellectual feasibility of contact and mediation; contact between individuals could be prolonged beyond a moment by a disciplined sense of intellectual receptivity; this appealed to a culture emerging from the uncertainty and lonely commitments of Existentialist philosophy and the modern philosopher's attempt to resolve the contradictions between individual and collective freedom (i.e., *Between Existentialism and Marxism*). The rise of the New Novel had brought with it a new age of pessimism. The distrust dominating human relationships and the impossibility of more than a momentary fusion between individuals, relationships wavering between domination and indifference, pervaded the novels of Nathalie Sarraute and Robbe-Grillet. Christopher Lasch expressed the passage of society through an age of narcissism and distrust:

> Poets and novelists today, far from glorifying the self, chronicle its disintegration. . . . personal relations take on the character of combat. . . .[32]

Thus, despite the path towards renunciation outlined by her concept of decreation, the development of her belief in the spiritual mediating power of 'attention' reaffirmed the possibility for collective freedom without the engulfment of individual intelligence. The power of attention, as the passive and receptive forces of controlled intelligence, led to mediation with detachment. Through this concept more than any other Weil has resolved the enigma of alienation and "déracinement."

The three functions of 'décréation'—purification through spiritual anonymity, mediation between the human and the divine, and a deeper and more effective sense of social commitment—are fulfilled in Weil's religious philosophy. The three-fold nature of her goal renders the entire question of 'déracinement' even more complex and more valuable. As in her non-religious writings, the ultimate point sought is mediation between the forces of uprootal and integration, through the power of attention.

Notes to Chapter 5

[1] Simone Weil, "La Personne et le Sacré," *Ecrits de Londres et dernières lettres* (Paris: Gallimard, 1957).

[2] John Hellman, *Emmanuel Mounier and the New Catholic Left, 1930-1950* (Toronto: University of Toronto Press, 1981), 189-90, 252.

[3] Roy Pierce, "Emmanuel Mounier (1905-1950): Tragic Optimist," *Contemporary French Political Thought* (London: Oxford University Press,1966), 63-69.

[4] Roy Pierce, "Biography of a Generation," *Contemporary French Political Thought*, 40.

[5] Emmanuel Mounier, *Le Personnalisme* (Paris: Presses Universitaires de France, 1950).

[6] Hellman, *Emmanuel Mounier and the New Catholic Left*, 256.

[7] Weil, "La Personne et le Sacré," 19.

[8] Michel Narcy, *Simone Weil, malheur et beauté du monde* (Paris: Editions du Centurion, 1967).

[9] Simone Weil, *La Condition Ouvrière*, (1951).

[10] Simone Weil, *L'Enracinement* (1949).

[11] Hannah Arendt, *The Human Condition* (Chicago: University of Chicago Press, 1958), 131.

[12] Janet Patricia Little, "Action et Travail chez Simone Weil," *Cahiers Simone Weil* 2d ser., no. 1 (March 1979).

[13] Ibid.

[14] René Girard, *La Violence et le sacré* (Paris: Editions Bernard Grasset, 1972).

[15] Roger Caillois had also published in 1939 a book treating a similar topic, the opposition of "le sacré" and "le profane" and the importance of this opposition in primitive ritual and ceremony. *L'Homme et le Sacré* (Paris: Gallimard, 1939).

[16] Weil, *La Pesanteur et la Grâce*, 41.

[17] Miklos Vëto, *La Métaphysique religieuse de Simone Weil* (Paris: Librairie Philosophique J. Vrin, 1971), 18.

[18] Ibid.

[19] Simone Weil, "Notes Ecrites à Londres–1943," *La Connaissance Surnaturelle* (Paris: Gallimard, 1950).

[20] Vëto, *La Métaphysique religieuse de Simone Weil*, 20. Wladimir Rabi in his study entitled "La conception weilienne de la création-Rencontre avec la Kabbale juive," describes more minutely the stages of the creation in Jewish mysticism. According to Rabi, Tsimtsoum is the concentrated position of the creator in one single point. The infinite creator withdraws into himself in order to make room for man. He leaves a space empty. "S'hevirath ha kelim" is the term used by Rabi to designate the breaking of the vases that he had created to contain the seminal light for the creation of vegetable, mineral and human life. When the vases break, the cosmic Drama begins and the seeds of life are dispersed, to be retrieved by the human creature. The retrieval of these seeds of life would free God from his exile and thus is the human creature's role in the cosmic drama. Rabi also underlines an important difference between the Kabbal's interpretation of the Creation and Weil's. For Weil, the Creation was divine sacrifice. For Jewish tradition, it was simply a gift, a good deed–"midrash," completely removed from the idea of sacrifice (*Simone Weil, Philosophe, historienne et mystique* [Paris: Aubier Montaigne, 1978]).

[21] Weil, *La Pesanteur et la Grâce*, 42.

[22] Ibid.

[23] Ibid., 20-21.

[24] Ibid., 26-28.

[25] Simone Weil, "L'Amour de Dieu et le malheur," *Attente de Dieu*, 98-121.

[26] Vëto, *La Métaphysique religieuse de Simone Weil*, 85-86.

[27] Weil, "L'Amour de Dieu et le malheur," 120.

[28] Simone Weil, "Réflexions sur le bon usage des études scolaires en vue de l'Amour de Dieu," *Attente de Dieu*, 85-98.

"Attente" in French can mean either "waiting for" or "in expectation of." The double meaning of the term is important for an understanding of Weil's use of the concept. "Waiting for" defines more precisely Weil's meaning. "In expectation of" fails to express the intensity of humility and worthlessness before God in the final stage of decreation.

[29] Ibid., 92-93.

[30] Ibid., 92. In all fairness, it should be mentioned that critics of Weil are divided as to whether her philosophy of decreation culminates in a successful abnegation of self and disappearance of will. Weil's own uncertainty is at the root of this divergency of interpretations; she evidently sought complete abnegation and therefore renunciation to personal will. This is a theme she repeats throughout her religious writings. Yet at the same time, she emphasizes the importance of the power of attention and individual intelligence in achieving this renunciation and passage to the Impersonal. Sacrifice contains in her analysis the elements of control and discipline, which are indications of active and willful action. Therefore, I and a minority of critics conclude that will remains important throughout Weil's entire experience and philosophy. I would venture even further and compare her uncertainty in distinguishing between the power of self and the power of exteriority or divine will to the ambiguity of her early views expressed in her diplôme-monograph on Descartes (cf. "Science et Perception dans Descartes," *Sur la Science*, and the first chapter of this book). It would be possible to conclude therefore that Weil retains the principle of will throughout her philosophy as an instrument of clarification in distinguishing between the power of self and the power of Others, either for the purpose of comprehending the creative potential of one's own autonomy or for the purpose of understanding the purifying function of self-imposed sacrifice. Those among the critics who would be in disagreement with me are André Devaux, président d l'Association pour l'Etude de la Pensée de Simone Weil, Eric Springsted, head of the American branch and his advisor Diogenes Allen of Princeton School of Theology. Janet Patricia Little is also among these critics; her studies have been among the most penetrating and objective: ". . . on use de son corps comme d'une chose morte. . . . *La volonté n'y a aucune part, mais le seul consentement.*" ("Action et Travail chez Simone Weil," *Cahiers Simone Weil*, [March 1979]). My own view of Weil, however, is closer to that expressed by Peter Winch, a critic of Wittgenstein who has also discovered parallels between Weil and Wittgenstein in his introduction to Price's translation of Weil's *Leçons de Philosophie*. In a presentation on Weil, "Le nécessaire et le bien," he stated: ". . .l'extention et le développement de la faculté de connaissance dépendent d'une sorte d'auto-discipline pratique. . . ." (Paris: Aubier Montaigne–Colloque de Cerisy-la-Salle, du 21 juillet au 1er août 1974, published 1978).

[31] Ibid., *Attente de Dieu*, 96.

[32] Christopher Lasch, *The Culture of Narcissism-American Life in an Age of Diminishing Expectations* (New York: Warner Books Edition, Norton & Co., 1969), 69.

Chapter 6
The Reintegration of Meaning, Through Language, History, Mythology, and Poetry

There is one final realm of Simone Weil's philosophy that is relevant to the theme of 'déracinement/enracinement'. Throughout her essays on language, history, science and literature, as well as in her extensive notes on mythology, Weil treats the problem of the reintegration of symbol with original meaning, as did Husserl, Valéry, and Arendt. In this chapter I will discuss Weil's exploration of this problem of the rediscovery of value. The first and most important section treats Weil's concern with the deterioration of precise language usage. She believed that consciousness and method positively determined private and public action in the propagation of symbols and could thus provide a basic means of demystification of the sources of violence and power. The sections which follow the main body of the discussion relate the problem of the reintegration of symbol with original meaning to history, violence, myth, and spirituality. In a short final section Weil's poetry is presented as the ultimate expression of her search for precision, mediation, and value.

THE RECONSTITUTION OF SYMBOL

Simone Weil's writings communicate the need for a re-evaluation of the rapport between the sign and its representative function, and the reintegration of symbol with its original meaning. She believed that our cultural dependency on symbols was self-imposed. In her essays on science she indicates that we have become strangers to ourselves by spiritual and intellectual abnegation and dependency. Since the major break at the end of the nineteenth century between Classical and Modern Science, the role of algebra progressively grew in importance to the point that physicists came to regard it as signified material in itself communicable only through itself. The devaluation of symbols and mathematical formulae in science expressed a general social phenomenon. Through this multiplicity of signs and symbols we have estranged ourselves from the patterns of our own thought and minds. Things are totally consumed by the presence of symbols which represent them. She believed that contemporary science, unintelligible to ordinary people, was obscure even to the scholars themselves whose specialization left them ignorant of scientific domains beyond their own field of expertise. The rapidly increasing specialization of science rendered control and verification of scientific theories more and more difficult. But I have also shown that Weil's commentaries on the divergencies between science and culture stressed the responsibility of the humanist as well as the scientist. The basic responsibility for the ignorance and misunderstanding alienating the sciences and the humanities lies in teaching. For this reason, Weil stressed the teaching of the history of the sciences and mathematics to young scholars in the humanities for a greater sense of coherency, unity and function. Weil's thought reappears in the writings of Arendt, notably in *The Human Condition*, in which Arendt also points out the increasing untranslatability of scientific symbols; even more than Weil she fears the manipulation of insufficiently comprehended symbols.

In his play, *La Guerre de Troie N'Aura pas Lieu*, Jean Giraudoux had treated the violence caused by Helen's presence as a symbol of the fatality of war. Weil defined it as a metaphor for the conflict and destruction caused by the disassociation of symbol from meaning and the deterioration of clear thinking that resulted from the imprecision and devaluation of language usage. Helen was the metaphor for all the undefined political absolutes polarizing groups of individuals.

A defined, precisely understood word ceases to be an absolute and subsequently ceases to be dangerous. Political entities and absolutes are built upon words devoid of precise meaning, that is, works whose representative value has been misperceived or lost sight of in the mind of the language user. The displacement of power and mystification into the realm of language has resulted in our loss of intelligence based on relation; this loss manifests itself in all domains of human action and thought; politics, science, labor and history. As a result, Weil believed that we had come to live in an unreal world, exclusively inhabited by mythical entities and monsters. Our political and social vocabulary consists of terms that evoke absolute realities, absolute in so far as they are assumed to be independent of the conditions which rendered possible their existence and of the goal towards which they are directed. As political and social entities, words as symbols become absolutes. Much of the demystification of power lies therefore in the re-establishment of relation as in the case of the misunderstanding of terms such as 'le capitalisme', 'la revolution', 'la lutte de classe', 'la nation', 'la lutte contre les trusts'. It concerns not only the rediscovery of rapport between meaning and symbol but it also concerns the rapport between words. Weil believed the mystification of language often exists in the form of antagonistic terms that come to represent the dichotomies of misperceived political reality. Weil uses as examples the ideological polarities between antifascism and anticommunism, between dictatorship and democracy, between 'ouvrier' and 'patron'.

Weil uncovers layers of displaced meaning contained within the notion of national interest. The demystification of meaning leads first to the denial of the concept of nation as an end in itself. As the exploration of the symbol 'nation' progresses, meaning is displaced; value is subsequently attributed to economic interests. Therefore the concept 'nation' retains meaning only in so far as it communicates a structural unit of economic power. As Weil progressively examines the depths of meaning, each uncovered layer of value invalidates those already examined. She again displaces the meaning of the concept of national interest when she denies both its function as a framework of sovereignty and as a structure of economic power; it is finally discovered to mean simply, the capability to make war.

Weil's exploration of the term 'national interest' has led to a complete denial of its representative value. In the attempt to reintegrate symbol and meaning, a political absolute has been shown. As Weil penetrates the layers of meaning attributed to the term 'national interest', she arrives at a meaning containing the project of self-destruction. Weil defines 'national interest' as the capacity to make war in order to maintain or increase the capabilities for destruction; besides the inevitable contagion of violence that reverberates upon all participants in warfare, Weil is also implying here that destruction as project and end in itself is a self-inflicted form of estrangement and death. Weil's point is to show that a meaning that contains the project of its own destruction is a dangerous source of alienation. "Nation" is only an example of uncomprehended terminology.

The opposed meanings attributed to the terms fascism and communism are also, in Weil's eyes, the result of the disassociation of language from precise meaning. She examines each of the terms and concludes that they are both expressions of the same political principles; they both represent state control of every domain of individual social life; they both represent the constraints of a military state, a one-party system, and the imposed system of slave labor. The closest possible similarity in political structure existed between Germany and the Soviet Union. Arendt developed this idea more fully in her book, *The Origins of Totalitarianism*, in which she maintained that fascism and communism were substructures of the same political anomaly.[1] Like Weil her argument was that the polarization between these two similar political structures was the true reason for the Second World War and the holocaust. Weil saw the irony that the similarity between political entities was a major factor in their opposition, in their polarization. This recalls her observations on violence and on the Other expressed in her earlier work, "Réflexions sur les causes de la Liberté et de l'Oppression Sociale."[2] In that essay she had noted, in the course of her discussion on the gradual displacement of force from nature and the resulting qualitative transformation of production, that the identity and similarity which one perceives in another challenges one's own freedom and power. As both Weil and Girard note, identity and similarity between individuals render them basically incompatible and lead to a denial of similarity through violent confrontation. Similarity and identity are a source of violence and polarization unless, as Weil observed in the *Iliad* and in her spiritual writings, the power of attention leads one's identification with the other to a state of empathy and comprehension of the necessary balance of forces between one's own freedom and that of the other. In the political realm of power contemporary to Weil, the terms fascism and communism represented the same political situation; therefore there was no representative value in the opposition built between the two terms, fascism and communism, nor in the corresponding polarization of the negative terms 'antifascism' and 'anticommunism'. Ironically, comprehension of their similarity was, in great part, a reason for their antipathy to each other; similarity and difference moving both together and against each other, as do the elements of "déracinement/enracinement".

The modern meaning attributed to the word dictatorship and democracy is also a misrepresentation. Although Weil considered the opposition attributed to the two concepts to have a valid basis in reality, the term had still been abused; their value as relative, referential measures of a social structure has been suppressed and they became political absolutes. Absolute democracy, absolute dictatorship do not exist. A political system is defined in terms of the degree of democracy and dictatorship it contains. The same misperception of relative meaning may be perceived in the opposition of the terms order and liberty. A disassociation of symbol from the reality it was meant to represent leads one to lose sight of the relational value of language.

Such misperceived realities and undefined objectives appear as well in the language of labor relations, where 'la lutte contre le patron' and 'la lutte contre les meneurs' had become the absolutes, the terms used during the labor struggle of the thirties, as France was emerging from this period of internal dissent.

The terms revolution and capitalism also evoke opposing absolutes, a deceptive polarization of terms meant to define the relative characteristics of a social and political structure, particularly important in a society whose economy is in a continual state of transformation.

The failure of language was, in Weil's opinion, the failure of individuals to think clearly and methodically. Weil considered misrepresentation of meaning through language a sign of deterioration in thought; the loss of a sense of clarity and relation revealed by the misrepresentation of meaning was the sign of an intellectual and spiritual vacuum.

Valéry's writings and commentary had expressed also this concern for the loss of a methodical basis for language, action, and thought, and like Weil, he believed that this had been caused by the estrangement of symbol from its original meaning. This was the basis of his criticism of the philosophical tradition. Terms and concepts were manipulated without full comprehension of their representative value. He believed that traditional problems in philosophy stemmed from the loss of original meaning as a true basis of representative value. Valéry feared that language had become an end in itself.

> ... on se trouve impuissant ... que devant un mot qui semble plus contenir que tout ce que l'on pense.[3]

The extent of Valéry's influence on Weil's views and critique of language is evident. Her early lectures at Roanne on language were supported by quotations from Valéry indicating both the positive and negative aspects of the symbol's power of 'dédoublement' (cf. Chapter 2). Her later critique of language and science reflect the influence of Valéry's views on semantics and poetry. His view that proper language use was the basis of logical action also greatly influenced Weil's own belief in methodical thinking and action. Judith Robinson perceived in Valéry's writing both his use of language and poetry as the expression of method and logic and his concern that symbol and language structures threaten the independence of individual thought and intelligence.

> Aux yeux de Valéry, pourtant, le language a un défaut... celui de nous imposer ... la pensée des autres. ...[4]

In his essay, "The Origin of Geometry," Husserl concerned himself with the quality of precision in language use as a vital means of mediation.[5] A rediscovery of the sedimentations of meaning in a linguistic symbol served to reactivate its original meaning and self-evidence, and to reactivate the mediating force between language and the individual user. The rediscovery of original meaning is conceived by both Husserl and Weil as a creative act, and imitative act of reconstitution of meaning; reactivation of the rapport between 'significant' and 'signifié' necessitates the recreation of the sign by an understanding of its basic value, what Husserl refers to as 'the activity of coaccomplishment'. For Weil, Valéry, Arendt, and Husserl, mediation through language is a form of active understanding. The absence of conscious precision and understanding in language usage nullifies the mediating function.

> There is a distinction ... between passively understanding the expression and making it self-evident by reactivating its meaning.[6]

Husserl interpreted this passivity in language use as a source of dangerous mystification and emphasized the consequent need for the reactivation of the logical and relative value of the sign within the user's consciousness.

> In view of unavoidable sedimentation of mental products in the form of persisting linguistic acquisitions, . . . such constructions remain a danger. . .[7]

Thinking out one's use of language and the necessary demystification of undefined symbols, however, did not lead Weil to devalue the poeticizing flexibility of symbol, in literature, particularly. She placed great value on the sign's power of 'dédoublement' and its subsequent capacity to transcend the fixity of meaning. Yet, for Weil, the flexibility and transcendency of the symbol still maintained the stability, the root of its value in the original meaning it transcends. A comprehension of that original transcended meaning was still essential, despite the inevitability and positive presence of opacity and transcendency. The problem of language is thus another manifestation of the complementarity of 'déracinement/enracinement'. Representation contains both the movements of cohesion and dispersion, integration and detachment. Robert d'Amico comments on the tension involved in representation and writing as a replacement for thought and speech.

> The reactivation and replication of meaning is inseparable from the threat of loss and crisis. . .[8]

THE RECONSTITUTION OF HISTORICAL MEANING

Simone Weil's hope for the reactivation of self evidence and original meaning as a basis of understanding and logical action in the different realms of politics, history, science, and philosophy parallels Husserl's efforts in the same direction. Husserl's thoughts on the subject are found in his unfinished work, *The Crisis of European Sciences and Transcendental Phenomenology*: relevantly included in this work is the previously mentioned article, "The Origin of Geometry." This essay summarizes and articulates most effectively the main theme of this work.[9] Both Weil and Husserl considered the rediscovery of original meaning the key towards confronting and resolving the crises of European civilization. Through discussion of geometry, Husserl stressed the need to distinguish between original meaning and the sedimentations of traditional meanings accumulated since the discovery and beginning of geometrical science. Both Husserl and Weil used their studies of geometry as an example of the need for a return to original meanings in all disciplines.

Husserl justifies a reevaluation of geometry through a return to its beginnings; Weil had done the same by her 'resuscitation' of Thales and a rediscovery of Greek mathematical principles.

Husserl sought to preserve the totality and continuum of historical meanings. He affirmed that a continual rediscovery of original meaning and self-evidence was necessary for rebuilding this sense of unity and continuity within individual consciousness. Although Weil did not consciously dignify the sedimentations of meaning developing after Thales' discovery of geometry, Weil also had examined the historical origin and meaning of geometry and of Greek Science in general for the purpose of rediscovering the principles of unity and continuum between language and meaning.

Thus, both strove to preserve the totality and continuum of historical truths. The essential value and meaning of cultural structures and symbols could be grasped by the discovery and disclosure of the historical origin of symbol and meaning.

> ...the whole of the cultural present...implies a continuity of pasts which imply one another...[10]

Weil's interest in rediscovering the historical origins of culture and thus maintaining the unified totality of historical meanings is shown in her numerous essays on Nationalism, History, and Colonialism. Much of our cultural alienation is based on our rupture with the past, our denial of historical meaning. As political absolutes, 'nation', 'revolution', have incompatible meanings in our minds. This is because each term, as absolute, denies the historicity of the other, its traditional historical meaning as well as its relative association with freedom. Weil's search for historical meaning is most profoundly illustrated, however, in an essay entitled, "A Propos de la Question Coloniale dans ses Rapports avec le Destin du Peuple Francais" (1943) where she recommends as true 'enracinement' the reassociation of Western and Oriental cultures.[11] This essay had been among Weil's papers in London written in fulfillment of her duties as writer and editor for De Gaulle's Free France Organization. Although previously published as an article, it was not included in the group of manuscripts that later comprised one of her first published works in 1949.[12] It was finally included in a collection entitled, *Ecrits Historiques et Politiques*, published in 1960.[13] The exclusion of this essay from the book, *L'Enracinement*, ironically removed what would have been one of the latter's most substantive sections.

Following the liberation and disappearance of the sense of purpose and solidarity found in the spirit of resistance and struggle, the French people were to be faced with the same spiritual and intellectual vacuum that had led to the Second World War. Weil believed that the problem of the necessary respiritualizaton of the French people was inseparable from the question of colonialism. What Germany had done to France, France had done to its colonial Empire.

Weil describes the different ways by which France imposed its own culture on Oriental civilizations and thereby denied them a sense of history and the dignity of a cultural identity. Her critique of a French foreign policy in Indochina before, during, and after the defeat of Japanese invaders, is of particular irony to us. It bears a striking similarity to the critiques and protests of American involvement during the more recent era of the Vietnam War. Weil's critique of the French presence and foreign policy in Indochina as well as her general criticism of French colonial policy may well have been considered too controversial in its time.[14]

The revitalization of the French people could be attained only by the revalorization of its historical beginnings. In support of her belief that Western culture began under the influence of the Orient, Weil alludes particularly to the historical contributions of Greece and Egypt. She challenges the extent of influence generally attributed to the Roman Empire.[15] Weil believed that the Latin influence had been glorified and exaggerated to the point that a sense of historical continuity had been lost along with the values of harmony, mediation, and equilibrium inherited from different civilizations of the Orient (cf. chapter on Deconstruction of Power: The State). This is consistent with Weil's thoughts on the development of Science (cf. chapter on Science, section on Greek Science). Although Classical Science marked the abandonment of Greek values of harmony and proportion, Classical Science owes many of its basic principles to discoveries made during the period of Greek Science.[16]

The uprootal and subjugation of Oriental civilizations and cultures was also a self-imposed form of estrangement because so much of European civilization had begun under the influence of the Orient. Both European colonial conquest of the Orient and American economic influence within Europe diminish our sense of historical continuum between the cultures and values of the past, the present, and the future.

A rediscovery of the historical influences of oriental civilization on Europe would help to rebuild a sense of cultural continuum between past, present, and future. Europe, by rendering itself more consciously secure of its historical identity would be less vulnerable to the forces of economic imperialism. In addition, by a reevaluation of its roots in Oriental culture, Europe would protect not only its own cultural identity but the more ancient cultures of the East and the younger and newer civilizations even further West who regard Europe as the treasury of their cultural past.

Hannah Arendt echoed Weil's and Husserl's concern for historical continuum as a necessary application of methodical thought and action in 1967 in her book, *Between Past and Future*, translated into French as *La Crise de la Culture*.[17] The use by Arendt of quotations from Weil in support of her own views on labor, science, language, and history and the similarity of their views on all these topics suggests Weil's possible contributions to the emerging New Left.

Violence and Language: In her critique of language and symbol, Weil expressed her belief that the need to demystify the power contained in the disassociation of meaning from symbol was rendered even more difficult by our refusal of superstition. The mystification of linguistic meaning was, in part, a displacement of violence and power provoked by our suppressed propensity for superstition. Language becomes dangerous in so far as it is an exteriorization of that which we refuse to recognize in ourselves. The presence of a mythological element in the determination of language is a form of violence, a disruption of logical thinking.

The violence of this disruption perpetuates itself because it forms the basis for a misrepresentation of meaning; in turn the misunderstanding and estrangement caused by the continual usage of the symbol carrying forth this misrepresentation often results in actual physical violence and destruction. The destruction of meaning and the subsequent destruction of ourselves is the vengeance of superstition; discredited and purged from our lives it reemerges in a more dangerous form. Ernest Cassirer presents the thesis in his book, *Language and Myth*, that language is the expression of myth as well as of logic.[18] Suzanne Langer, the interpreter and translator of this work concludes that, although language and myth are two different modes of thought and the potentialities of both must be recognized, language has the power to break the bounds of the myth-making phase of the mind and to take us to the phase of discursive logic and conceptualization of facts.[19] This is similar to Weil's conclusion concerning language; language as the tool and expression of logical thinking and action involves refinement of immediate perception, a turning back upon oneself in a conscious appraisal of the process of meaning.

Another form of violence, however, is imposed by efforts to demystify the power of language: "La chasse aux entités" that Weil undertakes is the attempted uprootal of the mythological determinant of language. Weil's purifying act of demystification is an attempt towards reintegration but at the same time a disruption that uncovers and releases the sources of violence. In her analysis on power (cf. chapter on Deconstruction of Power, section on Freedom and Oppression), Weil had already described the basic instability of power (or force), its volatile nature, and the impossibility of its containment. Attempts to possess and contain power only arouse a degree of violence that continually displaces itself. Weil had illustrated this aspect of her concept of power in her discussion of "L'Etoile Nord-Africaine" where the attempts to contain and localize the sources of violence through the arrest and imprisonment of Algerian leaders was a short-sighted, ineffective resolution of the problems incurred by the existence of a colonial empire. Her fear of the potential physical violence caused by misrepresented meaning and imprecise language usage is valid and essential but the purge she proposes must by necessity be affected by the disruptive quality of force and take its place in a series of repetitive violence, caused by the purge or suppression of a natural mythological factor in the determination of language meaning. Words cleansed of their mystifying element become an imitation of the violence they exclude in a repetition of disrupted meanings. There is an interesting contrast between the violence Weil fears from mythological misrepresentation and the violence to which she later returns in her comparative study of mythology, of which indications appear in her final notebooks.

Paradoxically, Weil fell victim to the contagion of violence contained in the notion of a purge, a phenomenon she had analyzed and denounced. Her shortcoming could be interpreted as the failure to extend this concept to semantics, in order to mediate the forces of logic and myth in language. Unfortunately she did not live long enough to do that. Still the difficulty for the reader of Weil is in deciding which is of greater immediacy—comprehension through the reassociation of symbol with original meaning, or the unsuppressed plenitude of creative imagination. The absence of either results in a new disruption of meaning. Weil's concept of methodical action and its application to precise language was unquestionably essential and could have served to diminish a serious intellectual and spiritual vacuum in our society. Yet the mediation Weil sought through methodical action imposed a new form of subjectivism. The project of language and literature is completed by a turning back upon oneself. Representation is fulfilled and valid only after the inward movement of interiorization and logic checks the initial exteriorization or objectification of the signified meaning. Language is thus verified as the creation of logic and reason. There is not a definite opposition between this more subjectivist view and those who affirm the materiality of language and literature; these latter critics point out the tendency of symbols and language to recreate themselves and build sedimentations of meanings through associative constructions. Weil was evidently aware that this tendency existed in language; the difference between Weil and Husserl and these latter critics was that Weil and Husserl feared and sought to control this influence on language whereas those who did not began to envision within this force and potential violence a rejuvenating mystery and enrichment of language, philosophy and science (i.e., Kuhn, Derrida, Cassirer). Suzanne Cunningham claimed that Husserl's concept of phenomenological reduction of the ego as a transcendent force and his search for self-evidence were identical elements of his Transcendental Phenomenology.[20] If one were to accept this view, one would logically consider Weil's concept of methodical and meditative action as a contradiction of her initial rejection of the Transcendental Ego. This would be inaccurate. Obviously, the element of 'retournement' was an effort to mediate the forces of mind and those of materiality. The conclusion is thus that mediation is a source of violence and uprootal in itself. The inexhaustibility of the dialectic is proof of the violence mediation triggers and contains. The symbol is a mediator. Therefore representation inevitably imposes violence on all human activity that it translates and mediates; this violence manifests itself through a devaluation, a disruption of meaning. As Derrida has demonstrated, this devaluation of meaning through representation is doubled when the symbol is written down.[21] This would suggest that Weil's and Husserl's efforts to traverse the depths of embedded meanings were futile, that their efforts at mediation and unity were futile also; in my opinion, they were not but that is a question of personal judgement. It is certain, however, that acquiescence to the force of estrangement and violence in the act of representation would have been against the Existentialist ethic. In her essay on oppression and freedom, Weil indicates that absolute freedom, that is, freedom from oppression and violence should be considered an ideal not a goal; it should be a measure by which to orient and appraise action. Absolute mediation or freedom without violence, without devaluation, is the impossible, the ideal. It follows that Weil and Husserl perceived the inevitability of the devaluation of meaning through representation but felt morally compelled to exert efforts to minimize that source of estrangement.

Mediation and Violence: The reintegration of symbol with original meaning is also pursued as a higher level of spirituality. In her religious writings, Weil expressed her belief in the existence of signs in the physical world, indicators of a higher universal reality. At the time of the creation these signs were dispersed in different forms throughout the universe. The process of decreation enables the individual to rise spiritually, and to reintegrate the dispersed indicators of a higher reality in a movement towards full reunification and 'enracinement'. Appearance is reintegrated with being; the

Actual is reunited with the Ideal. The forces of dispersion and reintegration are mediated through violence.

Mediation contains the forces of cohesion and dispersion, 'déracinement/enracinement', and therefore is a volatile image, the mediation of pause and arousal. In Weil's religious writings, acts of love, friendship, obligation, demand a degree of self-effacement, denial or sacrifice, the imposition of violence upon oneself for the sake of the Other. Mediation becomes a balance between the violence of one's ego and the violence of one's love for the Other. The Creation was an act of love by which the creator refused an extension of itself and stepped backwards. Friendship is a condition arrived at through denial of one's own plenitude and presence, allowing the Other's presence to enter one's consciousness, moving back to share space with the Other. The notion of obligation explained in *L'Enracinement* reflects the priority of the Other's presence and project in Weil's philosophy. An obligation exists independently of a right or privilege, independently of physical existence and reality. Obligation, eternal and unconditional, is an inward movement; violence in this sense, is absolute and sanctified. In contrast, the concept of privilege or right in Weil's philosophy is an outward movement; dependent upon the recognition of obligation, it is a reverberation of its inward movement; it is violence in a relative form. It is interesting that Weil attributes in part the misuse of language to a confusion between obligation and privilege by the revolutionaries of 1789, and a confusion between absolute and relative forms of violence.

This brings one to the conclusion that one form of violence is an imitation of the other. The creation was the supreme movement of obligation, self-denial and empathy for the Other. It was the violence of love in its absolute form. From this moment, the sources of violence were displaced, dispersed, and henceforth imitative acts. The assertion of a right or privilege, the extension of one's own freedom, is the expansion of self; violence here is in its relative form as an outward movement. This latter relative form is an imitation of the absolute. Therefore, in Weil's writing, all violence retains its reductive force as an imitation of the initial violence of the Creation. The difference between the human condition and the divine lies in the opposed directions of violence.

Violence and Myth: This leads us to another domain of Weil's writings. There is an interesting contrast between the violence Weil fears from political myths and misrepresentations, and the violence to which she returns in her comparative study of mythology of which indications appear in her notebooks (cf. *Cahiers* I, II, III, and *La Connaissance Surnaturelle (Cahiers d'Amérique)*, Intui-

tions Pré-Chrétiennes). The previous discussion has established that the latter is a dispersion of relative, imitative forms of violence.

Mircea Eliade had described mythology as the repetition of the primordial act of the Creation.[22] Although mythology cannot be entirely interpreted in this way, this expresses a central theme in the particular myths Weil chose to study and explicate in the last two years of her life. During this time, Weil concentrated on the reverberation of violence that appears in the myths of a multiplicity of different cultures.

Janet Patricia Little considers Weil's study of myth in these final years an illustration of her religious philosophy and interprets it within that framework. Citing the influence of Alain on Weil's own interest in mythology Little also indicates an essential difference. Whereas for Alain, myths were a source of creative difference, for Weil they were a sign of similarity and unity.[23]

Little categorizes the main body of myths appearing in Weil's writings as representative of particular stages in the decreation process. The details of her study are not important to this argument, but the main point she has discovered concerning Weil's usage of myth relates to the discussion of violence, to the seeming contradiction between relative and absolute violence discussed earlier as opposing movements of dispersion and reintegration. Myth, for Weil, is a culturally differentiating imitation of the Creation; the initial violence of the Creation is perpetuated through myth. As Little points out and most critics will agree, Weil had always been somewhat interested in the mythical source of literature, but had sought solutions to the problems of language, science, politics, philosophy, in reason and logic.[24] During her last years, the solutions she sought were rather in spirituality; the intensification of her religious beliefs and the comparative mythological study she began are indications of this; Weil turns finally from reason to the spirituality found in myth and religious studies for a greater understanding of the sources of violence. It is this dispersion and reintegration of the sources of violence that she sees as the function of myth, as the sources of both difference and fusion. Myths are a repetition of imitative acts of the Creation.

It is also important to remember in relation to the theme 'déracinement/enracinement' the coexistence of myth and specificity of belief in Weil's religious writing. In religious texts, such as the New Testament, the Koran, the Bhagavad-Gîtâ, and the Upanishads, she recognizes a mythical fertility that does not obstruct the form of the belief it represents. Other cultures and religions where myth reveals an image of the Messiah are not necessarily interpreted by Weil as early forms of Christianity. She retained the fierceness and strength of her belief in Catholicism while recognizing the influence of myth on the formation of Christian belief. This is another manifestation of 'déracinement/enracinement'. The presence of myth within Christianity provides a force of flexibility and mediation.

The folklore of a multiplicity of cultures is explored in Weil's notebooks: Spanish, Irish, English, American Indian, Japanese, Danish, Esquimo, Gypsy, Korean, Dutch, Turkish, Australian, Greek, Buddhist, Zen, Scandinavian, Scottish, Russian, Albanian, and others. One example of Weil's study of cultural myth or folklore is the Scottish tale of the Duke of Norway (or the Tale of Three Nights) whose Russian parallel would be "Fenist the Bright." It is the story of a prince who exists in animal form by day and human form by night. He marries during the day. That night his bride, distraught with the situation, destroys the animal skin of her husband and he subsequently disappears. After a long difficult search, she discovers him in a castle preparing to marry. She uses a magic hazelnut that she had found to bribe the bride-to-be; she thus purchases three consecutive nights with her husband but is unable to awaken him because the bride-to-be had drugged him. At the end of the third night he awakens and recognizes his bride and is thus reunited with her (cf. *Cahiers* II, p. 285, this version is slightly different from the one described by Little whose interpretation of the myth was based on a passage from *Intuitions Pré-Chrétiennes*).[25]

> Far hae I sought ye, near am I brought to ye,
> Dear Duke of Norway, will ye turn and speak to me?
> (Elle a chanté)...Till her heart was like to break, and over again like to break...[26]

In *Intuitions Pré-Chrétiennes*, a similar version of the same myth is told but with a slightly different interpretation. She interprets it as "La Quête de l'homme pour Dieu." Weil also generalizes and relates the myth to the general mythological theme of a princess or a prince who sets out in search of her or his mate, accompanied by a slave with whom she or he switches identities. At the last moment, true identities are discovered and the lovers are reunited.

> Les deux thèses... évoquant la Passion... la marche interminable,
> épuisante de l'épouse légitime, convient... à cette évocation.[27]

The violence of separation is followed by and demands the violence of reintegration.

Homer's poem on the myth of Demeter and abduction of Prospirpina or Persephone by Aidonnée (Hades) also illustrates this cycle of dispersion and reintegration. Weil considered Demeter, meaning "Mother of the Earth," to be identical to all mother goddesses whose cults are analogous to that of the Virgin Mary in the Catholic Church. Narcissus is the flower which represents the being of the same name, so beautiful that it could only be in love with itself. In Weil's interpretation, the Narcissus is divine beauty because the only form of beauty that can have itself as the object of its love is divine. In the form of mortal, earthly beauty, it exists as a lure, and entrapment of the soul.

> Il lui donna un grain de grenade doux comme le miel, à manger en cachette, Par stratagème, pour qu'elle ne demeurât pas pour toujours là-bas, près de la vénérée Demeter au voile bleu. . . .[28]

Once the soul is taken, it is allowed to return only after eating the seed of a pomegranate. Weil interprets the seed as consent, the soul's yielding to divine will.

> La croissance exponentielle d'un atome de bien pur, une fois qu'un tel atome est entré dans l'âme . . . c'est ce qui indique le grain de grenade. Le consentement de l'âme. . .[29]

One form of violence serves as the image of the other, as the source of reintegration. Weil notes also that these two successive moments of violence appear in the *Phaedrus* (Phèdre) and in the myth of the cave.

The story of Orestes and Electre also illustrates this cycle of dispersion and reintegration. This myth, however, also expresses another theme of myths used by Weil—the death or punishment and subsequent restoration of a god. There are two moments of violence which lead to the final moment of recognition, in my opinion: the murder of the rightful king and the violence of Electre's despair. Weil interprets this differently and finds instead opposing moments of violence in Electre's confrontation with the gardener: the gardener's announcement of the death of her brother, Orestes, and the restoration of her brother when the gardener reveals his true identity.

> . . .ce deuil mené sur l'urne et les cendres d'Orestes, . . . évoque . . . le thème du Dieu mort et ressuscité.[30]

It is interesting that Weil interprets what is normally conceived as a parable of vengeance and retribution, as mythical parallels of the story of the Incarnation and Redemption. The forms of relative and absolute violence oppose and resolve each other. In this category are many, many other myths discussed by Weil, all of which cannot be presented here. Among the most interesting is her use of American Indian mythology, of mythical figures from Hindu tradition (Upanishads) and from the traditional folklore of Buddhism, from Tibet and Japan.[31] She also draws parallels between the stories of Prometheus, Osiris, Dionysus, Krishna, Arjuna, Noah and Jesus. In her *Cahiers d' Amérique*, there is a particular concentration on American Indian mythology. Among the more emphasized Indian myths are: "Dirty-Boy"–the story of the Incarnation of the Sun and the Star for the love of two daughters of an Indian chief (Teit, Memoirs of American Folklore Society),[32] "Le Corbeau et la Lumière"--the story of the Incarnation of an Indian boy into the form of a crow to bring the Sun from the heavens to a world that was still in darkness (Tsimshiam: Boas).[33] She also uses Frazer's study as a source of various Indian tribal legends on resuscitation and Incarnation (i.e., 144–"Aztecs mangent le Dieu Vitziliputzli sous la forme d'une pâté de maïs modélée à l'image d'un dieu.[34] An interesting task would be to categorize and analyze Weil's comparative use of American Indian mythology.

Myths of all cultures express for Weil the universal search for mediation and integration. They are proof of cultural similarity and unity, not difference, by their expression of relative and absolute violence. They are expressions of a common hope for reintegration, for true 'enracinement'.

Violence and Poetry: Poetry is Weil's ultimate form of meditative thinking.[35] Excerpts from her *Cahiers* as well as a letter from Valéry appraising Weil's own poetry attest to the influence of symbolist poetry on Weil. In her *Cahiers*, Weil includes quotations from Mallarmé's poetry and at one point refers to him as "le poète par excellence."[36] Quotations from Valéry are much more numerous, however; they express Weil's beliefs in the cyclical process of purification and reversal, and suggest Weil's increasing interest in an artistic form of expression.

> . . .son idée d'un univers absolu des sons (purs, combinés) qu'évoque chaque fragment de musique. Cet univers absolu ne peut être que le silence–la musique part du silence et en retourne. . . .[37]

The affinity between Valéry's poetry and Weil's religious philosophy is evident. In fact, Weil's philosophy can be illustrated by much of Valéry's poetry. The evolution of Weil's and Valéry's philosophies have followed the same pattern. Both passed through similar stages of thought: the perception of chaos, the construction of conceptual order by the self to resolve that chaos, the revelation of myths and illusions in patterns of human thought, language, and philosophy, the challenge of structural concepts of time and space, a search for the absolute as a means of purification, clarity and reintegration.[38]

Both conceive of true existence as absence and aspire towards the purity of non-being and the absolute. Both perceive the negative as well as positive effects of the symbol's power of 'dédoublement'.

> Je ne me suis jamais référé qu'à mon moi pur, par quoi j'entends l'absolu de la conscience. . .[39]

The search for anonymity, purity is expressed by the act of writing, by the artistic endeavor of poetry. Weil noted particularly in her *Cahiers* the link between Valéry's notion of value reduction and the function of poetry (cf. *Cahiers* I, p. 10).[40] The reduction of value is part of a cyclical process of clarification.

The imposition of regular rhythm and rhyme in a poem is a form of violence according to Weil; this violence strengthens the poet's hold on the dimensions of time and space by transposing the harmony and eternity of the world into poetry or art.

> Poésie; vertu de la rime (et de la mesure, de toutes contraintes) arrêter, rompre par violence les associations. . . .[41]

There has been no analysis of Weil's poetry. This is probably because she wrote few poems. Neil Baldwin, however, an American poet who has collected and interpreted the poetry of William Carlos Williams, has translated Weil's poetry into English. It is significant to note that most of her best poetry was written during the last few years of her life ("A un Jour," "Les Astres," "La Mer," "Nécessité," "La Porte").[42] Her creative efforts had begun to focus more intensively on mythological and artistic expression in these final years. Weil's poetry is evidence that the play of violence and mediation in her philosophy culminated in a form of artistic expression.

In my opinion her finest poem is "A un Jour," written in 1938. More than any of her other poems or of the verses comprising her one-act play, "Vénise Sauvée," "A un Jour" reveals Weil's potential for poetic expression.[43]

> *Quel coeur ne fend si la subite*
> *Et douce atteinte du matin*
> *Défait l'ombre où tout bas s'agite*
> *Doute, remords, peur du destin?*

> *La Grâce lui fait mal; il saigne*
> *Devant les plaines où l'eau baigne*
> *Des plis de brouillard délicat,*
> *La ramure qui tremble nue,*
> *L'aile qui glisse suspendue*
> *L'air inondé d'un faible éclat.*[44]

When Weil began to compose this poem, she had just begun to turn towards Catholicism. In these verses it is already possible to perceive the beginnings of Weil's yet unconsolidated religious philosophy. Images of obscurity and violence are mingled together in her description of the sounds and sensations of the dawn. The mixture of beauty and pain gives tension to Weil's description of the day's beginning. Her pessimistic allusions to an essential state of sin infuses this tension.

> *Jour naissant, jour fait de rosée*
> *Si clair dans l'âme et dans les cieux*
> *Toute cette splendeur posée*
> *Comme une caresse en tous lieux*
> *Nous reviendra tendre et limpide.*
> *Le soir à travers l'air fluide*
> *En comblera le pré mouillé*
> *Mais avant que le soir descende*
> *Et parmi nous calme s'étende,*
> *O jour, que tu seras souillé.*[45]

The flow of time is described as a violent, indifferent equalizer of beings.

> *Pourquoi blesser de ton aurore*
> *Les yeux des vaincus, jour mort-né?*
> *Ils sont las qu'il leur faille encore*
> *Voir luire en soleil condamné.*
> *Un jour mort est trop long à vivre*
> *Mille fois milles âmes désertes*
> *Saluent ce jour déjà perdu*
> *Ces mille et mille jours inertes*
> *Sont un jouet vil et vendu. . . .*[46]

In *Eclair*, a poem of five stanzas of four verses each with alternating rhyme, the thunderbolt evokes for Weil the movement of destruction, cleansing and rejuvenation.

> Que le ciel pur sur la face m'envoie
> ce ciel de longs nuages balayé
> un vent si fort, vent à l'odeur de joie
> Que naisse tout de rêves nettoyé. . . .[47]

In the violence of the lightening and thunder, wind is the agent of purity, light, and clarity. As the poem progresses, this harmony and clarity take an increasingly oppressive form until the world is again plunged into obscurity and depression.

> Le monde est né; vent, souffle afin qu'il dure:
> Mais il périt recouvert de fumées.
> Il m'était né dans une déchirure
> De ciel vert pâle au milieu des nuées. . . .[48]

In the poems *Nécessité*, *La Mer* and *Les Astres*, the verses are organized so as to contrast the tension of physical suffering with the immobility and indifference of natural and human-made elements.[49] The purifying contact with necessity is described as a violent experience. It is significant that Weil's expression of necessity is conveyed through poetry. Three types of contact with necessity as separate layers of meaning are contained within Weil's poetry: the indifferent passing of time is the basic, natural contact with necessity, reducing the individual to a comprehension of her or his own finitude within the eternity of nature; the second contact with necessity is conveyed through work; poetic limitations of form and harmony constitute the third contact of necessity which is a medium for the other two. A sample of one of these poems follows where machine-like images deliberately obscure the distinction between natural and human-made necessity.

> Le cercle des jours du ciel désert qui tourne
> Parmi le silence aux regards des mortels
> Gueule ouverte ici-bas, où chaque heure enfourne
> Tant de cris si suppliants et si cruels. . . .[50]

Throughout all of Weil's poetry—and I have discussed only a few examples—as in all of her political and religious writing, violence is the centrality of experience. It is the agent of reduction, the equalizer, the source of transcendency. The sources of violence as essential contact with necessity determine and mediate our physical and spiritual experience, our movement from uprootal to reintegration, from dispersion to unity, and back again. Mythology and Poetry are the final expressions of Weil's philosophy of mediation between the forces of *'déracinement/enracinement'*.

Notes to Chapter 6

[1] Hannah Arendt, *The Origins of Totalitarianism* (New York: Harcourt, Brace, 1951).

[2] Simone Weil, *Réflexions sur les Causes de la liberté et de l'Oppression sociale* (Paris: Gallimard, 1955).

[3] Paul Valéry, *Cahiers* IV, 926. Passage noted in following cited article by Judith Robinson.

[4] Judith Robinson, "L'Analyse de l'esprit dans les 'Cahiers' de Paul Valéry" (Paris: Jose Corti, 1963), essay included in *Les Critiques de notre temps et Valéry* (Paris: Editions Garnier Frères). 36-47.

[5] Edmund Husserl, "The Origin of Geometry," *The Crisis of European Sciences and Transcendental Phenomenology* (Evanston: Northwestern University Press, 1970), 353-78. (Written in 1936 and published in 1939 in *Revue Internationale de philosophie*, Vol. I, No. 2 (1939) under the title "Der Ursprung der Geometrie als intentional-historisches Problem.") Discussed also in *La Voix et le Phénomène, Introduction au problème du signe dans la Phénoménologie de Husserl*, Jacques Derrida (Paris: Presses Universitaires, 1967).

[6] Husserl, "The Origin of Geometry," 361.

[7] Ibid., 362.

[8] Robert D'Amico, "Husserl on the Foundational Structure of Natural and Cultural Sciences," *Philosophy and Phenomenological Research*, 42 (no. 1, September 1981), 5-22.

[9] Husserl, "The Origin of Geometry," 361.

[10] Ibid., 371.

[11] Simone Weil, *Ecrits Historiques et Politiques* (Paris: Gallimard, 1960), 364-78.

[12] Simone Weil, *L'Enracinement* (Paris: Gallimard, 1949).

[13] Weil, *Ecrits Historiques et Politiques*, 364-78.

[14] "Quelque soulagement que doive probablement causer le départ des Japonais, une continuation de la domination française ne serait sans doute pas subie sans horreur, à cause des atrocités qui, d'après des témoignages concordants, ont été commises par les Français pour reprimer une rébellion au moment de l'accord franco-japonais. D'après l'un de ces témoignages, des villages auraient été anéantis par des bombardements aériens, et des milliers de personnes, accusées d'être les familles de rebelles, mises sur des pontons et coulées . . . ." Ibid., 369.

[15] Ibid., 370.

[16] "Toute la science classique est contenue déjà dans les travaux d'Eudoxe et d'Archimede. . . ." ("La Science et Nous," *Sur la Science*, 135). Eudoxus, a friend of Plato and one of the last of the Pythagoreans, is credited with the discovery of generalized number and with the invention of Integral Calculus. He built a mechanical model of the system of the stars based on all that was known in his time, by a combination of circular and uniform movements performed on one sphere but around different axles and with different speeds. Weil explains the modern application of this principle in cinematics, demonstrating the substitution by Classical and Modern Science of circular movement by straight lines, and the addition of the principle of acceleration. The theory of generalized number elaborated by Weierstrass, who invented Integral Calculus at the end of the nineteenth century, is identical to that of Eudoxus, Weil claimed ("Rêverie à Propos de la Science Grecque," *Sur la Science*, 263-64). Weil also states that Archimedes was the founder of statistical mechanics because of his invention of the lever, the center of gravity. His theory of the equilibrium of floating objects or bodies was the beginning of modern physics by the fact that fluids were conceived as a support ("La Science et Nous," 136-37).

[17] Hannah Arendt, *Between Past and Future* (Chicago: University of Chicago Press, 1954); Translated into French by Patrick Lévy,*La Crise de la Culture* (Paris: Gallimard, 1972).

[18] Ernest Cassirer, *Language and Myth* (New York: Dover 1953) (tr. from *Studien der Bibliothek*

Warburg 6, ed. Fritz Saxl).

[19]Ibid. "Translator's Preface," viii-ix.

[20]Suzanne Cunningham, *Language and the Phenomenological Reductions of Husserl* (The Hague: Nijhoff, 1976), 7. (I owe this reference to Peter Hutcheson, from his article, "Husserl and Private Languages," *Philosophy and Phenomenological Research*, 42: 1, pp. 111-18.).

[21]Jacques Derrida, *De la Grammatologie* (Paris: Editions de Minuit, 1967).

[22]Mircea Eliade, *Aspects du mythe* (Paris: Gallimard, 1963), 15. (I owe this reference to Little which she cited in the following article. Although Little does not relate Weil's myths to her concept of violence, Little's article provides the religious framework of Weil's studies of myths, which leads one to relate it to the concept of violence as an equalizer.

[23]Janet Patricia Little, "Signification de la mythologie et des contes chez Simone Weil," *Simone Weil—Philosophe, historienne et mystique* (Aubier Montaigne, Paris, 1978), 105-6.

Little further comments: "On pourrait parler de 'structuralisme' chez elle, puisqu'elle essaye de dégager ces uniformités de structure de mythes très divers. . . ., 107

[24]Ibid., 105. Little discussed Weil's early childhood work "Les Lutins du feu," which in Little's view is indicative of Weil's early appreciation for the creative source of myth for literature.

[25]Simone Weil, *Cahiers* II (Paris: Librairie Plon, 1972), 285.

[26]Ibid.

[27]Simone Weil, *Intuitions Pré-Chrétiennes* (Paris: la Colombe, 1951), 15.

[28]Ibid., 11.

[29]Weil, *Cahiers* II, 286, and *Intuitions Pré-chrétiennes*, 11-12.

[30]Weil, *Intuitions Pré-Chrétiennes*, 17.

[31]The main body of mythology taken from Hindu and Buddhist religion appears in *Cahiers* I, II, III. Interesting passages include those that compare the spirit of Bhagāvad Gita and the legend of Joan of Arc, with the subsequent discussion of war (". . . il fait la guerre quoique inspiré par Dieu, elle fait la guerre parce qu'inspiré par Dieu..."–*Cahiers* I-47). Another interesting passage is Weil's comparison of the four states of "conjecture, croyance, pensée discursive ou raisonnement, et entendement" (discussed by Plato) to the four states of Vedanta (Veille, rêve, lumière ou un, et le bien absolu). Also of interest are her various allusions and explanations of aspects of the story of Milarēpa's broken pot and its parallels with Plato's *Banquet* (*Cahiers* II, 120, 285). For a precise categorization and explanation of the influence of Hindu and Buddhist religion and myth on Weil's own religious philosophy, there is David Raper's stduy "L'Interprétation des Traditions Hindoues et bouddhiques chez Simone Weil," *Simone Weil, Philosophe, historienne, et mystique*, 93-100. This is a very important article because the influence of Oriental religion and mythology on the formation of Weil's religious philosophy has long been and is underestimated. ("Elle a . . . trouvé dans la philosophie des *Upanishads* le cadre moniste, ou non-dualiste, dont, comme mystique, elle avait soif. . . .)" 94.

[32]Weil, *Intuitions Pré-Chrétiennes*, 17.

[33]Simone Weil, *La Connaissance Surnaturelle-Cahiers d'Amérique* (Paris: Gallimard, 1950), 139-41.

[34]Ibid.

[35]Meditative thinking contains the principles of logic and method with the added dimension of spirituality. For both Weil and Heidegger, calculative or methodical thinking and meditative thinking marked consecutive stages of her philosophy (John M. Anderson and E. Hans Freund, trans., *Discourse on Thinking* (New York: Harper & Row, 1966 [English translation of Martin Heidegger, *Gelassenheit* (Pfullingen: Gunther Newke Verlag, 1959]), 46, 47, 53. See also John D. Caputo, *The Mystical Element in Heidegger's Thought* (Athens: Ohio University Press, 1978).

³⁶Ibid., 60.

³⁷*Cahiers*, I: 10.

³⁸Paul Valéry, "Au Sujet d'Euréka," *Oeuvres de Paul Valéry* I (Paris: La Pléiade, 1957), 854-67. "On peut resumer tout ceci en écrivant que les propriétes de la matière semblent dépendre seulement de l'ordre de grandeur. . . ." 859. Paul Valéry, "Le Philosophe et 'La jeune parque,'" *Oeuvres de Paul Valéry* I. Also see Judith Robinson's article, "Les Chances d'une logique," *Les Critiques de notre Temps et Valéry*. Paul Valéry, "Fragments du Narcisse," Charmes, *Oeuvres de Paul Valéry*, I:122-30, "Le Temps mène ces fous qui crurent que l'on aime Redire à tes roseaux de plus profonds soupirs: Vers toi, leurs tristes pas suivent leurs souvenirs. . . ." Also Georges Poulet, "La Conscience Valéryenne du Temps," *Etudes sur le temps humain*, chapt. 17 (Paris: Plon, 1950). Paul Valéry, "Sémiramis, mélodrame et trois actes et deux interludes," 82-96. *Oeuvres de Paul Valéry*. I: "A présent—je me coucherai sur la pierre de cet Autel, et je prierai le Soleil. . . ."

³⁹Paul Valéry, "Lettre-Préface au Père Rideau" (cited in an article by Marcel Raymond, "Le Refus d'être quoi que ce soit," *Les Critiques de notre temps et Valéry*).

⁴⁰*Cahiers* I: 10.

⁴¹Ibid., 184-85.

⁴²Simone Weil, *Poèmes, suivis de Vénise sauvée* (Paris: Gallimard, 1968).

⁴³Ibid., 25-30.

⁴⁴Ibid., 25.

⁴⁵Simone Weil, *Poémes, suivis de Vénise sauvée* (Paris: Gallimard, 1968), 25-26.

⁴⁶Ibid., 26-27.

⁴⁷Ibid., 21.

⁴⁸Ibid.

⁴⁹Ibid., 31-34.

⁵⁰Ibid., 33

Conclusion

A central preoccupation can be detected throughout Simone Weil's work. This basic concern is the loss of continuum. In Weil's description and reaction to this absence of wholeness and unity, the terms 'déracinement/enracinement' can be seen as operative in different forms and contexts. Their mobility and complementarity indicate that the rediscovery of continuum and reintegration of self with the universe is complex for Weil.

The simple opposition implied by Weil's own explicit usage of the terms leads the readers towards a false reduction or simplification of Weil's ideas. But Weil's philosophy, her search for continuum is not simple. I have, therefore, used the terms "déracinement/enracinement" to explore the complexity of her ideas.

Weil's later usage of the phrases "déracinement ouvrier" and "déracinement et nation" indicate certain types of alienation which had already become major themes in her writing before she eventually used these terms. These forms of alienation are discussed in the third chapter of this study. Thus the level at which Weil explicitly uses the terms "déracinement/enracinement" has influenced my perception of their meaning. This is the first level of meaning to be considered, "déracinement" representing a movement or condition that uproots and therefore alienates, "enracinement" meaning a force or state of being that implants and therefore causes unity, growth and a sense of cultural and spiritual belonging. Since this is the level of meaning at which Weil consciously uses the pair "déracinement/enracinement," it remains important and should not be discarded.

I believe, however, that these terms gain in value as the depth of Weil's thought is explored. Although Weil did not use them consciously beyond a categorization of the types of alienation in existence, they serve to describe conceptual movements within her own analysis. Two main features emerge from this study of her analysis: 1) throughout Weil's philosophy, ideas and phenomena normally perceived as opposing become complementary. The result is that one functions as the other and the ethical charge of each is not fixed: 2) the second feature can be deducted from the first; the subversiveness of the terms and the fact that one usually functions as the other reveals a pattern of deconstruction in Weil's analysis. In order to establish unity and continuum, one must disrupt or uproot, even if the disruption is only a partial and not a total denial of tradition.

Weil's rejection of the transcendental ego is an uprootal from Cartesian solipsism; but the rejection of subjectivism brings with it the inevitability of choice and involvement with the world. This early essay sets the pattern for the complementarity of "déracinement/enracinement" that appears in every domain of Weil's thought. Weil's lectures at Roanne discussed in the second chapter describe a stage of objectification, a redistancing of the conceptual self from the world. This is a form of detachment, of exile, but it functions as a force of integration because it provides the necessary distance for conceptualizing effective action. At this stage of her philosophy pure and unreflected action is gratuitous for Weil and the major cause of social alienation. In her lectures at Roanne, Weil defines existence and individual identity as the product of methodical action. The methodical approach to action which Weil envisioned demanded a more thorough comprehension of the reciprocal causal relation between language and action and the extent to which their rapport reflects and determines thought processes of the individual mind. Thus, a stage of regression follows the uprootal of self (cf. Chapter 2 to objectify one's involvement with the world and thereby render one's action more effective, more methodical. One's sense of identity and consciousness heightens as one relates oneself more effectively to the world. Consequently the movements of uproctal and rooting, "déracinement/enracinement" are complementary. This has been seen from two points of view. Within the essay on Descartes, there are conceptual movements of uprootal (rejection of the transcendental ego) and grounding (the encounter and tension between mind/body, a healthy balance of forces) which function together and move the individual towards a greater sense of integration with the world. "Science et Perception," and *Leçons de Philosophie* also, on a wider scheme can be viewed as representative of two complementary stages of thought; "déracinement," uprootal from Idealist tradition, the rejection of subjectivism, can be viewed as the dominant movement in the essay on Descartes. In the Roanne lectures, however, the stage of regression serves to reaffirm Idealism while valorizing also Materialist concepts. The dominant movement is that of a reintegration of both Idealist and Materialist traditions; methodical action, reflecting the reciprocity of mind/body is the stage in Weil's Existentialist philosophy which integrated both forces. Thus "déracinement" and "enracinement" are complementary. In these two early stages of Weil's philosophy, the polarization of the terms "déracinement/enracinement" fades away. They become inextricable.

In the third chapter, "Deconstruction of Power," "déracinement" expresses both the problem of cultural alienation and the deconstruction of myths that have caused alienation. That is, "déracinement" describes both the problem and the solution for the achievement of true "enracinement."

Weil's concept of freedom, her theory of oppression, and her study on the natural instability and displacement of power form the basis for her methodical deconstruction of social and cultural myths. By this deconstruction Weil hopes to restore individual identity and independence of thought. Deconstruction precedes reconstruction. Her new definition of freedom as understanding the objectives and stages of one's own action is an uprootal from the traditional antithetical structure of belief. She thus refuses the choice between interiority/exteriority, between mind/body, between Idealism/Materialism. "Déracinement" as uprootal, manifests itself also in Weil's analysis of oppression. The division of labor and the resulting qualitative transformation of production have displaced or 'uprooted' power from its original source in nature and thereby triggered the continual displacement of power among ourselves; the first form of "déracinement" as uprootal of power from nature, is negative; the second can be considered negative in so far as it defines a state of uncertainty, positive in so far as it provides a balance of forces between individuals; thus 'la course au pouvoir', as continual displacement or uprootal manifests itself both positively and negatively. There is also the obvious parallel between these two series of uprootal and the movements of 'création/décréation' in Weil's religious philosophy. One disruption serves to rectify another. Violence as an equalizer is both a force that disperses and fuse. A complementarity is therefore present between the forces of alienation and reintegration, "déracinement/enracinement."

In sections dealing with Weil's deconstruction of Myths, I have noted her perception of the concretizing of ideas and symbols. Nation and revolution, originally symbols and vehicles of freedom, had come to engulf or consume their meaning, and become ends in themselves. Freedom had become concretized within the framework of nation or of revolution. I perceive this as a form of entrenchment, inflexibility, a negative form of "enracinement" from which Weil tries to uproot the reader and herself. Weil perceived that ideals and meanings are constantly displaced between different structures and phenomena which lend to their expression as in the case of nation and revolution. This idea of displacement is an important feature of Weil's analysis which encompasses both the movements "déracinement/enracinement"; meaning uproots or displaces itself as soon as its symbol ceases to be a vehicle of expression and becomes an end in itself. This is a healthy, necessary form of displacement or uprootal in Weil's discussion of power, myth and language.

In the chapter on Science and Uprootal, "déracinement" meaning discontinuity, functions positively and negatively. In so far as discontinuity is a means towards achieving continuity it is justified (cf. section on Greek Science). When discontinuity, however, becomes the main principle in defining work, energy, and scientific formulae, Weil considers it a negative force (cf. section on Modern Science, discussion of Quanta Theory). A complementarity must exist between the forces of continuum and discontinuum before discontinuum can be conceived of as positive.

In the discussion of the crisis of determinism, both the extremes of empirical positivism and free will are forces, extreme points of alienation which Weil refuses in her essays on science. The rapport of the terms "déracinement/enracinement" expresses both the opposition but essential complementarity of chance and necessity, of non-determinist and determinist forces, of continuity and discontinuity.

Weil's religious philosophy of which her poetry is the ultimate expression centers around the principle of decreation. Decreation describes a process of uprootal, of separation of oneself from the world. It is at the same time a rediscovery of unity, oneness and a form of spiritual transcendency and reintegration with the divine. The decreation of self parallels Weil's deconstruction of myths of power. The two movements of creation/decreation, are opposed but complementary; creation creates duality whereas decreation leads to reunification; decreation compensates for the autonomy and absence brought about by the creation. Both the features of deconstruction and the complementarity of opposing terms are particularly dominant in Weil's religious philosophy. One uproots oneself from the appearances of being to integrate oneself into the reality of Ideal being. One transcends the relative towards the absolute. Decreation is both the antithesis of and the source of transcendent power beyond our limited, divinely-created state. One violent act of love and self-denial is met by another; the essential violence of decreation, basically an imitative act, provides the antithetical movement and force to restore true existence in Weil's final meaning of the term. Its synthesis is a greater sense of mediation between the realms of the human and the divine, between the forces of spiritual reintegration and detachment. The tension between the two acts of love merge into the final point of the "Creation/Decreation" cycle. The traversed depths of spiritual purity and anonymity provide the distance from the relative and direct it as closely as possible towards the absolute restorative point of Truth.

Weil's comparative study of mythology is also a form of deconstruction which parallels her religious philosophy and her commentaries on power, myth and history. Through an exploration and comparison of myths of various cultures, Weil discovers two moments of disruption. Violent acts occur in pairs, death is usually followed by resuscitation. Myth thus expresses the common tendency of all cultures to seek unity and presence. I find also that in Weil's religious writings, this pair of terms ("déracinement/enracinement") expresses the co-existence of myth and specificity of belief. The mythical fertility that Weil discovers within Catholicism and religious texts of various religions does not obstruct the strength of her belief; it provides instead a force of flexibility and mediation.

In this book I have found the theme "déracinement/enracinement" valuable at the level of Weil's conscious usage of the terms to indicate the opposing conditions of alienation, and spiritual and cultural reintegration. But I felt it necessary to extend the meaning of the pair as a metaphoric expression of important principles of Weil's analysis. Complementarity and Deconstruction are these principles. They characterize the patterns of Weil's analysis throughout her lifetime and manifest themselves in various ways. The central preoccupation with the restoration of continuum is present throughout her work. I have used the problematic binary opposition of "déracinement/enracinement" to express the various forms of her search for unity, continuum and presence, and to break away from the image of immobility and fixity implied by Weil's explicit usage of the term "enracinement." The value Weil attributes to displacement, disruption, discontinuum is essential to an understanding of her attempt to restore continuum. It is essential to her belief in integration with flexibility and detachment, qualities without which true "enracinement" cannot exist.

My study of Weil has been of great personal value to me. It is normal for one to write on an aspect of a writer or philosopher with which one can identify. The theme of alienation or exile is a common twentieth-century theme treated by scores of writers and individuals. But Weil's approach to the problem appeals to me particularly because of the distance and detachment of her commitment and philosophical search. I have attempted to portray this central feature of her thought through my discussion of "déracinement/enracinement." I have also tried in my discussion of Weil's ideas, as an expression of this principle of integration with detachment to valorize with distance and without praise the movement and variation of her thought. Perhaps at times a certain amount of subjectivism and emotion appears in my own writing, despite my aversion to hagiographical studies of Weil. Nonetheless I shrink from phrases used by such writers as T. S. Eliot who attributes to Weil "a kind of genius akin to that of saint,"[1] of the late Wladimir Rabi who describes her as "le plus grand écrivain spirituel que la France ait suscité au cours des cinquante prèmieres années de ce siècle,"[2] of Leslie Fiedler who calls her "the Saint of the Absurd."[3] "Ils me l'ont tuée," said Malou Blum of the hyperboles and references to sainthood continually used by admirers of Weil.[4]

This critical stance of detachment that I have tried to maintain, has, hopefully, guarded me from considering the study of Weil an end in itself, rather than the means to an end. A study of her philosophy has alerted me to the necessity of distance in the comprehension of objectives and values. I believe this critical stance helps me also in distinguishing between aspects of Weil's writing that further the comprehension of true values and those that do not. Thus, I have attempted to adopt Weil's own critical stance in order to discriminate for myself between the positive and negative aspects of her philosophy.

I do not accept everything that Weil says, i.e., her unequivocal contempt for Judaic theology; her statements concerning the legacies of the Roman culture and Medieval Christianity at times seem too categorical to me, especially since her particular view of true Christian spirituality leads her to devalue the profundity of St. Augustine's writings and the importance of the entire Thomist tradition. Her perception of Roman culture, however, as the source of the predominant value we place on force and victory is valid; her extension of this idea to literature is valuable; particularly original is her argument that literary works which are accorded more importance and which are generally chosen as subjects of study are those which reflect the cultural value we place on force and victory. I find great value in Weil's philosophy, but the metaphoric power of "déracinement/enracinement" whose rapport expresses for me Weil's concept of integration with flexibility and detachment, helps me to perceive and refuse her prejudices.

By the completion of this book, I have kept a promise made to myself more than a decade ago when I was exposed for the first time to the writings and biography of Simone Weil. I have attempted to communicate to the reader the essential value and profundity of her philosophy through a development of the theme "déracinement/enracinement."

Notes to Conclusion

[1] T. S. Eliot, "Preface," *The Need for Roots* (English translation of *L'Enracinement*). Reprint of original translation copyrighted by G.P. Putnam's Sons, 1952 (New York: Harper & Row, 1971), vi.

[2] Wladimir Rabi, "La conception weilienne de la création, Rencontre avec la Kabbale juive," *Simone Weil, philosophe, historienne et mystique* (Paris: Aubier, 1978), 141.

[3] Leslie Fiedler, "Simone Weil, Prophet out of Israel, Saint of Absurd," *Commentary*, 11:1 (January 1951), 36-46.

[4] In conversation with me, summer of 1980.

Bibliography

Angress, Werner T. *Stillborn Revolution—The Communist Bid for Power in Germany.* Princeton: Princeton University Press, 1963.
Arendt, Hannah. *Between Past and Future.* Chicago: The University of Chicago Press, 1954.
———. *La Crise de la Culture.* Paris: Editions Gallimard, 1972.
———. *The Human Condition.* Chicago: University of Chicago Press, 1958.
———. *Crises of the Republic.* New York: Harcourt, Brace & Jovanovich, 1969.
———. *The Origins of Totalitarianism.* New York: Harcourt, Brace & Company, 1951.
Augustine. *Confessions and Enchiridion*, Vol. 6. Translated and edited by Albert C. Cutler. Philadelphia: Westminster Press, 1974.
Auroux, Sylvain and Yvonne Weil. *Dictionnaire des Auteurs et des Thèmes de la Philosophie.* Paris: Librairie Hachette, 1975.
Avanzina, Guy. *La Contribution de Binet à l'Elaboration d'une Pédagogie Scientifique.* Paris: Librairie Philosophique J. Vrin, 1969.
Ayer, A. J. *The Origins of Pragmatism, Studies in the Philosophy of Charles Sanders Peirce and William James.* San Francisco: Freeman, Cooper & Co., 1968.
Bachelard, Gaston. *Le Nouvel Esprit Scientifique.* Paris: Librairie Félix Alcan, 1934.
Barrès, Maurice. *Les Déracinés.* Paris: Librairie Plon, 1935.
Barthélemy-Madaule, Madeleine. *L'Idéologie du Hasard et de la Nécessité.* Paris: Editions de Seuil, 1972.
Baudouin, Charles. *Le Triomphe du Héros.* Paris: Librairie Plon, 1952.
Benrubi, Isaac. *Contemporary Thought of France.* New York: Alfred A. Knopf, 1926.
Bergson, Henri. *Creative Evolution.* Translated by A. Mitchell. New York: Modern Library, 1944.
———. "Lettre à Léon Brunschvicg," *Ecrits et Paroles*, Vol. 3. Paris: P.U.F., 1957-59.
Brecht, Bertolt. "Les Visions de Simone Machard," in *Théâtre Complet*, Vol. 6. Paris: L'Arche Editeur, 1957.
Brunschvicg, Léon. "L'Actualité des Problèmes Platoniciens," *Actualités Scientifiques et Industrielles* No. 575: Conférences du Centre Universitaire Méditerranéen de Nice publiés sous la direction de M. Paul Valéry, 1937.
———. *Les Etapes de la Philosophie Mathématique.* Paris: Librairie Blanchard, 1912.
———. "La Physique du Vingtième Siècle et la Philosophie," *Actualités Scientifiques et Industrielles*, No. 445, 1936.
Burtt, E. A. *The Metaphysical Foundations of Modern Physical Science.* Chicago: Humanities Press, 1951.
Cabaud, Jacques. *L'Expérience Vécue de Simone Weil.* Paris: Librairie Plon, 1957.
Caillois, Roger. *L'Homme et le Sacré.* Paris: Editions Gallimard, 1939.
Camus, Albert. *L'Homme Révolté.* Paris: Editions Gallimard, 1951.
———. *Le Malentendu, suivi de Caligula.* Paris: Editions Gallimard, 1958.
Capek, Milic. *The Philosophical Impact of Contemporary Physics.* Princeton: D. Van Nostrand Co., Inc., 1961.
Caputo, John D. *The Mystical Element in Heidegger's Thought.* Athens, Ohio: Ohio University Press, 1978.
Cassirer, Ernest. *Language and Myth.* Translated by Fritz Saxl. New York: Dover Publications, Inc., 1953.
Char, René. *Feuillets D'Hypnos.* Paris: Editions Gallimard, 1946.
Chartier, Emile. *Les Idées et les Ages.* Paris: N.R.E., 1927.
Clark, Ronald. *Einstein, the Life and Times.* New York: World Publishing Co., 1971.
Cohen, Morris, and I. E. Drabkin. *A Source Book in Greek Science.* Cambridge, Massachusetts:

Harvard University Press, 1948.
Corte, Marcel. "La Pensée Sociale de Simone Weil," *Synthèses*, (1947): 309-20.
Cunningham, Suzanne. *Language and the Phenomenological Reductions of Husserl*. The Hague: Nijhoff, 1976.
D'Amico, Robert. "Husserl on the Foundational Structures of Natural and Cultural Sciences," *Philosophy and Phenomenological Research* 42 (no. 1, September 1981). Niagara Falls, New York: Brown University, 1981.
Dewey, John. *Reconstruction in Philosophy*. Boston: Beacon Press, 1920.
De Beauvoir, Simone. *Le Sang des Autres*. Paris: Librairie Gallimard, 1945.
―――. *Pyrrhus et Cinéas*. Paris: Editions Nagel, 1944.
De Broglie, Louis. *Continu et Discontinu en Physique Moderne*. Paris: Editions Albin Michel, 1941.
―――. *The Revolution in Physics*. New York: The Noonday Press, 1943.
Derrida, Jacques. *De la Grammatologie*. Paris: Editions de Minuit, 1967.
―――. *La Voix et le Phénomène, Introduction au problème du signe dans la Phénoménologie de Husserl*. Paris: Presses Universitaires, 1967.
Diderot, Dénis. "Lettre sur les Aveugles," *Oeuvres Philosophiques, Chronologie et Introduction par Antoine Adam*. Paris: Garnier-Flammarion, 1972.
Dujardin, Philippe. *Simone Weil, Idéologie et Politique*. Grenoble: Presses Universitaires de Grenoble, 1975.
Edie, James. "The Philosophical Anthropology of William James–An Invitation to Phenomenology," in *Studies in the Philosophy of Experience*. Chicago: Quadrangle Books, 1965.
"Education in Action–The Story of John Dewey," *The World Tomorrow*, 17 (no. 4, 1931): 10-12.
Ehrenberg, Victor. *From Solon to Socrates–Greek History and Civilization during the Sixth and Fifth Centuries, B.C.* London: Methuen & Co., 1968.
Eliade, Mircea. *Aspects du mythe*. Paris: Editions Gallimard, 1963.
Eliot, T. S. "Preface," *The Need for Roots*. (English translation of *L'Enracinement*). Reprint. New York: Harper & Row, 1971.
Fieldler, Leslie. "Simone Weil–Prophet out of Israel, Saint of the Absurd," *Commentary* 11 (January 1951):36-46.
Forman, Paul. *Weimar Culture, Causality and Quantum Theory, 1918-1927. Adaptation by German Physicists and Mathematicians to a Hostile Intellectual Environment* Historical Studies in the Physical Sciences, Vol. 3. Philadelphia: University of Pennsylvania Press, 1971.
Friedman, George. *The Political Philosophy of the Frankfurt School*. Ithaca: Cornell University Press, 1981.
Giniewski, Paul. *Simone Weil ou la haine de soi*. Paris: Berg International, 1978.
Girard, René. *La Violence et le Sacré*. Paris: Editions Gallimard, 1972.
Giraudoux, Jean. *La Guerre de Troie n'Aura pas lieu*. Paris: Librairie Larousse, 1960.
Goblot, Edmond. *Le Vocabulaire Philosophique*. Paris: Librairie Armand Colin, 1920.
Grand Larousse Encyclopédique, vols. 4, 8, 9. Paris: Librairie Larousse, 1961.
Heidegger, Martin. "La Question de la Technique," Essais et Conférences, traduction française de "Die Frage nach der Technik," in *Vortageund Aufsatze*. Prullingen: Neske Verlag, 1954.
―――. *Discourse on Thinking*. New York: Harper & Row, 1966. Translation of *Gelassenheit*, Translated by John M. Anderson and E. Hans Freund. Prullingen, Gunther Neske Verlag, 1959
Hellman, John. *Emmanuel Mounier and the New Catholic Left, 1930-1950*. Toronto: University of Toronto Press, 1981.
Hughes, H. S. *Consciousness and Society: The Reorientation of European Social Thought, 1890-1930*. New York: Alfred Knopf, Inc., 1958.
Husserl, Edmond. *Méditations Cartésiennes–Introduction à la Phénoménologie*. Paris: Librairie

Philosophique J. Vrin, 1953.

———. *The Crisis of European Sciences and Transcendental Phenomenology.* Translated by David Carr. Evanston, Ill.: Northwestern University Press, 1970.

Hutcheson, Peter. "Husserl and Private Languages," *Philosophy and Phenomenological Research*, 9 (no. 1, December 1981): 111-18.

Hutson, Arthur, and Patricia McCoy. *Epics of the Western World.* Philadelphia: Lippincott Company, 1954.

Huxley, Aldous. *The Devils of Loudun.* London: Oxford University Press, 1952.

James, William. *Psychology.* (Abridged version of *Principles of Psychology*) Cleveland: World Publishing Company, 1905.

Jammer, Max. *The Conceptual Development of Quantum Mechanics.* New York: McGraw-Hill, 1966.

Kafner, Frank A., and James N. Laux. "The Girondins (1791-1793)," *The French Revolution: Conflicting Interpretations.* New York: Random House, 1968.

Kant, Immanuel. *Critique of Pure Reason.* Translated by Norman Kemp Smith. Chicago: Humanities Press, 1950.

Kruks, Sonia. *The Political Philosophy of Merleau-Ponty.* Sussex: The Harvester Press, 1981.

Lamartine, A. D. *Premières et Nouvelles Méditations Poétiques.* Paris: Pagnerre-Furne-Hachette et Cie., Editeurs, 1870.

Langevin, André. *Paul Langevin, Mon Père.* Paris: Les Editeurs Français Réunis, 1971.

Langevin, Paul "L'aspect général de la théorie de la relativité," *Bulletin scientifique des étudiants de Paris*, 2 (1922): 6.

———. *La Pensée et l'Action*, textes recueillies et présentés par Paul Labérenne. Paris: Editions Sociales, 1964.

———. "La Valeur Educative de l'histoire des Sciences," *Bulletin de la Société de Pédagogie*, 22: (December, 1926): 2-8.

Laplace, M. Le Comte. *Essai Philosophique sur les Probabilité.* Paris: Mme. Ve. Courcier, Imprimeur Libraire pour les Mathématiques et la Marine, 1814.

Lasch, Christopher. *The Culture of Narcissism—American Life in an Age of Diminishing Expectations.* New York: Norton & Co., 1979.

Lewis, Roy. *Giraudoux: La Guerre de Troie N'Aura Pas Lieu.* London: Camelot Press Limited, 1971.

Lidolf, Luce Blech. *La Pensée Philosophique et Sociale de Simone Weil.* Berne: Herbert Lang & Cie, SA, 1976.

Liebknecht, Karl. *Militarisme, guerre, révolution.* Paris: François Maspero, 1970.

Little, Janet Patricia. "Action et Travail chez Simone Weil," *Cahiers Simone Weil*, 2 (No. 1, March 1, 1979): 10-19.

———. "Le Refus de l'Idolâtrie dans l'Oeuvre de Simone Weil," *Cahiers Simone Weil*, 2 (No. 4, December 4, 1979): 201-2.

———. "Signification de la mythologie et des contes chez Simone Weil," *Simone Weil—Philosophe, historienne et mystique.* Paris: Aubier Montaigne, 1978.

Luxemburg, Rosa. *Selected Political Writings.* Edited and introduced by Dick Howard. New York: Monthly Review Press, 1971.

Malan, Ivo. *L'Enracinement de Simone Weil.* Paris: Didier, 1956.

Marx, Karl, and V. I. Lenin. *The Civil War in France: The Paris Commune.* New York: International Publishers, 1940.

Merleau-Ponty, Maurice *La Phénoménologie de la Perception.* Paris: Editions Gallimard, 1945.

Meyerson, Emile. *La Déduction relativiste.* Paris: Payot, 1925.

Michaud, Régis. *Modern Thought and Literature in France.* New York: Funk & Wagnalls Company, 1934.

Möeller, Charles. "Simone Weil et l'incroyance des croyants," in *Littérature du XXe siècle et christianisme* Vol. 1, *Silence de Dieu*. Paris: Casterman, 1953.
Monod, Jacques. *Le Hasard et la Nécessité, essai sur la philosophie naturelle de la Biologie Moderne*. Paris: Editions du Seuil, 1970.
Mosse-Bastide, Rose Marie. *Bergson, Educateur*. Paris: P. U. F., 1955.
Mounier, Emmanuel. *Le Personnalisme*. Paris: Presses Universitaires, de France, 1958.
Narcy, Michel. *Simone Weil, malheur et beauté du monde*. Paris: Editions du Centurion, 1967.
O'Brien, Conor Cruise. "The Antipolitics of Simone Weil," *Simone Weil, Interpretations of a Life*. Edited by George Abbott White. Amherst: University of Massachusetts, 1981.
Pascal, Blaise. *Pensées*. Paris: Editions Garnier-Frères, 1958.
Perrin, Joseph-Marie, J. Danielou, G. Durand, J. Kaelin, I. Bochet, P. Hussar, J. M. Emmanuelle *Réponses aux questions de Simone Weil*. Marseilles: Aubier-Editions Montaigne, 1964.
Pétrement, Simone. *La Vie de Simone Weil*. Vol. 1, *1909-1934*, Vol. 2, *1934-1943*. Paris: Fayard, 1973.
Pierce, Roy. "Simone Weil: Sociology, Utopia and Faith," *Contemporary French Political Thought*. London: Oxford University Press, 1966.
Planck, Max. *The Philosophy of Physics*. Translated by H. W. Johnston. New York: W. W. Norton & Co., Inc., 1936.
Plato. *Gorgias-A Revised Text with Introduction and Commentary*. Translated and edited by E. R. Dodds. London: Oxford University Press, 1959.
———. *The Republic-A New Version Founded on Basic English*. Translated and edited by Ivor Armstrong Richards. New York: W. W. Norton & Co., Inc., 1942.
Price, Hugh, Trans. *Lectures on Philosophy by Simone Weil*. Cambridge: Cambridge University Press, 1973.
Prigogine, Ilya, and Isabelle Stengers. *La Nouvelle Alliance—Métamorphose de la Science*. Paris: Editions Gallimard, 1979.
Proudhon, Pierre-Joseph. *Les Confessions d'un Révolutionnaire pour servir à l'histoire de la révolution de Février*. Paris: La Voix du Peuple, 1849.
———. *Correspondances, La Guerre et la Paix—Recherches sur le Principe et la Constitution du Droit des Gens*. Paris: Librairie des Sciences politiques et sociales, 1927.
Reymond, Arnold. *History of the Sciences in Greco-Roman Antiquity*. New York: Biblo and Tannen, 1963.
Ritter, Alan. *The Political Thought of Pierre-Joseph Proudhon*. Princeton: Princeton University Press, 1969.
Robinson, Judith. "L'Analyse de l'esprit dans les 'Cahiers' de Paul Valéry," *Les Critiques de notre temps et Valéry*. Paris: Editions Garnier Frères, 1963.
Rosenthal, Sandra B. and Patrick L. Bourgeois. *Pragmatism and Phenomenology: A Philosophic Encounter*. Amsterdam: B. R. Gruner Publishing Co., 1980.
Russell, Bertrand. *An Essay on the Foundations of Geometry*. London: Dover Press, 1897.
———. *Principles of Mathematics*. New York: Norton Press, 1903.
Sartre, Jean-Paul. *Critique de la Raison Dialectique*. Paris: Librairie Gallimard, 1960.
———. *L'Etre et le Néant*. Paris: Gallimard, 1943.
———. *L'Existentialisme est un Humanisme*. Paris: Editions Nagel, 1965.
———. *La Liberté Cartésienne*, Vol. 1, *Situations*. Paris: Editions Gallimard, 1947.
———. *La Transcendance de l'Ego—Esquisse d'une description phénoménologique*, Vol. 6, *Recherches Philosophiques*. Paris: Librairie A. Hatier. 1936-37.
Seward, Desmond. *The Bourbon Kings of France*. New York: Harper & Row Publishers, 1976.
Simone Weil, philosophe, historienne et mystique. Colloque de Cérisy-la-Salle, du 21 juillet au 1er août 1974. Paris: Aubier Montaigne, 1974.
Spengler, Oswald. *The Decline of the West*. New York: Knopf, 1926.

Spinoza. Benoît. *Ethique*, Translated by Von Vloten. Paris: Librairie Plon, 1957.
Sprague, Elmer and Paul W. Taylor. *Knowledge and Introductory Readings in Philosophy*. New York: Harcourt, Brace & Co., 1959.
Valéry, Paul. *Oeuvres de Paul Valéry*. Paris: Bibliothéque de la Pléiade—Gallimard, 1957.
Vergez, André, and Denis Huisman. *Histoire des Philosophes Illustrée par des Textes*. Paris: Fernand Nathan, 1966.
Vëto, Miklos. *Métaphysique religieuse de Simone Weil*. Paris: Librairie Philosophique J. Vrin, 1971.
Weil, Simone. *Attente de Dieu*. Paris: Fayard, 1966.
———. *Cahiers*, vols. 1, 2, 3. Paris: Librairie Plon, 1951.
———. *La Condition Ouvrière*. Paris: Gallimard, 1951.
———. *La Connaissance Surnaturelle*. Paris: Gallimard, 1952.
———. *Ecrits historiques et politiques*. Paris: Gallimard, 1960.
———. *Ecrits de Londres et Dernières Lettres*. Paris: Gallimard, 1957.
———. *L'Enracinement—Prélude à une Déclaration des Devoirs Envers l'Etre Humain*. Paris: Editions Gallimard, 1949.
———. *Gravity and Grace*. Translated by Arthur Wills. New York: G. P. Putnam's Sons, 1952.
———. *Intuitions Pré-Chrétiennes*. Paris: la Colombe, 1951.
———. *Leçons de Philosophie*. Transcrites et présentées par Anne Reynaud-Ghérithault. Paris: Librairie Plon, 1959.
———. *Lettre à un religieux*. Paris: Gallimard, 1951.
———. *Oppression et Liberté*. Paris: Gallimard, 1955.
———. *Pensées sans ordre concernant l'amour de Dieu*. Paris: Gallimard, 1962.
———. *Poèmes, suivis de Vénise sauvée*. Paris: Gallimard, 1968.
———. *La Pesanteur et la Grâce*. Paris: Librairie Plon, 1948.
———, *Réflexions sur les Causes de la liberté et de l'oppression sociale*. Paris: Gallimard, 1955.
———. *The Simone Weil Reader*. Edited by George A. Panichas. New York: David McKay Corporation, Inc., 1977.
———. *La Source Grecque*. Paris: Gallimard, 1953.
———. *Sur la Science*. Paris: Gallimard, 1966.
Wells, H. G. *The Time Machine, An Invention*. London: William Heinemann, 1894.
Whitmarsh, Anne *Simone de Beauvoir and the Limits of Commitment*. Cambridge, Cambridge University Press, 1981.
Zemansky, Mark W. *Temperatures Very Low and Very High*. New York: Dover Publications, Inc., 1964.

Index

Action, 43-47, 50-51, 59, 65-66, 68, 75-77, 111, 122, 148-50: conscious, 65, 148-50; emotional, 47; Française, 111, 148-50, 101; methodical, 43-46, 59, 65-66, 68, 75-77, 245-47; methodology of, 74, 75; spontaneous, 65, 122; unreflected, 68; voluntary, 46. *See also* France, history of; Little, J[anet] P[atricia]; Marcel, Gabriel; Merleau-Ponty, Maurice; Necessity, Sartre, Jean-Paul; Weil, Simone; Work

Adorno, Theodor, 161-62. *See also* Frankfurt School; Friedman, George; Horkheimer, Max

Agadir, 115. *See also* Colonialism; France, history of

Alain, 26-27, 29-32, 39-40, 65, 70, 163, 165. *See also* Chartier, Emile

Albigensia, 109. *See also* France, history of

Alembert, Jean Le Rond, d', 173. *See also* Science, classical

Algebra, 11, 55, 165, 171-72, 235. *See also* Signs; Viète, François

Algésiras, Treaty of, 115. *See also* Colonialism; France, history of

Alienation, 61, 63, 100-1, 141, 176, 259, 261

Allemagne, L'Eternelle, 99-100

Alliance, la Nouvelle. *See* Prigogine, Ilya; Stengers, Isabelle

Alsace-Lorraine, 115. *See also* Colonialism; France, history of

Analogy, 165

Anticommunism, 236. *See also* Communism

Antifacism, 236. *See also* Fascism

Arendt, Hannah, 151, 172, 235; *Between Past and Future*, 243; *Crises of the Republic*, 151; *The Human Condition*, 172, 223; loss of meaning, 210; mediation, 239-40, *The Origins of Totalitarianism*, 237; similarity with Weil, 151; understanding, 239-40. *See also* Husserl, Edmond; Valéry, Paul; Weil, Simone

Arithmetic, 170

Associationism, 55. *See also* Body

Atomism, 55

Attente, 93, 120

Attente de Dieu, 144-45

Attention, 146

Augustine, Saint, 264, 207-8; *Confessions* 207; movement towards non-being, 208

Autonomy, 226

Babylonians, 167

Bachelard, Gaston, 165, 180

Baldwin, Neil, 251. *See also* Poetry

Barrés, Maurice, 176. *See also* Determinism

Barthelemy-Madaule, 201

Bataille, Georges, 65. *See also* "Le Cercle Communiste démocratique"

Baudoin, Charles, 88. *See also* *Triomphe du Héros*; Poetry, epic

Being: definition, 51; duality of, 21; plenitude of, 227

Bergson, Henri, 52, 53, 55, 56, 165, 180. *See also* Intuition

Bernanos, Georges, 100-1. *See also* *Grands Cimetières sous la lune, les*

Bernouilli, Jacques, 173. *See also* Science, classical

Béziers, 109. *See also* France, history of

Binet, Alfred, 165

Biranisme, le, 29-30, 33. *See also* Maine de Biran; Voluntarism

Blum, Malou, 158-59. *See also* Weil, Simone

Body, 21-23, 36, 38, 39, 45, 49, 54, 63, 80-81

Bohr, Niels, 190, 194

Boltzmann, Ludwig, 178, 196. *See also* Irreversibility

Bradley, Francis, 70. *See also* Pragmatism; James-Lange Theory; James, William

Brecht, Bertolt: *The Visions of Simone Machard*, 67

Brittany, 109. *See also* France, history of

Brun, Giordan, 186

Brunschvicg, Léon, 27, 39-40, 70, 165, 185. *See also* Hughes, H. S.; Positivism, logical; Wittgenstein, Ludwig

Bureaucracy: Germany, 63, 122, 126. *See also* Alienation

Bureaucratization: industrial, state, union, 134-38, 144

Burgundy, 109. *See also* France, history of

Cabaud, Jacques, 27, 116

Cahiers du Sud, les, 87; *See also* Weil, Simone

Camus, Albert: *l'Homme Revolté*, 38; le *Mythe de Sisyphe*, 38; passivity, 51; *la Peste*, 74

274   Index

Capek, Milec, 209, philosophical impact of contemporary physics, 193, 195. *See also* Time; Space
Capitalism, 128, 239. *See also* Marx, Karl
Cassirer, Ernest: *Language and Myth*, 243. *See also* Language; Myth; Langer, Suzanne
Catholicism, 145-48
Causality, 193
Cave, myth of. *See* Plato
Cercle Communiste democratique, le, 65. *See also* Bataille, Georges
Chance, 76, 193-94; 199. *See also* Determinism, crisis of; Hasard et Nécessité; Monod, Jacques
Charmes. *See* Valéry, Paul
Char, René, 106. *See also Feuillets d'Hypnos*
Charles V, 100. *See* France, history of
Charles VI, 100. *See* France, history of
Chartier, Emile, 27. *See also* Alain
Christianity, 145
Church, 145
Civil War in France, The, 123, 124. *See also* France, history of; Marx, Karl
Civil war, Spain, 166
Clark, Ronald, 184. *See also* Einstein, Albert
Clausius, Rudolf, 173, 175. *See also* Entropy
Colonialism, 113-20. *See also* "Qui est Coupable de Menées Antifrançaises?"; Weil, Simone
Comité de Vigilance des Intellectuels antifascistes, 119. *See also* Weil, Simone
Communism, 121, 238. *See also* Anticommunism
Complementarity, 264. *See also* Déracinement; Enracinement
Comte, Auguste, 77, 180. *See also* Positivism
Condition, Ouvrière, la, 121, 141. *See also* Weil, Simone; Factory work
Congo, French. *See* Colonialism; France, history of
Connaissance, Surnaturelle, la, 204. *See also* Weil, Simone
Consciousness, 15-16, 24-25, 33, 35, 45, 47, 55, 56, 57, 63, 66, 142-43, 260; structures of, 66, 28, 45, 55
Continuum, 60, 188, 189, 194, 195, 205, 210. 259, 264. *See also* Wave Theory; De Broglie, Louis
Creation, 13, 225, 246, 247, 260-64

Crises of the Republic, 151. *See also* Arendt, Hannah
Critique of Practical Reason, 29. *See also Critique of Pure Reason*; Kant, Immanuel
Critique of Pure Reason, 29, 39. *See also Critique of Practical Reason*; Kant, Immanuel
Critique Sociale, la, 129
Cross, 208-9
Cube, duplication of, 211
Cunningham, Suzanne, 245. *See also* Transcendental ego
Czechoslavakia: invasion of, 87

D'Alembert, *See* Alembert, Jean Le Rond, d'.
D'Amico, Robert, 240
Darwin, Charles, 77, 127. *See also* Marx, Karl
D'Aubigné, Agrippa. *See* France, history of; France, literature of
Daudet, Alphonse. *See Contes du Lundi, les*; France, literature of
De Beauvoir, Simone, 66-67; *Pyrrhus, et Cinéas*, 67; *le Sang des Autres*, 67. *See also* Action, methodical
De Broglie, Louis, 183, 189, 190, 203. *See also* Continuum, Wave theory
Deconstruction, 73-74, 149-50, 221, 260
Decreation, 221, 224-25, 226, 260-64
Dédoublement, 251. *See also* Baldwin, Neil; Poetry; Valéry, Paul
Déracinement, 11, 28, 34, 35, 37-38, 44, 57, 68-69, 81-85, 90-91, 98, 113, 116, 120, 134, 139, 143, 148-50, 161-62, 173, 177, 194, 198, 212, 221, 224-26, 238, 239-40, 247, 259, 260-64. *See also* Complementarity; Enracinement
Derrida, Jacques, 90, 245
Descartes, René, 11-12, 14-16, 20-21, 26-28, 31, 33, 35-36, 37, 48, 58-59, 60, 163, 173, 186, 260; *Bâton de l'Aveugle, le*, 21; inseparability of space from matter,207; contestation of logical priority of space, 207; ontological proof, 58; *Traité des Passions de l'Ame*, 48. *See also* France, literature of
Determinism, 58,176, 183, 185, 186, 191-92, 193, 199, 200, 204, 208; crisis of, 260-64
De Viau, Theophile. *See* France, literature of
Dewey, John, 70, 76-77
Dialectical materialism, 63. *See also* Marx, Karl
Diderot, Dénis, 33

Diophantus, 167, 169
Discontinuity, 177, 186-87, 188, 194, 197, 210, 260-64
Discours de la Méthode, 13-16. See also Descartes, René
Doubt, 18, 19, 26, 58
Dreyfus, Alfred, 116
Dujardin, Philippe, 128, 157. See also Weil, Simone
Durkheim, Emile, 147. See also Power, of the social; Church
Ecrits Historiques et Politiques, les. See Weil, Simone
Ecrits de Londres. See Weil, Simone

Effort, 174
Egypt, 115, 168. See also Colonialism; France, history of; Oppression
Einstein, Albert, 183, 189, 190, 193, 200-1, 208-10, 211. See also Clark, Ronard; Time, spatialization of
Electre, 116. See also Giraudoux, Jean; Myth
Electricity, 189
Elements, 169. See also Euclid
Eliade, 247. See also Myth
Emigrants: Algerian, 117; North African, 118-19; Tunisian, 119; Indochinese, 119
Emotion, 48, 54, 70
Empiricism, 12, 43, 64-65; radical, 65. See also James, William
Energy, 173, 175, 177, 178, 195, 198
Engels, Friedrich, 121, 130
Enlightenment, 165
Enracinement, 12, 13, 35-37, 38, 44, 68, 69, 81, 82-85, 107, 113, 116, 120, 148-50, 162, 166, 171, 177, 190-91, 194, 198, 201, 212, 224-26, 238, 239-40, 246-47, 259-64, 268. See also Complementarity; Déracinement
"L'Enseignement des Mathematics," 171
Entropy, 173, 175, 196, 198. See also Clausius; Science, classical; Work
Epic: deconstruction of, 90-91, 94-95; discontinuity of, 89-90. See also Tragedy, deconstruction; *Iliad*; Narration, continuity of
Essence, 66
Estrangement, 14-15, 245. See also Alienation; Déracinement
Etoile nord Africaine, L', 118-19, 244. See also Colonialism

L'Être et le Néant, 68. See also Sartre, Jean-Paul
Euclid, 169. See also *Elements*
Evil, localization of, 116
Exile, 69
Existence, 16-17, 19, 22, 27, 28, 30, 39, 43, 46, 63, 67
l'Existentialisme est un Humanisme, 35. See also Existentialism; Sartre, Jean-Paul
Existentialism, 11, 26-27, 31-32, 44, 65-66, 67, 181, 184, 205. See also *l'Existentialisme est un Humanisme,* l; Sartre, Jean-Paul; *Transcendance de l'Ego, la*
Expanse, 25
Exteriority, 14, 16-18, 19-20, 22, 23, 34-35, 40, 45, 47-48, 50-56, 59, 62, 64, 66, 68. See also Self

Factory work, 73, 121, 141-44. See also *Condition Ouvrière, la*; Weil, Simone
Fascism, 238. See also Antifascism
Feudalism, 79. See also France, history of; Oppression, Rome
Feuillets d'Hypnos, 106. See also Char, René
Feuilles libres, 113-14, 117. See also Colonialism
Fidéism, le, 57-58
Folle de Chaillot, la, 116. See also Giraudoux, Jean
Force, 79, 82-83, 85, 87-94, 98, 112-13, 244
Form, 52
France, 99, 100-3, 113-20; history of, 100-3, 106-12, 115-16, 123, 130, 152, 241-42
France, literature of, 101-3, 112, 115
Franco, Francisco, 118, 133
Frankfurt School, 161, 199; See also *Political Philosophy of the Frankfurt School*
Freedom, 13, 14, 15-18, 19, 27-28, 30, 31, 35, 38, 39, 43, 67, 71, 74-76, 79, 83-85, 149-50, 260-61
Free will, 45, 177, 199
Freud, Sigmund, 48, 56, 89. See also *Interpretation of Dreams*; Myth; Refoulement, le; Subconscious, the
Friedman, Georges, 161-62. See also Frankfurt School

Galileo, 195, 202-3
Games, 93

Generalization, 54
Geometry, 163, 168, 169
Germany, 99-101, 114-15, 121, 135, 242; and phenomenology of the mind, 104; and romanticism, 104; and workers movement, 135-38. *See also* Hegel, Georg Wilhelm
Germany: history of, 101-3, 104-6, 124, 133, 136-37, 155-57
Girard, René, 90, 151; tragédie, la, 151; violence, la, 151; *Violence et le sacré, la*, 151, 224
Giraudoux, Jean, 85-87, 116, 235-37; *Electre*, 116; *Folle de Chaillot, la*, 116-17; *Guerre de Troi n' Aura pas lieu, la*, 85-87, 117, 235-37; . *See also* Weil, Simone: language
God, 26, 58, 59,74; existence of, 19. *See also* Descartes, René; Ontological proof
Grands Cimetières sous la Lune, la, 133. *See also* Bernanos, Georges
Gravitation, 199
Gravity and Grace, 99. *See also* *Presanteur et la Grâce, la*; Weil, Simone
Great Beast, the, 96. *See also* Myth; Plato
Greece, 163
Green, T. H., 70. *See also* Bradley, Francis; James-Lange theory; James, William; Pragmatism
Guerre de Troie n'Aura pas lieu, la, 117, 151. *See also* Giraudoux, Jean; Lewis, Roy
Guerithault, Anne Reynaud, 43-44, 48. *See also* *Leçons de Philosophie*
Habit, 51
Hadj, Messali, 118-19, 153. *See also* *L'Etoile Nord-Africaine*
Hasard et Nécessité. *See* Chance; Monod, Jacques
Hegel, Georg Wilhelm, 104, 127-28, 181. *See also* Germany, and phenomenology; *Phenomenology of the Mind*
Heidegger, Martin, 30, 32, 205
Heisenberg, Werner, 184; and uncertainty principle, 191-92
Hellman, John, 222. *See also* Mounier, Emmanuel
Hésitations devant le Baptême, 145. *See also* *Attente de Dieu*
History, 260-64; notion of, 235-37. *See also* Little, Janet Patricia; Judaism, critique of; Time
Hitler, Adolf, 137

Hobbes, Thomas, 210
L'Homme Révolté, 38. *See also* Camus, Albert
Horkheimer,Max, 161. *See also* Frankfurt School; Adorno, Theodor; Friedman, George
Hughes, H. S., 71, 182. *See also* Brunschvicg, Léon; Merleau-Ponty, Maurice; *Obstructed Path, The*; Positivism, logical; Vienna Circle; Wittgenstein, Ludwig
Hume, David, 26-27, 39, 206. See also *Inquiry Into Human Understanding*; Space
Husserl, Edmund, 32, 33, 34, 44, 70, 165, 184; *Crisis of European Sciences and Phenomenology*, 240; geometry, 240; historical meanings, 241; language, 239-40, 245-46; mediation, 239-40; *Meditations Cartésiennes*, 27; *Origin of Geometry, The*, 239; understanding, 239-40
Hutson, Arthur, 88. *See also* McCoy, Patricia

Idealism, 12, 32, 35, 43, 44, 63, 65, 66, 70, 180, 260-64
Idealism, epistemological. See Bachelard,Gaston; Brunschvicg, Léon; Kant, Immanuel; Poincare, Henri
Iliade, ou le Poème de la Force, 85, 87-94, 120
Imagination, 14, 18-20, 21, 24, 29, 31, 51-52, 227
Impersonal, 221-22. *See also* Narcy, Michel; Simone Weil, *Malheur et Beauté du Monde*
Incommensurables, 170
Indeterminacy, 183, 193
Infinitude: spatial, 209; temporal, 209
Infinity, two chasms of, 226-27. *See also* Pascal, Blaise
Inquiry Into Human Understanding, 39. *See also* Hume, David
Instincts, 47. *See also* Pavlov, Ivan Petrovitch; Reflex
Instrumentalism, 76, 77
Intentionality, 21, 33, 34
Interiority, 14, 37, 40, 45, 55, 56, 59-60, 64, 66
Introspection, 46, 55
Intuition, 46
Intuitions Pré-Chrétiennes, 248. *See also* Myth; *Connaissance, Surnaturelle, la*
Irreversibility, 178, 198-99. *See also* Boltzmann, Ludwig; Science, modern; Zemansky, Mark

Israel et les Gentils. See Weil, Simone

James-Lange theory, 70. See also Bradley, Francis
James, William, 43, 48, 49,70. See also Materialism; Empiricism, radical; Pragmatism; Principles of Psychology, The
Jammer, Max, 182
Judaism, critique of, 148. See also History, notion of; Little Janet Patricia; Marcion; Time
Judgment, 57-58; analytical, 57; synthetic, 57. See also Kant, Immanuel
Jung, Carl, 89. See also Freud, Sigmund, Interpretation of Dreams; Myth; Rank, Otto

Kant, Immanuel, 26-27, 29, 32, 39,44, 67; a posteriori, 59; a priori, 59; categories, 59; judgment, analytical, 59; judgment, synthetic, 59; Kantian priorities, 82-83; neo-Kantian influence, 38. See also Force, reversal of
Kierkegaard, Sören, 181
Knowledge, 25-26, 33, 46, 55, 83, 175; complexity of, 79, 83. See also Existence; Pierce, Roy
Kruks, Sonia: Political Philosophy of Merleau-Ponty, The, 66
Kuhn, Thomas, 245

Labor, 14, 21, 23, 25, 31, 36, 173; division of, 79, 81, 260-64; specialization of, 79, 140-42. See also Work
Lagneau, Jules, 29
LaGrange, Charles, 173. See also Science, classical
LaMarck, Jean Baptiste de Monet, 127. See also Marx, Karl
Langer, Suzanne, 243. See also Myth; Language; Cassirer, Ernest
Langevin, Paul, 165, 213
LaPlace, Pierre Simon de: Essai Philosophique sur les Probabilities, 185. See also Determinism; Probability
Language, 59, 60-61, 235, 237; as expression of will, 61; as a recipient of action, 62; conscious use of, 62, 235-37; "dédoublement," 60-61; fixity of meaning, 60-61; loss of meaning, 62, 235-37; myth,

de Troie, 61, 65, 85; objectification, 60-62; violence, 90, 243-45. See also Cassirer, Ernest; Myth; Langer, Suzanne; Robinson, Judith; Valéry, Paul; Violence
Leçons de Philosophie, 14, 43-71; 260
Leibnitz, Wilhelm, 56, 59, 183; causality, 183
Lenin, Nikolai, 63, 64, 139; Materialism and Empiriocriticism, 64, 139
Leviathan, 210. See also Hobbes, Thomas
Lévinas, Emmanuel, 158-59. See also Relgion, critique of
Lewis, Roy, 151. See also Giraudoux, Jean; La Guerre de Troie n'Aura pas Lieu
Lidolf, Luce Blech, 64
Little, J[anet] P[atricia]: history, notion of, 148-49; Judaism, critique of, 148-49; "Refus de l'Idolatrie dans l'Oeuvre de Simone Weil," 147; Time, 148-49; myth, 247. See also Myth; Necessity; Work
Locke, John, 12. See also Empiricism
Louis XIV, 100-3. See also France, history of
Louis XIII, 152. See also Richelieu, Duc de; Seward, Desmond
Louis Philippe, 101
Love, 224, 246, 260-64
Luxemburg, Rosa, 124, 130. See also Germany, history of; Revisionism; Social Democracy; War credits

Machinism, 63,122, 126, 139-41, 144. See also Alienation
Madrid, Treaty of, 115. See also Colonialism; France, history of
Magnitude: relativity of. See Pascal, Blaise; Weil, Simone
Maine de Biran, Marie François, 29-30, 65. See also Voluntarism
Malraux, André, 67
Marcel, Gabriel, 66, 67, 184
Marcion, 148. See also Judaism, critique of; Weil, Simone
Marcoux,Camille, 38
Marxism, critique of, 126-28, 144, 223
Marx, Karl, 63, 77, 121, 139-41; 154-55; involvement with war, 130. See also Capitalism; Dialectical materialism; Engels, Fredrich; Value, surplus
Materialism, 35, 40, 43, 44, 63, 64, 77, 207, 260-64; 244-47; Ne Recommençons pas la Guerre

Materialism and Empiriocriticism, 63. *See also* Lenin, Nikolai
Mathematics, 11-12, 167; Greek, 163; history, 165. *See also* Science, history of; Russell, Bertrand
Maurras, Charles: *l'Action Française*
Maxwell, James, 173, 189
McCoy, Patricia, 88. *See also*; Hutson, Arthur
Meaning, 235-46; deconstruction of, 243; loss of, 245; reintegration of, 240, 246
Mediation, 245-46
Méditations, 13, 58. *See also* Descartes, René
Méditations Cartésiennes. See Husserl, Edmond
Memory, 51-52, 53
Menaechmus, 168
Merleau-Ponty, Maurice, 44, 66-67, 70. *See also* Action, methodical; Kruks, Sonia; Hughes, H. S.
Métaphysique religieuse de Simone Weil. See Vetö, Miklos
Meyerson, Emile, 165.
Miletus, 168
Milhaud, Gaston,165
Militarism, 126, 129-34, 144. *See also* War
Mind, 19-20, 36, 43, 45, 53, 55, 63, 64, 142-43. *See also* Body; Perception; Thought
Monod, Jacques, 200-1. *See also* Chance; *Hasard et Necéssité*
Montaigne, Michel Eyquem, 181. *See also* France, literature of
Morocco, 115. *See also* Colonialism; France, history of
Mounier, Emmanuel, 221-22. See also *Esprit*; Hellman, John
Movement, 14, 20, 21, 24, 36, 50, 52, 179
Munich Compromise, 87
Myth, 85-87, 246-50, 260-64; of the Cave, 96; critique of, 89; deconstruction of, 260-64; didactic interpretation of 89; Great Beast, the, 96; historic interpretation of, 88; Indian, American, 250; language, 244-47; Narcissus, 249; naturalistic interpretation of, 88-89; Orestes, 249; Phaedrus, 249; Prometheus, 250; Prosipirpina, 248-49; Ring of Gyges, 97; social, the, 98; Upanishads, the, 247. *See also* Camus, Albert; *Connaissance, Surnaturelle, la*; Eliade, Marcel;

Langer, Suzanne; language; Little, J[anet] P[atricia]; Plato; *Republic*

Napoleon, 101-3
Narcissus, 249. *See also* Myth
Narcy, Michel, 222. *See also* Impersonal, the; *Simone Wiel, Malheur et beauté du Monde*
Narration, continuity of, 89-90. *See also* Epic, discontinuity of; *Iliad*
Nation, 99; concept of, 103, 107; myth of, 99-101
Nationalism: French, 99, 107; German, 99, 104
National Socialists, 121, 136
Nature, 46
Necessity, 13, 15, 19, 31, 45, 58, 59-60, 64, 65, 166, 173, 174, 175, 193, 194, 198, 199, 223, 226; limits of, 27-28. *See also* Science, classical
New Left, French, 144
Ne Recommençons pas la Guerre de Troie, 61, 65, 85. *See also* Language
Newton, John, 173, 195, 206-7. *See also* Empiricism, logical priority of; Space
Nicomachus, 169
Nietzsche, Friedrich Wilhelm, 29, 186; time, concept of, 209; *Zarathustra*, 210
Noces, 67. *See also* Camus, Albert
Nominalism, 54
Non-being, 204, 205, 208. *See also* Augustine, Saint
Novis, Emile, 162

Obligation, 246. *See also* Right
Old Testament, 148
Oppression, 74, 79, 82-85, 126-28, 139-41, 149-50, 260-61; Egypt, in, 77-78; functional theory of, 77; Greece, in, 78; Rome, in, 78, 79; structure of, 81, 82, 139-41
Orestes, 249. *See also* Myth
Orient, 242
Origins of Totalitarianism, 237. *See also* Arendt, Hannah

Pacifism, 85-87, 130
Panichas, George, 96. *See also* Myth; Power; Social, the
Paris Commune, 153-54
Particularization, 54

Pascal, Blaise, 181, 205, 226-27. *See also* France, literature of; Infinity
Passivity, 47, 51
Patrie, la. *See* Nation
Patriotism, French, 107. *See also* Nationalism, French
Pavlov, Ivan Petrovitch, 48
Péguy, Charles, 114. *See also* Colonialism; War
Perception, 11-37, 39. "Connaître," 18, 28, 30; measure of depth, 52, pain, 15, 79; Pantheon, 24, 25; pleasure, 15, 79; "ressentir, 30
Perrin, Father Joseph-Marie, 73, 145, 158-59. *See also* Weil, Simone
Personalism, 221-22
Personne et le Sacré, la, 221-22. *See also* Weil, Simone
Perspectives—Allons-nous vers la Révolution Prolétarienne, 121, 138. *See also* Weil, Simone
Pesanteur et la Grâce, La, 199, 204, 208, 226. *See also* Weil, Simone
Peste, la, 74. *See also* Camus, Albert
Pétrement, Simone, 26, 30, 31, 39,40, 116, 119
Phenomenology, 33, 66, 104. *See also* Existentialism; Intentionality
Physics, 163, 177, 179, 196, 205, 207
Physicists, German, 182
Pierce, Roy: knowledge, complexity of, 83, 141
Planck, Max, 163, 178, 183, 188, 196, 210. See also *Initiations à la Physique*; Quanta theory; Ray, Black; Science, modern
Plato, 11-12, 169. *See also* Myth; *Republic*
Pleasure: *See* Sensation
Poetry, 235-37, 250-54; epic, 88-89. *See also* Baldwin, Neil; Baudoin, Charles; Dédoublement; *Triomphe du Héros, Le*; Valéry, Paul
Poland: invasion of, 87
Poincaré, Henri, 209. *See also* Reversibility, temporal; Time
Political Philosophy of the Frankfurt School, 161-62. *See also* Adorno, Theodor; Frankfurt School; Friedman, Georges
Positivism, 77
Positivism, empiric, 180. *See also* Comte, Auguste; Science, classical; Taine

Positivism, logical, 181. *See also* Brunschvicg, Léon; Hughes, H. S.; Vienna Circle; Wittgenstein, Ludwig
Power, 14, 15-18, 22, 23, 28, 30, 36, 38, 49, 77, 81-83, 126, 260-64; centralization of, 79, 83; deconstruction of, 85-87; displacement of, 23, 77, 235-37; equilibrium of, 99-101; instability of, 82, 83, 90-91, 98; social, of the, 144-45
Pragmatism, 44, 49,65,70, 76-77. *See also* James-Lange theory; James, William
Prigogine, Ilya, 198, 201. *See also Alliance,la Nouvelle*; Stengers, Isabelle
Principles of Psychology, 43, 48-9, 70. *See also* Empiricism, radical; James, William; Pragmatism
Priorities, Kantian: reversal of. *See* Force; Kant, Immanuel
Probability, 187, 193, 197, 199. *See also* LaPlace, Pierre Simon de
Project, 31-32, 178
Prometheus, 250. *See also* Myth
Property: private, 126. *See also* Marx, Karl; Value, surplus
Proportion: principle of, 168, 210. *See also* Geometry
Prospirpina, 248-49. *See also* Myth
Proudhon, Pierre Joseph, 130,154-55
Proust, Marcel: *Recherche du Temps Perdu, À la*, 53
Prussia: Frédéric II, 103-4; history of, 104-6; Napoleon Bonaparte, conquests of, 104; Napoleon III, conquests of, 104. *See also* Germany, history of
Psychology, Principles of, 43, 48-49, 70. *See also* Empiricism, radical; James, William; Pragmatism
Pyrrhus et Cinéas, 66-67. *See also* De Beauvoir, Simone
Pythagoras, 168, 169, 185. *See also* Proportion, principle

Quanta Theory, 177, 187, 189, 193, 194, 197, 260-64
Quantum Mechanics, 187-88; 211

Rabi, Wladimir, 158-59. *See also* Religion, critique of
Rank, Otto, 89
Rassemblement, Populaire, Le, 117, 119
Rationalism: French, 26

Index

Rationalization, system of, 140-42. *See also* Taylorization
Ray, Black, 178. *See also* Planck, Max; Science, modern
Realism, 32, 70
Recherche du Temps Perdu, A la. See Proust, Marcel
Reflex, 46-48; conditioned, 47; corporal 47, 48; Pavlov, Ivan Petrovich, 48; physical, 46
"Refléxions à Propos de la Théorie de Quanto," 162-63, 172. *See also* Quanta theory; Science
"Réflexions sur les Causes de la literté et de l'Oppression Sociale," 73, 121
"Réflexions sur l'Origine de l'Hitlerisme," 153. *See also* Weil, Simone
Reformism, 135
"Refoulement, le,' 56. *See also* Freud, Sigmund; Subconscious
"Refus de l'Idolatrie dans l'Oeuvre de Simone Weil," 147. *See also* Little, J[anet] P[atricia]
Relativity, theory of, 177, 202-3, 211. *Science, modern*
Religion, critique of, 158-59 *See also* Levinas, Emmanuel; Rabi, Wladamir; Weil, Simone
Renault, 166
Republic, 95-96. *See also* Plato
Resistance, 20, 32, 51, 65, 66, 67, 80. *See also* France, history of
Revisionism, 65, 122, 124-25; Luxemburg, Rosa, 124-25; Social Democrats, 121, 135-37. *See also* Germany, history of
Revolution, 121-22, 134, 144, 238; concept of, 98; France, history of, 131; myth of, 98,144; Roman influence, 113
Révolution Prolétarienne, 121, 137-38
Richelieu, Duc de, 101-3, 152. *See also* France, history of
Right, 246. *See also* Obligation
Ring of Gyges, 97. *See also* Myth; Plato
Roanne, lectures, 61, 65, 239, 260
Robespierre, Maximilien de, 132
Robinson, Judith, 239. *See also* Language; Valéry, Paul
Romains, Jules, 142; *Hommes de Bonne Volonté,* 142. *See also* Unconscious
Roman Empire, the, 114. *See also* Colonialism
210, 211; homogeneity of, 206-7; logical

Rousseau, Jean-Jacques, 181
Russell, Bertrand, 204. See also *Principles of Mathematics*
Russia: history of, 123, 124, 125, 131

Saint Augustine. *See* Augustine, Saint
Saint-Exupéry, Antoine de, 67
"Sang coule en Tunisie, Le," 117. *See also* Colonialism; Weil, Simone
Sang des Autres, Le, 67. *See also* De Beauvoir, Simone
Sartre, Jean-Paul, 11, 22, 27, 30, 33-34, 35, 66, 67, 184; collective freedom, 71; *Critique de la Raison Dialectique,* 71; *diable et le Bon Dieu, Le,* 71; *L'Etre et le Néant,* 43, 68; *L'Existentialisme est un Humanisme,* 67; individual freedom, 71; *Mouches, Les,* 71; "Transcendance de l'Ego, La," 16, 35; similarity with Simone Weil, 71. *See also* Existentialism; Freedom; Weil, Simone
Science, 75-76, 162, 260-64; classical, 173-77, 180, 210, 242; Greek, 166, 210, 242, 260-64; history of, 165; modern, 164, 177, 185-87, 210, 260-64; pedagogy of, 165. *See also* Determinism; Discontinuity; Entropy; Irreversibility; Necessity; Positivism; Quanta theory; Relativity, theory of
"Science et Nous, la," 162
"Science et Perception dans Descartes," 40, 43, 46, 51, 63, 66, 162, 163. *See also* Descartes, René
Self, 11-14, 16-18, 19, 20, 21, 22, 23, 26-27, 28, 30, 32, 33, 34, 36, 38, 45, 47, 57, 68, 161, 221, 224-25, 259, 260-64
Sensation, 48, 49, 50, 51, 57
Serge, Victor, 137-38
Series, 50, 76, 66
Seward, Desmond, 152
Signs, 171-72. *See also* Algebra
Similes: Homer's use of, 94
Social Democrats, 121, 135-36, 137
Socialism: critique of, 121-22, 125; scientific, 63
Social: the power of, 122. *See also* Myth, power of
Socrates, 170
Souvenier (le), 52-53
Souveraine, Boris, 137-38
Soviet Union, 137-38
Space, 51-52, 60, 174, 175, 201, 207, 209,

priority of, 204; temporal priority of, 205
Spain, 100, 132-33
Spartacus League, 130,155
Spengler, Oswald:*Decline of the West*, 183
Spinoza, Benoît, 26-27, 48, 54, 58, 186
Square: duplication of, 170
State: concept of, 98; myth of, 98
Stengers, Isabelle, 198-201. *See also* Prigogine, Ilya
Sur la Science, 11. *See also* Weil, Simone
Symbol, 90-91, 171, 210, 235-37, 238, 240, 245, 246. *See also* Derrida, Jacques
Synagogue, 145
Swift, Jonathan, 205

Tacitus, 105-6. *See also* Germany, history of
Taine, Hippolyte, 180-81. *See also* Positivism, empiric; Determinism
Taylorization, 142
Technocracy, 139-41, 144
Thales, 163, 168, 170, 211
Thibon, Gustave, 18. *See also* Weil, Simone
Thoughts, 17-20, 22, 28, 55, 176. *See also* Perception; Consciousness
Time, 174, 175, 201, 207, 208-9, 211; as an expression of necessity, 208; homogeneity of, 207, reversibility of, 208-9. *See also* Nietzche, Friedrich Wilhelm; Poincaré, Henri; Augustine, Saint
Tragedy: deconstruction of, 91-92. *See also* Epic, deconstruction of; *Iliad*
Traité des Passions de l'Âme, 48. *See also* Descartes, René
Transcendental ego, 11, 27, 33, 245, 260. *See also* Cunningham, Suzanne
Transcendance de l'Ego, (La), 16, 35, 44, 66. *See also* Existentialism; Sartre, Jean-Paul; Transcendental ego
Transcendental ego, 44, 66. *See also* Existentialism; Sartre, Jean-Paul; *Transcendance de l'Ego (La)*
Triomphe du Héros, Le, 88. *See also* Baudoin, Charles; Poetry, epic
Trotsky, Léon, 132. *See also* Weil, Simone

Uncertainty principle, 184. *See also* Heisenberg, Werner
Unconscious, 53, 56. See also *Hommes de Bonne Volonté*; Memory; Romains, Jules

Understanding, 18-20, 24, 28, 31
Unemployment, 121. *See also* Germany
Upanishads, the, 247. *See also* Myth
Uprootal, 13

Valéry,Paul, 116, 239, 250-51; *Charmes*, 204; mediation, 239-40; understanding, 239-40. *See also* Baldwin, Neil; Dédoublement; Language; Poetry; Robinson, Judith; Weil, Simone, language
Value, surplus, 126. *See also* Marx, Karl
Versailles, Treaty of, 100, 115-16. *See also* Colonialism, France, history of
Vĕto, Miklos: *Métaphysique religieuse de Simone Weil, La* 221, 225
"Vide, le," 203, 227. *See also* Void
Vienna Circle, 181. *See also* Brunschvicg, Léon; Hughes, H. S.; Positivism, logical; Wittengenstein, Ludwig
Viète, François, 165. *See also* Algebra
Vietnam, 241-42. *See also* Colonialism
Vigilance, 114. *See also* Colonialism
Violence, 90-91, 94-95, 223-24, 243-44, 246, 260-64; as an equalizer, 90-91; causes of, 116-20; contagion of, 94-95; language, 90, 243, 244-45; myth, 90, 244-45, 246-47; poetry, 250; repetition of, 246
Visions of Simone Machard, The, 67. *See also*Brecht, Bertolt
Void, 203. *See also* "Vide, le"
Voluntarism, 29, 32, 34, 40, 65. *See also* Alain; Maine de Biran, Marie François
Von Papen, Franz, 136

War, 113-15, 122, 129-34. *See also* Colonialism; France, history of; Militarism, Péguy, Charles; Revolution
Wave Theory, 188, 190. *See also* Continuum
Weil, Simone, 40, 43, 44, 46, 48, 65-67, 99, 113-14, 164, 184, 205; action, methodical, 6; anarchism, 73; *Attente de dieu*, 74; biography, 72-73; Blum, criticism of, 73, 158-59; *Cahiers*, 148, 149, 249-51; civil war, Spanish, 73, 166; CGTU, 138; *Condition Ouvriére, La*, 121, 141; *Connaissance, Surnaturelle, La*, 147, 204; death, 74, 106-7; DuJardin, Philippe, 157; *Ecrits historiques et politiques*, 74, 120, 241-42; *Ecrits de Londres*, 74; *L'Enracinement*, 73, 95-98, 241-42
"L'Enseignement des Mathématics," 171;

Factory work, 73, 142-43, 166; Free France, 73, 106-7, 241-42; "Guerre de Troie n'Aura pas Lieu, La," 117, 151; historical meanings, 241; *Iliade ou le poème de la Force*, 85-94, 120; *Intuitions Pré-Chrétiennes*, 248; "Israel et les Gentils," 147; language, 74, 239-40, 245-46; *Leçons de Philosophie*, 43 ff.; *Lettre à un Religieux*, 147; Marcion, 158-59; Marcoux, Camille, 39; mediation, 239-40; Munich 1938, 73; myth, 246-50; pacifism, 73; Perrin, Father Joseph-Marie, 73, 145, 158-59; "Perspectives–Allons-nous vers la Révolution Prolétarienne," 121, 138; "Personne et le Sacré, La," 221-22; *Pesanteur et la Grâce, la*, 73, 97, 147, 199,204, 208, 226; Plato, 95-96; poetry, 251-54; Popular Front, 73; pragmatism, 64; "Propos de la Question Coloniale, Á," 241-42; "Qui 'est Coupable de Menées antifrançaises?", 118; religion, critique of, 158-59; "Réflexions sur les Causes de la Libertéet de l'Oppression Sociale," 73, 237; Roanne, lectures, 46, 73; "Sang Coule en Tunisie, Le," 117; "Science et Perception dans Descartes," 162, 163; similarity with Hannah Arendt, 151; similarity with John Dewey, 70; similarity with Jean-Paul Sartre, 71; *Sur la Science*, 74; Thibon, Gustave, 73, 157; Trotsky, Léon, 132, 138-39, 157; understanding, 239-240; Vichy government, 166; Weil, Andre: correspondence with, 197

Weimar Republic, 182

Will, 17, 34, 39, 43, 55, 57, 120, 146

Winch, Peter, 14

Wittgenstein, Ludwig, 182. See also *Tractatus Logico-Philosophicus*; Vienna Circle

Women, French, 116-17. See also Giraudoux, Jean

Work, 21, 23, 25, 31, 34, 35, 64, 79, 173, 174, 175, 178, 179, 222, 223. See also Labor

Workers: Algerian, 120; Indochinese, 120; North African, 120; Tunisian, 120

World, 20, 32, 43, 59, 66. See also Exteriority

Xenophobia, 116-20

Zemansky, Mark, 198

Mary E. Giles

THE POETICS OF LOVE
Meditations with John of the Cross

American University Studies: Series VII, Theology and Religion, Vol. 18
ISBN 0-8204-0321-0   177 pp.   hardcover US $ 28,00

Recommended prices - alterations reserved

The Poetics of Love is a meditative commentary on John of the Cross's celebrated poem, the "Spiritual Canticle." The author responds to John's expression of the journey to God and unitive love by turning to everyday events to see them as context for an inner development which is truly mystical. Commenting strophe by strophe on the mystical process, she shows the potential for mystical consciousness in such experiences as falling in love, writing a poem, studying the stars and riding a horse. Desire, suffering, paradox, ecstasy, compassion, metaphor, virtue, solitude and joy are among the twenty-one subjects that mark the journey. The scholar will find in the meditations an example of reader response criticism while the student of mysticism may be encouraged to celebrate human relationships, nature, art and science as revelations of the divine.

PETER LANG PUBLISHING, INC.
62 West 45th Street
USA - New York, NY 10036

Lucy L. Melbourne

DOUBLE HEART
Explicit and Implicit Texts in Bellow, Camus and Kafka

American University Studies: Series III Comparative Literature, Vol. 21
ISBN 0-8204-0264-8   248 pp.   hardcover lam. US $ 39,00

Recommended prices - alterations reserved

What distinguishes fiction from non-fiction in first-person narratives? What is the difference between a novel and autobiography? What makes a first-person narrative a literary work of art? If fiction is a self-contained meaning structure, what frame of reference can we use to tell if the narrator is "lying?" Using a phenomenological approach to these questions basic to both literary theory and practical literary criticism, Dr. Melbourne develops a model of the unreliable first-person narrative. By applying it to three challenging works, Saul Bellow's *Dangling Man*, Albert Camus's *La chute*, and Franz Kafka's "Ein Landarzt," she shows us how to read between the lines" to discover the implicit text structuring first-person narratives into literary works of art.

Contents: Literary theory and criticism of the first person narrative applied to Saul Bellow's *Dangling Man*, Albert Camus's *La Chute*, and Franz Kafka's "Ein Landarzt."

PETER LANG PUBLISHING, INC.
62 West 45th Street
USA - New York, NY 10036

Natoli, Charles M.

NIETZSCHE AND PASCAL ON CHRISTIANITY
American University Studies: Series 5, Philosophy. Vol. 3
ISBN 0-8204-0071-8   197 pp.   hardcover/lam., ca. US $ 24,25

Recommended prices - alterations reserved

Although Pascal was one of the small group of thinkers who influenced Nietzsche profoundly, and although Nietzsche claimed to have Pascal's blood running in his veins, Pascal did not succeed in communicating to him his intense anxiety over the truth of the Christian faith. Instead, Nietzsche chose to focus his trenchant anti-Christian polemics on the value of its effects on humankind. This study, one of the very few on the Nietzsche/Pascal relationship, explores and appreciates the religious thought of each. It also assesses the nature and ground of their relationship and investigates the reasonableness of the Faith that divided them.

Contents: A study of the Nietzsche/Pascal relationship and of their disparate approaches to the problems each saw posed by Christianity. Truth or value – which is paramount in appraising religious belief?

PETER LANG PUBLISHING, INC.
62 West 45th Street
USA - New York, NY 10036

Steffen, Lloyd H.

SELF-DECEPTION AND THE COMMON LIFE
American University Studies: Series 7, Theology and Religion. Vol. 11
ISBN 0-8204-0243-5   415 pp.   hardback US $ 45.40 / s.Fr. 88.55

Recommended prices - alterations reserved

Self-Deception and the Common Life investigates the topic of self-deception from three points of view: philosophical psychology, ethics, and theology. Empirical evidence and an «ordinary language» analysis support the case that the linguistic expression 'self-deception' is literally meaningful and that the language of the common life can be trusted. After critically analyzing the cognition, translation, and action accounts, along with the contributions of Freud and Sartre, Steffen proposes a new synthetic «emotional perception» account, one that avoids paradox. Giving attention to relevant moral issues, he argues that self-deception is not immoral, but represents a peculiar form of *akrasia*. Finally, because theologians employ 'self-deception' to describe the cognitive component of sin, Steffen considers the logic of theological self-deception. His study seeks an «intimate acquaintance» with self-deception and exemplifies a method of analysis relevant to constructive theological inquiry.

Contents: «Ordinary language» analysis of self-deception — Accounts: cognition, translation, action, Sartre, Freud, «emotional perception»—self-deception and *akrasia*—theological self-deception: sin, pride, and Kierkegaard's «sin is despair».

PETER LANG PUBLISHING, INC.
62 West 45th Street
USA - New York, NY 10036